To you – our dear ~~"~~
shepherd – whom we
forget.

Janet Evelyn Noak
John Paul Claassen
Frank David Hamang
Jim L Hirsch
Nora Jean Anderson
Marilyn Smith
Mary Ann Bocca
Rae Belle Elliott
William Langbehn
Robert Schultz

THIS IS LUTHER

PLATE I

THE RIETSCHEL LUTHER

Ernst Rietschel, noted designer of the Luther monument at Worms, gets the credit for this reproduction of the Great Reformer's head. After Rietschel's death in 1861, his pupil Huettig completed the work of his master

This Is
LUTHER

A CHARACTER STUDY

by

Ewald M. Plass

CONCORDIA PUBLISHING HOUSE

St. Louis, Missouri

PRINTED IN THE UNITED STATES OF AMERICA

*TO
MY WIFE*

PREFACE

February 18, 1946, was the 400th anniversary of the death of Martin Luther. The world has not forgotten him. The amazing number of books and articles on the great Reformer has received a sizable accession at the quadricentennial of his death. Perhaps, then, these remarks ought to be a sort of justification and an apology. It may seem presumptuous to offer anything on a subject which has engaged the thoughts and the pens of great scholars for centuries. But the following is not another biography of Luther. It is intended to be a character study. It is to tell what Luther *was* rather than what Luther *did;* or, to express the same thought somewhat differently, it is interested in what Luther did only inasmuch as it serves as a revelation of what he was. There are enough biographies of the Reformer, and no doubt there will be more, but studies of his gigantic and versatile character are practically nonexistent in the English language.

The sketch here offered does not profess to have plumbed the depth of Luther's character. Its modest aim is merely to offer a few illustrations of the many-sidedness and the richness of one of the most remarkable men that ever lived. But if these lines stimulate others to take up their pens and give us a life-size portrait of Luther, such as the younger Holbein might have given us with his brush, they will have served one of their purposes. Then, too, we hope the reader will come to feel some of that admiration and reverence for Luther with which the writer of these lines has increasingly been filled during many years of reading his mighty writings. The undersigned would like humbly to lay the wreath of this little study on the tomb of this great man of God. The flowers in the wreath, at least the beautiful ones, grew in Luther's garden; they are quotations gathered from his own writings.

E. PLASS

Milwaukee, Wis., 1947

On Luther's birthday, November 10

CONTENTS

PLATES

Chronological Outline of the Age of Luther

(Projecting dates refer to Luther's life)

1483 Nov. 10, born at Eisleben.
1484–1497 at Mansfeld. Father a miner.
    1485 Aug. 25, Treaty of Leipzig divides Saxony into two parts, Electoral, or Ernestine, and Ducal, or Albertine.
    1485–1500 Duke Albert of Saxony.
    1487–1525 Elector Frederick the Wise.
    1492–1503 Pope Alexander VI.
    1493–1519 Emperor Maximilian.
1497–1498 at Magdeburg school under Brothers of the Common Life.
1498–1501 at Eisenach school; Frau Cotta.
    1500–1539 April 17, Duke George the Bearded.
1501 matriculates at University of Erfurt about May.
1502 B. A.
    1503–1513 Pope Julius II.
    1504–1567 Philip, Landgrave of Hesse.
1505 M. A.; enters Augustinian monastery, July.
1507 ordained priest; first Mass May 2.
1508 called to University of Wittenberg to teach Aristotle's *Ethics.*
1509 March, degree Baccalaureus ad Biblia.
1509 autumn, called to teach Lombard's *Sentences* at Erfurt.
    1509–1547 Henry VIII king of England.
1510 October–February, 1511, journey to Rome; December spent there.
1511 summer, returns to Wittenberg; lectures on Bible.
1512 October, Doctor of Theology.
    1513–1521 December, Pope Leo X.
1515 May, elected district vicar of Augustinian order.
    1515–1547 Francis I king of France.
1517 Oct. 31, posts 95 Theses on door of Castle Church, Wittenberg.
1518 Oct. 12–14, interview with Cardinal Cajetan, Augsburg.
1519 Jan. 4–5, interview with Miltitz at Altenburg.
    1519–1555 Emperor Charles V (elected June, 1519).
1519 July 4–14, debate with John Eck at Leipzig.
1520 June 15, Leo X signs bull *Exsurge Domine,* threatening to excommunicate Luther within 60 days.
1520 August, publishes *The Address to the Christian Nobility.*
1520 October, publishes *On the Babylonian Captivity.*
1520 November, publishes *On the Freedom of a Christian Man.*
1520 Dec. 10, burns papal bull and Canon Law.
1521 April 17–18, at the Diet of Worms. Edict signed May 26.

1521 May 4—March 1, 1522, at Wartburg.
    1522–1534, September, Pope Clement VII.
    1523 revolt of knights under Sickingen put down May 7.
    1524 Diet of Nuremberg.
    1524–1525 Peasants' War.
1525 June 13, marries Catherine von Bora (born January, 1499, Nimbschen; Cistercian cloister, 1508; leaves cloister April, 1523).
    1525 February, Charles V wins victory over Francis I at Pavia.
    1525–1532, August, Elector John the Steadfast.
    1526 May, Philip of Hesse and John of Saxony form League of Torgau.
    1526 June and July, Diet of Spires.
    1527 May 6, Rome sacked by imperial troops.
    1529 Feb. 26, Diet of Spires opens; Lutheran princes protest April 25.
1529 publishes catechisms.
1529 Oct. 2, conference at Marburg with Zwingli and others.
1530 April 23—Oct. 4 at Feste Coburg during Diet of Augsburg.
    1530 Diet of Augsburg; Augsburg Confession read June 25.
    1531 October, Zwingli falls in battle of Cappel.
    1532 Peace of Nuremberg between Protestants and Catholics.
    1532–1547 Elector John Frederick the Magnanimous; lived as Duke of Saxony till 1554.
1534 publishes the whole Bible in German (begun 1521).
    1534 Anabaptist rising in Muenster.
    1534 Ignatius Loyola founds Jesuit order.
    1534 English Act of Supremacy.
    1534–1549 Pope Paul III.
1536 signs Wittenberg Concord with leaders of German Zwinglians.
1537 Smalkald congress and Articles.
    1539–1541 August, Duke Henry the Pious. Reformation of Ducal (Albertine) Saxony.
    1541 John Calvin (1509–1564) introduces Reformation in Geneva.
    1541–1546 Duke Maurice of Albertine Saxony, made Elector 1546, died 1553.
1545 publishes *Against the Papacy at Rome Founded by the Devil.*
    1545–1563 Council of Trent.
1546 Feb. 18, dies in Eisleben; buried in All Saints' Church, the castle church, in Wittenberg.
    1546–1547 Smalkald War; battle of Muehlberg, April 24; Elector John Frederick captured and Maurice of Albertine Saxony given the electorate and some of his lands.
    1547–1553 Edward VI king of England.
    1547–1559 Henry II king of France.
    1552 Dec. 20, Catherine Luther dies.
    1555 Sept. 25, Religious Peace of Augsburg.

"The Word they still shall let remain"

THIS IS LUTHER

CHAPTER I

INTRODUCTORY

Blessed be the day of Martin Luther's birth! It should be a festival second only to that of the nativity of Jesus Christ.

Robert Southey, English poet

LUTHER'S CHARACTER IS ONE OF THE NOBLEST AND PUREST IN history. This statement is made deliberately. It is no snap judgment, dictated by blind partisan zeal and based merely upon the writings of the Reformer's friends and sympathizers. Over a period of twenty-five years we have carefully read the criticisms of Luther by those who are unsympathetic to him and to just about everything for which he stands. It need hardly be said that such writers have left no stone unturned, no corner unexplored, no incident in Luther's life, however trivial, unexamined. Perhaps no man's life has ever been looked into with such amazing thoroughness. But the life of Luther has stood the test. We owe a great debt of gratitude to the enemies of the Reformer. They have stimulated microscopic research; and their own investigations have proved the generally accepted picture of Luther's character to be the correct one. The old adage "Familiarity breeds contempt" does not apply to Luther. Gustav Freytag justly says: "His picture has the remarkable quality of becoming bigger and more lovable the closer it is approached." [1]

It is nothing short of a miracle of God's grace that a man of Luther's energy and intenseness consistently lived on a plane so high that his life must be microscopically examined to discover anything objectionable. Even then it is found that his faults were the failings common to men. "Wo viel Licht, da viel Schatten," the Germans say; that is: Where the light is bright, the

[1] Fr, L 5.

shadow is deep. Luther is a remarkable exception to the rule of this proverb. He was highly gifted and a veritable dynamo of energy. Such characters frequently do everything on a grand scale. They are men of extremes. There are great heights but also great depths in their characters, brilliant light but also grim shadows. Luther's character has shadows, but they are astoundingly light. We thank God for that fact.

THE WORD, NOT LUTHER, THE OBJECT OF FAITH

No one, of course, ought to accept Luther's Gospel because of the nobility of his character or the breadth and profundity of his learning. What Luther preached must stand entirely on its own merits. What Ambrose Blarer, a friend of Luther, said ought to be the confession of all who believe as Luther taught. When, in 1522, Blarer forsook the Benedictine monastery, he justified his step by publishing a defense. In this apology we find the following statement: "Therefore I will rather lose my body and life and all my fortune than be moved from my position; not on account of Luther, who is personally strange and unknown to me except by his writings — he also is human and therefore subject to mistake and error like other men — but on account of the divine Word which he carries in him so transparent and clear and proclaims and elucidates with such victorious and triumphant success and with such candid and unterrified spirit." [2] Blarer had the right approach to the "Luther problem." It is not a personal problem at all. Had the Reformer looked back upon a past stained with vice and immorality, as did Augustine and many of Luther's own critics, that deplorable circumstance would in no wise have detracted from the eternal verity of his message. Those who by blackening his character seek to discredit the Gospel he preached are engaged in a venture as futile as it is mean. Even if their strictures were justified, they would leave the point at issue entirely untouched. Just parenthetically be it remarked that *this* method of discrediting Lutheran doctrine comes with a peculiarly

---

[2] In Fr, L 68.

bad grace in particular from those who recognize such monsters of iniquity as John XXIII, Sixtus IV, and Alexander VI as their religious leaders. But we shall let that pass. Prejudice and inconsistency — to use no stronger term — are close relatives. To return to the main thought: The Gospel of a gratuitous salvation ought to be accepted not because Luther preached it, but because God revealed it. It is *God's* Gospel, not *Luther's*. "It did not grow in my garden," truly said the Reformer. Julius Hare, chaplain of Queen Victoria, correctly and pithily remarked: "The Reformation does not rest on the character of Luther, but on the Word of God." [3]

LUTHER'S WORK MORE IMPORTANT THAN HIS PERSON

And yet, the proclamation of that Gospel in apostolic purity has endeared Luther to millions as has nothing else that he was or did. Great as his character is, the Gospel he preached is infinitely greater. It is the shame and the tragedy of modern Protestantism that this truth is no longer recognized. In 1910, Preserved Smith published a *Life and Letters of Martin Luther*. We believe this to be one of the best English biographies of Luther. Particularly the judicious introduction of some of Luther's letters makes the Reformer live in this biography — though it is almost impossible to write an uninteresting life of so colorful and dynamic a character. But while Smith appreciates the heroic in Luther and testifies to the charm of his personality, he is quite unsympathetic to the Reformer's doctrinal position and principles. Smith closes his preface to the second edition of 1914 with the words: "After all, Luther's strongest appeal to us is his personality. His true originality is his character, his greatest work his life, his most remarkable achievement himself." [4] We believe Preserved Smith has entirely misunderstood Luther's greatest contribution to history. His "most remarkable achievement" is not "himself." It is the purification of Christendom; it is the restoration of the

---

[3] H, V 231.
[4] Sm, L XVIII.

Pauline, the Scriptural, doctrine of justification by faith. As we shall see, Luther himself considered that achievement his claim upon the memory of mankind. With characteristic modesty he considered it his only claim.

MUCH SOURCE MATERIAL AVAILABLE

So much is certain: if Luther is misunderstood, the fault must lie with the interpreter. Both primary and secondary sources offer an almost incredible wealth of material to the student of Luther. "A glance at the catalog of almost any great library — that of the British Museum for instance — will show that more has been written about Luther than about any man, save one, who ever lived"; [5] and that "One" was more than a man. He was the Son of Man and the Son of God. There are over 200 complete biographies of Luther. Many are available in every major language of the world. But it is not our intention to draw heavily upon such secondary sources. We shall concern ourselves primarily with source material. There is an amazing wealth of this, from Luther's *Sieben Busspsalmen* (Seven Penitential Psalms), his first production, in 1517, to his last letter to his wife, dated February 14, 1546. Few writers have been more prolific. In all Luther published over 350 works. These include a number of translations and many pamphlets. As a writer Luther has at times been accused of prolixity, but it must be borne in mind that many of his ideas introduced his contemporaries to a new world of thought. This made necessary a repetition which today impresses many as verbosity. His expressions and ideas are almost inexhaustible. Not inappropriately his words have been called "halfbattles." The still incomplete Weimar edition of his works now contains approximately 100 volumes, each averaging 700 pages in quarto format. Such literary productivity is not entirely unapproached. St. Augustine is credited with 232 works and the "literary behemoth" of colonial America, Cotton Mather, with 382. But these writers never attained the popularity of Luther. As

---

[5] Sm, L XX.

early as 1520 the Reformer writes: "I have printed so much there is danger that I shall weary the buying public at length." [6] But in the same year a friend of Erasmus wrote to Zwingli from Paris: "No one's books are bought more eagerly. A certain bookseller told me that at the last Frankfort fair he had sold fourteen hundred copies of Luther's works, which had never before happened with any other author." [7]

LUTHER'S "TABLE TALK" LARGELY AUTOBIOGRAPHICAL

The average non-Lutheran is perhaps most familiar with Luther's *Table Talk*. It offers much material and sheds much light on the Reformer's views concerning everything imaginable. From the Holy Trinity to tree grafting, from the resurrection to recipes, from the trivialities of daily life to the weightiest concerns of our eternal destiny — almost the entire field of human life and knowledge is covered by these off-the-record remarks of Doctor Luther. In the Weimar edition of his works no fewer than 6 volumes are devoted to these colorful titbits of the oracle of his day. I think it is Froude who somewhere calls the *Table Talk* of Luther "one of the most brilliant books in the world" and says it is as full of food for thought as the plays of Shakespeare. Probably few who have read the inimitable *Table Talk* will consider this assertion an exaggeration. The temptation to linger over the *Table Talk* is great. There is such a delightful bonhomie about it. It reveals the great Luther to us in a setting and an atmosphere of relaxation. And we find him to be thoroughly interesting as a man. There is a conversational dishabille about this *Table Talk* which makes it unique. In fact, the timid, social precisian Melanchthon at times cautioned some of Luther's friends against perpetuating *all* the remarks of the genial, candid Doctor. He thought they were too intimate and frank. Melanchthon held that a man ought never entirely shed a certain professional dignity lest he lose caste with his inferiors. Luther was never concerned about impressing

---

[6] S-J, LC I:290.
[7] S-J, LC I:383.

people in that way. "No man ever lived whose whole heart and soul and life have been laid bare as his have been to the eyes of mankind. Open as the sky, bold and fearless as the storm, he gave utterance to all his feelings, all his thoughts: he knew nothing of reserve: and the impression he produced on his hearers and friends was such, that they were anxious to treasure up every word that dropped from his pen or from his lips." [8]

HOW IT WAS PRESERVED

In our characterization of the Reformer we shall at times make use of the *Table Talk*. But it is to be quoted with care. It is important to remember as a matter of fact that Luther did not write this collection himself. Its assembling, arrangement according to subject matter, and its ultimate publication are to be credited to a small group of Lutheran Boswells. In the late 1520's they gathered around the supper table in the Black Monastery, Luther's home. Some were Luther's famuli, others tutors of his children, still others boarders in the Luther household. One of these boarders, Conrad Cordatus, first conceived the idea of recording these remarks of Luther. Soon others followed his example. Among them were Lauterbach, Roerer, Veit Dietrich, Johann Schlaginhaufen, and Hieronymus Weller, little Hans Luther's tutor. The circle grew and by the 1540's included Johann Aurifaber and Johann Mathesius, subsequently one of Luther's first biographers. At first there was no thought of publication. But in 1566 Johann Aurifaber gave to the press what for years had been one of his most prized treasures. In preparing the *Talk* for publication he naturally drew upon his memory to expand the notes hurriedly taken down at the Doctor's table. The resultant book was an immediate success. Thereupon arose a demand for the personalia found in the notebooks of the other "Boswells." When these were compared, it was of course found that there were discrepancies due to mishearing or misunderstanding. Since

---

[8] H, V 293.

that time the effort to establish the original version of these Luther remarks has been the Herculean task of scholars. But though they must, therefore, be used with care, this famous *Table Talk* of Luther gives us many an intimate glimpse, many a close-up of the man. At times it permits us to look as deeply into the soul of Luther as his letters do.

LUTHER'S LETTERS ESPECIALLY VALUABLE SOURCE MATERIAL

Luther's letters — what a gold mine for the man in search of source material for a picture of the real Luther! We shall see that the Reformer had all the attributes of an interesting correspondent. He possessed a fine command of language, had a keen sense of humor, and a very wide range of interests. In consequence we shall draw largely on the letters. We shall let Luther speak of himself and for himself as much as possible. And we can well afford to assume little more than the role of a master of ceremonies; for if ever a man laid bare his heart and his soul in his letters, that man was Martin Luther. Few men we know of could better afford to do so, for few have had less to hide from the eyes of their fellow men; few have lived closer to God. Writing to the philosopher Maeurer, Luther says: "It makes no difference if my letters to you are delivered to someone else. I do not fear to have them public property, for I write under God's sight." [9]

CANDOR OF LUTHER'S LETTERS

There are persons whose letters read like essays. There is an atmosphere of detachment about them which makes them almost impersonal. They are stiff and formal. This cannot be said of the letters of Luther. The Reformer possessed a vivid imagination. We recall the remark of a now deceased professor of homiletics: "Look at your audience while writing your sermon." Luther did that while writing his letters. He imagined the addressee present. His letters have all the spontaneity, informality, and warmth of

---

[9] S-J, LC I:377.

a personal conversation. There is nothing studied about them, nothing Chesterfieldian. Luther never strikes a pose. The Luther of his letters is "Luther, wie er leibt und lebt." Herder said of him: "He gives a picture of himself in every line." [10]

GREAT NUMBER OF LUTHER'S LETTERS

And how many lines there are! "It is probable that more than ten thousand letters might be found bearing on the German Reformation during this period," says Preserved Smith of the years 1521—1530 only.[11] Hundreds of these were written by Luther. The mass of Luther's correspondence is almost incredible. One wonders how a man so busy could write over 3,000 letters in about 30 years. And some of these letters are veritable pamphlets in size. "There are still 1,334 letters of Dr. Martin Luther extant, found in all parts of Germany and in foreign collections. . . . Luther's letter to Charles V was purchased by J. P. Morgan for about $25,000 and presented to Emperor William II as a gift." [12] This letter, dated April 28, 1521, may be found in an English translation in Smith's *Luther's Correspondence and Other Contemporary Letters*, Vol. I, p. 547 ff.

LUTHER'S IDIOMATIC LANGUAGE DIFFICULT TO TRANSLATE

The originals of Luther's letters are, of course, in either Latin or German. At times especially the idiomatic German of Luther almost defies translation. One is reminded of what Luther said while engaged upon his classic translation of the Bible. He remarked: "Good Heavens, how hard it is to make the Hebrew writers speak German! They withstand our efforts, not wishing to give up their native tongue for a barbarous idiom, just as the nightingale would not change her sweet song to imitate the cuckoo, whose monotonous note she abhors." [13] Again he said in

---

10 In Kr, C 82.

11 S-J, LC II:9.

12 *Lutheran Witness*, April, '34.

13 Sm, L 264.

a letter to his friend Spalatin: "Absolutely no translation except a very free one can reproduce figures of speech and the cogency of an argumentative style. I do not mention the extreme difficulty of giving the author's spirit." [14] If it be borne in mind that Luther possessed a "spirit" very much his own, the difficulty of rendering *him* into English that does justice to the peculiar genius of the man and captures and reproduces the vigorous "Lutheresqueness" of his idiom will in a measure be appreciated. Fortunately, this "spirit" is so strong in the case of Luther that even a mediocre translation cannot entirely dispel it. His was a very strong and very many-sided character.

LUTHER AMAZINGLY MANY-SIDED

The result is a versatility perhaps unique in history. Most men can at best be masters of one trade, however much they may be "Jacks-of-all-trades." Luther seems to have had enough talent and energy to become master in a number of fields of endeavor. He was at once the most popular and prolific author and the most celebrated pulpit orator of his day. Millions believe him to have been the greatest theologian of his age. Even the learned Erasmus had the highest respect for his scholarship. He was a brilliant conversationalist; and no less a person than Mendelssohn professed to have profited by studying his remarks on music. Such versatility was no doubt the result of a character in which a number of traits usually found alone and in part almost contradictory were strongly developed. Of all the men who have deeply affected the course of history perhaps no one is more paradoxical than Luther. But these very contradictions of his nature qualified him for the difficult task to which he was called by God. He had to be and was endowed with gifts and talents usually distributed among a number of men; for he had frequently to do the work of many singlehandedly. And so he possessed in a singular combination the qualities needed to renovate the Church and to make a new world. Luther had a nature that was profoundly deep and

---

[14] S-J, LC I:400.

intensely religious, but it was associated with a sparkling mother wit and a joviality that made him a delightful companion. The pulverizing strength of his blows was the terror of his enemies till he breathed his last, but at the same time he was so tenderhearted that the warm sympathy in his many letters of comfort brings healing to bleeding hearts to this day. That is the reason why Carlyle says of Luther: "Ah, yes, unsubduable granite, piercing far and wide into the heavens; yet in the clefts of it fountains, green beautiful valleys." [15] Dr. Krauth, in his *The Conservative Reformation and Its Theology,* quotes Heinrich Heine to this effect: Luther "had qualities which are very seldom found united, which we are accustomed to regard as irreconcilable antagonisms. He was at the same time a dreamy mystic and a practical man of action. . . . When he had plagued [?] himself all day long with his doctrinal distinctions, in the evening he took his flute and gazed at the stars, dissolved in melody and devotion. He could be soft as a tender maiden. Sometimes he was wild as the storm that uproots the oak, and then again he was gentle as the zephyr that dallies with the violet." [16] Such was the character which we shall try to examine a little more closely now.

THIS BOOK A CANDID PICTURE OF LUTHER

We offer nothing psychological or psychiatric. We have no thesis to prove. Our intention is simply to picture Luther as we find him reflected in his writings, especially in his letters. If we find contradictions in his character, we shall not consider it our duty to reconcile them. Nor shall we consider it our responsibility to defend the Reformer against all the aspersions of his enemies. Those curious to know to what length malice will go, we herewith refer to the books written by H. Boehmer and W. Walther, not to mention the earlier one by J. Hare. These books, the former by Germans, the latter by an Englishman, are unanswerable defenses of Luther's character against all who cannot appreciate what Lu-

---

[15] Ca, H 168.

[16] Kr, C 45.

ther *was* because they abhor what Luther *did*. As an obiter dictum we may add that from the days of the first Catholic biography of Luther, in 1549, by Johann Dobneck, better known as Cochlaeus, down to the large work of the wily Jesuit Hartman Grisar, the Reformer has not been charged with anything new. Perhaps the charges are made to appear more grievous and imposing by the use of scientific terms, such as "autochthonous complexes" and "endogenous neurosis." But they are the old charges, charges repeatedly exploded by the fairness and honesty of even Catholic scholars from Erasmus through Michelet to Lord Acton and Joseph Clayton. In 1937 Clayton said, under the imprimatur of Cardinal Stritch, then archbishop at Milwaukee, "Luther cannot be 'debunked' — if the expressive slang of these latter days be permitted. He revealed himself in his own lifetime too fully to be divested by posterity of masterful (and other pleasing and less pleasing) qualities known to his contemporaries. Masterful Luther was."

CHAPTER II

A MAN OF INFLUENCE

There are few, even of his own disciples, who
appreciate him highly enough.
Friedrich von Schlegel, Catholic critic

WHEN SPEAKING OF THE INFLUENCE OF LUTHER, IT IS
difficult to avoid superlatives. We do not at present
have in mind his influence on world affairs. That was
great and enduring. Preserved Smith holds that "no man in history has . . . more completely dominated his time." [1] The Frenchman Taine thought: "There was no province of human intelligence and action which was not refreshed and fertilized by this universal effort" (the Lutheran Reformation).[2] The Catholic historian Michelet contends: "It is not incorrect to say that Luther has been the restorer of liberty in modern times." [3] The German Goethe says: "We do not know for how much, in a general way, we must thank Luther and the Reformation." [4] And Gustav Freytag tells us: "Domestic devotion, marriage, and education of children, municipal life, and school affairs, manners, recreation, all sentiments of the heart, all social pleasures, were consecrated by his teachings and writings. Everywhere he strove to set new goals and to lay deeper foundations. Not a department of human duty about which he did not compel the people to reflect. His influence spread far and wide." [5] Such tributes to the world influence of Martin Luther could be multiplied almost indefinitely. Whether men consider his influence a bane or a blessing, they cannot honestly deny that it created a new order of things. Luther dominated his age as few before or after him have ever ruled over theirs. But that fact does not concern us now.

[1] S-J, LC I:6. [3] Mi, L xii. [5] Fr, L 105.
[2] In D, L 35. [4] In Be, M viii.

STRONG INFLUENCE EXERTED BY LUTHER'S PERSONALITY

We are interested in determining what manner of *man* Martin Luther was. What he did was no doubt an index to what he was. Therefore the acts of the man cannot be ignored, but at present they interest us only in so far as they furnish a key to his character and reveal his personality. And we shall find that Luther possessed one of those strong personalities over against which neutrality is almost impossible. Such characters either strongly attract or strongly repel one. The reaction of Erasmus to the influence of Luther furnishes an interesting illustration of this fact. The great scholar had an honest reverence for Luther. But it made him uneasy. He tried in vain to get away from the influence of Luther. The Reformer's heroic decisiveness was an irritation to the timid Humanist, because he felt it to be a silent rebuke as well.

LUTHER NOT CARRIED TO FAME BY FAVORING CIRCUMSTANCES

But is the gigantic stature of Luther in history perhaps to be accounted for on the theory that he received credit that belongs to the greatness of the cause for which he contended? Such a transfer of greatness is not altogether unheard of. At times a man of mediocre ability achieves signal success because he is peculiarly favored by circumstances. In the light of his success he may then appear greater than he is in reality. Probably it is idle, if not impossible, to determine how much the personal element contributed to the success of the Reformation. Did Luther make the Reformation or did the Reformation "make" Luther? The Reformer himself would have been the last to boast, as did Napoleon, that circumstances did not make him, but that he made the circumstances. But nonetheless there are many who believe that the Reformation would be as unthinkable without Martin Luther as the American Revolution would be without George Washington. "The Reformation is Luther," says John Morley.[6] So much is certain: Luther was, in his own days, the

---

[6] In D, L 26.

best-loved and the best-hated man. Nor has the situation changed much in our times.

Surely, the German poet Lessing had little sympathy with the doctrines of the Reformer. He was notorious for his liberalism — perhaps radicalism would be the more fitting term. Nevertheless Lessing said of Luther: "I have been in imminent danger of making him an object of idolatrous veneration." [7] Upon reading such a tribute from such a source one wonders what sort of language will be used by those who, unlike Preserved Smith, have recognized Luther's work to be even greater than his character, who venerate him as the God-sent Reformer of Christendom.

HIS COMPELLING PERSONALITY RECOGNIZED BY CONTEMPORARIES

To some men recognition comes belatedly. Years after their death has made both the censure and the praise of men mean nothing to them, they come into their own. The afterworld erects monuments to their memory, and beautiful epitaphs tell of their worth. The greatness of J. S. Bach was not generally appreciated until, a century after his death, Felix Mendelssohn opened the ears of the world to the beauty and profundity of his music by performing the *St. Matthew Passion*. But this was certainly not the fate of Luther. As early as 1519 Melanchthon addressed Luther in the following manner in a Greek poem: "Holy Nazarite of Israel, . . . elect servant of uncorrupted truth, protector of souls, . . . faithful and sleepless shepherd of the temple of the all-merciful God, . . . thou champion of the truth, smite with the wonder-working staff of Moses the doting brains of the enemies of the Word, . . . fight steadfastly, and unceasingly follow light-bearing Jesus. . . ." [8] Nor were the talents and the work of Luther unknown beyond his circle at this early date. In the same year (1519) the printer John Froben wrote to Luther about a friend of his, a bookseller of Pavia, Italy, that "he has promised to send epigrams written in your honor by all the learned in Italy; so much does he like your constancy and skill." [9]

---

[7] In Kr, C 45.   [8] S-J, LC I:144.   [9] S-J, LC I:162.

TESTIMONY OF ERASMUS AND OTHERS

At the same early date a friend of Erasmus wrote to Zwingli in Switzerland: "How great will be the indignation of posterity if they read that Luther was a good man, of a life miraculously pure, brilliant, learned, candid, a good Christian, and a German patriot, and yet that when he first, in this age of perverse theologians and detestable monkish tyranny, dared to warn them and to vindicate Christ, whose worship had been stained and almost wiped out by human doctrines, he was crushed not by arguments or texts of Holy Scriptures, with which he always invincibly defended his own innocence, but by a fraudulent and tyrannical conspiracy of scoundrels!" [10] At the very beginning of the Reformation these words aptly describe both the character of Luther and the manner of his work. In the following year, 1520, the papal legate Aleander wrote from Worms that pictures of Luther were being offered for sale in that city on which the Holy Spirit was seen to hover over the head of the Reformer. On other pictures the halo of the saint had been given Luther. Such appreciation of him continued as long as he was recognized to be the restorer of purity to the Church. This is the view that is ever in the foreground in Mathesius' sermonic lectures on the life of Luther, published in 1576. Mathesius had been a disciple of Luther and a guest at his table. He had hung upon his lips and had studied him closely. In his biography of the Reformer he calls him the "man of marvels," God's "holy instrument" for the purification of the Church, "our beloved prophet," [11] and many similar names of admiration. In subsequent centuries such tributes to Luther continue. Entire volumes could be filled with them. Of course, as the emphasis on purity of doctrine grew less, the significance of Luther was estimated differently. But there were always some, even among non-Lutherans, to whom he was chiefly significant as Reformer. Among these was Robert Montgomery, who wrote an epic poem called *Luther*. About seventy-five years ago this

---

[10] S-J, LC I:271.   [11] Ma, M vii, 2, 186.

difficult to follow their head whither their heart does not lead, to differentiate with scholarly fairness and objectivity between persons and problems. A man's heart travels faster than his head. We commonly feel before we think; and when we do think, the temptation is great to permit our feeling to influence our thinking. Many, it seems, just cannot rise to the scholarly level on which full justice is done to the personal purity and nobility of the character of a man with whose views they do not agree. What to normal biographers means one thing turns into its very opposite for them. Their prejudice acts like a historical alchemy in the reverse. It turns golden motives into dross. Such biographasters are not even like horses with blinkers; for they (the horses) at least see clearly what is in the direct line of their vision. But the prejudiced make it impossible for themselves to see anything as it is or as it was. Their mind is like a convex mirror: it distorts all the lines which it reflects. Thus Luther's much-acclaimed courage is bullheadedness; his modesty must be the result of a distrust in the goodness of his cause; his prayers for his enemies are hypocritical window dressing. In short, his motives must have been normally bad, however innocent or good they may appear on the surface, because such an apostate monk and renegade priest must necessarily have been a moral pervert.

> All seems infected that th' infected spy,
> As all looks yellow to the jaundiced eye. — Pope

A striking illustration of this effect of prejudice is furnished by Mathesius. He tells us of a Venetian Catholic who was asked to authorize the printing of a manuscript which was a translation into Italian of Luther's sermons on the Lord's Prayer. But the Reformer was not identified as the author of the sermons. Upon reading the manuscript the good Catholic exclaimed: "Blessed are the hands that wrote this, blessed the eyes that read it, blessed the hearts that believe it and thus cry to God." [15] No doubt even such bitter enemies of Luther as John Eck and Jerome Emser

---

[15] Ma, M 299.

would have endorsed many a view of the Reformer if only it had come from someone else; they would have considered many acts noble and heroic if they had been performed by anyone but Martin Luther.

EXCEPTIONAL RECOGNITION FROM HONEST OPPONENTS

Fortunately there are some notable exceptions. Some enemies of his Gospel *did* recognize the purity of his character. To the famous English statesman-cardinal, Thomas Wolsey, the Catholic Erasmus wrote: "The man's [Luther's] life is approved by the unanimous consent of all, and the fact that his character is so upright that even his enemies find nothing to slander in it, must considerably prejudice us in his favor." [16] Dr. Johann Doellinger, whom Lord Bryce calls "that glory of Catholic learning," declared before his breach with Rome in 1870: "I see in Luther a great and noble character, against whose person I would not cast one stone." [17] And at the head of this chapter stands a quotation of the German Catholic Friedrich von Schlegel. These are by no means the only tributes honest Catholic scholars have paid to the nobility of Luther's character.

LUTHER STILL ABUSED

Why, then, the continued vilification? One is not surprised to read that a Spanish soldier gave Luther's effigies in the Castle Church two stabs with his dagger when, a year after the Reformer's death, Charles V came to Wittenberg. Such action is quite in keeping with the attitude and the temper of a soldier, especially a Spanish soldier, of the sixteenth century. But one does expect a little more from men of thought, from scholars and theologians. However, the following outburst is credited to the head of a Dominican monastery in 1520. "Would that I could fasten my teeth in Luther's throat; I should not fear to go to the Lord's Supper with his blood on my mouth." [18] Nor let anyone

---

[16] S-J, LC I:187.   [17] In D, L 24.   [18] S-J, LC I:376.

think that this bitter hatred disappeared with the age of controversy. Two hundred years later, in 1723, a Strassburg priest, Nikolaus Weislinger, published a book in which he "reads such a text to the godless heretic, the stinking profligate, the filthy ragamuffin, the ribald brawler, the obscene, slanderous and execrable Luther and all the verminous Lutheran rabble of filthy vagabonds that the reader's senses are almost overwhelmed." [19] Almost two hundred years later, as recently as November, 1914, the then Pope, Benedict XV, delivered himself of the following. He referred to Protestants as "the emissaries of Satan, who set up pestilential pulpits and, like Luther and Calvin, by diabolical machinations commit abominable robbery of the people's faith and seek their perdition." [20] Such ravings remind one of Erasmus' statement "It is much easier to conquer him [Luther] with bulls and with smoke than with arguments." [21] Fortunately the enemies of the truth found the one as impossible as the other. As to making Luther squirm under such verbal castigation — he always thanked God when he was considered worthy to endure anything which might make his life a more faithful imitation of Christ's. Therefore, were he living today, he would rejoice that men should still revile him and speak all manner of evil of him falsely, for Christ's sake. And as to Luther's revilers, such outbursts, offered without proof or evidence, betray a weak cause, for the man who lapses into mere calling of names proclaims either his prejudice and ignorance or the weakness of his cause. Indeed, the case against Luther's character is so weak that Erasmus' verdict, although written in 1520, is just as true in 1947. The great Catholic Humanist says: "All who have written against him [Luther] have composed nothing worth reading." [22] This is applicable to slanderous statements about Luther's character no less than to the principles he so successfully vindicated. As to refuting in detail all the shameless accusations brought against Luther by enemies whose exasperation grew in direct proportion

---

[19] Bo-P, L 19.   [21] S-J, LC I:401.
[20] In Ba, L 269.   [22] S-J, LC I:403.

to their increasing inability to silence him — well, the Reformer once wrote: "I should need much leather to muzzle all the mouths [that slander me]. It is enough that my conscience is clear before God; He will judge what I have said and written." [23] Those are the words of a man who is sure of himself. Such men make good leaders.

HIS TALENT OF LEADERSHIP RECOGNIZED BY FRIEND AND FOE

Even the enemies of Luther hesitate to question his talent for leadership. His was one of those strong, forceful characters that compel confidence. Men remarked about his decisiveness, his positiveness. People may call it blind dogmatism, to which, indeed, it may be closely related. But we shall see that it was not so in the case of Luther. And that fact was known. Luther was entirely too conscientious and too scholarly to defend a view which he had accepted at a venture, without thoroughly examining into its merits. Men admired such conscientiousness and were impressed by the definiteness with which he stated his case. There was never any doubt about Luther's position. He made himself unmistakably clear. Only malice could misunderstand him. He never hedged about an issue, never expressed himself ambiguously, so as to leave a back door for an escape. This ringing positiveness was no doubt one of his greatest assets as a leader. Men knew exactly what he wanted and whither he was leading.

AN ILLUSTRATION OF HIS LEADERSHIP

Luther's compelling leadership can be seen nowhere, probably, to better effect than upon the occasion of his return from the Wartburg. During his absence confusion had begun to spread at Wittenberg. The great principle of Christian liberty proclaimed by Luther was being abused and misunderstood by souls who, like the old bottles in the Gospels, were not strong enough to hold the new wine. Elements of disorder within Luther's circle

---

[23] S-J, LC II:320.

at Wittenberg were being outbidden for leadership by elements of still greater disorder from without. The excitable Carlstadt and his confreres were joined by fanatical pretenders to prophetic visions who came from Zwickau. All was confusion. No one knew how to handle a situation so obviously charged with dynamite. At this critical moment all eyes instinctively turned to the Wartburg. Nor in vain. Informed of the state of affairs at Wittenberg, Luther, in spite of papal curse and imperial edict and though not entirely against, yet certainly without, the advice and consent of Elector Frederick, returns to Wittenberg. Ranke justly calls this one of the great moments in history.[24] Would this lone monk, condemned and outlawed, be able singlehandedly to close the flood gates of radicalism? He *was* able. Perhaps even Luther never preached more important sermons than the eight he delivered in troubled Wittenberg during that spring of 1522. At his voice the uproar was hushed, the frothy waves of fanaticism were calmed, and peace was restored. Thomas Lindsay says: "It is the fate of most authors of revolutions to be devoured by the movement which they have called into being. Luther occasioned the greatest revolution which Western Europe has ever seen, and he ruled it till his death. History shows no kinglier man than this Thuringian miner's son." [25]

HIS GUIDANCE SORELY MISSED AFTER HIS DEATH

How completely Luther had dominated the scene was revealed after his death. The disintegrating doctrinal controversies which then unsettled the Lutheran Church perhaps would never have occurred had Luther still been there to combat error with his mighty blows. He sensed the coming of these sad aberrations and earnestly warned against them. So long as his sturdy arm still swung the sword of the Spirit, which is the Word of God, error ventured not to rear its head too boldly. His compelling personality was a unifying power sufficiently strong to hold the wavering in line. But after his decease began the distressing doc-

---

[24] Ra, D II:22.   [25] Li, H I:389.

trinal controversies within the Lutheran Church which, by God's grace, finally, after thirty-four troubled years, were settled in large part by the famous *Book of Concord*. Meanwhile, however, Melanchthon and others had at times come within an ace of selling the precious heritage of Luther's Reformation for the pot of beans of Catholic toleration and Calvinistic co-operation. We are told that the delegates at the Council of Trent appeared radiant with smiles on the morning of February 22, 1546. A horseman had arrived from Germany at dawn. Luther was dead. Twenty years ago the Elector had been told by Hans von der Planitz, his representative at the Diet of Nuremberg: "The cardinals at Rome are really afraid of Martin." [26] They had good reasons to be afraid.

ERRORS AND CORRUPTIONS DEEPLY INTRENCHED

Truth had a fearful account, an account of long standing, to settle with Rome. The work of Luther was like the excision of a malignant tumor. It involved the removal from the body of Christian doctrine and practice of a mass of corruption that was threatening the complete extinction of spiritual life, a corruption that, like a tumor, had at one time seemed too insignificant to warrant any alarm. But it had grown steadily and slowly, so that the body of Christendom became so habituated to the poison it was feeding into its system that it was scarcely aware of its deadly presence. Rome likes to telescope the canonization of her errors and push them into the distant past. This makes it possible for her to impress people with the spurious claim of her antiquity, of her practical agelessness. Then, too, it is so much easier to hide in the haze of long-forgotten ages. But it is unhistorical to picture the body of Romish doctrine as a fixed entity at any time before almost the twentieth century. While some of her errors were hoary with an age greater than that of Methuselah, other departures from Scriptures were of comparatively recent date at Luther's time. And yet, all were animated by a

---

[26] S-J, LC II:119.

common spirit, all radiated from a common center, like the roots of a tumor. But many people did not see this connection and considered Luther a radical for cutting so deeply into the body of Catholic doctrine. Then, too, some of the heresies Luther had to oppose had actually endeared themselves to the people. They were religious sanctionings of permanent tendencies in corrupt human nature. Since they were so deeply rooted, it was difficult to eradicate them. Successfully to do so required a process rather than an act. It was a matter of education rather than mere legislation. But many people could not see this fact and accused Luther of going too slow. We shall mention only a few of the grosser departures from Scripture of which Christendom had become guilty in the course of centuries and to remove which certainly required the skill of a very exceptional man.

THE SUPERSTITION OF PURGATORY

At the time of Gregory the Great († 604) the doctrine of purgatory was so generally held as to be considered a teaching of the Church at large. A few years ago Cardinal O'Connell of Boston said of it: "It is of faith that there is a place we call purgatory, where petty faults, or the temporal punishment due to sin, are expiated." [27] It may be pointed out that some such place of purging became a doctrinal necessity after the adulteration of justification by faith. As O'Connell intimates, Scripture knows nothing of purgatory. Therefore it is not at all a matter of faith but rather of superstition.

In 1075 Gregory VII declared all clerical marriages invalid. A generation later Canon XXI of the First Lateran Council of 1123 decreed: "Our judgment upon marriages contracted by persons of this kind [the clergy] is that they must be broken." We have no desire to dwell upon the unspeakable immoralities which this enforced celibacy caused. Those interested in this shameful chapter of Catholic history may satisfy their curiosity by merely browsing in H. Lea's *An Historical Sketch of Sacerdotal Celibacy*.

---

[27] In En, P 201.

OTHER PAPAL HERESIES

At the beginning of the thirteenth century the Inquisition was established. Of the purpose of this institution the bull *Ad Extirpanda,* published in 1252 by Pope Innocent IV, says: "When those adjudged guilty of heresy have been given up to the civil power by the bishop or his representative, or the Inquisition, the podesta, or chief magistrate of the city, shall take them at once and shall, within five days at the most, execute the laws made against them." These laws as a rule called for the burning alive of the hapless victim. In the same century, the thirteenth, often referred to by Catholics as the "century of faith," since Rome had then reached the zenith of her power, other heresies were approved as the official doctrines of the Church. Thus 1215 saw transubstantiation made public doctrine. Eleven years later we hear of the inevitable doctrinal corollary of transubstantiation, the idolatrous custom of the adoration of the host (the bread) as the material body of Christ and therefore God. Perhaps it was no mere coincidence that this century also saw the Council of Toledo (1229) place the very Bible of God on the *Index Librorum Prohibitorum,* the list of books Catholics are not allowed to read. This is one of the gravest of all the crimes of the Roman hierarchy: keeping famished souls from the bread of life. Nor has she ever repented of this sin. In the *Catholic Encyclopedia,* in volume II, on page 545, we read the following under "Bible Societies": "The attitude of the Church toward Bible Societies [American and British Bible Societies] is one of unmistakable opposition. Believing herself to be the divinely appointed custodian and interpreter of the Holy Writ, she cannot, without turning traitor to herself, approve the distribution of Scripture 'without note or comment.' It would be the violation of one of the first principles of the Catholic Faith — a principle arrived at through observation as well as by revelation [!] — *the insufficiency of the Scriptures alone* to convey to the general reader a sure knowledge of faith and morals."

Came the fourteenth century and Pope Boniface VIII. This ambitious man published the official document on the political aspirations of the hierarchy. In his bull *Unam Sanctam* he contends: 1. that it is necessary to salvation that every man submit to the Pope; 2. that the material sword is to be drawn *for* the Church, the spiritual *by* the Church; 3. that the supremacy of the Pope, also in temporal affairs, is to be enforced; 4. that the temporal power is subordinate to the spiritual, as to the higher.[28] This claim of political supremacy as well as spiritual autocracy is good canon law to this day. In theory Rome has never receded a step from this position, although circumstances have often forced her reluctantly to forego their entire realization.

THE WORST OF HERESIES: CONDEMNATION OF JUSTIFICATION BY FAITH

The most critical time for Rome came with the dawn of the sixteenth century and the Reformation. Would she repent and accept correction, or would she harden herself against the call to return to Scripture and the truth? Emperor and princes and theologians found it difficult to get her clearly to define her position at all. She evaded issues whenever possible. She compromised when she had to. She temporized and played for time whenever and wherever she could. Finally even her ability to think up subterfuges was at an end. Then came the Council of Trent. Whoever called it must have done so with his tongue in his cheek. The Council was attended by only three cardinals and forty bishops. These were mostly Italian and mostly nonentities. It was the year before Luther's death, and the Reformer clearly foresaw the outcome of that "reforming" conclave. He asked his friends to increase the intensity of their prayers, since "the devil again rages at Trent." His gravest apprehensions proved to have been only too well founded. Not only did this Council decree that "tradition" was of equal authority with Scripture, but in its sixth session it reached the very climax of antichristian blasphemy. The most fateful canon ever passed by Rome was the twelfth of this session. It reads thus: "If anyone saith that justifying faith is

---

[28] Gieseler, J., *Lehrbuch der Kirchengeschichte*. Bonn, Marcus, 1846. Band II, Teil II, S. 203 f.

nothing else but confidence in the divine mercy which remits sins for Christ's sake or that this confidence alone is that whereby we are justified, let him be anathema" (that is, cursed by God).[29] The die had been cast. Placed squarely before the cardinal doctrine of Christianity, the Roman hierarchy cursed it. Henceforth Rome was to be a sect and, judged solely by her official pronouncements, the Church of the very Antichrist.

HERESIES OF INDIVIDUAL POPES

"Her *official* pronouncements," we say. By these she is to be judged. There are those who dwell at length on the gross heresies of individual Popes. Of the city and court of Leo X († 1521) it was said: "One was not considered a cultured man if one did not harbor erroneous opinions about Christianity."[30] "Petrarch said that the court of the Popes at Avignon was a place where the hope of heaven and the fear of hell were regarded as old fables ... and sin was looked upon as a sign of manly independence."[31] When Pope Clement VII († 1534) was reminded upon a certain occasion of his illegitimate birth, he laughingly replied he shared that misfortune with Christ.[32] But we shall let the heresies of individual Popes pass. We are concerned with the official position of the papal Church.

IMMORALITY AND DEMORALIZATION COMMON

How had Christian life fared amid this increasing adulteration of Christian faith? Badly enough, as was to be expected. Men spoke of the "Augean stable of the Papacy." Gibbon tells us that at the time of John XII († 963) devout women hesitated to visit the supposed tomb of Peter "lest ... they should be violated by his successor."[33] Shall we quote from the *Ecclesiastical Annals*

---

[29] *Canons and Decrees of the Council of Trent;* tr. by J. Waterworth. Chicago, Christian Symbolic Publ. Soc., n. d. P. 46.

[30] In Ranke, Leopold v., *Die roemischen Paepste;* 9. Aufl. Leipzig, Duncker & Humblot, 1889. I:49.

[31] Ba, L 60.   [32] Ra, D IV:108.   [33] In Ba, L 31.

of the Catholic Cardinal Baronius († 1607)? Of the Papacy as early as the ninth century he says: "The palace of the Lateran was become a disgraceful tavern, in which ecclesiastics of all nations disputed with harlots the price of infamy." [34] It is neither necessary nor edifying to quote this passage any further. Nor is it necessary to call upon any of the host of available witnesses to prove that, generally speaking, conditions in this respect did not improve during subsequent centuries. The sacredness seemed to have passed out of everything. Highest church offices were sold. It was said: "One can get at Simon Peter only through Simon Magus." The deceit practiced upon the gullibility of the ignorant and superstitious public with relics, genuine and otherwise, were ludicrous, were its implications not so sad. At one time "an imperial law had to prohibit corpses of martyrs from being cut into pieces and offered for sale" as relics. There were on exhibition at various places Noah's beard, Paul's thorn in the flesh, plumage from the archangel Michael's wings, some ashes from the bush Moses had seen burning, some of the earth of which Adam was made and innumerable similar reliquian absurdities, to say nothing of some that were revolting, if not sacrilegious. The holy collection of Frederick the Wise, numbering no fewer than 5,005 items, the aggregate indulgence power of which meant a 1443 years earlier departure from purgatory, is well known. So widely spread and so deeply rooted was the holy humbug — no milder word adequately characterizes this traffic — and so far were the departures from Christian doctrine and life that cried for reformation in the days of Luther. And then he came. When Dr. Fleck, who had been present at the dedication of the university at Wittenberg in 1502, read the Theses, he exclaimed: "Ho! Ho! the man who will do the work is here."

---

[34] In Ba, L 47.

CHAPTER III

THE BACKGROUND

You are known to me, but you daily appear
greater and greater.—*Crotus Rubeanus,* Catholic
co-author of the *Epistolae Obscurorum Virorum.*

W HO WAS MARTIN LUTHER? PERHAPS THE NAME NEED
not be examined. "What's in a name?" And need the
ancestors be disturbed? Some wit once remarked: The
man who boasts of his illustrious ancestors is like the potato: the
better part of him is underground. Little danger of such boasting
in Luther's case. To begin with, Luther was not given to boasting;
and secondly, he came from lowly, though honorable, parents.
The etymology of the family name has caused much speculation.
Luther himself offered various derivations at different times.
Modern etymologists seem to be agreed that the name developed
from the surname Lothar. Variant spellings were Lother and
Lotther. Originally Lothar is said to have been written Chlo-
tachar. This designated a man who was renowned (hlut = famous)
in the army (chari = German *Heer, army).* Surely, a singularly
appropriate meaning for the name of a man who became one of
the most renowned champions in the Church Militant of Jesus
Christ. But this could scarcely be foreseen. Modern sociologists
are suggesting that the biography of a man be begun with a study
of at least his grandparents. When asked how to train a boy most
efficiently, Victor Hugo is credited with having answered: "Begin
with his grandmother." It is commonly held that many characteristics are inherited from one's grandparents, particularly from the
maternal side. If continued observation were ever to prove this
to be a reliable key to the secret of a man's personality, it would
unfortunately contribute little to the tracing of the roots of Luther's character. We do not know as much as the name of Luther's
maternal grandmother. We are merely told that she was a towns-

woman from Smalkald. Such a dearth of information may seem strange; for it is known that almost a tenth of the landowning farmers about Moehra were members of what one may call the Luther clan. They were an energetic and sturdy stock. They more than held their own in that community, and even at the turn of the present century, more than four hundred years after Luther's birth, six Luther families were still living in those parts.

ONLY "ONE" LUTHER

It may in consequence seem peculiar that only one Luther achieved more than local renown. But still, how many famous men are there in history who were the sons of equally renowned fathers or whose own sons followed in their footsteps? There are no more than a few. The Bach family is one such notable exception. For centuries the name Bach and the word musician were synonymous in Germany. In England the younger Pitt occurs to one as a son who was his father's chief competitor for highest honors. "A chip of the old block," someone said while young Pitt was delivering his maiden speech in Parliament. "No," Burke replied, "the old block himself." But who ever heard of the illustrious ancestors of our Miltons and Shakespeares, our Washingtons and Lincolns? And as to sons: many scarcely recall whether they had any. So Martin Luther blazes forth a lone star of the first magnitude, runs his brilliant course in history, then disappears. To many this has seemed providential. God had work that needed to be done. He raised up and prepared the man who was to do it. And that man could have a successor in his peculiar work as little as could the Apostles. However much the lack of a second Shakespeare is unexplainable, there could, in the very nature of the case, be but one Luther.

LUTHER'S PARENTS

Where did he come from? Who were his immediate antecedents? Who and what were his father and mother? The elder Cranach did two portraits of Hans and Margarete Luther. Perhaps they are still hanging in the Luther room at the Wartburg.

Upon these pictures of Luther's parents biologists, sociologists, phrenologists, and other more or less genuinely scientific students of man's antecedents have been exercising their ingenuity ever since. Hans and Margarete are called "small, short persons, a tan folk" by contemporaries. Luther's close friend Spalatin assures us that the Reformer was the image of his mother. Of his father Melanchthon says: "For his integrity he was greatly beloved by all good men"; and of the mother: "While there were in her the other virtues which become an honorable matron, yet in her were especially conspicuous modesty, the fear of God, prayerfulness; and other honorable women looked up to her as an example of virtue." [1] It is well known that the discipline in Hans Luther's family of seven children (Martin was the oldest) was strict to severity. Neither father nor mother spared the rod. Upon one occasion, Luther tells us, his father beat him so severely that for some time there was an estrangement between them. Upon another, his mother took matters in hand and flogged him till the blood flowed. He added: "They meant it heartily well, but they could not discern dispositions, according to which corrections should be tempered." [2] According to Luther's well-known remark "The apple should lie beside the rod," there should be a judicious use of severity and kindness, or, if you will, of Law and Gospel. It appears, then, that Luther's parents found it as difficult to divide these pedagogically as their son did theologically for many years.

HOW LUTHER IMPRESSED A CONTEMPORARY

Meanwhile Martin received his primary education at Magdeburg and Eisenach, matriculated at the University of Erfurt in 1501, entered the Augustinian cloister in 1505, and became priest in 1507. In 1508 he was called to the University of Wittenberg, became Doctor of Divinity in 1512, and in 1517 began to shake the world with his 95 Theses. These brought on the famous debate at Leipzig in 1519. Peter Schad, better known as Mosellanus,

---

[1] In Be, M 120.   [2] Erl 61:274.

from his birthplace on the river Moselle, presided at this historic encounter and has given us what we are anxious to hear: the first fairly detailed description by an eyewitness of Luther's appearance at this time. He was now thirty-six years old. Mosellanus writes: "Martin is of middle height with slender body, worn out both by study and care, so that you can almost count his bones. He is in the vigor of manhood; his voice is sharp and clear. He is so wonderfully learned in the Bible that he has almost all the texts in memory. He has learned enough Greek and Hebrew to form a judgment of the translations. He has no lack of matter in speaking, for an immense stock of ideas and words are at his command. Perhaps you miss in him judgment and method in using his stores. In daily life and manners he is cultivated and affable, having nothing of the stoic and nothing supercilious about him; rather he plays the man at all seasons. He is a joker in society, vivacious and sure, always with a happy face no matter how hard his enemies press him. You would hardly believe that he was the man to do such great things unless inspired by the gods. But what most men blame in him is that in answering he is more imprudent and cutting than is safe for a reformer of the Church, or than is decorous for a theologian."[3] About the criticism contained in this description of Luther's manner of defending himself more will be said anon. Naturally the Luther of, let us say 1539, was in more than one respect no longer the Luther of 1519, although the basic traits of his character and even certain external characteristics remained with him to the very end. Thus he carried himself peculiarly erect, slightly elevating his left shoulder above the right and tilting his head backward. If this created an impression of self-importance, it was belied by Luther's entire demeanor, which, while increasingly self-confident, was genuinely modest and unassuming. It was observed that when engaged in an animated discussion while seated, he would lean forward and rub his hands over his knees, as though seeking also a physical outlet for the intense activity of his mind.

---

[3] S-J, LC I:261.

PLATE II

LUTHER'S BIRTHPLACE

The house in which Luther was born in Eisleben, Saxony, stands at the top of a street bearing his name. All except the first floor burned in 1689, but was restored by voluntary contributions. In 1693 and for a number of years thereafter it was used as a public school for orphans. In 1817 the government took charge of this historical shrine. The bust of Luther above the entrance is, of course, a modern addition

PLATE III

LUTHER'S FATHER

This painting of Hans Luther, the Reformer's father, was done by
Lucas Cranach, the German artist and personal friend of Luther,
in 1527

PLATE IV

LUTHER'S MOTHER

Lucas Cranach also painted Luther's mother in 1527. Her maiden
name was Margarete Ziegler. Contemporaries tell us that Martin
resembled his mother rather than his father in appearance

PLATE V

LUTHER IN HIS DOCTOR'S ROBE

At the comparatively early age of 29 Luther had taken the degree of Doctor of Sacred Theology. This painting, by Cranach, was apparently made somewhat later, for it indicates a moderate portliness, which certainly did not characterize Luther in 1512

LUTHER'S PHYSICAL APPEARANCE

Luther's head was massive, but because of the breadth of his shoulders appeared to be smaller than it was in reality. Again, his forehead seemed to be lower than it really was, partly because of the light-brown hair which in later life was permitted to fall down over it and partly because of the great development of the lower half of the face. With the increasing corpulence of middle age Luther developed a double chin. Considered as a whole, his head is that of a man of intense feeling, of dauntless courage, and of an iron will. He is the man of action rather than the purely speculative genius. But it is no small mind and no cramped soul that look out upon the world through those black eyes. Perhaps nothing about Luther's appearance is more frequently referred to by his contemporaries than his eyes. They were black, deep-set, and slanted slightly downward toward the bridge of the nose. They were unforgettable eyes, marvelously expressive. The papal emissary Cajetan, who had felt their penetrating power, shudderingly exclaimed: "I will no more discuss matters with this beast; he has deep eyes and marvelous speculations in his head." At Worms the gleam of those falcon eyes chanced to fall upon an Italian. The man moved uneasily in his seat, as if "the evil eye were upon him." [4] The Swiss Kessler, who met Luther at an inn on his way to Wittenberg, says: "His eyes were black and deep-set, shining and sparkling like stars, so that one might not well bear to look into them." [5] The eyebrows were really not arched but rather ran upward toward the temples, like the outspread wings of an eagle. Some students hold that from a purely artistic point of view Luther's mouth was the most striking feature of his face. One artist says that it eloquently expresses both firmness and kindness. The voice of the Reformer was not deep, resonant, and booming; it was rather high-pitched — a spoken tenor, one may say — but clear and penetrating. The chin of Luther, though square and well developed, did not protrude belligerently. The comfortable corpulence of later life added to its fullness.

---

[4] Li, H I:280.   [5] Cp. K-K, M I:500.

LUTHER PORTRAITS AND BUSTS

Those interested in portraits of Luther, done by his contemporaries, notably by his friends, the Cranachs, father and son, may read Appendix A in H. Boehmer's *Luther and the Reformation in the Light of Modern Research,* 5th edition, translated by E. S. G. Potter. It is not necessary to list and to evaluate the Cranach Luther portraits. It is enough to remark that they are inferior as drawings to the productions of their contemporaries Holbein and Duerer. A pity that neither of these masters has given us a likeness of the Reformer. Boehmer says that also Rietschel's famous Luther head shows us a rather idealized Luther. Since we possess no good authentic portraits of the later Luther by a first-class artist, it is perhaps as easy to make this statement as it is difficult to prove it. We do know that Luther put on weight in later life. He refers to himself as "ein fetter Doktor." Just how much his portliness and the wear and tear of life altered his features it is impossible accurately to determine. Probably we shall always have to be satisfied with the judgment of painters and sculptors in this matter. While we are aware of the fact that, after all, it means little to Luther's character how his face looked, we nonetheless like to think that his features continued to express something of the greatness of the soul within him. In consequence, as far as we are concerned, we are willing to accept Rietschel's Luther as coming as close to the real Luther of later life as it is possible to reconstruct from the data that have come down to us. If Luther did *not* look like that in later life, he certainly might have. The adamant in his character, together with the imperturbability of his heroic faith, is written all over the face of Rietschel's head of Luther. Notice that tilt upward of the head, before remarked about. And though, unfortunately, no sculptor can reproduce those "windows whence a man's soul looks out," as eyes have been appropriately called, only a moderately active imagination is necessary to think Luther's leonine eyes into Rietschel's masterpiece. And there he stands, "unsubduable granite," as Carlyle says. Pope and Emperor, devil and hell, combine against him; vile enemies traduce and slander him; false friends betray the cause of Christ and His Church; but Martin Luther "continues the even tenor of his way." For the "peace of God which passeth all understanding," that deep peace in Christ Jesus which Luther's enemies know not, has breathed a great calm into his big soul. He is far too much of a realist to underestimate the dangers by which he is constantly surrounded, but the grand thing about the man is this, that he knows "Groesser als der Helfer ist die Not ja nicht." If those determined lips of Rietschel's Luther could speak, one would expect them to say:

> Though devils all the world should fill,
> All eager to devour us,
> We tremble not, we fear no ill;
> They shall not overpower us.

LUTHER DEEPLY RELIGIOUS

One of the first impressions one gets of Luther is this: here is a man who is deeply religious. This impression is confirmed upon closer study. His character is essentially religion-centered. Spiritual relations and religious truths are his chief concerns. Naturally, this does not mean that there was any affinity between Luther's soul and the Gospel of saving grace. The leaders in the field of specifically Christian thought and the heroes of Christian faith are the products of a spiritual rebirth, not the results of ordinary births. It may be true that our Bachs and Beethovens are born musical geniuses. But our Sauls can become Pauls by regeneration only. When, therefore, a natural bent in Luther toward religion is spoken of, the reference is not to the content of religious belief, but to an active interest in religion as such. What is meant is simply this, that Luther did not only not neglect the religious interest that lives in every heart by nature, but carefully and actively cultivated it. Perhaps he ought to be called a religious introvert, but that term is not adequate. It is too narrow. He listened with awe to the voice of his conscience. The strict parental discipline developed a very sensitive conscience within him and made him think much about right and wrong.

To young Luther the great end of life increasingly seemed to be the adjustment of the relation between a man's soul and his God. That is, indeed, the basic problem of every religion: the proper relation between the temporal and the eternal, the visible and the invisible, the natural and the supernatural, the sinful and the holy. Says the great German Luther student Dr. Wilhelm Walther: "In so far as Luther's character was shaped by his own bent and determination, it was entirely religion-centered, and only he can correctly understand him who seeks to appreciate him as a religious hero." [6] The judicious Leopold von Ranke remarks: "Never was a man permeated in a more lively manner by the feeling of the immediate presence of the Divine Being." [7] Perhaps the best appreciation of this intense religiousness of Luther by a non-Lutheran comes from the pen of Julius Hare. He says: "You can hardly read a single letter, however slight and short . . . without being impressed with the conviction that religion with Luther is not a thing of words and phrases, not a thing of habit or custom, of convention or tradition, not a thing of times and seasons, but an intense, vivid reality, which governs the pulses of his heart and the motions of his will." [8] But let Luther reveal the intensity of his religiousness to us himself.

HIS LOVE FOR THEOLOGY

In 1508 he had been called to the University of Wittenberg. The following year he wrote to a certain Johann Braun, priest of the Church of the Virgin at Eisenach: "If you wish to know my condition, I am well, thank God, except that my studies are very severe, especially philosophy, which from the first I would willingly have changed for theology; I mean that theology which searches out the meat of the nut, and the kernel of the grain and the marrow of the bones." [9] The German mind has been called "ponderously metaphysical" and "exasperatingly thorough." Whether this is right or wrong, a merit or a demerit, need not be ventilated here. So much, however, is certainly true: the

---

[6] Wa, L 5 f.   [7] Ra, D III:191.   [8] H, V 89.   [9] S-J, LC I:24.

German Luther was never satisfied unless he had penetrated to the very heart of a matter. He wanted to look into the inner soul of things. Nor did he, from the first, hesitate to look deeply and searchingly into his own soul. This practice at times caused him moments of spiritual wretchedness. In one of these the earnest soul writes: "I beg you to pray the Lord for me, for I confess to you that my life daily approaches nearer to hell." [10] To this letter he signs himself "an exiled son of Adam," indicating what was troubling him: a lively awareness of human corruption, of which we shall have more to say somewhat later. In a similar strain he pours out his heart to Melanchthon: "Pray for me, wretched and despised worm that I am, vexed with a spirit of sadness by the good will of the Father of mercies, to whom be glory even in my wretchedness. . . . I seek for nothing else and thirst for nothing else than a gracious God." [11]

Luther's approach to life as a whole is distinctly religious. Things are of importance to him in direct proportion to their convertibility into religious values. Not only do "the heavens declare the glory of God and the firmament show forth His handiwork" (Ps. 19:1), but the most unpromising situations in life minister spiritual benefits to him, and the most trivial matters remind him of some eternal truth. The world is full of silent but eloquent preachers for Martin Luther. He is so saturated with religious truth that his mind's eye discovers it everywhere, just as the world takes on the color of the glasses through which we look out upon it. In reality Luther is listening to himself. The lessons his surroundings preach to him are echoes of the great truths that are moving in his soul; the illustrations he sees in them are reflections of his own inner life. A few instances may make this clear. Luther had a bowling green prepared for the many young men who frequented his home. He loved himself to roll the first ball, which perhaps would go in a direction not at all intended by the Doctor. In the general laughter which followed he heartily

---

[10] S-J, LC I:50.   [11] S-J, LC II:419.

joined, then, sobering, he remarked how often in life a man was certain he could perform miracles in Church and State, could, as it were, lay low all nine pins with the first ball, nay, fancied he possessed such wizardly talents as to bowl down an even dozen of the nine pins and then saw his ball roll — into the gutter, that is, failed ignominiously to make good his boast. Upon one occasion Luther expressed his interest in chemistry, because, aside from its importance to medicine and metallurgy, it always suggested a picture to him of how God on the day of universal resurrection and judgment would restore our bodies from the dust of the grave and would separate with unerring accuracy the good and the evil. One day a pet dog, sitting on his haunches, eyed with intense desire a piece of meat which Luther was holding in his hand. The Doctor observed his eloquently pleading look for a while, sighed and remarked: "Oh, that I might pray the way the dog can look at that meat!" From the Wartburg he wrote to his friend Spalatin: "Last week I hunted two days to see what that bitter- sweet pleasure of heroes was like. We took two hares and a few poor partridges — a worthy occupation indeed for men with nothing to do. I even moralized among the snares and dogs, and the superficial pleasure I may have derived from the hunt was equalled by the pity and the pain which are a necessary part of it. It is an image of the devil hunting innocent little creatures with his gins and his hounds, the impious magistrates, bishops and theologians. I deeply felt this parable of the simple and faithful soul. A still more cruel parable followed. With great pains I saved a little live rabbit and rolled it up in the sleeve of my cloak, but when I left it and went a little way off, the dogs found the poor rabbit and killed it by biting its right leg and throat through the cloth. Thus do the Pope and Satan rage to kill souls and are not stopped by my labor."[12]

We shall see in a different connection that Luther's interest in the fine arts was not aesthetic. He knew nothing of "art for

_____

[12] S-J, LC II:53 f.

art's sake." These things were of value to him in direct proportion to the service they rendered, or could be made to render, to
religion. Luther's first, last, and constant interest in life was
religion.

IN PROSPERITY AND IN ADVERSITY RELIGION OF SUPREME INTEREST

But what is the ultimate goal of the Christian religion? It is
so to live in this life as to prepare for that to which this is merely
introductory. "Our citizenship is in heaven." Old Cotton Mather
said of John Eliot, the famous "Apostle to the Indians": "He was
one who lived in heaven while he was on earth." He might have
said as much of Luther; for if ever it could be said of a man that
his feet were planted firmly on the earth, while his heart was in
heaven, that man was Martin Luther. There are enough people
whose interest in that other life is aroused only if and when this
life begins to pall on them. Not so Luther. He thoroughly enjoyed the good things of this life. After he had found his Savior
and had discovered the Christian philosophy of life, there was
nothing of the pseudo spirituality of a cramping asceticism about
him despite his deep religiousness. Yet, in 1541 he wrote to his
sick friend Friedrich Myconius: "I have received your letter saying that you are sick unto death, that is, if you interpret it rightly
and blessedly, unto life. It is a singular joy to me that you are so
unterrified by death, that sleep into which all good men fall, nay,
that you are rather desirous of being freed and living with Christ.
We should have this desire not only on the bed of sickness but in
the full vigor of life, at all times and in all places and circumstances, seeing that we are Christians who have risen, revived,
and ascended into heaven with Christ." [13] This does not mean
that Luther never longed for that other life because of the misery
of this one. His sensitive nature keenly felt the troubles here
below. Nor does the heroism of faith for which he is justly noted
make a man's soul insensible to the sorrows of this life. On the
contrary: the Christian faith makes one understand the troubles of

[13] Sm, L 391.

life in all their depth and breadth; for it reveals their deadly root, sin. But it knows of no cure-all that will finally usher in the millennium for human society. The Christian knows that in spite of his strenuous efforts to dry the tears and bind up the wounds of his suffering fellow man, this world will continue to be full of headaches and heartaches to the very end. For that blessed consummation he therefore longs. His burdened soul is full of a heavenly homesickness. Luther's soul was. In 1530 his father lay critically ill. He wrote to him: "This execrable life is nothing but a vale of tears; the longer a man lives, the more sin and wickedness and plague and sorrow he sees and feels, nor is there respite or cessation this side the grave; *there* is repose, and we can then sleep in the rest Christ gives us until He comes again to wake us with joy. Amen." [14] Upon reading these words one feels that they must have welled up out of the very depth of the Reformer's heart. Nevertheless, there is no note of defeatism in them. Luther does not long for heaven merely because he is tired of fighting against sin and evil, but because he is tired of sin and evil as such and longs for the perfection of that other life. "No *Weltschmerz,* no melancholy discontent, lay at the root of this calm and for the most part wonderfully cheerful longing for death. With Luther, as with all great Christians from St. Paul to Johann Sebastian Bach, it sprang directly from the conviction which governed his whole feeling and thoughts: 'For to me to live is Christ, and to die is gain.'" [15]

---

[14] S-J, LC II:515.
[15] Bo, L 187.

CHAPTER IV

"HERE I STAND"

We owe you much, Martin, for having led us
from the husks of swine back to the pastures of
life and the words of salvation.

Johann Staupitz, abbot of a Benedictine cloister

THERE IS SOMETHING ALMOST PATHETIC ABOUT THESE WORDS of Staupitz. As is well known, he was the first dean of the theological faculty at Wittenberg, was named vicar general of the German Augustinian monasteries, and in this capacity became acquainted with Luther, whose talents he quickly discovered and appreciated. As vicar general Staupitz encouraged the study of the Scriptures and, as this would lead one to expect, at first abetted Luther in his protest against the departure of Rome from its standards. But, like Erasmus, he was timid by nature and seems to have fancied that the reformation of the Church might be effected gently, gradually, and privately. Luther was too bold and aggressive for Johann Staupitz, and so they slowly drew apart. The quotation above is from his last letter to Luther. Eight months later Staupitz was no more. His motto had been: "Jesus, Thine am I; save me." There is reason to believe that he had recognized both the formal and the material principle of the Reformation: the sufficiency of God-inspired Scripture and justification by faith. The pathetic thing about the man is — and in this respect he was one of many — that he did not possess the courage of his convictions. But he is at least to be credited with having clearly seen the pivotal truths of the movement.

FORMAL PRINCIPLE OF THE REFORMATION

The first was *sola Scriptura:* the all-sufficiency of Scripture as the inspired Word of God. The Reformation is often spoken of as that period of history during which the mind of man was liberated. In a certain sense this is true enough. The mind of man was freed from priestcraft and hierarchical tyranny. But it is not true that Luther meant to emancipate human reason from all control in the sense of Nietzsche: that "der Mensch ist das Mass aller Dinge," that is, man himself determines the truth or the falsehood, the right or the wrong, of everything, so that there is no appeal to any higher court from the decisions of his mind. The forces of radicalism in our times are known to have claimed Luther — who has *not* claimed him? — as the apostle of their position, at least in principle. "In principle," we say, because, not quite daring to represent the Reformer as the preacher of an absolute liberty, of anarchic individualism, they contend that it was only an unfortunate inconsistency that Martin Luther stopped short where he did. But this is not being true to the facts in the case.

WARNING AGAINST MISUSE OF REASON IN RELIGION

Neither explicitly nor implicitly did Luther ever preach that liberty consists in an exemption from all external control whatsoever. Such a practical deification of human reason was no less than abominable idolatry in the eyes of Luther. As early as 1518, after defending his position against the theologians of the University of Erfurt, he wrote to his intimate, Spalatin: "In vain is a story told to a deaf man; they obstinately stick to their own little ideas, though they confess that these ideas are supported by no other authority than natural reason, which we consider the same as dark chaos." [1] It is evident that from the very beginning Luther considered human reason, whether in a Christian or in a non-Christian, unsafe as a guide into the truth. Nor did he ever recede from this position. In the last sermon he was to preach at Wittenberg, a few weeks before his death, he says in part: "Human reason disgraces and insults God. . . . Therefore reason is, in kind and in nature, a ruinous prostitute. . . . See to it, then, that you bridle reason and do not follow her pretty

---

[1] S-J, LC I:85.

notions. . . . [Tell her:] You cursed harlot, would you mislead me into practicing prostitution with the devil? . . . This struggle [against reason] goes on till the Last Day. . . . Nothing is quite so pleasing to one as *philautia*, the enjoyment of one's own wisdom." [2] The Lutheran emphasis in this passage is nothing artificial, no cheap pulpit fanfare. We know that especially toward the end of his life the Reformer viewed with grave apprehension the symptoms of an incipient rationalism. This alarm was increased by finding the "cult of reason" rearing its ugly head in the inner circle of his friends. Notably the philosophically inclined Melanchthon was weakening in this respect. That boded no good for the Church. Therefore the increased emphasis on the deadly danger of dabbling into the mysteries of revelation with the "cursed harlot" reason. If, after his decease, those who were to carry on his work would introduce the vicious principle of rationalism, Luther would make certain that at least *he* could be quoted by no one in defense of that "fruitful mother of all heresies." As such he looked upon reason. He was firmly convinced that no specifically Christian doctrine could and would survive the reign of reason in religion. In his *Commentary on the Letter to the Galatians* he had said: "If we will follow the judgment of reason, God setteth forth absurd and impossible things when He setteth out unto us the articles of the Christian faith." [3] Thereupon he lists the principal doctrines of Christianity and points out that they seem "absurd and foolish" to "that most cruel and pestilent enemy of God" reason. The development of the thought is occasioned by the interpretation of Gal. 3:6: "Abraham believed God." Also the patriarch, Luther points out, had to believe against reason and in the face of the evidence of his senses. "But," he continues, "faith killeth reason and slayeth that beast. . . . So all the godly . . . do kill reason, saying: Reason, thou art foolish; thou dost not savor those things which belong unto God; therefore speak not against me, but hold thy peace; judge not, but hear the Word of God and believe it." [4]

---

[2] Erl 16:143-145.   [3] Lu, G 195.   [4] Lu, G 195.

UNDUE AUTHORITY CONCEDED TO FATHERS AND SCHOOLMEN

Luther expected this subordination of reason to revelation from all men, including the post-Apostolic Fathers and the Scholastics of the subsequent Middle Ages. He was willing enough to listen to them in the witness box, but he would not tolerate them in the chair of the judge. Naturally, Luther thought more of the Church Fathers than he did of the Schoolmen, since many of the Fathers were still fairly orthodox. Thus he wrote to a certain Dungersheim, who carried on a private controversy with him by mail: "You and Eck are accustomed to accommodate the words of the Bible to the words of the Fathers, as though they did not desire to draw us to the Bible rather than to themselves. But contrariwise it is my custom, following the example of Augustine, but reverently, rather to follow up the streams to the source, as Bernard boasts that he did." [5] Throughout his life Luther thought highly of Augustine. In the introduction which he wrote for the publication of his German works in 1539, he first says it is *not* a pity that, by the grace of God, the books of many of the Fathers and Councils have been lost. Yet, he continues, he likes to use the writings of the Fathers as books of reference, and "by this manner of using them I am following the example of St. Augustine, who is among the first, nay, who is almost the only one who wants to remain unfettered by the books of all the Fathers and saints and be subject to Holy Writ alone. On this score he had a rough skirmish with St. Jerome, who threw up to him the books of his predecessors. But St. Augustine paid no attention to them. And if one had only followed this example of St. Augustine, the Pope had never become the Antichrist, and innumerable books would not have come into the churches like swarms of countless bugs and insects; and the Bible would nicely have remained in the pulpit." [6] But the trouble was that St. Augustine's example was *not* followed; and Luther was severely criticized in his days for daring to impugn the authority of the time-honored schoolmen. He unburdens himself thus to Staupitz

---

[5] S-J, LC I:255.   [6] Erl 1:69.

in 1518: "My adversaries excite hatred against me from the scholastic doctors, because I prefer the Fathers and the Bible to them; they are almost insane with their zeal. I read the scholastics with judgment, not, as they do, with closed eyes. Thus the Apostle commanded: 'Prove all things; hold fast that which is good.' I neither reject all that they say nor approve all. Thus those babblers make the whole of a part, a fire of a spark, and an elephant of a fly. But with God's help I care nothing for their scarecrows." [7] S. T. Coleridge, who was a great admirer of the Reformer, tells us how it came about that Luther freed himself from the servile deference to the Schoolmen and the Fathers which was so characteristic of his age. He says: "Luther was too spiritual, of too heroic faith, to be thus blinded by the declamations of the Fathers." [8]

LUTHER DID NOT EXPECT MEN BLINDLY TO ACCEPT "HIS" WORD

This spirituality and heroic faith of Luther also kept him from having faith in himself, from relying on his own judgment or encouraging anyone to accept anything as true or right merely because he, Martin Luther, taught and thought it was so. In the introduction to his German works, just adverted to, Luther says: "Whoever wants my books at this time ought, whatever he does, not let them be an obstacle to studying the Bible itself." [9] Men were not to believe even the Bible because Luther believed it, though they might follow Luther because they had satisfied themselves that he followed the Bible. "No one is bound to believe me; let every man search [Scripture] for himself," [10] he bluntly told the Christians of Strassburg. Such words prove that Martin Luther was not, and could not be, the founder of a mere sect. He and Mohammed were poles apart. He was so far removed from expecting or hoping that his writings would become a sort of Lutheran Koran that he wrote to the printers in 1523: "I had hoped that people would henceforth pay more attention

---

[7] S-J, LC I:78.   [9] Erl 1:68.
[8] In H, V 80.   [10] S-J, LC II:276.

to the Holy Scriptures themselves and let my books go now that they have served their purpose and led men's hearts into and up to the Scriptures, which was my reason for writing my books. What is the use of making many books and yet always staying away from the chief book? Drink rather from the fountain itself than from the rill that has led you to the fountain." [11] But perhaps the grandest thing Luther ever wrote on this subject is to be found in a letter to a friend and relative of Franz von Sickingen, Hartmuth von Cronberg. To this man the Reformer wrote: "There are many who believe on my account, but the only true believers are those who would continue to believe even if they heard (which God forbid!) that I had denied the faith or fallen away from it. These are they who pay no heed to the bad, the terrible, the shameful things they hear about me and about our people, for they do not believe on Luther, but on Christ Himself. The Word has them, and they have the Word; as for Luther, they care not whether he is a knave or a saint. God can speak by Balaam as well as by Isaiah, by Caiaphas as well as by Peter; nay, He can speak by an ass. I myself do not know Luther and will not know him. I do not preach about him, but about Christ. The fiend may fly away with him, if he can; but if he leaves Christ in peace, it will still be well with us." [12] No, Martin Luther expected no man blindly to follow him whithersoever he led.

Nor did Luther ever profess that God favored him with visions and private revelations. As is well known, this has been the claim of "enthusiasts" (*Schwaermer*) from the days of the Montanists down to Joseph Smith, Mary Baker Eddy, and others. Perhaps it is not necessary to refute the accusation that Luther at times confessed to having received his Gospel directly from Christ. He did, indeed, write to his Elector: "I have received my Gospel not from men but from heaven only, by our Lord Jesus Christ." [13] However, only an almost unpardonable ignorance or a still more culpable malice can see anything in this but the assertion that it was the exalted Christ Himself who opened the eyes of Luther

---

[11] S-J, LC II:189. [12] S-J, LC II:108. [13] S-J, LC II:94.

to the correct understanding of the Gospel as it is revealed in Scripture. But this is true of every Christian. "No man cometh unto the Father but by Me," [14] said Jesus. This religious soberness of the Reformer appears the more remarkable when we bear in mind the fervor and intensity of his faith. There was nothing of the frothy irresponsibility of the religious enthusiast about him, nothing of the religious autointoxication of the mystic. Luther persistently held that every supposed revelation of God outside and above and beyond God's Word was a satanic delusion and a snare. Deservedly well known are his words in the Smalkald Articles: "In a word, enthusiasm inheres in Adam and his children from the beginning to the end of the world, having been implanted and infused into them by the old dragon, and is the origin, power, and strength of all heresy, especially of that of the Papacy and Mahomet. Therefore we must constantly maintain this point, that God does not wish to deal with us otherwise than through the spoken Word and the Sacraments. It is the devil himself whatsoever is extolled as Spirit without the Word and Sacraments." [15] In his *Table Talk* Luther tells us that one day, while he was engaged in his room in fervent prayer and meditation on the Passion of Christ for us, a glowing light appeared on the wall opposite him. In it was visible a majestic figure of Christ with His five wounds. At first Luther imagined it to be something good, but it soon occurred to him that Christ appears to us only in His Word and in the lowliness of a suffering Savior. Therefore, turning to the apparition, he exclaimed: "Be gone there, you shameful devil." Thereupon the vision disappeared.[16] Take the story for what you think it is worth. And it *is* worth something. Whether the apparition had objective reality or not means little or nothing for our purpose. It was real to *Luther;* and his refusal to accept as God-sent any revelation aside from His revealed will is strikingly illustrated by this anecdote.

---

[14] John 14:6.

[15] Erl 25:140 (*Concordia Triglotta* translation).

[16] In K-K, M II:517.

There was a good reason for this loyalty of Luther to Scripture. It has been called an afterthought; and it is true: Luther was more or less involuntarily crowded into this position by the course of events. But at a date earlier than is usually supposed, Luther recognized the all-sufficiency of the Bible as well as its verbal inspiration. The latter doctrine had, indeed, not suffered so much at the hands of Rome as had the former. To begin with, it is more theoretical; we mean: one's attitude over against it does not become so readily evident. Then, too, a man may adhere to the inspiration of Scriptures and still deny its all-sufficiency. This, in a general way, became the official position of Rome; and it was also Luther's position at first.

A few years before the posting of the Theses, during Luther's lectures on the Psalms, delivered 1513—1515, his students heard and noted the following from him: "What pasture is to the beast . . . the nest for the birds, the stream for fish, the Scriptures are for the believing souls. . . . It cannot be otherwise, for the Scriptures are divine; in them God speaks, and they are His Word." [17] These words express both the necessity and the inspiration of Scriptures and find the former rooted in the latter. "And yet Luther did not at this time regard the Scriptures as the sole authority. . . . To the Church and the Church Fathers Luther still surrendered his own and independent understanding of Scripture." [18] It was not until the year 1518 that Luther, by his public appeal to a future general Church Council, showed that he no longer regarded the Pope as an authority beside or above Scripture.

Then came the great Leipzig Debate during the summer of 1519. In the course of preparing for this and during the debate itself, Luther cut himself loose also from the authority of the Councils. He now had come to recognize clearly the sole authority

---

[17] Wei 3:640; 41, 6; 451, 26, in Re, L 17.   [18] Re, L 18 f.

and all-sufficiency of the written Word. In the early months of 1519 he wrote: "I honor the Roman Pontiff and his decrees. None is above him, without exception, save the Prince of this vicar of Christ, namely, Jesus Himself, Lord of us all and of all men. I prefer His word to the words of His vicar, and have no doubt that we should judge all the words and deeds of the vicar by *His* word. For I desire him to be subject to this universal rule of the apostle: 'Prove all things; hold fast that which is good.' I will suffer none to withdraw his neck from this yoke, whether in the name of the mother or of the mistress of all churches. I have the more reason for this position as in our time we see some councils rejected and others accepted, theology treated as a matter of mere opinion, the sense of law depend on the arbitrary opinion of one man, and, in short, everything so confounded that almost nothing certain is left to us. But it is clearer than day that many decretals are repugnant to the Gospel, so that we are simply forced to fly for refuge to that solid rock of Scripture, and not to believe anything, no matter what, that speaks, commands, or does anything without this authority." [19] This supreme authority of Scripture Luther henceforth urged with an emphasis and a persistency that are, we believe, in a class by themselves.

A few illustrations will serve to make this clear. In 1521 he wrote: "That is truly a carrying of the sword in the scabbard when we do not take the naked sword by itself but only as it is encased in the words and glosses of men. This dulls its edge and makes it obscurer than it was before, though Emser calls it smiting with the blade. The bare sword makes him tremble from head to foot. Be it known, then, that Scripture without any gloss is the sun and the sole light from which all teachers receive their light, and not the contrary." [20] The same year witnessed the dramatic climax of the development of Luther's attitude to Scripture. On April 18, in the presence of an august host of witnesses, Martin Luther made this immortal statement: "Unless I am overcome with testimonies from Scripture or with evident reasons

---

[19] S-J, LC I:158 f.   [20] Wei 7:638, 26 ff., in Re, L 144 f.

— for I believe neither the Pope nor the Councils, since they have often erred and contradicted one another — I am overcome by the Scripture texts which I have adduced, and my conscience is bound by God's Word. I cannot and will not recant anything; for to act contrary to one's conscience is neither safe nor sincere. God help me! Amen." [21] Thus before all the world, as it were, Luther took his stand on the Bible alone. Nor is the expression "evident reasons" a modification of the position, introducing a second principle of authority, human reason. The words "my conscience is bound by God's Word" make such an interpretation impossible. By "evident reasons" Luther means plain deductions which are drawn from Scripture passages, such as the following. The Bible teaches that "the wages of sin is death," but infants are subject to death; therefore infants, too, must be sinful. "Here I stand" — whether Luther concluded his heroic address with these words or not, whether the "here" was meant literally or figuratively, need not concern us. The fact is — thank God! — that he *did* stand, stand there bodily and boldly, and freely and firmly took his stand on Scripture alone. Henceforth — depend upon it — Martin Luther will never fail to improve an opportunity to press home that indispensable prerequisite of orthodoxy: *sola Scriptura*.

"ALL" HUMAN AUTHORITY REJECTED

In his mighty *Commentary on the Letter to the Galatians,* which appeared during these years, this thought recurs at frequent intervals. Thus Luther writes: "A goodly argument, forsooth: I approve the Scripture; ergo, I am above the Scripture. John Baptist acknowledgeth and confesseth Christ and pointeth to Him with his finger; therefore he is above Christ! The Church approveth the Christian faith and doctrine; therefore the Church is above them! For the overthrow of this their wicked and blasphemous doctrine thou hast here [Gal. 1:9] a plain text like a thunderbolt, wherein Paul subjected both himself and an angel

---

21 K-K, M I:417.

from heaven, and doctors upon earth, and all other teachers and masters whatsoever under the authority of Scripture; for they ought not be masters, judges, or arbiters, but only witnesses, disciples, and confessors of the Church, whether it be the Pope, Luther, Augustine, Paul, or an angel from heaven. Neither ought any doctrine to be heard in the Church besides the pure Word of God, that is to say, the Holy Scriptures; otherwise accursed be both the teachers and hearers together with their doctrine." [22] Towards the end of his commentary Luther again presses home the *sola Scriptura* and says it is to be upheld even though it be charged with causing divisions in Christendom.

ADHERENCE TO SCRIPTURE NOT NARROW-MINDEDNESS

The specious objection that such an uncompromising adherence to Scripture is a breach of Christian love and charity — how modern that sounds! — has given us the following classic passages from the pen of Luther. One may well imagine the verve and energy with which he dashed them off. He says: "Our enemies object against us that we are contentious, obstinate, and intractable in defending our doctrine, and even in matters of no great importance. But these are the crafty fetches of the devil, whereby he goes about utterly to overthrow our doctrine. To this we answer therefore with Paul that a little leaven leaveneth the whole lump. In philosophy a small fault in the beginning is a great and foul fault in the end. So in divinity one little error overthroweth the whole doctrine; wherefore we must separate life and doctrine far asunder. The doctrine is not ours but God's, whose ministers only we are called; therefore we may not change or diminish one tittle thereof. The life is ours; therefore, as touching that, we are ready to do, to suffer, to forgive, etc., whatsoever our adversaries shall require of us, so that faith and doctrine may remain sound and uncorrupt. . . . Doctrine is heaven, life is the earth. In life is sin, error, uncleanness, and misery. . . . There let charity wink, forbear, be beguiled, believe, hope, and

---

[22] Lu, G 51.

suffer all things; there let forgiveness of sins prevail as much as may be, [just] so that sin and error be not defended and maintained. But in doctrine, like as there is no error, so it hath no need of pardon; wherefore there is no comparison between doctrine and life. One little point of doctrine is of more value than heaven and earth; and therefore we cannot abide to have the least jot thereof to be corrupted. . . . Our doctrine — blessed be God! — is pure; we have all the articles of our faith grounded upon the Holy Scriptures; those the devil would gladly corrupt and overthrow; therefore he assaileth us so craftily with this goodly argument, that we ought not to break charity and the unity of the churches." [23] But Luther was not to be taken in by this "goodly argument." His responsibility was to remain scrupulously loyal to the Word and to teach and preach it in all its purity. Whether men accepted or rejected that Word was no responsibility whatever of Martin Luther. "The word of God, in whatever form, whether a simple promise, or a promise embodied in a sacrament, or a series of revelations made by God's Spirit to the soul of man, as recorded in the Bible, is the grand reality which, in Luther's view, dwarfed all other realities on earth. It must needs do so, if it be a reality at all; but scarcely any one has grasped this truth with such intense insight as Luther. Consequently, in his view, the Anabaptist, who held himself emancipated from the authority of God's word on the one side, was as grievously in error as the Romanist on the other, who superseded its authority by that of the Church; and in applying his great principle and working out the Reformation, Luther's task consisted in upholding the due authority of the Scriptures against the extremes on both sides." [24]

SOLE AUTHORITY OF SCRIPTURE DENIED BY THE VAST MAJORITY

Now, this attitude of sole and sober loyalty to Scripture was something new to the church at large. It is true enough that theoretically the Word of God had never been removed from its

---

[23] Lu, G 446, 448.   [24] W, P 195.

supreme position by the public voice of the Church. But for practical purposes this meant little enough. The lack of general education, which the hierarchy did little to remedy, the great cost and the scarcity of books, left the people at large for the most part dependent upon the mere hearing of the Word of God in public worship. That the spirit of the hierarchy was opposed to the free and private study of Scripture became increasingly evident. The Bible came to be looked upon as a professional book, a book for priests and monks, beyond the need, if not the comprehension, of mere laymen. By 1229 this attitude had become so generally accepted that, as we have seen, the Council of Toledo could venture officially to forbid its reading without fear of troublesome protest. Still it is true that ever and again during these darkening centuries voices would be raised in defense of the inspiration and sufficiency of Scripture. To many they must have sounded like voices from the dead. Like John the Baptist's voice, they certainly were voices crying in the wilderness. In this case it was the wilderness of an ossified traditionalism, a wilderness in which a pretentious hierarchy had been polluting and filling in the wells of the Water of Life with the dross and the rubbish of human speculations. But as the night of Scholasticism wore on, certain voices became louder, like the harbingers of a new day. One of these voices was the famous Franciscan Schoolman William Occam († 1349). Luther thought rather highly of some of his writings, notably those on the Lord's Supper. About Scripture, Occam said: "What is not contained in the Scriptures, or cannot with necessary and obvious consistency be deduced from the contents of the same, no Christian needs to believe." [25] One would like to believe that it was for statements such as this that Occam came to be called Doctor Invincibilis, but we fear that would be wishful thinking. Towards the end of this century, just one hundred years before Luther's birth, John Wycliffe died (1384). Especially in his work *Of the Truth of Holy Scripture* he taught the sole authority of the Word of God.

---

[25] In Re, L 14.

This, if nothing else, makes the name he has been given, "the Morning Star of the Reformation," peculiarly applicable. But it need hardly be said that because of this view the Englishman met with emphatic opposition and was called an adherent of the "heretic Occam."

LUTHER VOICED THE CONVICTION OF A MINORITY

When we turn to the century in which Luther himself was born, we come upon the testimony of the chancellor of the University of Paris, a bishop and a cardinal, Pierre D'Ailly († 1420). He was active particularly at the Council of Constance in 1415. But though the minority of which men like him and Gerson were leaders was vocal, its testimony could not penetrate. D'Ailly himself was convinced that only a thoroughgoing "reformation in the head and members" could save the Church from ruin. Of the supremacy of Scripture he said: "A declaration of the canonical Scripture is of greater authority than an assertion of the Christian Church." [26] The conclusion, then, at which we arrive, is this: While the Bible was not entirely neglected in the Church Luther sought to reform, it was studied by her theologians like the writings of an Augustine or a Thomas Aquinas — only not so frequently and zealously; and its passages were quoted in proof of a certain position just as citations from ecclesiastical writers were adduced — only not so frequently. But this did not at all satisfy Martin Luther. He wrote in his vigorous reply to Henry VIII of England: "I oppose the quotations of all the Fathers, the craft and word of all angels, men, and devils with the Scripture. . . . Here I take my stand, am obstinate and proud and say: The Word of God is supreme to me, and the majesty of God supports me; in consequence I care a fig for it though a thousand Augustines and a thousand churches of Henry were opposed to me. I am certain that the true Church clings to the Word of God with me." [27]

---

[26] In Re, L 14.   [27] Erl 28:379.

ALL-SUFFICIENT SCRIPTURE THE ONLY SAFE REFUGE

Indeed, is it so difficult to see that this attitude toward the Bible was the only alternative? The issue was plainly this — nor has it changed today —: either a blind submission to the pronouncements of the Church or an intelligent conviction gained by personal study of the revelation of God in Scripture. The only other alternative was — and is — agnosticism and atheism. Luther tells us in his *Table Talk* that at times when he could not sleep at night and began to think about life and world affairs, the devil would suggest all manner of unsolvable problems to him. He calls these wrestlings his "night battles" and assures us that they were more grueling than his battles by day. There, says the Reformer, in the solitude and stillness of the night, the old evil Foe would tempt him to doubt the very existence of God. Then he adds: "When I think about the Turk, the Pope, and the princes without viewing them and their doings in the light of God's Word, the devil is quick to discharge fiery arrows of temptation into me, but when I oppose him with Holy Writ, I have conquered." [28] Luther means that history does not make sense to natural man. In the face of all the misery and injustice in this world he cannot understand how God, if He really exists and is the Righteous and the Omnipotent One, can look on this world tragedy without forthwith correcting its glaring contradictions. The Reformer holds that the only escape from this pessimism is flight into Scripture. No man, no decrees of councils, but only Scripture can convince the worried heart that in a very real sense "God's in the heaven, and all's well with the world," that God sees everything and controls everything in the interest of His glory and the welfare of His loved ones. There is no reason whatever to be alarmed about anything.

SCRIPTURE SATISFIES BECAUSE OF ITS GREAT CLARITY

Luther would not have been able to have this confidence in Scripture had he doubted the *clarity* of God's revelation. Just this was an open sore in the Church of his day. The clearness of

---

[28] Erl 59:124 f.

Scripture was impugned. Daniel Webster somewhere says that to deny the general clarity of Scripture is to impugn either the love or the intelligence of God. He holds that if the good God had a revelation to make that was indispensable to man's salvation, it must be supposed that He who created the human mind would and could express Himself clearly enough to be understood by man. Webster says that, entirely aside from any revelation of Scripture on this head, this assumption is a moral necessity. It must be granted that the great defender of the American Union has both logic and Scripture on his side. But this clarity of the Bible, a necessary prerequisite for its efficiency, was not at all generally accepted in Luther's times. Nor is it conceded by Rome today. The American Catholic cardinal J. Gibbons († 1921) wrote in his *The Faith of Our Fathers:* "The Scriptures alone cannot be a sufficient guide and rule of faith . . . because they are not of themselves clear and intelligible, even in matters of the highest importance, and because they do not contain all the truths necessary for salvation." [29] One wonders what Paul would have said to Gibbons, Paul who wrote to young Timothy that even in his childhood he (Timothy) had been acquainted with the Scriptures, "which *are* able to make thee wise unto salvation." [30] The fact that Paul refers to the *Old* Testament only makes the statement still stronger. Luther believed Paul and therefore wrote to Erasmus, who, as a Romanist, was inclined to take him (Paul) less seriously: "I have hitherto determinately set myself against the Pope, in whose kingdom nothing is more common or more generally received than this saying 'that the Scriptures are obscure and ambiguous; and that the Spirit, as the Interpreter, should be sought from the apostolic see of Rome!' than which nothing could be said that was more destructive. . . . That saying is no human invention but a poison poured forth into the world by a wonderful malice of the devil himself, the prince of all demons." [31]

According to Luther there is something satanic about the

---

[29] In En, P 155.   [30] 2 Tim. 3:15.   [31] Lu, B 102.

denial of the clearness of Scripture. If the old evil Foe succeeds in persuading men that, although the Bible is God's book, it is unfortunately too obscure and too deep to be understood by the average man, he will in a large measure have nullified the purpose of its inspiration. Luther was right. This delusion made it possible for a designing hierarchy to lead the "faithful" whithersoever it pleased. And yet, though the scheme might well have originated in the nether regions, it found a traitorous ally in the spiritual and mental inertia of natural man. It is so much easier to follow the lead of others than to pick one's own way, blindly to accept as the truth the cut and dried formulae of the Church than to search the Scriptures to see "whether those things are so." But while this is an explanation, it is no excuse; for according to Scripture a *Christian* faith exists only where there is a personal conviction of the truth as revealed in Scripture. The sole basis of saving faith is *God's* Word. Relying upon the word of man as a warrant for the truth of anything spiritual is not faith at all but mere superstition. Therefore Luther told Erasmus: "We affirm that all spirits are to be proved in the face of the Church by the judgment of Scripture. For this ought, above all things, to be received and most firmly settled among Christians, that the Holy Scriptures are a spiritual light by far more clear than the sun itself, especially in those things which pertain unto salvation or necessity." [32] Again, in his exposition of the Thirty-seventh Psalm Luther says: "It is a horrible and great insult to, and crime against, Holy Writ and all Christendom to say that Scripture is dark and not clear enough for everyone to understand, so that he might be instructed by Scripture what to believe and might prove his faith by quoting it." [33]

LUTHER'S DEFENSE OF SUCH CARDINAL DOCTRINES WAS PAULINE

This was the formal principle of the re-formation: a call to prodigal Christendom to *return* to the light of Scripture, to come back to its first love, the Word of God. The spirit of the early

---

[32] Lu, B 104. [33] Wal V:334 f.

Church had revived in Martin Luther. His entire approach to theology was apostolic. There was the same emphasis upon the great cardinal doctrines of sin and grace. It was an appropriate coincidence that the patron saint of the faculty of theology at Wittenberg was none other than St. Paul. Though almost fifteen centuries had passed since the martyrdom of Paul, Martin Luther was raised to continue his work. One may call him a post-Apostolic Church Father. If not in point of time, he certainly was such in point of doctrine. Julius Hare says of the Reformer: "Though Luther was not what is technically termed a Father and could not be so from the period when for the good of mankind it was ordained that he should be born, yet it has pleased God that he, above all other men since the days of the Apostles, should, in the truest and highest sense, be a Father in Christ's church, yea, the human father and nourisher of the spiritual life of millions of souls, for generation after generation." [34]

SOME DOCTRINES CARICATURED BY LITERALISTIC FANATICS

As was to be expected, there were travesties of this reliance upon the clear, literal sense of Scripture, and Luther was unfairly made responsible for all of them. Unfortunately this sort of logic neither was nor is anything new. The great principles for which a man stands are misunderstood and caricatured, and his enemies cry out in malicious delight: "Did we not tell you so? We always knew that no good could come from such noxious views." Luther had preached that the Bible is to be accepted at face value, is to be understood in its clear, literal sense. Thereupon certain fanatical literalists arose and actually burned the Bible. The warrant for this they professed to have found in the words of Scripture "The letter killeth, but the spirit giveth life." [35] Promptly the enemies of Luther accused *him* of having incited men to this irresponsible fanaticism. Other enthusiasts were seen shouting their harangues from the roof of a house. They had read in Scripture: "Preach ye upon the housetops." [36] Yet

[34] H, V 83.   [35] 2 Cor. 3:6.   [36] Matt. 10:27.

others reacted in a very literalistic manner to the exhortation to "become as little children." [37] To express their understanding of this exhortation some adult Anabaptists might be discovered skipping about and clapping their hands in childish fashion on the public streets, while others played with dolls or made mud pies. Of course, Luther was blamed for all and everything. But enough of this pseudo logic of malice. If this sort of deduction is to be employed, our heavenly Father would Himself be charge-able with the fearful abuse to which men put even His choicest gifts. It is sad to see to what subterfuges men will stoop to dis-credit a cause with which they are out of sympathy.

Perhaps there was nothing about Luther with which the papal hierarchy was more utterly out of sympathy than the man's insist-ence upon the complete *sufficiency* of the Bible. That was Brother Martin's unpardonable sin. Nor is this contradicted by the famous ironical answer of Erasmus to the question of Elector Frederick about Luther. The Catholic scholar replied that Luther had made two mistakes: he had touched the crown of the Pope and the bellies of the priests. But what made the papal crown secure and what insured for the priest a life of ease and indolence? It was the ignorance and neglect of Scripture doctrine and Scrip-ture standards and practices. The leaders of the hierarchy saw this clearly enough. Whether they condemned the *sola Scriptura* sincerely, in spiritual blindness, or in conscious opposition to the truth makes little difference. The fact is they denied that any position could be conclusively proved by an appeal to Scripture alone. In a letter dated November 25, 1522, Pope Adrian VI said: "Almost all the things on which Luther differs from others have already been rejected by General Councils, and there ought to be no doubt that whatever has been approved by General Councils and the Church Universal, must be held as an article of faith; for anyone who casts doubt upon things that have once been rightly settled, insults a Synod of the Church." [38] The entire lengthy letter need not be quoted, but it should be mentioned that

---

[37] Matt. 18:3.   [38] S-J, LC II:145.

nowhere in it is there a reference to Scripture in refutation of Luther's doctrines. The changes are rung on "saints" and "Fathers" and "Councils." These Luther had dared to contradict. Passages from Scripture are indeed introduced to illustrate the corruption of the Church; and after a reference to the moral rot in the Roman curia, the Pope's court, Adrian confesses: "The whole world eagerly desires . . . a reformation." But nowhere is it intimated that the reform which Adrian himself considered a crying need consisted simply in heeding the call to return to the Word of God in doctrine and life. Rome would have no *sola Scriptura.*

TO THIS DAY ROME DENIES THE ALL-SUFFICIENCY OF THE BIBLE

And this spirit has been perpetuated in her. The Anglican Henry Manning († 1892), who apostatized to Rome during the Oxford Movement (1851), wrote: "We neither derive our (Catholic) religion from the Scriptures, nor does it depend upon them." [39] Now, this is an extreme statement, but it is simply extremely honest. In spite of the attempts of papal spokesmen to create the impression at times that Rome adheres to Scripture as it is interpreted by her official head, even this is, in reality, not the case. In *practice* the theory of Rome results in the complete abolition of the Bible as the source of doctrine and life. According to Roman doctrine the Catholic Church is in a very real sense the *Pope's* Church. Nor is this view of recent date. It is true, it was not proclaimed publicly as the official doctrine of Rome until the Vatican Council decrees of 1870. But the spirit of it was in the Papacy even in Luther's days. The Catholic professor Sylvester Prierias felt himself constrained to enter the arena of controversy against Luther's 95 Theses. He called his attack a *Dialogue on Papal Authority.* In it Prierias said: "Whoever does not rest upon the teaching of the Roman Church and the supreme pontiff [the Pope] as an infallible rule of faith, from which even Holy Scripture draws its vigor and authority, is a heretic." [40]

---

[39] In En, P 155.   [40] In Ho II:73, note 5.

More than that. The Professor contended that whatever the Pope may say or do in his official capacity is always true and always right though he may be so wicked as to lead people to hell in droves.[41] After a few more exchanges between Prierias and Luther, the Reformer transmitted a note to the Professor advising him to stop writing books that were making him ridiculous in the eyes of the world. But however ridiculous or monstrous the principal views of Prierias may appear to others, the hierarchy has never repudiated them, although, as Luther reported, the Dominicans at the time sought to suppress the *Dialogue* by buying up copies wherever they could find them.[42] But the views of Prierias finally carried the day: the Pope is the supreme, infallible source of truth and right; from his decision there is no appeal; he is the mouthpiece of God. Against this antichristian exaltation of man, any man, any group of men, anywhere, any time, Luther protested to the very end. He was never tired of teaching, preaching, and writing "in season and out of season" about the sole authority of Scripture. "Neither am I to be believed," says he, "nor the Church, nor the Fathers, nor the Apostles, no, nor an angel from heaven, if we teach anything against the Word of God; but let the Word of God abide forever." [43] The Englishman Peter Bayne is right in saying: "With all the earnestness of which he was capable he [Luther] disclaimed any other office than that of leading men back to the fountainheads of inspiration." [44]

MANY MODERNISTS CONSIDER LUTHER'S POSITION A MISFORTUNE

But, strange as it may seem, this insistence on complete conformity to Scripture is converted into a charge against Luther by many who find the papal claims as spurious as he did. They feel that the Reformer did not go far enough in his emancipation of the human mind. While crediting him with much that is original and heroic, they hold that he unfortunately could not — perhaps could not be expected to — slough off the medieval spirit of deference to some sort of authority. Therefore, we are told, he in

---

[41] Wal XVIII:314 f.   [42] Wal XV:2410.   [43] Lu, G 58.   [44] Bay, M I:25.

reality merely exchanged masters, substituting the supremacy of a dead book, the Bible, for the supremacy of a living man, the Pope. But the Bible is no "dead book." Jesus said: "The words that I speak unto you, they are spirit, and they are life," [45] and in Heb. 4:12 we are assured: "The Word of God is quick and powerful." It is plain that these critics want what Byron calls "that heritage of woe," the emancipation of man from all external control. They feel that holding a man to complete conformity to Scripture is clapping him into a doctrinal strait jacket. Man's spirit, they hold, ought to be allowed free play. As long as his teaching and life are according to the "spirit" of Scripture, we ought not legalistically insist upon his being "cribbed, cabined, and confined" by and in its letter. One wonders just where these people expect to discover the "spirit" of Scripture except in its "letter," in its plain, grammatical sense. They seem to be playing with words and on words. It is Lessing who somewhere says that Luther has successfully freed us from the tyranny of the Papacy and then asks: Who will now free us from the tyranny of the letter of Scripture? Lessing is at least candid. Others mean about the same thing but express it more cautiously. As one of Luther's English biographers puts it: "If religious thought in our day were exactly what it was in Luther's day, then would it be certain that Luther had toiled in vain." [46] We do not like these words. They seem to imply that Luther "toiled" to make doctrinal change and development possible. He did not. Luther labored to free the souls of men from *human* authority — including themselves — so that they might now freely surrender themselves to that utter obedience to Christ and His Word which is the truest liberty. In short, while the reform Luther achieved was, in a sense, radical, it may just as truly be said to have been conservative.

LUTHER A GREAT CONSERVATIVE

No one less than von Ranke says: "We see Luther directing his weapons on both sides — against the Papacy, which sought to reconquer the world then struggling for its emancipation, and

---

[45] John 6:63.   [46] Bay, M I:vii.

against the sects of many names which sprang up beside him, assailing Church and State together. The great Reformer, if we may use an expression of our days, was one of the greatest conservatives that ever lived." [47] It has frequently been said that "Luther was the Reformation." This is particularly true of the Reformation in Germany. Perhaps in no great movement of history has the personal element been more prominent. Therefore it is to be expected that the German Reformation reflects the character of the man who was its guiding spirit. This it certainly does to a remarkable degree. The Reformation in Germany was pre-eminently conservative. In consequence it ought not to be called a revolution or a revolt. These designations are, of course, not complete misnomers, but they do have connotations which are too negative as characterizations of Luther's work. Luther's approach to the problems of the day was not negative. He did not set out with the purpose of destroying Rome but of saving souls. "The spirit of the Reformation was no destroying angel who sat and scowled with a malignant joy over the desolation which spread around." [48] This dare never be lost sight of, or many positions occupied and defended by Luther in the course of the movement are certain to be inexplicable or will inevitably be misinterpreted. Luther's life's passion was to find and to defend the truth, no matter what might rise or fall in the effort. The desire to startle and to shine by proposing something new and unheard of, the passion to impress his age by the originality of his genius, was entirely foreign to Martin Luther. He knew nothing of the wild satisfaction of the radical to whom the old and the traditional look good only when they lie shattered at his feet. "Whatever Lutheranism may be, seeing that it has exercised a vast power over mankind, its principle or form, the kernel of its true definition, must be something positive, not something negative, an assertion, not a denial. The assertion will indeed involve a denial or, it may be, many denials; and these will be the limits of the definition; but a No has little power unless it be the

---

[47] Ra, D IV:5.   [48] Kr, C 202.

rebound of a Yes, the thunderclap following the lightning flash. Erasmus' No, Voltaire's No, merely awakened echoing Noes in the hollow caverns of men's hearts, and the latter at least gnawed at men's hearts, dried up the fountains of tears and turned their smiles into sneers. Luther's shook the world, but shook it in order to steady it." [49]

LUTHER CALLED CHRISTENDOM BACK TO THE BIBLE

Had Luther's approach been merely negative, history no doubt would have a very different tale to tell about him. We would perhaps hear in comprehensive studies of that age that a certain hot-tempered monk, Lother or Luther by name, recklessly attacked Holy Mother Church. Remaining stubbornly impenitent, he and a few fanatical adherents were finally burned alive at the stake for the glory of God and the Blessed Virgin and to the great satisfaction of all the faithful. But fortunately for Christendom, Luther's approach was different. The strongest weapon the Reformer wielded against the Papacy was the truths she still confessed. He persistently and consistently said it was his intention to cleanse, not to crush the Church. That is why he had no desire to leave the Church. As a matter of fact, he never did leave it. The Church left him, forsook him, even while he was cleansing it of the incrusted corruptions of centuries. Men speak of the new Church Martin Luther founded. He founded no new Church. It was "new" only in the sense in which an oil painting can be said to be new from which a skillful artist has removed the dust and the grime of ages. "Where was your Church before the Reformation?" a Catholic is said to have asked a Lutheran. "Where was your face before you washed it this morning?" came the answer as a counterquestion. Perhaps the illustration is homely, but it entirely answers the purpose. Therefore not Luther but Rome was (and is) guilty of introducing novelties. It was not unusual during the Middle Ages to seek to give such departures from Scripture a Biblical veneer by quoting the words of Jesus: "I have yet

---

[49] H, V 110.

many things to say unto you, but ye cannot bear them now." [50]
It was brazenly contended that the exalted Jesus was revealing
these "many things" to His Church from time to time through the
saints and the Councils and the Pope. Luther removed these
impertinent un- and anti-Scriptural additions, while carefully and
lovingly conserving the original body of revealed truths. Of
course, this body of Scripture doctrine seemed strange and new
to many; but the restorer assures them: "People say my teaching
is contrary to the old, traditional faith. But what sort of faith is
this? It is the faith of the Pope together with his priests and
monks. How old is this faith? Two or three hundred years, since
even in my own recollection many papal articles of faith have
arisen and forced their way into the Church; for I recall the times
when [the adoration of] St. Anne was unknown in these churches
and communities. . . . All this is called the 'old, traditional faith'
by them. Truly, a pretty faith, not as old as a man of sixty! But
is it not provoking that the Word of the Lord, yea, the word of
the holy Fathers and prophets from the beginning of the world,
is to be called a 'new faith' by those who call themselves Christian? But so it is; for we preach and desire to preach nothing
but what you yourself read in the Scripture of the Prophets and
Apostles." [51]

The position, then, which Luther took was this: Everything
within the Church, all her doctrines and all her practices that
could not be proved to be false and sinful by Scripture, may
be retained as long as it is not open to patent abuse and misunderstanding. Now, this conservatism of Luther lost him many
a friend, and to this day there are those who deplore what they
consider vestiges of medievalism in the body of Luther's doctrine.
Just in passing, his teaching of the real presence of Christ's body
and blood in the Lord's Supper may be mentioned. Both Lindsay and Smith hold that Luther's teaching on this head was conditioned far less by Scripture than by "medieval philosophy." [52]
But something may be medieval historically and nonetheless true

---

[50] John 16:12.　　[51] Erl 17:142 f.　　[52] Sm, L 241; Li, H I:354.

doctrinally. The standard of judgment is Scripture alone, not time. Luther was indeed historically minded and had that respect and consideration for age which is the mark of a thoughtful mind. Not being intoxicated with his own ability, he did not ignore the views of those who had gone before him. To him the new was not necessarily the better, and change not necessarily progress. Luther looked at the structure of Christian doctrine erected by the Prophets and Apostles and founded on Jesus Christ, and was content to repair and to restore it; the radicals and fanatics of his age meant to burn it to the ground, like the Chinese who burned his house to the ground to rid it of rats. If and when Luther kept anything, it was because he was firmly convinced that it could not be condemned on Scriptural grounds and principles and that its proper use was helpful to Christian life and faith. We think in this connection of the entire field of the fine arts: music, sculpture, and painting, and of clerical vestments and liturgical usages. Von Ranke says: "Luther attacked the dominant doctrines [of Rome] with the weapons of a profound learning." [53] That is, he went to work soberly and thoughtfully. He rarely did anything rashly. He never hesitated to retain anything because Rome held it, nor ever was tempted to espouse error because it might more effectively injure the hierarchy. In singleness of heart he sought and retained the truth, looking neither to the right nor to the left.

Perhaps a little digression would be in order at this point. It is not unusual to find men who declare themselves able to prove that Luther flatly contradicts himself. Now, it must be granted that the Reformer not only wrote much but frequently expressed himself so strongly and brought out the point he wished to make into such bold relief that he seemed to deny or contradict something no less true, though perhaps under different conditions. Nor is this all. It must be borne in mind that it was impossible for Luther to shed overnight all the false doctrines and views which he had absorbed during his heretical Catholic training.

---

[53] Ra, D II:18.

In a very real sense Luther *developed* into the Reformer. While his conversion, his recognition of the central doctrine of Scripture, justification by faith, was instantaneous, the many implications of this great truth were fully appreciated by him only gradually. That is the reason why it is indeed possible to "quote Luther against Luther," that is, to find that Luther changed his position on certain points in the course of his career. But to refer to this fact in order to prove that the Reformer lacked decisiveness and consistency is, to put it mildly, unfair. Luther often refers to his progress in the grasp of the truth. With characteristic candor he does not hesitate to ask his readers to use his earlier writings with care and to exercise charity in their judgment on him.[54]

MANY OF LUTHER'S EARLIER OPINIONS MODIFIED

In consequence of all this it is indeed possible at times to ask: *Which* Luther said this or that? Does this statement reflect the standpoint of Luther at the beginning or toward the end of his career? But this circumstance has a very slight effect upon the picture of Luther's *character*. The fact as such does, it is true, reveal the man's conscientiousness and candor. But the basic traits of his character were the same in 1509 as in 1539. Naturally his character was purified and ennobled when he found the Savior of Scripture. Particularly his motivation was changed. He was as zealous as ever to be good and to do good, but the driving power was no longer his desire to make sure of his salvation. Now it was the wish to express the deep gratitude of his heart for the salvation Jesus Christ had secured for him.

These considerations must also be borne in mind in order to appreciate Luther's attitude toward government. In this relation, too, his sober conservatism is seen at work. As may be expected, Luther had much to say about government. Only the references to this institution fill six columns in the large index volume of the St. Louis-Walch edition of his works. Entire books

---

[54] Wal XIV:439.

have been written on Luther's political theories. We are interested only to know to what extent they reflected his character. The relation of Church and State was such in his days that the Reformation movement as represented by him could not escape contact with the political powers. In 1523 appeared Luther's treatise *Secular Authority, to What Extent It Should be Obeyed.*[55] This writing was sober and conservative throughout. It showed, to begin with, that secular authority is ordained by God; secondly, that its sphere is this life and that it ought never invade the sphere of faith and conscience; and, thirdly, that the princes ought to conduct themselves according to this nature of State and Church. We have here an ethical defense of government over against the medieval theory that all authority ultimately rests in the Church. The publication so pleased the Elector Frederick that he had it copied by hand, had it beautifully bound, and made a close study of it. And well he might; for as Luther did not hesitate to say: "My opinion is that no teacher before my times has written so powerfully on secular authority as I have. It was so good that also my enemies had to thank me for it." [56]

LUTHER DID NOT RECOGNIZE THE RIGHT TO REVOLT

But it was particularly the Peasants' War of 1525 that brought into bold relief Luther's attitude toward government. The roots of this upheaval have been traced back into the fourteenth century and beyond. The Reformation of Luther was at most the occasion, but it can never be considered to have been the cause, of this outburst of the oppressed. If the peasants drew the deduction of a wild license from Luther's gospel of Christian liberty, the fault lay with them, not with either the Gospel or its restorer. Three years before the rebellion began the Reformer could sincerely say: "They who read and understand my teaching correctly will not make an insurrection. They have not so learned from me. But who can prevent men from assuming our name when they make insurrection? How much that Christ has forbidden, how

---

[55] Ho III:222-273.　　　　[56] Wal XVI:358.

much that even destroys Christ, are the papists doing in the name of Christ! . . . The devil tries in every way possible to find an excuse for slandering our teaching." [57] Luther's judgment of the entire Peasants' War is found in a letter to his friend Nikolaus Amsdorf. Under date of May 30, 1525, he writes: "My opinion is that it is better all the peasants be killed than that the magistrates and princes perish, because the peasants took the sword without divine authority. . . . Even if the princes of this world go too far, nevertheless they bear the sword by God's authority. . . . Therefore no pity, no patience, is due the peasants, but the wrath and indignation of God and men should be visited upon those men who heed no warnings and do not yield when just terms are offered them, but with satanic fury continue to confound everything. . . ." [58] Nor let anyone say Luther took this position after he sensed the outcome of the War. In 1522 he had written to Elector Frederick: "No one should oppose authority save Him who ordained it; otherwise it is rebellion and displeasing to God"; [59] and while the rebellion was in progress, Luther already wrote against the peasants at a time when they were still successful everywhere. [60]

LUTHER NO LICKSPIT IN HIS RELATION TO THE AUTHORITIES

But this does not mean that Luther was the toady and the tool of the princes. While his conservatism, grounded on Scripture, made him condemn the use of force by citizens against their government, he was as far as possible removed from condoning tyranny and oppression. After the fire of the rebellion had been extinguished in the blood of its instigators, Luther wrote: "The recently ended rebellion has made us wiser, and the great losses then suffered have taught us by experience what a confusion arises if one does not carefully see to it that the common man is appeased and harmony is maintained as much as possible. Therefore it is necessary to contribute to these ends not merely

---

[57] Ho III:213.
[58] S-J, LC II:320.
[59] S-J, LC II:95.
[60] Erl 53:291 f.

by force, as is now being done, but also by reasonableness. For mere force cannot hold its own; it keeps the subjects in eternal hatred of the government, as all history testifies." [61] These are the words of a man who was neither a wild-eyed revolutionist nor an ossified traditionalist but a clear-visioned, fair-minded conservative. If either radicalism or reaction have reared their heads in Church and State, they have no right to claim descent from Martin Luther.

In our times the former charge is perhaps the more common. It is held that Luther, without being aware of the consequences involved in the principles for which he contended, began the liberation of the human mind. Others followed him in Church and State who, we are told, drew the logical conclusions from his premises. These led to modernism in the Church and radicalism in the State. To quote Preserved Smith: "Luther was, contrary to his intentions, the father of modern undogmatic Christianity, and through that, to a degree, of modern rationalism. Emerson quite rightly stated that had Luther known his Theses would lead [!] to Boston Unitarianism, he would rather have cut off his hand than have posted them. But once the avalanche was started, he was impotent to stop it. Having pushed men but a little way from the unstable equilibrium of ideal Catholic faith, he put them in a condition necessitating [!] further motion. Indeed, not only was he the spiritual ancestor of many Christian sects which he would have anathematized, but even, to a certain extent, of infidelity [!]. There is a measure of truth in Nietzsche's assertion that the great Saxon first began to teach the Germans to be un-Christian [!]." [62] We pause for breath. This *is* a strange situation. Luther the father of both modern unbelief and — according to Lessing and others — at the same time of a slavish worship of the letter of Scripture! Certainly an amazingly versatile influence! We have seen Luther credited and charged with about everything except such catastrophes in nature as earthquakes and floods. But in all seriousness: here is a classic instance of

---

[61] In Wa, F 402.　　　　　[62] Sm, L xvi f.

historical stone-blindness. However, it ought perhaps not to be considered surprising. It is to be doubted whether Preserved Smith, Ralph Emerson, and Friedrich Nietzsche ever understood the true nature of Christianity. Both the formal and the material principle of the Reformation were therefore mysteries to them. Perhaps they could gather accurate factual information relating to the movement, but as interpreters they were necessarily failures. Martin Luther, the "father of modern undogmatic Christianity" — whatever that is —! Shades of Marburg! Henry Wace has answered this stupid charge so conclusively in his *Principles of the Reformation* before Smith ever advanced it that we shall quote him at length.

LUTHER WOULD GIVE EVERY MAN THE RIGHT TO OBEY THE WORD

Henry Wace has this to say: "The general effect of [Luther's] teaching upon the condition of the world is evident. It restored to the people at large, to rulers and to ruled, to clergy and to laity alike, complete independence of the existing ecclesiastical system, within the limits of the revelation contained in Holy Scriptures. In a word, in Luther's own phrase, it established Christian liberty. But the qualification is emphatic, and it would be to misunderstand Luther utterly if it were disregarded. Attempts are made at the present day to represent him as a pioneer of absolute liberty, and to treat it as a mere accident of his teaching and his system that he stopped short where he did. But, on the contrary, the limitation is of the very essence of his teaching, because that teaching is based on the supremacy and sufficiency of the divine word and the divine promise. If there were no such word and promise, no such divine revelation, and no living God to bring it home to men's hearts and to enforce His own laws, Luther felt that his protest against existing authority, usurped and tyrannical as it might be, would have been perilous in the extreme. But when men shrank from the boldness of his proclamation, and urged that he was overthrowing the foundations of society, his reply was that he was recalling them

to the true foundations of society, and that God, if they would
have faith in Him, would protect His own word and will. The
very essence of his teaching is summed up in the lines of his
great psalm,
    'Das Wort sie sollen lassen stahn
    Und kein'n Dank dazu haben.' " [63]

"HERE [ON SCRIPTURE] I STAND"

To summarize: at an early date in his career Luther recognized Scripture to be the verbally inspired Word of God. He
therefore held that not reason — including his own — not Church
Fathers, not church councils, and not Popes but *Scripture alone*
must be regarded as the infallible guide into all truth concerning
Christian faith and life. He believed it to be clear enough to convey this truth to any reader or hearer honestly and prayerfully
in search of it. If to some this seemed reactionary, Luther rather
considered it a conservatism expressly demanded by God and
the only escape from agnosticism and atheism on the one hand
and a degrading, unthinking obedience to papal tyranny on the
other. "Here I stand," he could say in challenge to the powers
of darkness and to a world of snarling enemies: "Here I stand:
on the Bible, all of the Bible, only the Bible."

---

[63] W, P 202 f.

CHAPTER V

A HERO OF FAITH

There is not another doctrine by which he revealed himself so completely permeated and
filled as the doctrine of justification by faith.

Leopold von Ranke, celebrated historian

B Y COMMON CONSENT IT IS CONSIDERED A PART OF GOOD
breeding not to speak of our gifts and talents. Perhaps
they are so undeniable that they are generally acclaimed
and have been conceded by our very enemies. But to speak
freely about our endowments is usually looked upon as an indication of poor manners. Even when others praise us in our
presence, good breeding demands, we are told, that we modestly
decline the compliment or at least appear to ignore it by remaining silent. At the very most, one may thankfully accept it while
expressing the conviction that it is a decided overstatement of our
merits. Now, Martin Luther did not at all conform to this pattern
of behavior. It had indeed been strange had he not soon discovered that the gracious Lord had given him gifts of head and
heart rarely found together in one man. That he was fully aware
of his exceptional endowments his writings and conversations
amply testify. Naturally this has been called intolerable conceit.
But it need not be that. The conventional standards above referred to may conceivably be transgressed without justly exposing
oneself to the charge of smug self-complacency. No one less than
the modest Paul laid a lengthy catalog of his achievements and
endowments before the Corinthians,[1] because his personal defense was necessary to protect from discredit the cause for which
he stood. We shall have occasion somewhat later to point out that
the problems confronting Luther and those Paul had to wrestle

---

[1] 2 Cor. 11:16; 12:1 ff.

with in his days were surprisingly similar. Luther himself saw this and at one time wrote to his Elector: "I must boast, as St. Paul, too, had to boast, though it is folly, and I would rather not have done it, if the lying spirits had let me. . . . I know and am certain, by God's grace, that I am more learned in the Scriptures than all the sophists and papists, but so far God has graciously preserved me and will preserve me from the pride which would make me refuse to give answer to the most insignificant Jew or heathen or anybody else. . . ." [2]

LUTHER MODESTLY ACKNOWLEDGED HIS GREAT GIFTS

But another consideration must not be lost sight of. There are people who, generally accepted standards of ethics notwithstanding, can speak of themselves and their success without offending anyone, because one senses their sincere modesty in spite of their candid self-appreciation. More than that. Very frequently such people speak just as freely of their limitations and failures. That was precisely the case with Martin Luther. It is no doubt one of the most remarkable traits of his character that these two, deep humility and lively self-appreciation, dwelt within him without weakening each other. Also this marks him as one of the truly great men of history. To quote only one of his many statements which reveal both his self-appreciation and his genuine modesty. He once remarked to those gathered at his table: "In view of the superabundance of gifts which God has bestowed upon me — of which I must confess and say that they *are* God's gifts, because they are not *mine* — I should have fallen into the abyss of hell had trials and temptations not been there [to keep me humble]." [3]

The Church of Jesus Christ has reasons to thank God that a man with Luther's gifts was satisfied to use them in the service of truth and righteousness. Had he permitted his talents to "go to his head" and fallen into that arrogance which is so common among the supremely gifted, the damage he might have done in

---

[2] S-J, LC II:246.   [3] In Wa, L 90.

Church and State and society is incalculable. He might have developed into a second Arius, to mention only the field of theology. Luther was aware of this. One evening after supper the tumults caused by the fanatical Anabaptists were the subject of comment. Thereupon Luther remarked: "If I were minded to accept three bishoprics from the Pope and to deny Christ, I could do great hurt to Christendom; for the devil has proposed other, more pointed arguments to me, of which they [the fanatics] are not as yet aware and cannot advance. But God keep me from it!" [4] Luther means, if for the sake of ease he would accept advancement and place his gifts at the disposal of antichristian error, he could propose arguments of such shrewdness in its defense that it would be difficult to meet them. Thank God, Martin Luther was satisfied to live the life of the hunted and to "bring into captivity every thought to the obedience of Christ." [5]

After the Diet of Augsburg in 1530 the outlook for the Reformation was dark. It is true, the Emperor had permitted the Augsburg Confession to be presented, but, according to some witnesses, had shown so little interest in giving it his personal attention as to fall asleep at one time during its reading. At the end of the Diet (November 19) the Lutherans were threatened with force and penalties and war unless they would conform. Luther, it seems, expected the worst for a while. So he wrote his *Warning to His Dear Germans*. In this he said: "If I were to be murdered in such a papistical and priestly uproar, I shall take a host of bishops, priests [*Pfaffen*], and monks along with me [into death], so that one should say: Doctor Martin was conducted to his grave by a great procession; for he is a great doctor, superior to all bishops, priests, and monks." [6]

His superiority consisted particularly also in his pulpit eloquence. He descended to the level of his hearers. He preached neither *over* nor merely *to* the heads of his audience but spoke to the heart. When at the conclusion of the conference that produced the Wittenberg Concord both Luther and Bucer preached

---

[4] Erl 61:116.   [5] 2 Cor. 10:5.   [6] Erl 25:7.

in the presence of each other, the following characteristic conversation is said to have taken place: Luther: "I like your sermon right well, friend Bucer, and yet I think mine was better." Bucer: "I gladly admit your superiority, Doctor." Luther: "I don't mean to boast; I know my weakness and that I am not so acute and learned as you in my sermons. But when I enter the pulpit, I consider my audience, mostly poor laymen and Wends, and preach to them. Like a mother I try to give my children milk, and not some fine syrup from the apothecary. You preach over their heads, floating around in the clouds and in the 'shpirit.'" [7] Luther was mimicking Bucer's pronunciation of the German word *Geist* [spirit] as "Gaischt."

To his very end this candid self-appreciation characterized Luther. But to all who really had gotten close to the man it was as inoffensive as that of a child. It was not childish, but childlike in its harmless and artless openheartedness. Years before he came to die he could look back upon a career of unparalleled influence and service. And he freely confessed his joy at it. Thus he wrote to the Christians in Strassburg in 1524: "I hope you have seen in my writings how simply and certainly I treat the Gospel, the grace of Christ, the Law, faith, love, the cross, doctrines of men, the Pope, and monastic vows; in short, the main heads of Christian doctrine. In these I think I am found blameless and cannot deny that, though unworthy, I am an instrument of God by which He has helped many souls." [8] Ten years later Luther could write with that peculiar mixture of bantering humor and dead earnestness which makes his writings such delightful reading: "The papists say they want to remain unreformed by a beggar like me. But in spite of all, this same beggar has done a fairly good job of reforming around on them — I must praise myself a bit, but secretly, so that they are certain not to find it out. Thank God, I have reformed more with my Gospel than they perhaps would have done with five councils." [9] On what he considered to be his deathbed, in 1527, Luther was heard to mutter:

---

[7] Sm, L 294.　　　　[8] S-J, LC II:276.　　　　[9] Erl 31:389.

"Oh, what a time the fanatics will make after my death." He clearly saw and did not hesitate to confess that it was largely his mighty influence that was stemming the muddy flood of radicalism. How true subsequent history proved this to be everyone knows. Upon the same occasion he prayed: "O dearest God and Father, Thou hast given me many thousand gifts above what Thou hast given others; I would have liked still to be used for the honor of Thy name and the good of Thy people; but Thy will be done, that Thou mayest be glorified by life or death." [10] Who has the heart to find any conceit in these words of honest self-appreciation, spoken, as they were, in the very presence of God? Proud people do not pray like that.

ABOVE ALL LUTHER CONFESSED TO HAVE REDISCOVERED SAVING TRUTH

The German critic and dramatist Lessing said that if God were to offer him either the possession of the truth or the endless quest after the never-quite-attainable truth, he would choose the search for the truth and not its possession. The statement has become famous — or ought we to say notorious. Luther might have called it that. To him the most prized possession was the conviction that he had found the truth; upon this he humbly prided himself. To our age of skepticism and agnosticism this characteristic of the Reformer may seem very presumptuous and unscholarly. History has repeated itself, and many men are again saying what philosophers in the days of Cicero said: We can be certain of only this, that we can be certain of nothing — and perhaps we cannot be certain of that either. This is subjectivism with a vengeance. Because of his attitude toward the Bible, Luther was spared this "hell of uncertainty." He knew where the truth was to be looked for, and he found it. Lessing's choice would never have been his. Shakespeare may say: "All things that are, Are with more spirit chased than enjoy'd," but to the soul that is in search of assurance and peace this makes no sense. Martin Luther had achieved his most immediate life's ambition when he found the truth as it is in the Christ of Scripture.

---

[10] S-J, LC II:406.

LUTHER CONVINCED BY A CAREFUL STUDY OF SCRIPTURE

He was immovably certain that he *had* found the truth. The passages one may quote from his writings in proof of this are legion. Naturally, there was progress in Luther's grasp of the truth. The marvel is that the progress was so rapid. This is to be accounted for by the fact that when once he had found Scripture, he fairly saturated himself with it. He worked it as a miner digs for gold; and perhaps the stillness of the cloister was punctuated by Brother Martin's joyful cry at coming upon another nugget of exceptional preciousness. During these early years his own reformation took place, so to speak. There were matters which were still unclear to him. He candidly confesses in a letter to his adversary, Albert, Archbishop and Elector of Mayence, under date of 1520: "Jesus Christ, the Judge of all, is witness to my soul that I am conscious of having taught nothing save Christ and the commandments of God and, again, that I am not so obstinate but that I desire to be instructed and, when I see my error, to change my mind." [11] Five years passed, years during which Luther not only did into German the entire New Testament and part of the Old, but during which he spent many hours diligently searching Scripture and fervently praying over it. His constant prayer was that he might find in the Bible what the Spirit of God had revealed there and that he might never read his own views into God's Book. He became so convinced that God had granted him this unprejudiced, self-effacing approach to His revelation that he wrote to Spalatin in 1525: "It is certain that our view is the true one, no matter whether I or they or everybody else shall desert it." [12] The immediate reference of these words is, it is true, to the doctrine of the Lord's Supper. But if Luther could speak with such certainty concerning this controverted matter, his convictions in the entire field of Christian doctrine must now have been clear and deep. So they were.

When, in 1535, he gave to the world his second and comprehensive explanation of the Letter to the Galatians, he said in it:

---

[11] S-J, LC I:282.   [12] S-J, LC II:282.

"So we with Paul do boldly pronounce all such doctrine to be accursed as agreeth not with ours. For neither do we seek by our preaching the praise of men or the favor of princes or bishops, but the favor of God alone, whose only grace and mercy we preach, despising and treading under foot whatever is of ourselves. Whosoever he be, then, which shall teach any other gospel or that which is contrary to ours, let us be bold to say that he is sent of the devil and hold him accursed." [13] It must be granted that these words are unmistakably clear. To some they have appeared arrogant. But Luther summarily disposes of that specious charge in one of his other writings. He says: "I will not waste any words arguing whether I am a haughty man or not, since that does not concern my teaching but my person. I have said repeatedly: Assail my person if you will and in any way you will; I do not claim to be an angel. But I will allow no one to assail my teaching with impunity, since I know that it is not mine but God's." [14] These words breathe that certainty of possessing the truth for which Luther became famous and his name proverbial. The Reformer is so certain of having found the truth that, like Paul, he calls down God's curse upon *himself* were he ever to depart from the doctrine he is teaching.[15] That *is* objectivism. Luther tells us how he achieved it. The immediate reference here is to the Augsburg Confession, the first public proclamation of the Lutheran doctrinal position. Luther writes: "I am concerning myself with this matter day and night, turning it over and over in my mind, arguing it out and *passing through the entire Bible;* and the longer I do this, the more my faith in our doctrine and cause increases and is strengthened within me, so that — please God — I shall permit nothing [no point of doctrine] to be taken from me, no matter what happens in consequence. . . . If He [God] is not with *us,* my dear friend, where in the entire world is He? . . . If *we* do not possess the Word of God, who are its possessors?" [16]

---

[13] Lu, G 52 f.

[14] Ho III:294.

[15] Lu, G 51.

[16] Erl 54:176 f.

HOW LUTHER TREATED THE DEVIL, WHO TEMPTED HIM TO DOUBT

One feels something like shame in the presence of such certainty. What pigmies we are in comparison with this hero of faith! But lest a sense of futility and defeatism come over us, it should be pointed out that also Luther had his hours of trial. He was not free from the temptation to doubt God's Word and his correct apprehension of it. To picture Luther as living in a constant heaven of blissful certainty would be creating a false picture; and he would be the first one to call it so. In his *Table Talk* Luther has much to say about temptations in this respect. "If the devil finds me at ease and not engaged upon the Word of God and armed with it, he seeks to disturb my conscience as though I had taught falsely, had disturbed the former state of the Church, which under the Papacy was nicely quiet and peaceful, and had caused great offense and excited discord and sects [*Rotten*] by my doctrine. Now, I cannot deny that he often makes me fear and tremble because of this. But as soon as I take to the Word of God, I have won. This is how I meet the clever knave with the Word: [I say] the doctrine I have brought to light through the grace of God by my teaching, preaching, and writing is not mine but the pure and unadulterated Gospel of Jesus Christ, God's Son, that abides forever; wherefore neither you nor the world — whose prince and god you are — can or should obstruct it." [17] At times Luther's treatment of the old evil Foe was less civil. He relates: "When the devil approaches to plague me during the night, I give him this reply: Satan, I must sleep now; for that is God's command and order: Work during the day and sleep at night." But frequently this summary dismissal did not prove effective, Luther continues. The devil continued to remind him of his sins and shortcomings. Finally, in impatience and righteous ire Luther contemptuously said: "Dear Satan, pray for me; you have never done anything amiss, you alone are holy. Go to God and earn grace for yourself; and if you try to make me holy, I tell you: Physician, heal thyself." [18] Someone has

---

[17] Erl 60:83.   [18] Erl 60:101.

well said: The devil, like a wayward boy, does not bother to knock down rotten apples; he is after the good fruit. The greater the saint, the severer the temptation. If the old evil Foe can cause the mighty ones in the Kingdom to fall, he has slain his thousands. It was Paul, the hero of the faith, who had the "thorn in the flesh"; and Martin Luther was tempted by many devils. He was writing part of his life's history when he penned the words

> The old evil Foe
> Now means deadly woe.
> Deep guile and great might
> Are his dread arms in fight;
> On earth is not his equal.

But in heaven is his equal, and in Scripture he has found his match; for "one little word can fell him." And the Word, Martin Luther had on his side; this "Word they still shall let remain."

NO HOPE FOR THOSE WHO REJECT THE "LUTHERAN" GOSPEL

Luther was so certain that he had indeed restored doctrine to apostolic purity that he did not hesitate to tell his contemporaries that unless they would accept "his Gospel," they would be lost forever. In 1522 he replied to the attack of Henry VIII on him. After having listed the principal heads of Christian doctrine, Luther told His English Majesty: "Whoever differs from my teaching on these points or condemns me, condemns God and must remain a child of hell." [19] He concluded this writing with the following blast: "You papists will never accomplish what you intend, do what you will. Before this Gospel which I, Martin Luther, have preached, there shall give way and by it there shall be subdued Pope, bishops, priests, monks, kings, princes, devil, death, sin, and everything that is not Christ and in Christ. Nothing can help them escape [their doom]." [20]

To anyone so firmly convinced that he was in possession of God's unadulterated truth the refusal of so many to open their hearts to it might possibly have seemed strange and puzzling. Perhaps this circumstance might even have moved him to doubt

---

[19] Erl 28:347.   [20] Erl 28:387.

the correctness of his position. The power of public opinion is
very strong; and the advertising value of some such slogan as:
ten million people use our product; can they be wrong? is well
known. But the sad fact that the purified Gospel did not meet
with universal acclaim did not disturb Luther, though it saddened
him. The reason why, after years of writing and preaching on his
part, the majority continued in the Church of Rome, Luther found
not in "his Gospel" but in the heart of natural man. The German
theologian Schleiermacher once said that every man is a born
Catholic. This is correct. That is, the way to salvation which the
Gospel proposes to man seems foolish and unworthy to him; and
in so far as he retains his corrupt nature, even the Christian looks
with favor upon the Catholic scheme of salvation by co-operation.
That is why Luther wrote: "They [the papists] adorn themselves
with extraordinary works and ways, go about in gray garments,
look sour, and are hard and strict with their fasts and mortifica-
tions of the body and hard sleeping quarters, and do not live at
all like ordinary people. That has a great influence upon the
people and quite charms them, so that they follow after this in
droves." [21] When such a life of supposedly superior sanctity is
commended to people by a clever preacher, Luther continues,
he might ruin with one sermon what perhaps ten years of instruction in Gospel truths have built up. This is possible because
human nature is flattered to believe what it wishes: to be credited
with at least a part of its own salvation. Luther adds: "I have
the easy confidence that, should I want to, I could by two or
three sermons preach my people back into Papacy and could
arrange for new pilgrimages and masses . . . for the mob is, as
said, easily persuaded to adopt such things."

Luther keenly felt the price he was paying in earthly values
for preaching the Gospel. It distinctly pained him to have to
preach the Word against a world of dissent, pained him to be cut
off from former associates and to be accused of going his *own* way.
He had no passion for controversy. He would have liked to remain

---

[21] Erl 43:316.

within the church organization in which he had been reared, which had become dear to him in many respects. But he found that the price he had to pay for such membership was too high. He was expected to deny his Savior by not being permitted publicly to confess and to preach Him. He could not and would not pay this price. To his close friend Spalatin he again unburdens himself: "It is a hard thing to dissent from all prelates and princes, but no other way is left of escaping hell and God's wrath." [22] Though the separation made his heart bleed, he had to go through with it. So firmly was Martin Luther convinced that he possessed the very truth of God, immutable forever. At the end of his large dissertation on the Lord's Supper he lists the doctrines of Christianity seriatim and then concludes: "This is my creed; for thus all true Christians believe, and thus Holy Scriptures teach us. But of that which I have not fully treated here my other writings will bear sufficient testimony, especially those which have been issued within the last four or five years. I pray that all pious hearts will bear me witness and unite their prayers with mine that I may persist in this faith and conclude my life in its maintenance. For though, in consequence of persecution or the pangs of death, I may say something different — which God, I hope, may prevent — yet let such expression be disregarded; and by this declaration I wish to have it publicly known that any such expression will be incorrect, resulting from the influence of Satan. In this determination may my Lord and Savior Jesus Christ assist me. Blessed be His name forever. Amen." [23]

LUTHER FAITHFUL TO THE VERY END

The Lord Jesus Christ did assist him, nor did He ever leave him. When, in the early morning hours of February 18, 1546, He called His faithful, battle-scarred servant to his eternal home, He heard him answer His call with this prayer: "O my heavenly Father, God and Father of our Lord Jesus Christ, Thou God of all comfort, I thank Thee that Thou hast revealed Thy

---

[22] S-J, LC I:386.   [23] Erl 30:373.

dear Son Jesus Christ to me. On Him I believe, Him I have preached and confessed, Him I have loved and exalted. Him the miserable Pope and all the godless dishonor, persecute, and blaspheme. I pray Thee, my Lord Jesus Christ, let my little soul be commended to Thy care. O heavenly Father, though I must leave this body and be torn out of this life, I nonetheless know of a certainty that I shall eternally abide with Thee and that no one can pluck me out of Thy hands." [24] Thus died Martin Luther, triumphantly convinced that he had found his God, had walked with Him, talked with Him, and would go to Him forever. "Who dieth thus dies well."

WHAT LUTHER THOUGHT OF FAITH

Where lay the secret of this man's great certainty? In his faith. But what was this faith like? What did Luther believe? How did he define faith? An exhaustive answer to these questions would require an entire volume. There are literally thousands of references in Luther's works to faith. No uninspired writer is known to us who has entered so deeply into the meaning of faith as did Luther, and few who have exemplified in their lives its beauty and transforming power to the degree in which the Reformer did. Thomas Lindsay says: "Men could *see* what faith was when they looked at Luther." [25] In consequence one desires to linger here and to trace in detail the growth of Luther's mighty faith. That his very definition of the word differed essentially from that of the medieval Church is to be expected. But we are not so much concerned with the act of faith as such. It is the object of faith that deserves particular attention; for at this point came the parting of the ways between Luther and Rome. The Reformer says: "It is a very necessary and profitable doctrine really to know what it means to believe aright, namely this: to have God's Word and promise and firmly to cling to it, [convinced] that it will surely so come to pass as the Word predicted; for to believe anything without [the sanction of] God's Word is

---

[24] K-K, M II:623.   [25] Li, H I:191.

not faith but a false fancy of which nothing will ever come." [26] Again he says: "Whoever wants to believe must disregard what his five senses comprehend and show." [27] According to these statements Luther held that faith consists in the confidence that whatever God has revealed in Scripture is true, irrespective of any and all appearances to the contrary. However, to accept anything as true and right that could *not* be proved by Scripture is not faith at all to Luther, but mere superstition. Faith, then, is the "Amen" of man to the voice of God speaking to him in Scripture.

SAVING FAITH IMPLIES CHRIST AS ITS OBJECT

But why was Scripture inspired? Chiefly to make men "wise unto salvation." Therefore faith according to the most common use of the Bible implies Christ as its saving object. In this inclusive sense it is most frequently used also by Luther, who had so deeply entered into the spirit of Scripture. By faith he usually means the faith that justifies because it clings to Christ. This became the center of Luther's teaching and preaching. Here lies the reason for his love of Paul's Letter to the Galatians.

SIMILARITY BETWEEN LUTHER AND ST. PAUL

We have no less than two commentaries by Luther on this Epistle, one from the years 1516—1519, the other, longer one, from the year 1531—1532. In his sermons and other writings he quoted from this Epistle and referred to it with disproportionate frequency, considering its shortness. He said of it: "The Epistle to the Galatians is my Epistle; I have betrothed myself to it; it is my Catherine von Bora." Luther's love for this letter is understandable. It is the Magna Charta of Christian liberty, the impregnable Gibraltar of justification by faith. Luther's famous explanations are homiletical lectures rather than critical comments. But this very fact enabled him to bring out the innermost spirit of St. Paul better than a dozen atomistic critics and gram-

---

[26] Erl 5:211. [27] Erl 51:125.

marians. John Bunyan's remark that next to the Bible itself he treasured Luther's *Galatians* most highly has to many not at all seemed an overestimation of this classic. Paul and Luther were kindred spirits. Their very work tended to make them so. God raised both to establish the doctrine of grace within a world peculiarly hostile to it. The very churches that in Paul's and Luther's days ought have proclaimed this message from the house-tops would have none of it and bitterly persecuted its champions. This silenced neither Paul nor Luther; for both had experienced in their own lives that Christ is indeed man's only hope. For both, it is true, the road to this experience was peculiarly long and rugged. For many years neither knew what Christian faith really is.

There is much autobiography in Paul's letter to the Galatians; and there is still more autobiography in Luther's commentaries on this Epistle. Concerning his monkish ignorance of the meaning of saving faith, Luther says: "I crucified Christ daily in my monkish life and blasphemed God through my false faith, wherein I then continually lived. Outwardly I was not as other men, extortioners, unjust, whoremongers; but I kept chastity, poverty, and obedience. . . . Notwithstanding, in the mean time I fostered, under this cloaked holiness and trust in mine own righteousness, continual mistrust, doubtfulness, fear, hatred, and blasphemy against God. And this my righteousness was nothing else but a filthy puddle and the very kingdom of the devil. For Satan loveth such saints and accounteth them for his dear darlings, who destroy their own bodies and souls and deprive themselves of all the blessings of God's gifts." [28] As Luther says: he never quite trusted his exemplary achievements as a monk. His conscience was too sensitive for that. He just would not fit into the pharisaic pattern of monkery, and soon we hear bitter complaints about his sin. They were mere peccadilloes, infractions of cloister laws, we are told. But this is not the entire picture. They *were* great sins; for Brother Martin was beginning to recognize the *spirit* of the Law of God ever more clearly: the

---

[28] Lu, G 61 f.

love of the heart, the willing surrender of one's inner self. This ideal he could not realize, and so we hear him moan: "My sins! My sins!" The lively consciousness of the damnable nature of sin, all sin, every sin, even the smallest sin, unless atoned for to the full, characterized Luther to the very end. This is another point in which he resembled Paul. Nor is it a mere coincidence. Only he who has felt the burden of sin crush all peace and hope out of his panting soul, will look up with love and gratitude to Him who alone can remove the incubus of his guilt. Only he who has looked into the depth of human nature and has seen the foul, slimy, creeping things that slink about and snarl there, can appreciate Him who alone can cleanse that stable of unclean things, the heart of man. When William Gladstone, Victoria's great prime minister, was asked what ailed the world of his days, he replied: "The sense of sin, that is the great want in modern life." Luther had to see sin in all its hideousness before he could preach the Savior in all His beauty. As Julius Hare put it: "Seeing, therefore, that the exceeding sinfulness of sin, the sinfulness underlying, even when it does not rise up and show itself in every human feeling and action, was manifested to Luther more vividly than perhaps to any man who lived between him and St. Paul, *conscientia* with him usually means the consciousness of our sins and of our sinfulness; a consciousness under the crushing misery of which, when a man has once been awakened to a spiritual conviction of this sinfulness, he cannot find rest in anything except the atoning sacrifice of the Savior." [29] Luther said in later life that the anguish of soul he had suffered during these early years was such that it often brought him to death's door. Even after having found peace in the wounds of his Savior, Luther never lost this deep awareness of the damnableness of sin. Thus he wrote to his friend Justus Jonas in 1527: "He [Christ] will not leave the poor sinner at the end, though I believe that I am the least of all men. Would that Erasmus and the sacramentarians might feel the anguish of my heart for a quarter of an hour; I can safely say that they would be converted and saved thereby." [30]

---

[29] H, V 127. [30] S-J, LC II:421.

UNDER POPERY CHRIST SEEMED A STERN TASKMASTER TO LUTHER

Did Luther know nothing of Christ in these early years? We are at times told by Catholic historians that Luther's anguish must have been either feigned in part or caused by abnormal mental and spiritual conditions. Christ was well known in the Church, and pictures and crucifixes were common, we are assured. This is true enough, but it means very little. The question is not *whether* Luther knew of Christ but *what* he knew of Him; and about this we need not guess. Luther says: "[In the cloister] I was often frightened at the very name of Jesus, and when I looked at Him on the crucifix, He seemed like a bolt of lightning to me," and again: "In popery I feared Christ more than I feared the devil." [31] For many weary years Luther knew Christ the Savior only as Christ the Judge. His active conscience raised his sins as a heavy veil of darkness before him, so that the Sun of Righteousness turned into a ball of angry fire for him.

Of course, there had ever been those in the Church of Rome who had recognized the beautiful Savior in spite of all the distorting and disfiguring superstitions and heresies that had come between Him and the anxious sinner. Rome had her St. Bernards in the dark twelfth century and her Johann Wessels in Luther's own century; and there were others before and after these witnesses to God's saving grace. But the very enemies of the Reformer testified that the doctrine of justification by faith was new to the church at large. Desiderius Erasmus († 1536) of Rotterdam was by many considered the greatest scholar of his day. In 1516 he published the Greek New Testament, critically edited by himself. We know that he studied it. In 1524 he published his *Paraphrases* of the New Testament. But to the end of his life the great Humanist apparently remained spiritually blind. Had he appreciated the centrality of justification by faith, perhaps even he might have "screwed his courage to the sticking point." It is understandable that a man, by nature timid and retiring,

---

[31] Wal VII:1329, 913.

who fancied that the Reformation movement was, after all, concerned with improvements that were in the main nonessential to Christianity, however desirable they might be, and that could, moreover, be introduced by gentle stages, would not, because he could not, appreciate the bold and unbending position of a Luther. To be willing to expose oneself to the peril which a clear confession of the Gospel involved in those days, one had clearly to see and firmly to believe its absolute necessity for salvation. As far as we are able to determine, Erasmus never did this. Even his defense of the papal position that man has the moral faculty to appropriate the grace of God to himself, is sufficient proof. But far more direct evidence is available. About 1523 Erasmus wrote to the Swiss Ulrich Zwingli: "Luther proposes some riddles that are absurd [!] on the face of them: . . . a man is justified by faith alone, and works have nothing to do with it." [32] So the *sola fide* (by faith alone) of Scripture seemed ridiculous to this great scholar. At another time, perhaps in 1525, Erasmus wrote an undated and unaddressed letter, which was probably intended to be maneuvered into position under the Emperor's eye. In this he said: "Whether works justify or faith justifies matters little, since all allow that faith will not save without works." [33] When, in the same year, Erasmus wrote to an acquaintance: "Luther . . . says I do not understand theology," [34] he had both correctly quoted Luther and characterized himself. Erasmus has been introduced here at some length because it is again becoming customary in certain circles to refer to him as the ideal, gentlemanly, conciliatory reformer. But James Froude correctly said: "Times come when rough measures alone will answer, and Erasmian education might have made a slight impression on the Scarlet Lady of Babylon." [35] Quite aside from Erasmus' cowardice, his failure to recognize the doctrine of justification by faith made him simply impossible as a reformer; for this was the lever with which Luther lifted the Church out of the "slough of despond."

---

[32] S-J, LC II:196 f. [33] Fro, L 344. [34] Fro, L 341. [35] Fro, L 238.

LUTHER'S REDISCOVERY OF JUSTIFICATION BY FAITH

This is the greatest achievement of Luther. For doing this many generations have blessed him. With this doctrine his name has become identified. Because of it he has been called the "legitimate son of Paul," and "Paul's voice in German." The Modernist Preserved Smith confessed: "Justification by faith has been rightly selected as the cardinal doctrine of Lutheran theology"; [36] and even Webster's Collegiate Dictionary says under "Lutheranism": "The cardinal doctrine is that of justification by faith alone." In consequence, no one can appreciate the character of Martin Luther in its innermost being who does not know what he taught and wrote and lived on this point. To begin with, Luther held that faith in this plan of salvation is so uncongenial to natural man that God Almighty Himself must create it within him. The Reformer said: "In our conversion or justification before God we do or perform nothing, not the most insignificant thing, within ourselves, by our own powers and free will, but we are passive only and let the Holy Spirit prepare us by means of the Word and mold us as a potter does his clay." [37] If, then, a sinner finds Christ, it is because Christ has found him, has rescued him from despair of himself or from that miserable idolatry, the worship of his own works. Particularly this false confidence in one's own works always drew the fire from Luther's pen. He had seen so much of it in popery, and he observed, after the Gospel was again being preached, how sadly true the Savior's remark was, that moral wrecks and social outcasts would accept the glad tidings more readily than the smugly self-satisfied, supposedly saintly Pharisees. In his *Galatians* Luther minces no words. He writes: "Therefore this opinion of the righteousness of the Law is the sink of all evils and the sin of the whole world. For gross sins and vices may be known and so amended or else repressed by the punishment of the magistrate. But this sin, to wit, man's opinion concerning his own righteousness, will not only be counted no sin, but also will be esteemed for a high

---

[36] Sm, L 15.   [37] Erl 58:225.

religion and righteousness. This pestilent sin, therefore, is the mighty power of the devil over the whole world, the very head of the Serpent and the snare whereby the devil entangleth and holdeth all men captive. For naturally all men have this opinion that they are made righteous by keeping the Law." [38] But all such attempts are futile. They remind one of the man who tried to pull himself out of a morass by tugging vigorously at his hair.

THE GREAT PRINCIPLE OF SUBSTITUTION: CHRIST IN OUR STEAD

Moreover, they are unnecessary and insulting to the God who has made Christ "to be sin for us." [39] The doctrine of substitution Luther brought out with apostolic clarity. He wrote: "All the Prophets did foresee in spirit that Christ should become the greatest transgressor, murderer, adulterer, thief, rebel, and blasphemer that ever was or could be in the world. For He being made a sacrifice for the sins of the whole world, is not now an innocent person and without sins, is not now the Son of God born of the Virgin Mary; but a sinner which hath and carrieth the sin of Paul, who was a blasphemer, an oppressor, and a persecutor; of Peter, who denied Christ; of David, who was an adulterer, a murderer, and caused the Gentiles to blaspheme the name of the Lord; and, briefly, who hath and beareth all the sins of all men in His body: not that He Himself committed them, but for that He received them, being committed or done of us, and laid them upon His own body, that He might make satisfaction for them with His own blood." [40] There are those who have objected to what they call the gross literalism of Luther's view of the substitution, but their quarrel is with Scripture, not with Luther. One of the most concise and at the same time comprehensive statements of Luther on the way to salvation was called forth by his exposition of Gal. 3:16. It deserves to be quoted at length. "The doctrine of the Gospel (which of all other is most sweet and full of singular consolation) speaketh nothing of our works or of the works of the Law, but of the inestimable mercy and

---

[38] Lu, G 270.   [39] 2 Cor. 5:21.   [40] Lu, G 242 f.

love of God towards most wretched and miserable sinners: to wit, that our most merciful Father, seeing us to be oppressed and overwhelmed with the curse of the Law and so to be holden under the same that we could never be delivered from it by our own power, sent His only Son into the world and laid upon Him all the sins of all men, saying, Be Thou Peter, that denier; Paul, that persecutor, blasphemer, and cruel oppressor; David, that adulterer; that sinner who did eat the apple [?] in Paradise; that thief who hung upon the cross, and briefly, be Thou the Person who hath committed the sins of all the men; see therefore that Thou pay and satisfy for them. Here now cometh the Law and saith: I find Him a sinner and that such an one as hath taken upon Him the sins of all men, and I see no sins else but in Him; therefore let Him die upon the cross; and so he setteth upon Him and killeth Him. By this means the whole world is purged and cleansed from all sins and so delivered from death and all evils. Now, sin being vanquished and death abolished by this one Man, God would see nothing else in the whole world, if it did believe, but mere cleansing and righteousness." [41]

FAITH APPROPRIATES BENEFITS OF CHRIST'S VICARIOUS SATISFACTION

"If it did believe," wrote Luther; for the settled and established fact of universal forgiveness, or, to use the theological term, objective justification, will benefit the individual only if and when he makes it his own, by a personal faith writes his name into the blank check of God's grace which the Gospel places before him. Luther found in Scripture that the penitent sinner is justified personally the moment he clings to Christ. Of this instantaneous justification he wrote: "St. Paul everywhere teaches that justification comes about not by works but solely by faith, without all works, not piecemeal [*mit Stuecken*] but all at once [*auf einem Haufen*]. . . . It is also come into possession of entirely at one time, not in piccemeal fashion." [42]   All, then, that is necessary is the connection of personal faith. Though this

---

[41] Lu, G 245.   [42] Erl 7:253.

connection may be weak, it nonetheless completely and instantaneously justifies the sinner as long as it ties him to Christ; for strictly speaking not faith, but the object of faith, Christ, justifies. Though the strong may hold a treasure more firmly than the weak, the value of the treasure is the same, if only it is held.

JUSTIFICATION BY FAITH THE VERY HEART OF LUTHER'S TEACHING

This *sola fide* (by faith alone) was the material principle of the Reformation. Whoever attacked that, Luther told Erasmus, was flying at his throat, was striking at the nerve center of his entire Reformation. This has been generally recognized by students of history. Julius Hare wrote: "He [Luther] retained his conviction with regard to the doctrine of justification by faith unshaken till the end of his life. In all his writings, from the moment when he first caught a lively perception of this primary truth, down to his last year, it is the animating principle of his whole teaching." [43] And Peter Bayne tersely summarizes: "To a Europe spiritually moribund he [Luther] preached the Gospel of omnipotent grace; and as that Gospel flashed on him from every page of Holy Writ, he told men to trust to no human authority but seek it there for themselves. Write that on his monument." [44] Yes, engrave in his monument especially the *sola fide*. Since the days of Paul the world had not heard this so strongly emphasized. There was a good reason for emphasizing it. The doctrine was indispensable for salvation. Important and vital as the inspiration of the Bible is, one may conceivably be saved without having clearly recognized it; but "he that believeth not [on Christ] shall be damned." [45] Like Paul, who professed to know nothing "save Christ, and Him crucified," [46] Luther exalted Christ above all. Thomas Lindsay appreciated this and wrote: "With Luther all theology is really Christology; he knew no other God than the God who had manifested Himself in the historical Christ and made us see in the miracle of faith that He is our salvation." [47] To Erasmus

---

[43] H, V 34.   [45] Mark 16:16.   [47] Li, H I:473.
[44] Bay, M I:60.   [46] 1 Cor. 2:2.

Luther wrote: "Take Christ out of the Scriptures and what will you find remaining in them?" [48] In the introduction to his second *Commentary on Galatians* appears the passage beginning with the oft-quoted words: "In my heart this article is sole ruler, namely, faith in Christ." [49] However, no statement of the Reformer on this point is better known and more famous than his ringing words in the Smalkald Articles. After having quoted a number of passages from Scripture which treat of justification by faith, Luther continues: "Of this article nothing can be yielded or surrendered, even though heaven and earth and whatever will not abide should sink to ruin. . . . Upon this article all things depend which we teach and practice in opposition to the Pope, the devil, and the world. Therefore, we must be sure concerning this doctrine and not doubt." [50] So deeply was the Reformer convinced of the centrality of the doctrine of justification by faith alone. Every beclouding of this teaching was high treason to him. Every substitute for it was an unspeakably damnable thing.

At times he would inject the remark *"Experto crede!"* (Believe one who has tried and experienced it) into his vigorous defense of this doctrine. In later life he often remarked, while reminiscing, that heaven itself seemed to have opened its gates to him when the Holy Ghost granted him the correct understanding of the "righteousness of God" as revealed in Christ and the Gospel. This certainty of personal salvation became one of Luther's outstanding characteristics. Dr. C. F. W. Walther used to tell his students at Concordia Seminary, St. Louis, that no uninspired writer made a man more triumphantly certain of his own, personal salvation than Martin Luther. This is true; and it is true largely because Luther had himself found the way to this certainty. But he found it forsaken and practically untrod. The official teaching of Rome on this head was then and is now that no man can be certain of his personal salvation unless God directly reveals it to him, since neither the Scriptures nor the

---

[48] Lu, B 26.   [49] Wal IX:8.

[50] Erl 25:115 f. (*Concordia Triglotta,* translation).

Church can give a man the desired assurance of spiritual security. John Moehler († 1835), an outstanding defender of the papal system, said in his days he would feel a bit uncomfortable in the presence of a man who professed to be certain of his salvation; such a claim would seem demoniacal to him. Moehler's remark is typically Catholic. But to call certainty of personal salvation spiritual arrogance, and uncertainty a proper modesty and humility, is intolerable. It is an insult to the Christ who has promised: "Neither shall any man pluck them out of My hand." [51] Luther was in doubt about his spiritual state until the Gospel breathed into his troubled soul the "peace of God, which passeth all understanding." Then he enjoyed that security of faith which is rooted in the certainty and reliability of God's Word and promise. "Faith," Luther wrote, "is, and indeed should be, a firm conviction [*Standfest*] of the heart that neither wavers nor wobbles, trembles, fidgets, nor doubts, but stands fast and is certain of its cause. . . . Wherever this Word [of God] comes into the heart with genuine faith, it makes the heart like itself, also firm, erect, and hard against all temptation, devil, death, and whatever it may be called, so that it stubbornly and proudly despises and scoffs at everything that would make it doubt, tremble, become evil and angry; for it knows that God's Word will not give it the lie." [52]

Naturally, also Luther was tempted to doubt the grace of God. Which child of God has not been so tempted and has not sometimes yielded? Luther says: "It is beyond measure difficult for a man to believe that God is gracious to him for Christ's sake although he is a great sinner. Ah, the heart of man is too narrow to admit such [a message] or to be able to comprehend it." [53] In his *Galatians* Luther confessed that his heart was not an exception to the rule. Even he, the great post-Apostolic apostle of justification by faith needed constantly to reassure himself by fleeing into Scripture that justification by faith without works of any kind at any time is indeed God's very own, astounding way of

---

[51] John 10:28.   [52] Wal III:1886.   [53] Erl 58:361.

accepting the penitent. Luther confessed: "The matter of justification is brittle, not of itself, for of itself it is most sure and certain, but in respect of us. Whereof I myself have a good experience. For I know in what hours of darkness I sometimes wrestle. I know how often I suddenly lose the beams of the Gospel and grace, as being shadowed from me with thick and dark clouds. Briefly, I know in what a slippery place even such also do stand as are well exercised and seem to have sure footing in matters of faith." [54] Fortunately Luther knew where to go to regain or to keep his footing. Nothing but the man's dogged faith saved him from despair, faith in Scripture as God's inerrant revelation, faith in Christ as man's all-sufficient Savior, and faith in God as Him who would never forsake His own.

LUTHER'S FAITH IN HIS GOD TRULY HEROIC

This childlike trust in the providence of God is another trait that both shames and inspires one. It was not a blind trust. It, too, was Christ-centered. Well might it be; for had not Paul said: "He that spared not His own Son, but delivered Him up for us all, how shall He not with Him also freely give us all things?" Again he says: "All things work together for good to them that love God." [55] To a friend who was fearful of the future, Luther wrote: "I know not what will happen, nor am I anxious to know, for I am sure that He who sitteth in heaven takes care of all things and has foreseen the rise, progress, and end (which I wait for) of this affair from eternity. Whichever way the lot falls, it will not move me; for it only falls where it falls by God's excellent will." [56] Luther was no Cicero or Seneca, whose lives often exhibited shaming contrasts to the good advice they had given others. The letter he wrote to the Elector Frederick while on his way to quiet the disturbances of the radical reformers at Wittenberg is an instance of this. His very going there was an act of heroic faith in God's providence. The Elector had emphatically advised him to stay in his Wartburg retreat. He told Luther he doubted whether he could save him from the penalties

---

[54] Lu, G 56.   [55] Rom. 8:32, 28.   [56] S-J, LC I:361.

of the imperial edict of Worms, which had declared him an out-law. To this Luther replied: "I have written this to Your Grace to inform you that I am going to Wittenberg under a far higher protection than that of the Elector. I do not intend to ask Your Grace's protection. Indeed, I think I shall protect you rather than you me. If I thought Your Grace could and would defend me by force, I should not come. The sword ought not and cannot decide a matter of this kind. God alone must rule it without human care and co-operation. He who believes the most can protect the most, and as I see Your Grace is yet weak in faith, I can by no means regard you as the man to protect and save me." [57]

Strange indeed would it be to read that Martin Luther never had moments in his trying career during which even he lost heart. The marvel is that we do not read of more. How upon one such occasion his wife Catherine dramatically revived the depressed Reformer's confidence in God's providence, has been versified by F. W. Herzberger.

> One day, when skies loomed the blackest,
>   This greatest and bravest of men
> Lost heart and in oversad spirit
>   Refused to take courage again,
> Neither eating nor drinking nor speaking
>   To anxious wife, children, or friends,
> Till Katharine dons widow garments
>   And deepest of mourning pretends.
> Surprised, Luther asked why she sorrowed.
>   "Dear Doctor," his Katie replied,
> "I have cause for the saddest of weeping,
>   For God in His heaven has died!"
> Her gentle rebuke did not fail him,
>   He laughingly kissed his wise spouse,
> Took courage, and banished his sorrow,
>   And joy again reigned in the house.[58]

How thoroughly religious Luther's entire approach to life was has already been mentioned. This character trait stood him in good stead many a time. Nature is full of sermonets on the providence of God if man will but listen and look. Luther did

---

[57] S-J, LC II:95.   [58] Po, M 41.

this. During the meeting of the Diet of Augsburg in 1530 he was put up at the Feste Coburg. This diet put a tremendous strain on the faith, the patience, and the firmness of the reforming party. But at this time of need God imbued Luther with a confidence in His care that refreshed the drooping spirits at Augsburg and has since then reassured many a troubled child of God. Preserved Smith called the following letter "one of the most wonderful letters he [Luther] ever wrote." It was addressed to Dr. Gregor Brueck, chancellor of Elector John. He read the Augsburg Confession before the diet and was one of the few who never lost heart during those trying days. Luther wrote to him: "I have recently seen two miracles. The first was that, as I looked out of my window, I saw the stars and the sky and the whole vault of heaven, with no pillars to support it; and yet the sky did not fall, and the vault remained fast. But there are some who want to see the pillars and would like to clasp and feel them. And when they are unable to do so, they fidget and tremble as if the sky would certainly fall, simply because they cannot feel and see the pillars under it." [59]

Now, that very frame of mind was Melanchthon's trouble. He had to *see* before he was quite willing to believe. But, as Luther often told him, such faith would be no faith at all. The very nature of faith is to rest on the invisible and intangible; it is a "conviction of the reality of things which we do not see." At Augsburg poor Philip was in the very depth of despondency. Luther tried to infuse a little of his heroic confidence into the timid man. He wrote a letter to him which is no less than a classic. If an excuse be needed for citing it at some length, may that be the excuse. Luther wrote: "Those great cares by which you say you are consumed I vehemently hate; they rule your heart not on account of the greatness of the cause but by reason of the greatness of your unbelief. . . . If our cause is great, its Author and Champion is great also, for it is not ours. Why are you, therefore, tormenting yourself? If our cause is false, let us

[59] Sm, L 259.

recant; if it is true, why should we make Him a liar who commands us to be of untroubled heart? Cast your burden on the Lord, He says. The Lord is nigh unto all them that call upon Him with a broken heart. Does he speak in vain or to beasts? I too am quite often smitten, but not all the time. It is not your theology which makes you anxious, but your philosophy, the same which has been gnawing at your friend Camerarius. What good can you do by your vain anxiety? What can the devil do more than slay us? What after that? I beg you, so pugnacious in all else, fight against yourself, your own worst enemy, who furnishes Satan with arms against yourself. Christ died once for sinners, and will not die again for truth and justice, but will live and reign. If He be true, what fear is there for the truth? . . . I pray for you earnestly and am deeply pained that you keep sucking up cares like a leech." [60] This was in June. In July Luther again wrote to his friend. Melanchthon's timid anxiety was still gnawing at his heart; in fact, we know it to have been largely congenital. It remained with him to the end, and after Luther's strong arm was no longer there to buoy him up, Melanchthon caused much trouble in the Church because of it. Luther wrote: "You are fearful because you cannot comprehend how this matter will end and what will be its ultimate result. But if you could comprehend it, I should not relish taking part in it or being related to it, much less being a prime mover of it. God has put the outcome of this matter in a place about which one finds nothing in your rhetoric or philosophy. The name of the place is Faith. Here all things stand that are invisible and do not appear; and if one took it upon himself (as you do) to make such a matter visible and comprehensible, he would come away with no other reward than worry and fear, as is indeed happening to you, although we have — in vain, however — defended and cautioned you against this. . . . May God increase your faith and the faith of all of us. If we have that, what can the devil and all the world besides do to us?" [61]

---

[60] Sm, L 257 f.   [61] Erl 54:177.

LUTHER CERTAIN THE REFORMATION WOULD ENDURE

Luther, it is plain, believed in the ultimate triumph of the cause, because he recognized it to be God's own cause. Thus he wrote in 1524: "We shall not fight or conquer any better if we are anxious and fearful, nor will things be worse for us if we are glad and joyful. . . . Let us fight like men who are fighting another's battle. The cause is God's, the care is God's, the work is God's, the glory is God's; He will fight and conquer without us. If He deigns to take us for His weapons, we shall be ready and willing." [62] As time went on, the Reformer became ever more firmly convinced that the Reformation was certain to remain, though millions might reject its purified Gospel and others again fall away from it. God would see it through. God would provide a place for it. His reply to Henry VIII is typically Lutheresque in its dramatic forcefulness. "All right, then, all together, the way you are together and belong together, devil, papists, and enthusiasts in one mass, come at Luther briskly: you papists from the front, you enthusiasts from the rear, you devils from everywhere! . . . In the name of God I bid defiance to all. Whoever regrets [having sided with the Gospel], let him forsake it; whoever is afraid, let him flee. He who backs me up is strong and reliable enough; that I know. Though the entire world cling to me and fall away again, that makes no difference whatever to me; and I am thinking it did not cling to me either while I stood alone. . . . I pray you just once more for God's sake: if possible do not become entangled with Luther. It is truly not Luther whom you are chasing; you should and must and will let Luther's doctrine stand and stay, though you numbered ten worlds together." [63]

SHAMEFUL ABUSE OF THE GOSPEL DID NOT SILENCE LUTHER

Such words make it abundantly clear that Luther did not permit the abuse of the Gospel to offend and to silence him. He freely confessed and deeply deplored that the precious Gospel

---

[62] S-J, LC II:274.   [63] Erl 30:12 f.

was being shamefully abused by many. Thus he wrote: "When the common people hear out of the Gospel that righteousness cometh by the mere grace of God, through faith only, without the Law and without works, they gather by and by of it, as did the Jews in times past: If the Law do not justify, then let us work nothing; and this do they truly perform. What shall we then do? This impiety doth indeed very much vex us, but we cannot remedy it. For when Christ preached, He must needs hear that He was a blasphemer and a seditious person; that is to say, that through His doctrine He deceived men and made them rebels against Caesar. The selfsame thing happened to Paul and all the rest of the Apostles. And what marvel is it if the world in like manner accuse us at this day? Let it accuse us, let it slander us, let it persecute us and spare us not; yet must not we therefore hold our peace, but speak freely, that afflicted consciences may be delivered out of the snares of the devil. And we must not regard the foolish and ungodly people in that they do abuse our doctrine; for, whether they have the Law or no Law, they cannot be reformed." [64] Towards the end of his commentary he reverts to this subject and says: "If grace or faith be not preached, no man can be saved; for it is faith alone that justifieth and saveth. On the other side, if faith be preached (as of necessity it must be), the more part of men understand the doctrine of faith carnally and draw the liberty of the spirit into the liberty of the flesh; this may we see in all kinds of life, as well of the high as the low. All boast themselves to be professors of the Gospel, and all brag of Christian liberty; and yet, serving their own lusts, they give themselves to covetousness, pleasure, pride, envy, and such other vices. No man doeth his duty faithfully; no man charitably serveth the necessity of his brother. The grief hereof maketh me sometimes so impatient that many times I wish such swine, which tread precious pearls under their feet, were yet still remaining under the tyranny of the Pope; for it is impossible that this people of Gomorrah should be governed by the Gospel of peace." [65]

---

[64] Lu, G 268 f.   [65] Lu, G 455.

In order properly to evaluate these strong words a number of things must be borne in mind. Above all it must be remembered that Luther frequently emphasized truths so strongly that one might get a false impression if the other side of the picture were neglected as entirely as, for the time being, he ignores it. Many no doubt abused the Gospel. But many also used it as the good Lord intended it to be used. But because of his sensitive conscience and his ardent love of the Gospel the abuse often loomed larger before the eyes of the Reformer than the correct use. Yet, he did not fail to see the fruits of the pure Gospel. He wrote the Elector of Saxony and his brother John in 1524, when the disturbances at Wittenberg were causing some apprehensions: "By the grace of God I can point to many spiritual fruits among our people . . . if boasting is to be done." [66] Then, it should also be borne in mind that conditions in the Church of Rome were, generally speaking, still worse, as the very enemies of Luther, men like Jerome Emser, testified.[67] Naturally, many of the older generation were so steeped in Romish error and superstition, or in spiritual indifference and carnal security, that little could be done with them. They scarcely allowed evangelical pastors and teachers an opportunity to preach the Gospel to them. Of this class Luther wrote: "If the older people do not want them, they may go to the devil." [68] The Reformer's hopes were settled on the younger generation. And not in vain. He lived to see it well indoctrinated; and he rejoiced at it, saying: "Tender youth, boys and girls, are growing up so well equipped by Catechism and Scripture that it warms my heart (*dass mir's sanft im Herzen tut*) to be privileged to see that now boys and girls can pray, believe, and speak more of God and of Christ than formerly all foundations, cloisters, and schools could do and more than they can do today. Truly, such young folk are a paradise the like of which is not to be found in the world." [69]

At the same time Luther did not fancy that a millennium was

---

66 Erl 53:264.

67 In Wa, F 339 f.

68 S-J, LC II:383.

69 Erl 54:148.

about to begin. He knew human nature — and the devil's nature besides — entirely too well to indulge in such overoptimism. There is a passage in his *Galatians* which subsequent events proved to have been sadly accurate in its prophecy. Luther foretold: "When we are dead and gone . . . many shall rise up who will be masters and teachers, who under a color of true religion will teach false and perverse doctrine and will quickly overthrow all that we in so long time and with so great travail have builded. We are no better than the Apostles, who, whilst they yet lived, saw (not without their grief and sorrow) the subversion of those churches which they themselves had planted through their ministry. . . . And yet, notwithstanding, Christ shall remain and reign to the end of the world, and that marvelously, as He did under the Papacy." [70]

NEITHER PRESENT TROUBLES NOR IMPENDING STORMS UPSET LUTHER

The mighty faith that inspired those last words gave Martin Luther the equanimity which so many have admired in him and for which they have envied him. To many people, superficially acquainted with him, he may appear unpredictable, impulsive, and temperamental. But his intimate friends tell us this was not at all the case. In spite of the intensity of his love and resentment he possessed a paradoxical imperturbability and evenness of temper. Especially clergymen may well envy Luther for being able to sit down after a heated controversy and perhaps pen a letter of sympathy to some sufferer that breathed nothing but the deepest calm and the very peace of heaven. He did not have to wait upon moods. Thus, when Henry VIII had written contemptuously to him, and George of Ducal Saxony had again demonstrated his hatred of the Gospel, and false friends were rising up against him, Luther wrote to his friend Wenzel Link about these things. One might expect them so to have filled his mind and to have harrowed his soul as to make him lose interest

---

[70] Lu, G 362.

in everything else. Intense, dynamic characters like Luther's often react in this manner. They are often so absorbed in the affairs they have made their life's work as to be or to become one-track minds. Not so Luther. In the midst of a world of problems and troubles he wrote to Link: "I am glad you promise me seed in the spring. Send as much as you can; I want it and am looking for it. If I can do anything in return, command me, and it will be done. For though Satan and his members may rage, I will laugh at him and will turn my attention to the garden, that is, to the blessings of the Creator, and enjoy them to His praise." [71]

MELANCHTHON AND LUTHER CONTRASTED

Melanchthon affords a striking contrast to Luther in this respect. He was constantly unsettled and worried about something. Theodore Schmauck has well described this difference between the two reformers. "Nowhere does the distinction between Luther and Melanchthon loom up more clearly than in a great crisis. Luther gave himself with all his soul to communion with the Lord; Melanchthon gave himself to innumerable consultations, plans, policies, and arrangements for turning the tide of events in accord with the methods of men. As a result, Luther was mighty in the strength of God in every critical moment; Melanchthon was weak, careworn, unsettled, and unnerved, fearful lest the plans he had laid would miscarry and the worst would befall. Round about the soul of Luther there swayed the atmosphere of heavenly peace." [72] To this we may add: While Luther was keeping his spirits at an even keel amid the storms of life by fervent prayer, Melanchthon might even be consulting astrological charts.

THE WORLD WAS FULL OF SUPERSTITIONS IN LUTHER'S DAYS

In view of the age during which he lived, Martin Luther was comparatively free from superstitions. His generation and many that had gone before were notoriously superstitious. The dominant Church had done little to dispel these fancies. She finally

---

[71] S-J, LC II:388.   [72] Sc, C 439.

fell under the spell of some of them herself and reverenced what her heads had at one time almost ridiculed or had tolerated with good-natured contempt. Then, too, the Church might use some of these superstitions to increase the awe of the "faithful" at the mysterious and the supernatural. This would broaden her field of operation and make the protective and curative means on which she claimed to have a monopoly more indispensable. The atmosphere amid which Luther grew up was therefore heavily charged with goblins and mischievous imps; it was full of devils and witches. The evil eye might kill and doom, and the mysterious incantation might blast and wither at any time. There were superstitions too numerous to catalog. Some were as harmless as they were childish; others rested like a torturing nightmare upon the people. Many were so old that in tracing them back one loses the thread of their origin in the haze of the distant past. Others, again, had sprung up — no one knew when or where or how — in the shadow of some Scripture teaching or historical fact and had become so inextricably interwoven with it that scarcely anyone knew — and perhaps fewer cared — just where fact ended and fiction began. And as though earth had not enough superstitions, the heavenly bodies were also invested with mysterious influences on human destiny. This was astrology. Melanchthon was under its spell, as were many of his contemporaries. When Luther wished to leave Smalkald in 1537, because he thought he felt his end approaching, Melanchthon would have none of it because of the evil influence of the new moon. Luther paid no attention to the moon and left. Of astrology he said: "To put faith in the stars is idolatry." [73] In his *Table Talk* he proves on both natural and Scriptural ground that astrology is heathen superstition.

LUTHER WAS COMPARATIVELY FREE FROM THEM

But in certain other respects Martin Luther was a child of his day. This does not necessarily reflect either on his character or his intellect. It merely implies that his views in certain fields

---

[73] Erl 57:374.

of knowledge were those of his class, the better educated of the first half of the sixteenth century. To laugh at some of the things in which, at the time, even this class put faith is as easy as it is unfair. Particularly some of the remedies prescribed by the medical science of Luther's day make strange reading. At times it is difficult to determine which was worse, the sickness or the prescribed cure. At Smalkald a brew of garlic and horse dung was prescribed for Luther.[74] He drank it in good faith. Frequently the patient remained alive in spite of the medical science. More will be said about this later.

Quite in keeping with the views prevalent in his days Luther regarded strange phenomena and exceptional occurrences as signs of future events of importance. Thus he wrote to the poet Paul Speratus, after having referred to the persecutions of Lutherans in the Low Countries: "But God has given them [the persecutors] an omen of death, if perchance they may come to themselves and repent; for a sea monster has been cast ashore at Haarlem. It is called a whale and is seventy feet long and thirty-five wide. By all the precedents of antiquity this prodigy is a sure sign of God's wrath. The Lord have mercy on them and us."[75] In 1525 that good man Frederick the Wise died. In a letter by which Luther announced the decease of his Elector to a friend he said: "The sign of it [the death] was a rainbow that Philip [Melanchthon] and I saw over Lochau one night last winter and a child born here at Wittenberg without a head; also another with club feet."[76] A few years later Luther wrote to another friend about the unjust measures introduced by Pope and Emperor to exact money from the Germans. Thereupon he concludes the letter by saying: "It is just and right that they who oppose Luther, their defender, should, under their own preserver, lose everything they have and be destroyed in the wrath of God. At Cronberg in Hesse an unborn child cried out twice in the bathroom in the hearing of the whole family. This is a bad sign."[77] Julius Koestlin

---

[74] K-K, M II:387.

[75] S-J, LC II:125.

[76] S-J, LC II:318.

[77] S-J, LC II:512.

has related other extraordinary appearances which Luther and his friends regarded as supernatural signs of coming events.[78] They need not detain us. Nor is it necessary to determine just how much of all this was superstition. At the same time it need not be denied that vestiges of medieval superstition did cling to the Reformer to the end of his life. Nor is that at all surprising when one remembers the eager and receptive soul of young Martin and the manner in which the line of demarcation between faith and superstition had been blurred and smeared, if not entirely obliterated, by the Church of Rome.

LUTHER'S VIEWS OF THE MENTALLY DERANGED

Then, too, there are what one may call borderline cases, cases which cannot be decided by an appeal to Scripture, since Scripture does not pass a categorical judgment on them, nor by an appeal to reason, since man's researches have not been able to find anything that is conclusive and final. As an example the relation between the mentally deranged and the powers of darkness may serve. To Luther the insane were possessed by the devil. He was not dogmatic about this, but he expressed his view clearly enough when he wrote: "My opinion of lunatics is that all idiots and insane persons are possessed by devils, though on that account they will not be damned." [79] To some this identification might seem an overstatement. But this entire subject is a matter by no means easy to decide. In spite of modern progress in the study of the structure and functioning of the human mind, we have still very much to learn. There are mysterious depths of the soul, of the inner life of man, which no psychologist or psychiatrist has as yet fathomed. It becomes us to speak modestly of this matter and to hold to no views that contradict the teaching of His revelation who has created the human mind and soul and knows what is in them.

Now, the details Scripture gives us are not enough definitely to determine whether the possessed were also insane. However,

---

[78] K-K, M II:203.   [79] S-J, LC II:447.

so much is clear: no honest interpretation of the New Testament stories in which possessed are introduced can make these unfortunates out to have been merely epileptic or insane, however similar certain symptoms may appear to be. But Modernists convert this similarity into an identity and hold that in former centuries men considered the mentally afflicted possessed by a personal spirit of evil simply because they were ignorant of psychology and psychiatry. Today, they hold, we can explain on natural grounds what once was considered supernatural because it was unknown and therefore mysterious. Their argument runs like this: since even those who believe in a personal spirit of evil now grant that many formerly regarded by them as having been possessed are now discovered to have been merely mentally deranged, it follows that all the supposedly possessed may very well have been and still may be simply cases of mental affliction and disorganization. In this way the fact that the dividing line between the mentally deranged and the possessed is frequently somewhat fluid and indeterminable is quoted to cast doubt upon the existence of that troublesome being, a personal devil.

LUTHER BELIEVED IN A VERY ACTIVE PERSONAL DEVIL

But the devil "will not down" that easily. Naturally, Luther's faith in the very existence of a personal devil is quite generally regarded as a vestige of medieval superstition. Preserved Smith wrote without any qualifications: "One part of Luther's religion, borrowed from the popular superstition of the age, was his belief in a personal devil." [80] It is true, Luther considered the devil at the bottom of all sin and mischief, both directly and indirectly — usually directly. Freytag has summarized the case like this: "In Luther's *Table Talk* . . . he [the devil] sits under a bridge in the form of a nixe and draws girls into the water, whom he forces into marriage. He serves in the convent as a domestic sprite, blows the fire into a blaze as a goblin; as a dwarf he puts his changelings into the cradles of man; as a nightmare he misleads

---

[80] Sm, L 339.

the sleepers to climb the roof and as a noisy hobgoblin tumbles things around in the rooms. By this last thing he particularly disturbed Luther several times. The ink spot in the Wartburg is not sufficiently authenticated, but Luther did tell of a disagreeable noise which Satan made at that place by night with a bag of hazelnuts. In the monastery at Wittenberg also, when Luther studied in the refectory at night, the devil kept up a noise in the church hall below him until Luther packed up his books and went to bed. Afterwards he was vexed because he did not defy the 'buffoon.' " [81]

In reply to this direct and implied criticism the following ought to be said. Luther's faith in a personal devil is proved to have been based on grim facts by dozens of Bible passages.[82] To call this "superstition" is unworthy of a theologian and a Christian. If no such being as a devil actually exists, what are we to make of Christ's testimony? Did He not know better? Then He is an unsafe Guide. Did He consciously deceive people? Then He was not honest. The entire body of Christian doctrine is imperiled by the denial of a personal devil. Perhaps Luther's dramatic imagination often found the old evil Foe personally present when and where he was not present. Possibly, though, the devil was more noticeably active than usual in the days of Luther, because he sensed how much was at stake. From the Gospels it is evident that he exerted himself particularly also in the days of Christ, when the Gospel was being established. Would he permit its re-establishment in the age of the Reformation without seeking to thwart it and to discredit it in every possible manner? But be that as it may: if Luther's attitude is an unwarranted extreme, it is assuredly to be preferred to the denial of the very existence of a devil. If Luther saw the devil in too much of what was going on, our sophisticated generation sees him in too little of what is happening, and that is by far the worse of the two extremes.

---

[81] Fr, M 118 f.

[82] See Matt. 13:39; Luke 8:12; John 8:44; 1 Tim. 3:6.

Certainly, any superstitious medieval accretions to the Scripture doctrine of the devil should be recognized and scored, but they do not in the least invalidate the doctrine as such. When Luther wrote to Spalatin of the scandalous disturbances caused by the fanatics at Wittenberg "I know it is the doing of Satan, for as he cannot hurt the Word of God, which is now returning to us, he seeks this way to disparage it," [83] no believing child of God can find the slightest superstition in these words. Furthermore, when Luther traced much of the misery and woe of the world to the direct agency of the devil, no one who takes God's Word at its face value will find anything to criticize in that. Luther once gave a good, succinct account of his views on this matter in a letter to Wenzel Link. "Physicians may attribute such things to natural causes and sometimes partly cure them by medicine, but they are ignorant of the power of devils. Christ did not hesitate to say in the Gospel that the old woman bowed down with infirmity was bound by Satan . . . so I am forced to believe that many are made dumb, deaf, and lame by Satan's malice, nor can I doubt that pestilence, fever, and other severe illnesses are caused by devils, who also bring on tempests, conflagrations, and blights in fruit and grain. What wonder if these wicked angels scourge the human race with all kinds of harm and peril as much as God permits! If some are cured by herbs and other natural remedies, it is by God's mercy. I suppose a physician would have said the sufferings of Job were due to natural agents and could be cured by natural remedies." [84]

That Satan was eager to destroy Luther in particular is to be understood. His attacks upon the Reformer have been mentioned above. Luther's vigorous counterattacks are a matter of history. When Preserved Smith says of Luther, "His fury resembled a personal hatred more than a philosophic detestation of an abstract principle," [85] he is quite correct. The devil was no "abstract principle" to Martin Luther. "Abstract principles" do not "as a roaring lion walk about, seeking whom they may devour"; [86] and that is

---

[83] S-J, LC I:339.   [84] S-J, LC II:447 f.   [85] Sm, L 339.   [86] 1 Pet. 5:8.

what Satan was attempting to do with both Luther and the Reformation; he wanted to destroy both.

One of his strategies was the attempt to dishearten the peace-loving Reformer by pointing to the strife the preaching of the Gospel was causing. Perhaps the devil thought this very subtle, but he certainly did not impress Luther by it; for the Reformer knew both Scripture and history too well. He was acquainted with these tactics of the "father of lies." It is true, Christ had said: "I came not to send peace, but a sword," [87] and then had gone on to predict that the most intimate bonds of relationship would be torn asunder when His Gospel would be preached. But the fault of the family strife would not be chargeable to the Gospel. The guilt would rest upon the unbelief and hatred of man. When cold water and unslaked lime come into contact, the heat that is generated is due to the nature of the lime. Just so the strife caused by the preaching of the "Gospel of peace" is due to the unbelieving, corrupt nature of man. The very fact that man blames the Gospel for causing disturbances in the world is an evidence of this corruption. But the tactics employed by fallen man in Paradise lost have become almost his second nature. "The woman whom Thou gavest me," — blame her; nay, blame Thyself for giving me the woman. "The serpent beguiled me," — blame that creature, intimated Eve. To shift the blame to someone else, even to God, if need be, that is what corrupt man has been attempting to do ever since. The devil knows this and therefore never misses an opportunity to suggest that the strife occasioned by the preaching of the Gospel must lie in the nature of the message. He tried to tell Luther that, too, but the Reformer refused to be taken in by it.

LUTHER'S VIEW REGARDING DISTURBANCES OF THE REFORMATION

Luther rather regarded the strife that followed upon his Gospel preaching as an additional proof that his message to the world was indeed the very truth of God. With his prototype Paul

---

[87] Matt. 10:34.

he was ready to say: "If I yet pleased men, I should not be the servant of Christ." [88] Therefore the combined opposition of Church and State, Pope and Emperor, to his Gospel only convinced him the more of its Scriptural character; for had not the Psalmist predicted: "The kings of the earth set themselves, and the rulers take counsel together, against the Lord and against His Anointed"? [89] This very passage Luther quoted in a letter to his philosopher friend Maeurer as early as 1520. Preceding the citation are the words: "Dear Michael, you would hardly believe how much I am pleased to see enemies rise against me more than formerly. I am never prouder and bolder than when I hear that I displease them. They are doctors, bishops, princes — what then? If the Word of God were not assailed by them, it would not be the Word of God as it is written (Ps. 2:2)." [90] Particularly the timid Erasmus charged Luther with having disturbed the peace. Luther did disturb the peace, as policemen may be said to disturb it when they interrupt robbers who are plundering a home in which they have killed some and drugged and gagged others. In this manner the papal hierarchy was carrying on in the house of God when Luther, in the name of the Law and the Gospel of God, interrupted their spoliation and exploitation. It is understandable that certain people should resent this and call it a disturbance. Luther therefore told Erasmus that his charge did not impress him. The disturbance as such he liked as little as Erasmus did; but there was something worse than this disturbance: it was the peace of spiritual death and stagnation. But let Luther again state his case in his own words: "By the grace of God I am not so great a fool or madman as to have desired to sustain and defend this cause so long, with so much fortitude and so much firmness (which you call obstinacy), in the face of so many dangers of my life, so much hatred, so many traps laid for me; in a word, in the face of the fury of men and devils — I have not done this for money, for that I neither have nor desire; nor for vainglory, for that, if I wished, I could not obtain in a world

---

[88] Gal. 1:10.   [89] Psalm 2:2.   [90] S-J, LC I:376.

PLATE VI

FREDERICK THE WISE

Elector Frederick the Wise of Saxony was painted a number of
times by Cranach. This picture shows him in his last years. He
died in 1525 at the age of 62

PLATE VII

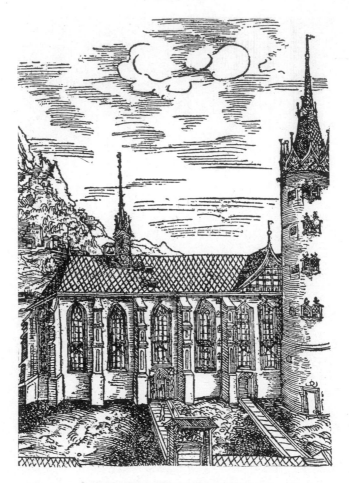

CASTLE CHURCH IN WITTENBERG

To the door of the Castle Church at Wittenberg Luther nailed his
famous Ninety-Five Theses on October 31, 1517. In 1760, during
a war with Austria, the doors of this historic church were destroyed
by fire. In 1858 they were replaced by iron ones, bearing the
original text of the theses

PLATE VIII

INTERIOR VIEW OF CASTLE CHURCH

Luther was buried in a leaden coffin on February 22, 1546, at the
foot of the pulpit, at the right. This picture was taken after the
renovation of 1885—1892

PLATE IX

PHILIP MELANCHTHON

This miniature oil painting comes from the brush of Hans Holbein, one of the best portrait artists of that day. It is the prized possession of the Royal Art Gallery of Hanover

so enraged against me; nor for the life of my body, for that cannot be made sure of for one hour. Do you think, then, that you only have a heart that is moved by these tumults? Yet I am not made of stone. . . . But since it cannot be otherwise, I choose rather to be battered in temporal tumult, happy in the grace of God, for God's Word's sake." [91]

Luther never hesitated to confess that the preaching of "his Gospel" was the occasion of many disturbances, but he very definitely denied that it was the *cause* of the strife. In his exposition of Gal. 4:29 he said: "Verily, it is no small grief unto us when we are constrained to hear that all things were in peace and tranquillity before the Gospel came abroad, but since the preaching and publishing thereof all things are unquiet and the whole world is in an uproar. . . . When a man that is not endued with the Spirit of God heareth this, by and by he is offended and judgeth that the disobediences of subjects against their magistrates, that seditions, wars, plagues, and famines, that the overthrowing of commonweals, kingdoms, and countries, that sects, offenses, and such other infinite evils do proceed altogether from the doctrines of the Gospel. Against this great offense we must comfort and arm ourselves with this sweet consolation, that the faithful must bear this name and this title in the world that they are seditious and schismatics and the authors of innumerable evils." [92] And Luther did so "comfort and arm himself." The unfair charges against him and his Gospel never cooled the ardor of his faith, never slowed the quick tempo of his pen, and never silenced the mighty voice of his testimony. He was aglow with a living, dynamic faith. That made a man with a personality like his a prophet of fire.

---

[91] Lu, B 54.   [92] Lu, G 406.

CHAPTER VI

A PROPHET OF FIRE

Obiit auriga et currus Israel, qui rexit ecclesiam
in hac ultima senecta mundi.

Melanchthon, at Luther's death

THE WORDS QUOTED ABOVE WERE WRITTEN BY MELANCHTHON when he announced the death of Luther to his students in a bulletin on February 19, 1546. He told them: "He who was the charioteer and the chariot of Israel has died, the man who guided the Church in this final period of the world's old age." [1] Melanchthon was neither the first nor the last to have discovered a similarity between Elijah and Luther. The Old Testament prophet was raised by God to call back an idolatrous people to the worship of the true God. It was a Herculean task, and for many years Elijah had to carry it on against the powers of both Church and State almost singlehandedly. But he did it with a zeal that has earned him the name "the prophet of fire." In fact, his zeal was such that there are those who feel that at times he might have attained his objectives just as well by more conciliatory words and more moderate actions.

Substitute the name Luther for Elijah and you have a sketch of the task of the Reformer, the manner in which he performed it, and the criticism some have had to offer. To all who know anything at all of Martin Luther the title "prophet of fire" will seem very appropriate. Not that the Reformer ever advocated autos-da-fé and the fiery stake for heretics. Such antichristian barbarism he left to Rome. But perhaps no one of his age spoke more flaming words, wrote more scorching condemnations of error and sin, and penned more fiery defenses of the Gospel than did he.

---

[1] Sc, C 586.

LUTHER A MAN OF INTENSELY DEEP AND ACTIVE CONVICTIONS

Luther was intense by nature. He could do nothing half-heartedly. He threw his entire energy into whatever he took in hand. In the language of today: he went all out for a thing. This trait was observed in Luther even as a youth, and it steadily grew upon him, as his character developed. His zeal as a monk has been adverted to above. He all but killed himself by the energy with which he observed the rigorous monastic rules and counsels. His zeal for the entire Papacy was exemplary. They who hold that Martin Luther left the Church of Rome because he never had been enthusiastic about her, are either uninformed or dishonest. Luther was a zealous Catholic. He assures us that before the light of the Gospel dawned upon him, he was willing at any time to do to death anyone who would refuse to accept as the truth any syllable the Pope might speak.[2] The burning zeal he showed against the Papacy subsequently can never honestly be ascribed to some personal grudge or peeve that had "gotten under Luther's skin." The first notice we have of Luther's character shows us a lad of intense and deep feeling. Preserved Smith is right: "Luther could bear anything better than lukewarmness."[3]

But Luther was no berserker. Naturally, intense characters such as his are peculiarly liable to outbursts of flaming anger. But Luther would never fly into an irresponsible rage during which, as some of the great in history, he would shiver chinaware and smash furniture. As H. Boehmer put it: "His [Luther's] anger had always very real grounds and, further, always expended its whole force at the writing table. Senseless and groundless fits of rage never occurred with him. Also, he had a great capacity for moderation. This appears not only in the moderation with which he behaved, notwithstanding his naturally impatient disposition, at the Diet of Worms, but also in his whole bearing during the progress of the Reformation, from 1522 to 1546, and his really remarkable forbearance towards the many extravagances which Magister Philippus permitted himself after 1532."[4]

---

[2] Wal XIV:439.   [3] Sm, L 392.   [4] Bo, L 195.

At the same time, however, the intensity with which Luther would grasp a truth, the way in which he would concentrate upon it, until it filled his entire soul, made it possible for careless or malicious hearers and readers to misconstrue him. He would so deeply enter into the spirit of an idea that for the time being it filled his entire mental horizon. An illustration might make this clearer. Someone has said: Live as though there were no Gospel; die as though there were no Law. The latter thought frequently occurs in Luther's writings. At times a passage may so strongly express it that, considered by itself, it almost appears as though Luther were depreciating and despising God's holy Law. One must never lose sight of the context, of the fact that Luther is speaking of the Law only as a possible means of salvation. As such it is worthless, nay, dangerous, and murderous. Or take the vital subject of substitution. Certain passages in Luther's writings so strongly emphasize this that, viewed apart from their connection, they seem disrespectful to the Savior, as Albert Barnes, for instance, actually holds them to be. But in his treatment of this matter in his *Notes on the New Testament* Barnes does not see that Luther has simply entered deeply into the thought of Scripture and consistently carried out its evident implications. Though strong, Luther's statement is not exaggerated. Thank God it is not. Luther says: "All the Prophets did foresee in spirit that Christ should become the greatest transgressor, murderer, adulterer, thief, rebel, and blasphemer that was or could be in the world." [5] These words can seem offensive only to a man who has never clearly thought through what the Scripture doctrine of substitution necessarily involves. To the man who has done that the words of Luther will contain the very center of the work of atonement: the vicarious satisfaction of Christ. Julius Hare has aptly said: "He who is familiar with Luther's writings, with their tone and spirit, their practical sense and spiritual wisdom, if he falls in with one of these stones of offense, will not stumble, but will suspend his judgment, trusting that what in its separation

---

[5] Lu, G 242.

may seem as shocking as a hand or eye, when severed from its body, will be proved on examination in its original place to fit aptly into the great body of truth from which it has been torn."[6] To the group gathered about his hospitable table the Reformer is recorded to have said: "I, Martin Luther, have done to death all the peasants in the sedition [Peasants' War]; for I directed that they be put to death; all their blood is on my neck. But I refer it to our Lord God; He told me to say that."[7] This statement is clear and inoffensive enough if taken in its entirety, but the expressions in it are so pointed and strong that malice may with comparative ease twist them into a charge against the Reformer. Luther lived to see this done, but never altered his original way of expressing himself. He insisted upon being himself, misinterpreters notwithstanding. To the very last his literary style reflected the intenseness of his character. In this respect age had no mellowing effect at all upon him. His scathing book *Against the Papacy at Rome, Founded by the Devil* was penned in 1545. He was then 62 years old.

LUTHER'S FIERY INTENSENESS WON PEOPLE'S HEARTS

Now, many people do not like such intenseness, no matter in which field a man's work may lie. They hold that a man, particularly one in a position of prominence and religious leadership, ought to be cool, deliberate, and serene. No doubt such sedateness is attractive in a way. Perhaps it were better called impressive. But such personalities rarely make reformers who gather an enthusiastic following. John Calvin ought not be quoted in disproof of this; for, as we shall see, Calvin was far from being the dispassionate man he is often imagined to have been. Unemotional characters, then, may certainly gain our respect, but they rarely win enthusiastic love and personal devotion. They are not human enough, so to speak. Men may defend to the death the cause for which they stood, but their person does not call forth such demonstrations of attachment. It was different in

---

[6] H, V 72 f.　　　[7] Erl 59:284 f.

the case of Luther. He had a twofold hold on men: the charm of his personality gave men's attachment to the Gospel he preached an almost personal character. Luther never took unfair advantage of this, but he could hardly avoid keeping men from loving him as much as they respected him. The intenseness, the whole-heartedness, of the man made him so human, so colorful. It is said that all who knew George Washington respected the dignified man; and that all who really knew Abraham Lincoln loved the man. Luther was like Lincoln, but he also commanded the respect given to Washington.

Luther's *love* was intense. Since his character was essentially religion-centered, as we have seen, the objects of his deep affection were religious and spiritual. He ardently loved his God. Here, again, we are impressed especially by the intensely personal nature of Luther's love to God. Some people, even some theologians, have found it difficult to personalize their love to a God whom their senses have never seen or heard. But Luther was not troubled in this respect. His relation to God was peculiarly intimate and personal. This will appear particularly in his prayer life. We hear him saying to his God: "My entire life serves Thee and not me; for I seek not myself but Thee and what is Thine." [8] This loving consecration and intense devotion to God was the direct result of Luther's appreciation of the grace of God in Christ. Men marveled at the clarity with which he preached that grace and the fervor with which he embraced it. But Luther himself was satisfied with neither. He once said: "I do indeed love Christ, who by His blood has redeemed me from the power and tyranny of the devil, but my faith ought really to be much greater and much more ardent. Ah, my Lord, enter not into judgment with Thy servant." [9] In a sermon delivered only ten days before his death, Luther deplored the fact that his love to God, as revealed in Christ, was still not as intense as it ought to be and as he should like it to be. If the fervor of our love were com-

---

[8] Erl 37:441.   [9] Erl 58:397.

mensurate to the greatness of God's grace, Luther said, we should be simply transported (*entzuecket*) with joy.

Julius Hare has well said: "The very intensity of Luther's convictions, the vehemence with which he contended for them, cannot but seem utterly extravagant to those who do not participate in them, or feel what questions of weal or woe, of life or death, for the whole race of man were at stake." [10] These words deserve to be underlined. Only the person who appreciates them will find nothing offensive in the famous remark with which Luther bade farewell to the people of Smalkald in 1537. When seated in the wagon and about to depart, he made the sign of the cross over those who gathered to see him off and solemnly said: "May the Lord fill you with His blessing and with hatred against the Pope!" [11] Luther had recognized the Pope to be the "very Antichrist." As such he could but hate and abominate his falsification and persecution of that Gospel of Christ which he (Luther) had learned to love so deeply. His words at Smalkald are usually quoted to reveal his deep-seated hatred of the Papacy, but we would submit that they may with equal right be adduced to prove Luther's great love for the Savior and His Gospel. This is only the reverse side, so to speak, of the same affection. He who loves holiness necessarily hates wickedness; he who loves Christ can but hate Antichrist.

Luther's *hatred* was always intense. It was also categorical and generic. Any falsehood or sin anywhere in anyone — very definitely including himself — aroused his intense resentment and protest. He said: "This is the greatest part of the grief and the sadness which the Christians have, that they must see that God's name (in His Gospel) is everywhere so shamefully desecrated and blasphemed, God's kingdom persecuted, and His will despised and trodden under foot, and that they must feel such things within themselves, that the devil fights against these things in their hearts with his hellish thoughts of unbelief, blasphemy, despair, etc. . . . This is the very torture of hell to them." [12]

---

[10] H, V 3.   [11] Tr., Intr. 49.   [12] Erl 50:127.

LUTHER'S HATRED NEVER BLIND OR IRRATIONAL

Luther felt that righteous anger against error and sin could scarcely be overdone. His little book against Duke Henry of Wolfenbuettel, entitled *Against Jack Sausage* (Hans Worst), is one of his bluntest writings. But some time after its publication he wrote to Melanchthon: "I have again read my book and wonder what happened to me that I was so moderate. I ascribe it to the suffering in my head. This did not permit a brisker and more vigorous attack." [13] Nor let anyone think Luther became confused and incoherent when writing while aroused, that he dealt savage blows indiscriminately, beat about in a blind fury, like the proverbial bull in the china shop. There are men who have done and said things in a fit of uncontrolled anger that they have lived deeply to regret. But, as H. Boehmer has pointed out, Luther's anger was never irrational. As a matter of fact he never thought more clearly than when aroused to white heat. His zeal seemed to stimulate and sharpen his mental powers. He once remarked: if he wanted to compose, write, pray, or preach well, he had to be moved by a righteous anger and zeal. Then, said he, his entire system was refreshed, and his intellect became alert.[14]

AN EMPHATIC CRITIC OF ALL ERROR

In the then conditions of Christendom there was enough and to spare to arouse the fiery zeal of anyone even less energetic than Martin Luther. Falsehood and superstition were to be found everywhere. The "truth as it is in Jesus" had not only to be clearly restated, but it had to be defended to the left against old heresies and to the right against new misrepresentations and distortions. This polemical activity often showed Luther at his best. He had the ability not only to state the truth so clearly that even children could grasp it — as in his Catechism — but also to expose the untenableness of contradictory views and to point out why they must be rejected. Luther's polemical writings

---

[13] In Wa, L 147.   [14] Erl 58:428 f.

have, in consequence, earned him the undying gratitude of many and the continued criticism of more. Among the statements of his views on this point the following is representative. "A preacher must not only feed the sheep so as to instruct them how they are to be good Christians but, besides this, must also guard against the wolves, lest they attack the sheep and lead them astray with false doctrine and introduce error such as the devil would not find fault with. But there are many people to be found at the present day quite ready to tolerate our preaching of the Gospel if we would not cry out against the wolves. . . . The wolf can very readily endure to have the sheep well fed . . . but this he cannot endure: the hostile bark of the dogs." [15]

OBJECTIONS TO LUTHER'S CONSTANT POLEMICS

Many did, indeed, take exception to Luther's "bark." Many people still do. They criticize him for what they like to call his censoriousness. He spent too much time finding fault with others, they tell us. This is said to be uncharitable and not in keeping with the spirit of the gentle Jesus. Luther, they hold, ought to have emphasized the points of agreement more and those of disagreement less. After all, many of those whom he takes to task so severely were apparently Christians at heart. Now, these specious objections are not new. Luther heard them, one and all, and disposed of them, one and all, with his customary thoroughness. What amazes one is the fact that they are at times still advanced and that people are taken in by them. What would be said of a man who would fault a physician for always calling attention to the sicknesses and diseases of people? And as to the spirit of the "gentle Jesus" — what about Matthew 23 and John 2:12-17? Do these keen critics not know that a spirit of love is compatible with righteous anger and zeal? The Jesus pictured by Modernists never existed, he is the creation of their imagination, and their unbelief wielded the brush and the pen that produced their caricature of the real Jesus.

---

[15] Wal IX:1275.

The condemnation of error is the inevitable theological corollary of the confession of truth. To separate the two is like trying to tear the front side from the back side of a piece of cloth. The two are one. Just so the thesis of a truth inevitably posits its antithesis. Why, then, should it not be expressed? Must the implications be left undeveloped for fear of hurting someone's feelings? That is a poor sort of charity which fails to identify certain definite heresies with certain definite church bodies in order to appear irenical and conciliatory. A patient were poorly served if his physician were earnestly to caution him against certain disease germs but would carefully avoid telling him where they are to be found. But enough of this. One is frequently at a loss to decide which is the more astounding: the fact that men are found who decry polemics or the fact that ever and again people are taken in by their arguments.

LUTHER'S REPLY

Luther correctly held polemics to be unavoidable. He said, in his original, drastic way, that whenever a man prayed the Lord's Prayer he cursed. "No one," wrote he, "can pray the Lord's Prayer aright without cursing in the act of doing so; for when he prays: 'Hallowed be Thy name; Thy kingdom come; Thy will be done,' etc., he must include in one class (*auf* EINEN *Haufen*) whatever is opposed to this and must say: 'Cursed, confounded, disgraced ought all names and all kingdoms become that are against Thee.'" [16] But among such antichristian powers the Papacy is the most prominent. Therefore the Reformer did not hesitate publicly to preach: "If someone now curse [asking] God to eradicate and destroy the Papacy, priestcraft, monkery, and nunnery with their foundations and cloisters, all the world should say, 'Amen,' because God's Word and grace (*Segen*) are cursed, damned, and hindered in all the world by such spectres from hell." [17] So, then, Luther considered it the sacred and, withal, unavoidable duty of the Christian clearly to expose and emphati-

---

[16] Wal VII:460 f.   [17] Wal XII:351.

cally to refute error. Nor, thought he, ought a man ever hesitate to call a spade a spade and to designate errorists by name. In this respect, too, Martin Luther certainly practiced what he preached; in fact, many have felt that in this direction the good man went too far.

No doubt the commonest charge against Luther is the *vehemence of his language*. There are many who hold that he becomes positively abusive at times and permits his intense feelings to run away with his discretion. It must indeed be granted that few have used stronger, more vitriolic language than Martin Luther. Perhaps merely the ability, not the desire, was lacking in others. But be that as it may, Luther's verbal blows are frequently annihilating. His enemies and some apologetic friends have called this characteristic his *furor Teutonicus,* but we doubt whether it was so generic. Luther never exhibited the irresponsible frenzy that is thought to be an active ingredient of the Teutonic fury. At times he called names, strong names, untranslatable names. But that was incidental. One may say it was the condiment in his dish. The main fare consisted of right meaty and weighty arguments.

Of course, it is easy to lift the titles he conferred upon the adversaries out of the argument in the development of which he used them. In this way a very impressive list may be compiled. Because of the weakness of their defense, caused, perhaps, by the mediocrity of their mental equipment no less than by the indefensibleness of their position, Luther does not hesitate to call his opponents asses. The defenders of Rome had scored Luther for inserting the word "alone" into his German translation of Romans 3:28. Luther, well aware of the fact that it is easy to see that his rendering is demanded by the genius of the German language, finally lost patience with his criticasters and bluntly said: "If your papist wants to make such a fuss about the word *sola,* 'alone,' tell him this: 'Dr. Martin Luther will have it so and says that a papist and an ass are the same thing.'" [18] At the

---

[18] Ho V:12.

end of his writing *On Translating: an Open Letter,* from which the words just quoted are taken, Luther says: "Nay, dear asses, come along and say that this [what Luther had stated] is the teaching of the Church — these stinking lies which you villains and traitors have imposed by force upon the Church and over which you archmurderers have slain many Christians." [19] In his *Commentary on the Letter to the Galatians* Luther calls the Papacy "the slaughterhouse of consciences and the very kingdom of the devil," [20] because of the unanswerable manner in which it urged monks to suicidal rigor of discipline and yet told them that they could never be quite certain of having earned the favor of God. As early as 1520 Luther wrote: "I think that at Rome they have all become mad, silly, raging, insane fools, stocks, stones, and devils of hell." These strong words occur in a letter to Spalatin in which he deplored the publication of Prierias' *Epitome,* the bluntest assertion of the theory of papal power that had, till then, appeared. Luther said of it: "See now what we have to hope from Rome, who allows this infernal writing to go out against the Church." [21] The Reformer's reply, in part, was one of the most famous and powerful of all his writings: *To the Christian Nobility.* In it there is this blast: "Hearest thou this, O Pope, not most holy, but most sinful? Oh, that God from heaven would soon destroy thy throne and sink it in the abyss of hell! . . . Through thy throat and pen the wicked Satan doth lie as he hath never lied before. Thou dost force and wrest the Scriptures to thy fancy. O Christ, my Lord, look down, let the day of Thy Judgment break and destroy the devil's nest at Rome! Here sitteth the man of whom St. Paul hath said that he shall exalt himself above Thee, sit in Thy Church, and set himself up as God — the man of sin and the son of perdition!" [22] This publication appeared in August, 1520. For a full quarter century thereafter Luther exposed the heresies, the chicaneries, and the corruptions of the Papacy in a manner that has put him into a class by himself among the champions of the truth against Rome.

---

[19] Ho V:26.   [20] Lu, G 346.   [21] S-J, LC I:329.   [22] Ho II:139.

HIS FINAL BLAST AT PAPAL ERROR AND CORRUPTION

As time went on, it became ever more evident that the Church of the Pope would go her own way, refusing to heed the call to come back to Scripture and to bow in humble obedience to its all-sufficient revelation. A lucid presentation of apostolic doctrine came in 1529 in Luther's two catechisms; the clarion voice of the Augsburg Confession sounded a reveille in the following year. Then came the still unrefuted Apology of the Confession and the Smalkald Articles. But every additional testimony of the truth seemed only to harden and stiffen the opposition of Rome. She *would* not confess her apostasy from the truth, though she had to canonize the baldest error. And that is the tragic position in which she finally found herself. Forced by pressure from within and without, she began to meet at Trent in 1545 to tell the anxious world where she stood. Luther now was convinced that she had hardened herself beyond reclamation. He therefore released his last and perhaps his mightiest broadside against her, his famous book *Against the Papacy at Rome, Founded by the Devil*. To appreciate its devastating impact, it ought to be read at one sitting. It is a veritable atomic bomb among polemical writings. A translation can hardly do justice to it. It seems to have welled up out of the depth of a soul surcharged with a mixture of grief and anger at the perverseness of apostate Rome. Luther's vehemence of language reaches its climax in this publication. After listing the doctrinal subversions and perversions of Rome, the Reformer says: "I must stop. I have no desire to puddle around in the blasphemous, hellish filth and stench of the devil. Let someone else also read. Whoever wants to hear God speak, let him read Holy Writ; whoever wants to hear the devil speak, let him read the Pope's dirty decrees [Luther spells it *Dreket* instead of *Dekret*] and bulls. Oh, woe, woe, woe, to him who finally comes to be Pope or cardinal! It were better for him never to have been born. Judas has betrayed and killed the Lord, but the Pope betrays and ruins the Christian Church, which the Lord considered more dear and precious than Himself or His blood. Woe to you, Pope!" [23] Somewhat later he says: "If the devil himself were to reign at Rome, he could not do worse; indeed, if he himself reigned, we could secure ourselves against him (*koennten uns fuer ihm segnen*) and flee from him, so that he could not affect us. But now the Pope has surrendered himself to him as a mask, trimmed with God's Word, under which one could not recognize him [the devil] — that is [a visitation of] God's wrath. Now it happened: everything (was done) which his bitter, devilish, hellish grudge against Christ and His Church could think up. Thereupon he became our idol whom we worshiped under the name of St. Peter and Christ together with all his lies, blasphemies, and idolatries." [24] As Luther stops to think about this, his indignation becomes such that he painfully feels the inadequacy of language to express the damnableness of it all. He gropes about for words and terms, finds all so tame and flat and mild, and then explodes into these words: "May God punish you, I say, you shameless, lying, and blaspheming jaw (*Luegenmaul und Laestermaul*), you mouthpiece of the devil." He concludes his book with these words: "I must let it go at that. If it please God, I shall do better in another booklet. If I were meanwhile to die, God grant that another [man] may be a thousand times worse [for the Papacy than I was]. For the devilish Papacy is the final calamity on earth and is closest to what all the devils can do with all their might. God help us. Amen." [25] One is tempted to quote from this writing of Luther at length, but the above is sufficient to indicate the white heat at which it was written. Moreover, there are expressions in it that would be shocking and unbearable to the more refined tastes — would sophisticated be the better term? — of today.

There is no need whatever to hide the fact that some of Luther's contemporaries deplored the vehemence of his language. The reference is to his friends or to those at least who were sympathetic to his cause. The impression Peter Mosellanus received

---

23 Erl 26:182.   24 Erl 26:189.   25 Erl 26:228.

of Luther at the Leipzig Debate was, as we have seen, a favorable one on the whole. But in relating it he says: "What most men blame in him is that in answering he is more imprudent and cutting than is safe for a reformer of the Church or than is decorous for a theologian."[26] Of course, this was decidedly the view Melanchthon took of Luther's strong language. Nor did he merely take exception to the names by which Luther at times called his opponents, such as liars, asses, scoundrels. Melanchthon was constitutionally opposed to strong statements of any kind. In a letter to his future biographer, Camerarius, he referred to the controversy carried on between Erasmus and Luther about the freedom of the will. We suspect that Melanchthon sighed when he wrote: "I hoped that with advancing years he would grow used to these things and be somewhat milder, but I see that he is becoming more and more vehement when confronted with such battles and such opponents. The matter causes me great anguish of mind."[27] Melanchthon's strictures alone are not enough to impress us. His excessive timidity takes much of that weight from them which ordinarily would attach to the testimony of an intimate friend. But his complaint is not the only one heard from the circle of Luther's friends. The energetic wife of Luther, Catherine von Bora, has never been suspected of fastidiousness and prudishness, but she too thought that at times her Doctor was too violent in his language.[28] After 1520 the Elector Frederick frequently requested Luther through Spalatin, his secretary, to be more moderate in his writings.

While some of his friends and intimates merely deplored, his enemies, of course, severely condemned Luther's vehemence of expression. Some claimed that it alone was sufficient to disqualify Luther for any reforming activities. Between the gentle Melanchthon and one of these opponents of the Reformer there was a certain kinship of spirit. This was Erasmus. Personal danger all but paralyzed him with fear. To Justus Jonas, Luther's close

---

[26] S-J, LC I:261.   [27] S-J, LC II:370.   [28] Bo, L 183; Sm, L 407.

friend, he wrote: "I do not even listen to those, Jonas, who say that Luther was unable to practice Christian moderation on account of the intolerable provocation of his antagonists. Whoever undertakes to do what he undertook ought to stand fast no matter how others act." [29] This reminds one of the story told about the fiery Andrew Jackson. Upon one occasion his temper had gotten away from him even more than was usually the case. A phlegmatic friend took him to task for this, stating that a man ought to control himself. Jackson turned upon him and said curtly: "Listen, friend, I control more temper every day than you do in an entire year." Erasmus had "easy talking." At the same time it is true that he actually thought, whether from temperamental or other reasons, that a reformation of the Church might be effected gently. Perhaps it never occurred to him that under certain conditions only a thunderstorm with its attendant lightning, strong winds, and other disturbances can purify the stagnant air. Did he not know that the method advocated by him had been tried unsuccessfully for entire centuries?

There is something majestic and awe-inspiring about a thunderstorm; and there was something equally awesome about the vehemence of Luther. Some of his enemies were virile enough to appreciate the qualities of a good fighter in him, while they condemned the use to which he put them. They never denied that his blows were those of a Hercules. One may say that they ruefully confessed to the unique vigor of his blow while rubbing the spot where it had fallen. The French Catholic bishop Bossuet († 1704), the "eagle of Meaux," was a bitter enemy of Protestantism but felt constrained to pay the following tribute to Luther: "It is not alone his followers, the Lutherans, who have lavished upon him the highest praises. Calvin frequently admires his virtues, his magnanimity, his constancy, the incomparable industry which he displayed against the Pope. He is the trumpet, or rather, he is the thunder — he is the lightning which has

---

[29] S-J, LC I:566.

roused the world from its lethargy: it was not so much Luther that spoke as God, whose lightnings burst from his lips. And it is true he had a strength of genius, a vehemence in his discourses, a living and impetuous eloquence which entranced and ravished the people." [30] At times there is almost an undertone of envy in the criticism of Luther's enemies. If they had only possessed Luther's command of language and the wealth of his vocabulary! Some of them learned to rue the day they imagined themselves qualified to write him down. Many tried it. In fact, the enemies of the Reformer must fairly be said to have begun the use of *violent* language and bitter invective.

ABUSIVE EXPRESSIONS OF FOES OF THE REFORMATION

The first writings in that age of heated controversy which employed vulgarities came from the pens of the Catholics Sylvester Prierias and Johann Eck.[31] The 95 Theses of Luther, which called forth these outbursts, were couched in the conventional language of academic disputation. While the expressions were intentionally somewhat paradoxical and challenging, there was nothing vehement about them. But after the appearance of Prierias' and Eck's productions this violent manner of controversy continued unchecked, so that Luther could write to Elector John in 1531: "Yes, my writings may be looked upon as sharp and vehement; but when will the other party take a hold of its own nose and judge the writings of their own people to be sharp?" [32] Thereupon Luther lists the various princes and dukes in whose countries violent and abusive attacks upon him had been published without any effort having been made either to stop such scurrility or at least to insist upon moderation. The following may serve to illustrate this point.

We shall pass by vilifications by lesser lights although some of them are extremely nasty. Perhaps their authors hoped in this manner to become famous. We shall do nothing to perpetuate

---

[30] In Kr, C 52 f.   [31] Wa, F 218.   [32] Erl 54:225.

their *in*famy. One is curious to hear what Pope Leo X had to say about Luther. He was an unspiritual and worldly-wise man besides being Pope. Therefore one is prepared for the worst. In a letter to Elector Frederick, dated 1518, Leo called the Reformer "this son of perdition or of damnation . . . this infected, scrofulous sheep . . . this wicked Martin" [33] and in the same year termed him the "only son of Satan" in a letter to Spalatin.[34] Similarly violent were the expressions employed by Leo's diplomat, Aleander, who called Luther "the dog," "this Satan," the "Lutheran Mohammed," [35] and a variety of other names.

Perhaps Luther never had a more bitter enemy than Duke George of Saxony. Many are the anecdotes told of this man's savage anger against the Reformer and his work. The pressure of this consuming passion finally rose so high that the Duke found it impossible to contain himself any longer. He must give vent to his ducal ire. However, lest his princely dignity suffer from the fumes and the smoke of it all, he penned the following sulphurous denunciation of Luther under an assumed name. The offering of Duke George is in part literally untranslatable. We submit the original German and translate merely a few of its vigorous terms and phrases. Luther is thus characterized: "Er ist gewiss mit dem Teufel besessen, mit der ganzen Legion, welche Christus von dem Besessenen austrieb und erlaubte ihnen in die Schweine zu fahren. Diese Legion hat dem Luther seinen Moenchsschaedel hirnwuetig und wirbelsuechtig gemacht. Du unruhiger, treuloser und meineidiger Kuttenbube! Du bist allein der groesste, groebste Esel und Narr, du verfluchter Apostat! Hieraus kann maenniglich abnehmen die Verraeterei und Falschheit deines blutduerstigen Herzens, rachgierigen Gemuets und teuflischen Willens, so du, Luther, gegen deinen Naechsten tobend, als ein toerichter Hund mit offenem Maul ohne Unterlass wagest. Du treuloser Bube und teuflischer Moench! . . . Du meineidiger, treuloser und ehrenblosser Fleischboesewicht! Pfui

---

[33] S-J, LC I:126.　　　　　[34] S-J, LC I:127.　　　　　[35] S-J, LC I:419 f.

dich nun, du sakrilegischer, der ausgelaufenen Moenche und Nonnen, der abfaelligen Pfaffen und aller Abtruennigen Hurenwirt! Ei, Doktor Schandluther! Mein Doktor Erzesel, ich will dir's prophezeit haben, der allmaechtige Gott wird dir kuerzlich die Schanze brechen und deiner boshaftigsten, groebsten Eselheit Feierabend geben. Du Sauboze, Doktor Sautrog! Doktor Eselsohr! Doktor Filzhut! Zweiundsiebzig Teufel sollen dich lebendig in den Abgrund der Hoelle fuehren. Ich will machen, dass du als ein Hoellenhund sollst Feuer ausspruehen und dich endlich selbst verbrennen. Ich will dich dem wuetenigen Teufel und seiner Hurenmutter mit einem blutigen Kopf in den Abgrund der Hoelle schicken." [36]

This really ought have relieved the emotional pressure on Duke George. It will be observed that he merely calls Luther all sorts of names. There is no disproof of any Lutheran doctrine. This is typical of much that was written against the Reformer; and it is very significant as well. Erasmus somewhere says: It is easier to call Luther names than to prove him wrong. Duke George certainly found the name calling easy. Among other things he called the Reformer "possessed by the devil . . . the greatest, coarsest ass and fool, the damned apostate . . . a foolish dog . . . a devilish monk . . . a beast . . . a perjured, faithless, honorless villain . . . Doctor Utterly Ass . . . a hell hound. . . ." The Duke closes this writing with the promise: "I shall send you into the abyss of hell with a bloody head to the raging devil and his prostitute mother."

As might have been foreseen, the associates of Duke George caught his savage spirit. A certain Johann Hasenberg, one of his proteges, felt constrained also to write to Luther in an effort to reclaim the "damned heretic." In his letter Hasenberg said: "Obstinate and contumacious wretch, abandoned to your own desires, proceed from bad to worse. . . . Be merry until you descend into hell, as you surely will, where, infernal brand! you will burn

---

[36] Wa, L 148 f.

forever and be eaten by the never dying worm." [37] It may be added: Luther informed the bearer of the letter that after its perusal he had put it to a very private use.

The controversy between Henry VIII of England, before his own breach with Rome in 1527, and Luther is well known. Also his English Majesty used language so violent that only rarely does one find anything similar in Luther. He says Luther is inspired by the devil and is spewing forth the poison of serpents. He calls him a terrible, hellish wolf. He says his mouth fairly drips with bloody gore and that he is a scoundrel.[38] Henry's minister, Thomas More, author of the famous *Utopia*, did not intend to permit His Royal Majesty to carry off all the honors. He, too, was eager to break a lance with Luther. More did it in a variety of ways. After having called Luther names for a while, he predicted that after a few thousand [!] years, people would relate that once upon a time there was a notorious crook and scamp by the name of Luther. He excelled the very devil in wickedness, the houses of ill fame in immorality, and the rogues in craftiness, etc. etc.[39]

For a while the optimistic of those days saw a ray of hope for the Church of Rome in the election of Pope Adrian VI in 1522. This Pope clearly saw and publicly confessed the necessity of a reformation of the Church. Adrian was, moreover, favorably known as a man of mild disposition. But his mildness forsook him when he wrote of Luther, whom he calls a snake that infects heaven and earth with its poison, a wild boar of the forest, a thief who breaks the holy Cross of Christ with his wicked hands and tramples on it with his filthy feet, this buffoon, this utterly faithless apostate, this devil, with his godless, pestiferous mouth, etc. etc.[40]

---

[37] S-J, LC II:451 f.

[38] In Wa, F 208.

[39] In Wa, F 212 f.

[40] Wal XV:2110—2123.

LUTHER'S REACTION TO SCURRILOUS ATTACKS

In view of such raving on the part of Luther's enemies, such wild, unproved, indiscriminate charges against him, is it to be wondered at that the Reformer wrote to Elector John of Saxony in the letter quoted above: "When did the Catholics ever punish the scurrilous writings published against us? . . . Your Grace may see that these people think it right and fine for a thousand authors to write against us, every sheet of whose voluminous works is full of poison and gall. . . . But if I, poor man, alone cry out against these monsters, then no one has written sharply but only Luther! . . . In short, whatever I do or say is wrong, even if I should raise the dead; whatever they do is right, even if they should drench Germany with innocent blood! Yet one must fight these people with cotton wool, bow to them and say: 'Gracious sirs, how pious and fair you are!' " [41]

Luther, it is to be noted, did not deny that he often wrote "sharply." In fact, at one time he deplored it and asked pardon for it in a letter to Cardinal Cajetan at Augsburg. He wrote: "I confess, as I have before confessed, that I was assuredly unwise and too bitter and too irreverent to the name of the Pope. And although I had the greatest provocation, I know I should have acted with more moderation and humility and not have answered a fool [!] according to his folly. For so doing I am most sincerely sorry and ask pardon and will say so from the pulpit, as I have already done several times, and I shall take care in future to act differently and speak otherwise by God's mercy." [42] This letter was written in 1518, at a time when even Luther still hoped that the Pope and his Church would prove to be reformable if and when the matters in controversy would be placed squarely before them. For this reason, Luther felt, they might indeed be dealt with more gently. But as time went on he became undeceived. Four years later he complained to an unnamed correspondent: "Now, as you know, I have written many little books without any

---

[41] Sm, L 274 f.   [42] Sm, L 52.

severity, in a friendly and gentle tone; I have made the most humble overtures and run after those men, and appeared before them at great difficulty and expense, and have borne their measureless lies and slanders. But the more I have humbled myself, the more they rave and slander me and my doctrine, until they have become hardened and can neither hear nor see. If anyone is so minded that he disregards and despises my long patience and my many offers, why should I care if he takes offense at my rebukes?" [43]

After six years of disillusionments he wrote to Erasmus: "I too am irritable and quite frequently am moved to write caustically, though I have only done so against hardened men, proof against milder forms of admonition. Otherwise I think my gentleness and clemency toward sinners, no matter how far they are gone in iniquity, is witnessed not only by my own conscience but by the experience of many." [44]

By 1531 it was clear to him that the only way in which he might hope to make an impression upon the foe was to deal with him severely. In a publication of that year, written against his inveterate enemy Duke George, he wrote: "This should henceforth be my glory and honor, and I want it so to be, that one should say of me how full of bad words, scoldings, and cursings about the papists I am. For more than ten years I have often humbled myself and given the best of words. . . . I will ring the death knell for them with my thundering and lightning." [45] In the same year he received an admonition from his Elector John to write more moderately. This drew the reply from him: "The two writings [complained about] are sharp and vehement, that is certainly true; nor did I write them so that they might be soft and gentle. I am only sorry that they are not sharper and severer." [46]

How did Luther justify the severity of his language? The

---

[43] S-J, LC II:133. [45] Wal XVI:1718.

[44] S-J, LC II:229. [46] Erl 54:225.

earliest comprehensive statement we have from him occurs in
a letter to his confidant Spalatin in 1520. It is this: "I cannot
deny that I have been more vehement than I should; but as they
knew that I would be, they should not have irritated the dog.
You know yourself how hard it is to moderate an angry pen. . . .
But they act against me and God's Word so criminally and fiercely
that were I not moved to write warmly, even a mind of stone
might be moved to war by indignation. Far from having such
a mind, however, I am naturally warm and have a pen which is
not at all blunt. So I am carried beyond the bonds of moderation
by these monsters. Moreover, I wonder whence this new scru-
pulousness is born, which calls all that is said against an opponent
scurrility. What do you think of Christ? Was He scurrilous when
He called the Jews a perverse and adulterous generation, offspring
of vipers, hypocrites, and children of the devil? Paul speaks of
dogs, vain babblers, seducers, unlearned, and in Acts 13 so rages
against a false prophet that he might seem insane, saying: 'O full
of guile and all villainy, thou son of the devil, thou enemy of all
truth.' Why did not Paul rather flatter him to convert him than
thus thunder? The consciousness of truth cannot be patient
against the obstinate and unconquered enemies of the truth." [47]

A number of things ought to be emphasized in this connection.
To begin with, Luther's harshness was motivated by hatred of
sin, not by hatred of the sinner. He fought measures, not men.
His treatment of poor Tetzel demonstrated that fact. He assured
his age: "I had rather be frank and deceive no one by flattery, of
that I can assure you. My outer bark might, perchance, be somewhat rough, but within I am softhearted and loving; for I want
to harm no one." [48] Therefore even in Luther's stern words one
senses his love for the sinner. He had Prierias' defense of papal
power, his *Epitome*, reprinted and wrote a preface of his own
to it. This contains the well-known dramatic words: "Farewell,
unhappy, hopeless, blasphemous Rome! The wrath of God hath
come upon thee, as thou hast deserved! We have cared for

---

[47] S-J, LC I:288 f.   [48] Wal XVIII:1063.

Babylon, and she is not healed; let us, then, leave her, that she may be the habitation of dragons, specters, and witches, and, true to her name of Babel, an everlasting confusion, a new pantheon of wickedness." [49] Paul once wrote to the Philippians (3:18 f.): "Many walk, of whom I have told you often, and now tell you even weeping, that they are the enemies of the Cross of Christ; whose end is destruction." Why did a strong character like Paul weep? No doubt because he loved the souls of the blind fools who by their denial of Christ were destroying themselves forever. Luther might well have written that passage. He was moved by the same spirit; his most blazing anger at the stubborn perverseness of men was full of sadness. One is reminded of the tears Jesus shed over Jerusalem.

But Jesus not only wept at the unbelief of His people and at the thought of their coming doom. In flaming words He castigated particularly those "blind leaders of the blind" who were largely responsible for this sorry spiritual condition of Israel. And Paul followed in His footsteps. There was no reason why Martin Luther should not appeal to such examples in justification of his vehemence of language. We have heard him do so in his letter to Spalatin. To the thoughts there expressed we may add those of the letter to Leo X with which he prefaced his classical *Treatise on Christian Liberty*. Luther wrote: "Who is more biting than the Prophets? Nowadays, it is true, our ears are made so delicate by the mad crowds of flatterers that as soon as we meet with a disapproving voice, we cry out that we are bitten, and when we cannot ward off the truth with any other pretext, we put it to flight by ascribing it to a fierce temper, impatience, and shamelessness." [50]

But Luther had still more to say in answer to the charge of rudeness of language. He called attention to its constant use by his opponents and correctly argued: If it *is* a fault so to express oneself, any criticism of my doing so comes with a peculiarly

---

[49] Wei 6:329, in Ho II:58.   [50] Ho II:302.

bad grace from *them*. They of all people have in that event forfeited every moral right to complain. If, however, they *are* permitted to use it, because it is not necessarily wrong, why am I singled out for criticism?

Then, too, it must be remembered that the enemies of Luther delighted in nothing more than to tease and torture him into such outbursts of anger and thereupon to quote them against him and his work. When one considers this and the intenseness of Luther's character, one is inclined to speak of his moderation rather than his rudeness. The complaints of his enemies were frequently sent to his Elector with the request to command Luther to be more gentlemanly in the treatment of his opponents. To the Elector therefore he as frequently wrote to give an account of himself. Thus he said: "As I acknowledge my fault in this matter, I hope that pardon will be denied me by no one who once considers what lions of Moab, what Rabshakehs of the Assyrians, how many Shimeis I alone have long been forced to bear with." [51] Lest anyone fancy only Luther thought that if he was to be blamed for his violent outbursts, his enemies ought, in fairness, to be made to carry much of the guilt, the testimony of Erasmus might be adduced. That timid man dared to write to Luther's bitter enemy, Albert, Elector of Mayence, as early as 1519: "I think it is *their* fault if Luther has written too intemperately." [52] In the following year Erasmus wrote to an unnamed correspondent: "If he [Luther] has gone mad in writing, they are madder in their answers." [53]

DISHONEST STRATEGY OF LUTHER'S ENEMIES

Perhaps it will be of interest briefly to illustrate some of the strategy which so aroused the righteous ire of the Reformer. His opponents would, for instance, quote certain of his passages only in part, or they would draw together passages separated by as much as an entire page. This might produce a meaning the very opposite of the one intended by Luther, or it might result

---

[51] S-J, LC I:479.   [52] S-J, LC I:242.   [53] S-J, LC I:403.

in contradictory nonsense. If this method be employed, even the Holy Bible may be made to teach robbery and murder. By omitting verses 31-36 of Luke 10 and drawing together verses 30 and 37 we arrive at this thought: "The thieves stripped him of his raiment and wounded him and departed, leaving him half dead. Go, and do thou likewise." At the same time we could honestly say, our words were all taken from the Scripture record of the story. Luther's enemies no doubt depended upon the inherent laziness of some of their readers and upon the inability of others to keep them from verifying the fairness and the accuracy of their quotations. That men still stoop to such tactics in order to discredit Luther and his work has been amply proved by Dr. W. Walther in his irrefutable defense of Luther.[54] Is Luther so much to be blamed for taking fire at such things? At the same time and just in passing, what a light such a procedure throws upon the goodness of Luther's cause and the effectiveness of his defense! The opponents must indeed be hard pressed to have to resort to this sort of strategy to make out a case against the Reformer.

Another "strategy" which aroused the mighty anger of Luther was the constant appeal to the Fathers, councils, and Popes, as though anything in the Christian Church could be settled by appeals to merely human authorities, however old and honored. But this way of "proving" things had become the second nature of the theologians in the age of Luther. Thus Aleander wrote from Worms in plain exasperation to a cardinal at Rome: "To refute him [Luther] I cited many sayings of the ecumenical councils and of the Greek and Latin Fathers, without daring to take a word from the theologians of the last seven centuries, for Luther will have nothing to do with them. So I, poor man, wasted the good time which otherwise I would have devoted to the study of Peter Lombard or St. Thomas Aquinas or the Nominalists in testing [!] the doctrines of this wretch. I must consider this time as good as lost. Thus we see how baneful is this assassin to everyone." [55]

---

[54] Wa, F 170 f., 174, 180, 263, 533, et passim.   [55] S-J, LC I:426.

Right here lay the very crux of the entire matter: where was the ultimate authority? Luther saw the issue very clearly and very soon. At the conclusion of his Latin answer to the book of Henry VIII he plainly says as much.[56] He often expresses his impatience and exasperation at the failure of the opponents to prove him wrong from *Scripture*.

The fact that his adversaries failed to do this was sufficient reason, Luther held, to suspect that they had hardened themselves against its clear testimony. This too put fire into his pen. To Erasmus he therefore wrote words we wish again to quote: "I too am irritable and quite frequently am moved to write caustically, though I *have only done so against hardened men*, proof against milder forms of admonition." [57] By his vehemence he was trying to make an impression on men who, he felt, were rapidly approaching spiritual insensibility, were passing into a spiritual coma from which there would be no awakening. "*Blunt wedges rive hard knots*," Luther once said, referring to his activity. With equal bluntness J. Froude says in answer to the Erasmian plea for a mild and gradual reformation: "But the devil is not expelled by rose water." [58]

WHAT ARE WE TO SAY ABOUT LUTHER'S RUDENESS OF LANGUAGE?

Now, what are *we* to say to this trait of Luther's character? There are a number of considerations which, it seems to us, place this mooted subject into its proper light. To begin with: violence is a relative term. Few people would see eye to eye on the question as to where it begins. The dividing line between emphasis and violence of language has not been laid down in textbooks with mathematical exactness, wherefore criticism on the point will always be more or less subjective.

Again, to some extent Luther's vehemence or emphasis of expression was the natural result of an intense character. Luther wrote and spoke with exceptional liveliness and emphasis on any-

---

[56] Wal XIX:348.   [57] Sm, L 205.   [58] Fro, L 193.

thing and everything. He "just was that way." He believed the mission of Christian faith was to sanctify, not to destroy peculiarities of temperament and disposition. Christians were never intended to be robots, dispassionate automata. Therefore, as one of his non-Lutheran American biographers, McGiffert, says: "As well apologize for the fury of the wind as for the vehemence of Martin Luther." [59]

Then, too, the times must be considered. In more than one respect it was a rude, inelegant age. Much of what sounded as a tame commonplace to ears of the sixteenth century would be considered fit to be printed only in wood-pulp magazines today. How common particularly rudeness of language was has been shown above. Perhaps an additional illustration will not be out of place, the less so since it refers to so famous a person as Calvin. Isaac D'Israeli says of him in his *Curiosities of Literature:* "Calvin was less tolerable [tolerant], for he had no Melanchthon! His adversaries are never others than knaves, lunatics, drunkards, and assassins! Sometimes they are characterized by the familiar appellatives of bulls, asses, cats, and hogs! By him Catholic and Lutheran are alike hated. Yet, after having given vent to this virulent humor, he frequently boasts of his mildness. When he reads over his writings, he tells us that he is astonished at his forbearance; but this, he adds, is the duty of every Christian! At the same time he generally finishes a period with — 'Do you hear, you dog? Do you hear, madman?'" [60] Today, it must be granted, such expressions would be considered something worse than bad taste. The enemies of Luther, it is true, were slow to lose their taste for such language. The bull that canonized the founder of the Jesuits, Ignatius Loyola, in 1623 called the Reformer "a horrible monster and a detestable pest." [61] Dr. W. Walther quotes instances of such language from Catholic authors of even the nineteenth and twentieth centuries. [62] We have no desire to quote them.

---

[59] In Da, L 22 f.　　　　[61] Kr, C 62.
[60] In Kr, C 62.　　　　　[62] Wa, F 369, 617 f.

The question has often been asked whether the poor health from which Luther suffered for many years had anything to do with his irritableness and consequent rudeness of expression. Perhaps it did. It certainly might have. But we feel it was mental or spiritual distress rather than the increase of physical disability that called forth some of the Reformer's most violent outbursts. The tremendous strain under which Luther lived the greater part of his life it is impossible for us to conceive. Some of us may consider the constant threat of death alone sufficient to unnerve a man. But this was the least of Luther's worries. He was consumed by zeal for the cause of Christ. For thirty years he taught and preached and printed and pleaded and prayed and coaxed and threatened. He left no legitimate means untried to call prodigal Rome back to Scripture and its Savior. His reward? He was threatened, persecuted, banned, outlawed, and slandered. No name was too vile for him, no damnation too severe. His words were misconstrued, his writings misquoted, his noblest motives misinterpreted. Yet all the while he was wearing himself out in the service of others. For himself he wanted nothing but a gracious God and the right to bring His peace to anxious, earnest souls everywhere. But the Church would have none of this; and as time wore on, the Reformer saw that the Gospel of God's grace was a rock of offense also to his age. This saddening discovery, though Scripture taught Luther to expect it, was a bitter disillusionment to a character as intense as his. In his later years it tended to add a note of bitterness and weariness to his writings. When this spirit was upon him, his message was that of Cassandra. Perhaps it were better to say: He was deeply moved by the spirit that spoke out in the words of Jesus over apostate Jerusalem: "Whereunto then shall I liken the men of this generation? and to what are they like? They are like unto children sitting in the market place and calling one to another and saying, We have piped unto you, and ye have not danced; we have mourned to you, and ye have not wept." [63]

---

[63] Luke 7:31-32.

We are not interested in making Martin Luther out to have been perfect and beyond reproach. Dr. W. Dau covered the case well when he wrote: "In the writings of Luther there occur terms, phrases, passages that sound repulsive. The strongest admirer of Luther will have moments when he wishes certain things could have been said differently. Luther's language cannot be repeated in our times." After all legitimate allowances have been made, it must, in justice, be granted that at times Luther went too far in his use of violent and rude language; and though, since it was done in the interest of truth and right, it was a "failing that leaned to virtue's side," it *was* a failing. But it ought also to be said that the failing has been grossly exaggerated. No one less than the man who had frequently complained about the harshness of Luther's language, Philip Melanchthon, pointed, four hundred years ago, at the corpse of Luther, lying before him in the Castle Church at Wittenberg and said: "Every one who understood him aright must witness that he was a very kind man, in all speech gracious, kind, lovable, and not at all forward, stormy, self-willed, or quarrelsome. And yet there was an earnestness and bravery in his words and actions, as should be in such a man. His heart was true and free from guile. *The severity which he used in his writings against enemies of the doctrine came not from a quarrelsome or spiteful mind, but from great earnestness and zeal for the truth."* [64] The loud sobs which interrupted his words bore testimony to their truth.

But what of Luther's intolerance? There are those who hold that Luther did not only fail at times to practice what he preached, but that he actually never held those views of religious liberty which today are associated with his name by many people. They say the principle of complete religious liberty was perhaps implied in many of his statements, but Luther himself did not consistently carry it out. Thus Preserved Smith says: "The Wittenberg professor never doubted the right and duty of the State to persecute for heresy. While still fighting for the op-

---

[64] Fr, M 127.

portunity to express his own opinions, indeed, he took a liberal view, and one of his early propositions condemned by the bull *Exsurge Domine,* was that it was contrary to the will of the Holy Spirit to put heretics to death. Again, in 1525, he said: 'The government shall not interfere; a man may teach and believe what he likes, be it Gospel or lies.' But a very few years of success convinced him and Melanchthon of the untenability of this attitude. In 1529, with the consent of the Elector John and of Melanchthon, who were present, an imperial edict was passed at Spires condemning Anabaptists to death. In pursuance of this law, a regular inquisition was established in Saxony with the 'gentle' Melanchthon at its head, and a hideous persecution began. In a short time several of the nonconformists were put to death, and many others imprisoned for long terms. Melanchthon wrote a paper to justify this course; this he did by asking: 'Why should we pity such men more than does God?' who, it was believed, sent them to eternal torment for their opinions. Luther signed this document, with a postscript showing that he was a little sorry for the poor people." [65]

LUTHER'S VIEWS ON REBELLIOUS HERETICS

Now, what are the facts in the case? To begin with: it is demonstrable that Luther's views on this subject were not the same throughout his career as reformer. In the year after the publication of the imperial edict against the Anabaptists,[66] Luther said the following in his exposition of the Eighty-second Psalm: "Since the gods, or rulers, beside their other virtues, are to advance God's Word and its preachers, are they also to put down opposing doctrines, or heresies, since no one can be forced to believe? The answer to this question is as follows: First. Some heretics are seditious and teach openly that no rulers are to be tolerated; that no Christian may occupy a position of rulership; that no one ought to have property of his own, but run away from wife and child and leave house and home, or that all property

---

[65] Sm, L xiii f.   [66] Wal XVI:261, 277.

shall be held in common. These teachers are immediately and without doubt to be punished by the rulers as men who are resisting temporal law and government (Romans 13). They are not heretics only, but rebels, who are attacking the rulers and their government, just as a thief attacks another's goods, a murderer another's body, an adulterer another's wife; and that is not to be tolerated." [67] Here Luther teaches that it is the duty of government to suppress by force all religious sects that are guilty of political rebellion under the cloak of religion. The government penalizes their political, not their religious views. This procedure ought not to be called religious intolerance and persecution.

LUTHER HELD THE STATE SHOULD NOT PERMIT "BLASPHEMY"

But Luther continues in his exposition of the Psalm: "Second. If some were to teach doctrines contradicting an article of faith, clearly grounded in Scripture and believed throughout the world by the whole Church (*Christenheit*), such as the articles that we teach children in the Creed — as, for example, if anyone would teach that Christ is not God, but a mere man and like other prophets, as the Turks and the Anabaptists hold — such teachers should not be tolerated but punished as blasphemers. For they are not mere heretics, but open blasphemers, and the rulers are in duty bound to punish blasphemers, as they do those who curse, swear, revile, abuse, defame, and slander." From these words it appears that Luther conceded a broader jurisdiction to government than is done in the modern state in which there is a complete separation of Church and State. The words just quoted do not, viewed by themselves, necessarily reveal a confusion of Church and State in the mind of the Reformer. Luther's state was not the modern state. It was granted greater latitude of jurisdiction, so that not merely perjury but also blasphemy was considered an offense political or civic no less than theological or religious. Adultery may be considered a somewhat analogous case. Both Church and State punish it.

---

[67] Wei 31, Part 1:208 f.; Wal VII:717 f.; Ho IV:309 f.

But this interpretation does not square with *all* the facts in the case. Luther goes on to say: "In like manner the rulers should also punish — or certainly not tolerate — those who teach that Christ did not die for our sins, but that everyone should make his own satisfaction for them; for that too is blasphemy against the Gospel. . . . They should be treated in the same way who teach that the resurrection of the dead and the life everlasting are nothing, and that there is no hell, and the like things." Here Luther teaches that the State ought to deny every man the right to proclaim and to seek to spread his views, if they deny fundamental doctrines of the Creed. It is true, Luther continues: "By this procedure no one is compelled to believe, for he can still believe what he will; but he is forbidden to teach and blaspheme." This means: liberty of conscience is, indeed, to continue, but *public* worship and propaganda are to be prohibited by the State. This position is at variance with the one held by Luther in 1525. In that year he had said, as quoted above: "The government shall not interfere; a man may teach and believe what he likes, be it Gospel or lies." [68] But this is not a flat contradiction. Luther had simply meanwhile been called upon to determine what was meant by "blasphemy" which the German Imperial Laws of 1495, 1512, 1530, and 1532 had recognized as punishable, but had not defined in detail. Luther defines blasphemy as the public denial or rejection of the well-known articles of the Christian Creed. He says: "In this case there ought not to be much disputing, but such open blasphemers should be condemned without a hearing and without defense . . . for these common articles of the whole Church have had hearings enough." [69]

MORE TOLERANT THAN THE CHURCH OF THE MIDDLE AGES

This is not the modern concept of religious liberty, though it certainly is an improvement over the heresy laws of the Middle Ages. H. Boehmer says: "No! He [Luther] does not recognize or desire any Inquisition, any *ecclesiastical* proceedings for heresy;

---

[68] Wei 18:298 f.   [69] Wei 31, Teil 1:209 f.

he recognizes only a *secular* criminal action for disturbance of the peace of the Church by dissident teaching, for seditious agitation against the existing organization of the State, and for public blasphemy; and he considers the death penalty necessary only in those cases in which the prevailing law also requires it — sedition and public blasphemy. Private faith, however, still remains free. What a man believes in his own mind shall never be made the object of legal proceedings." [70]

MAN CANNOT BE CLUBBED INTO THE CHRISTIAN FAITH

Luther appears at his best when he insists upon the use of persuasion and not power against the heretic. The following passage in his *Letter to the Christian Nobility* is one of his earliest (1520) and best known: "We should vanquish heretics with books, not with burning. . . . If it were a science to vanquish the heretics with fire, then the hangmen would be the most learned doctors on earth; we should no longer need to study, but he who overcame another by force might burn him at the stake." [71] Luther's attitude toward religion was too personal to admit of religious persecution as an effective *converting* agency. He might hold that the use of force would confer a negative benefit upon the Church, in that it would silence the public voice of blasphemous error. But he was firmly convinced that the positive benefit of conversion could come to a man solely by the preaching of the Word. Nor would he ever, in consequence, have been satisfied with achieving a medieval outward conformity to the doctrinal position of his Church by the fear of punishment. To Luther the seat of religion was the heart, not the knees. The heart was to go out to God in loving self-surrender. The relation of a man's soul to his Maker was first of all and above all a personal, not a corporate responsibility, taught Luther; wherefore it is wrong to put mere heretics to death. When, therefore, Leo X published his criticisms of Luther's position in the bull of 1520, the Reformer was not surprised to find point thirty-three con-

---

[70] Bo, L 295.   [71] Ho II:142.

demning his assertion that it is contrary to the will of the Holy Ghost to burn heretics.[72]

Two years later the Zwickau "prophets" were making life miserable for Nicolaus Hausmann. Luther gave his friend the following sound and characteristic advice: "What our friends attempt by force and violence must be resisted by word only, overcome by word and destroyed by word. It is Satan who urges us to extreme measures. I condemn masses held as sacrifices and good works, but I would not lay hands on those who are unwilling to give them up or on those who are doubtful about them, nor would I prevent them by force. I condemn by word only; whoso believes, let him believe and follow, whoso does not believe, let him disbelieve and depart. No one is to be compelled to the faith, but to be drawn by word, that he may believe and come of his own accord."[73] This letter indicates that Luther had occasion in the same year to teach his own circle this vital lesson. The spirit of radical intolerance became rampant at Wittenberg. Hastening thither from his Wartburg retreat, he preached his famous eight sermons to his disturbed people. In the second sermon occurred a passage descriptive at once of Luther's reforming methods and of his personal character. To an hushed audience the Reformer said: "I will preach it, teach it, write it, but I will constrain no man by force, for faith must come freely, without compulsion. Take myself as an example. I have opposed the indulgences and all the papists, but never by force. I simply taught, preached, wrote, God's Word; otherwise I did nothing. And then, while I slept or drank Wittenberg beer with my Philip and with Amsdorf, the Word so greatly weakened the Papacy that never a prince or emperor inflicted such damage upon it. I did nothing; the Word did it all. Had I desired to foment trouble, I could have brought great bloodshed upon Germany. Yea, I could have started such a little game at Worms that even the Emperor would not have been safe. But what would it have been? A fool's play. I did nothing; I left it to the

---

[72] Wal XV:1438.   [73] S-J, LC II:110.

Word. What do you suppose is Satan's thought, when an effort is made to do things by violence? He sits back in hell and thinks: How fine a game these fools will make for me!" [74] On the following day he began his third sermon with the blunt remark: "I can drive no man to heaven with a club." [75]

But there were those to whom the patient and tolerant treatment of heretics seemed inadequate. Its results were too meager and too slow in coming. In their impatience and exasperation they resorted to intolerance, persecution, and death. Luther therefore published a letter to two clergymen in which he pleaded: "It is not right, and I am truly sorry to see that such miserable people [as the Anabaptists] are so pitifully murdered, burned, and horribly done to death; one ought to permit everyone to believe whatever he likes. If his faith be false, he has punishment enough from the eternal fire in hell. Why, therefore, does one want to torture them also here in time, as long as they err only in the faith and are not seditious besides or resist the government in some other way? . . . With Scripture and God's Word one should restrain and resist them; with fire one will accomplish little." [76] This letter was written in 1528.

THE STATE IS NOT TO ALLOW ANY CHURCHES TO COME TO BLOWS

Naturally, Luther had no intention to suggest that the fanatics be permitted to carry on in their own violent way. But no one will consider the advice he wrote to his Elector Frederick and his brother John intolerant, since he expressly included himself and his own party in it. Luther wrote: "If they will fight with anything more than the Word, if they will break and smite with the fist, then Your Grace should interfere, whether it is we or they who do it, forbid the offenders the land, and say: 'We shall gladly look on and allow you to fight with the Word, that the true doctrine may be preserved; but keep your fists to yourselves, for that is our affair; or else get out of the land.'" [77]

---

[74] Ho II:399 f.   [76] Erl 26:256.

[75] Ho II:401.   [77] S-J, LC II:246.

LUTHER FAR AHEAD OF HIS TIMES IN RELIGIOUS TOLERATION

Now, as has been pointed out, the Reformer unfortunately did not always fully live up to this lofty standard of toleration. But by falling into inconsistencies of speech and action he proved no more than that, though among the best of men, he was but a man at best. The surprising thing is not that he was still intolerant to some extent, but that a man reared in the murderous Church of Rome, "drunk with the blood of saints," should come so close to the Scriptural position of religious liberty as did Martin Luther. A famous English author once had his portrait painted. Out of deference to him the artist did not picture a slightly disfiguring birthmark on his face. Upon noticing the omission the author said: "Put it on, man. Paint me, wart and all. Men will be interested to see what I looked like, not what I should like to have looked like." This was spoken in the spirit of Luther. The Reformer would be the first to declare some of the pen pictures given us by his ardent admirers since 1546 flattering idealizations.

G. FREYTAG'S TESTIMONY

And yet, after all deductions have been made, one cannot but regard the portrait of the Reformer, penned by Gustav Freytag, no blind partisan, to be true to life. If a man is to be given the credit of his better self, if he is to be judged by the general tenor and bent of his life and influence, Freytag did not overdraw Luther's picture when he wrote: "In a savage age, accustomed to kill with fire and sword, this man conceived those spiritual battles loftier and purer than all else. Any employment of physical force was hateful to him, even during the time of his greatest personal danger; he would not be protected by his sovereign; nay, he wanted no human protection for his doctrine. He fought with a sharp quill against his enemies, but the only pyre which he lighted was for a paper; he hated the Pope as he did the devil, but he always preached peace and Christian tolerance towards papists; he suspected many of being in secret league with the devil, but he never burned a witch. In all Cath-

olic countries the fires blazed over those who professed the new
faith, even Hutten was strongly suspected of having cut off the
ears of some monks; Luther had hearty compassion for the
humiliated Tetzel and wrote him a letter of consolation. So
humane was his sentiment." [78]

ROME LUSTED AFTER LUTHER'S BLOOD

Unfortunately one may say as much of only a very few of his
enemies. Many were the things the "prophet of fire" had to
endure for the sake of Christ's Gospel. At the Diet of Worms the
end of Luther's meteoric career seemed to have come. The papal
diplomat Aleander presented the imperial ban against the Reformer, declaring him an outlaw, to the Emperor after the Sunday
service in the church. Then and there Charles V signed what to
many seemed to be the death warrant of the bold monk. Handing
it back to Aleander, Charles asked smilingly: "Are you contented
now?" Aleander offered fulsome thanks. He "despatched the
document to Rome with an exultation which could only find due
expression in a quotation from Ovid's *Art of Love.* (!) Pope Leo
celebrated the arrival of the news by comedies and musical en-
tertainments." [79] For twenty-five years thereafter Luther lived in
almost constant expectation of a sudden and violent death. But
the prospect of such an end held no terror for the Reformer. He
wrote: "They threaten us with death; if they were as wise as they
are foolish, they would threaten us with life. It is a laughable
threat when they try to frighten Christ and His Christians with
death, for they are victors over death. It is like trying to frighten
a man by saddling his horse and putting him up to ride." [80]

LUTHER WILLING TO SUFFER MARTYRDOM

However, years passed, and God's providence so controlled
political and religious developments in Europe at large and Germany in particular that the murderous enemies of the Gospel
never quite succeeded in doing Luther to death. In 1529, after

---

[78] Fr, M 95 f.   [79] Li, H I:298.   [80] S-J, LC II:105.

the second Diet of Spires, the situation again became acutely critical for the Reformation. A war of religion seemed imminent. Luther wrote to his Elector, John of Saxony, who was openly and staunchly Lutheran: "We must keep our hands clean of blood and violence, and if it were to come to pass (though I think it will not) that the Emperor actually attacks us and demands that I or the others be given up, then, by God's help, we shall appear and not put Your Grace in any danger, as I have often told Your Grace's pious brother, my gracious Lord, Duke Frederick." [81] Throughout his life Luther, though unwilling to make others suffer for their faith, was ready to sacrifice his very life for the Gospel he had restored. In fact, the Reformer regretted not having been thought worthy by God to die a martyr's death. In keeping with the view of Scripture on this point,[82] he looked upon "persecution for righteousness' sake" as a distinction and a badge of honor. Therefore, when he imagined, during a serious illness in 1527, that his end was near, he prayed: "Lord, if it be Thy will that I die in my bed, Thy will be done; I would rather have shed my blood, but John the Evangelist, who also wrote a good strong book against the Pope, died thus, according to Thy will." [83]

These words breathe a death-defying courage no less than an heroic faith. Both were characteristic of the Reformer. Luther has become very famous for his leonine courage. Old Alexander Bower thinks that courage is the key to his character and career. Bower wrote back in 1813: "If among the numerous virtues of Luther we seek for that which more particularly characterized him, we shall fix, without hesitation, on his contempt for the terrors of power. It was to this undaunted spirit that he was chiefly indebted for his usefulness and celebrity. To maintain the cause of truth as a servant of God was a task in which no danger could appal him. His courage arose from no hasty resolution and still less from any hidden ambition — it was a firm, deliberate determination, founded on thorough conviction

---

[81] S-J, LC II:506.   [82] Cp. Matt. 5:11; 1 Pet. 4:14.   [83] S-J, LC II:407.

and unconscious of abatement under the most embarrassing circumstances. Regardless of the threats of foes or the expostulations of friends he persevered in his course and looked forward, with patience and confidence, to 'reap in joy what he had sown in tears.' " [84]

Luther's courage appeared, of course, particularly in his heroic acts; but there are many passages in his writings which fairly radiate the dauntless spirit for which his name has become all but synonymous. In the early months of 1521 the outlook was dark enough for Luther. The Diet of Worms was to convene, and only God knew into what that might develop. The enemies of the Reformer were spending sleepless nights plotting his utter destruction. His friends were becoming alarmed and urged moderation and compromise. And Luther himself? In March he flung this defiance at Jerome Emser, private secretary of Duke George: "My great and joyful courage hurts you to your very heart. But in spite of you and Eck, the Pope and your whole crew, yea, in spite of the devil too, I am and, please God, will remain in a constant, fearless, proud state of mind, defying and despising you all as fools and blind men and malignant liars." [85] At the same time he picked up his pen to write a devout exposition of Mary's Magnificat (Luke 1:46-55), as though Worms had nothing whatever to do with him.

LUTHER AT WORMS, "THE GREATEST SCENE IN MODERN HISTORY"

In April the Diet met. Knightly friends and sympathizers urged Luther not to venture into that den of lions, but to discuss matters with the Emperor's father confessor, Glapion, in a near-by castle. Other friends reminded him of the fate of poor John Huss, burned at the stake during the Council of Constance in 1415 in spite of Emperor Sigismund's pledge of safe-conduct. But to the one he answered: If the Emperor's confessor had anything to tell him, he could do so in Worms; and to the others he wrote the immortal words: "Though there were as many devils

---

[84] Bow, L 290.   [85] Ho III:293.

in Worms as tiles on the housetops, I will nonetheless enter there." Though Huss had been burned, the truth had not been burned, said Luther. And the truth was his primary concern, not his own poor body. His body might be done for quickly enough, but the truth had to be confessed.[86] The dramatic part which Luther played at that Diet has engaged the pens of men and moved their spirits ever since. The dullest chronicles that have come down to us have caught a bit of the exalted spirit that animated Luther during his appearance and defense before that august assembly. Carlyle's well-known words are: "The Diet of Worms, Luther's appearance there on April 17, 1521, may be considered as the greatest scene in modern history."[87] Robert Montgomery has put it into poetry.

> But there he stands! — in superhuman calm
> Concentered and sublime. Around him pomp
> And blaze imperial; haughty eyes, and tongues
> Whose tones are tyranny, in vain attempt
> The Heaven-born quiet of his soul to move.
> Crowned with the grace of everlasting truth,
> A more than monarch among kings he stood;
> And while without, an ever-deep'ning mass
> Of murm'ring thousands on the windows watched
> The torchlight gleaming through the crimsoned glass
> Of that thronged hall, where Truth on trial was,
> Seldom on earth did ever sun go down
> Or evening mantle o'er a grander scene.
> There priests and barons, counts and dukes were met,
> Landgraves and margraves, earls, electors, knights,
> And Charles the Splendid, in the glowing pride
> Of princely youth, with empires at his feet;
> And there — the miner's son, to match them all!
> With black robe belted round his manly waist,
> Before that bar august he stood serene,
> By self-dominion reining down his soul.
> Melanchthon wept; and Spalatinus gazed
> With breathless wonder on that wondrous man.
> While, mute and motionless, a grim array
> Of priests and monks, in combination dire,

---

[86] Se, A 326 sq.; K-K, M I:408.   [87] Ca, H 158.

On Luther fastened their most bloodhound gaze
Of bigotry. But not one rippling thought disturbed
The calm of heaven on his commanding face.
Meek but majestic, simple but sublime
In aspect, thus he braved the wrath of Rome,
With brow unshrinking and with eyes that flashed
As if the spirit in each glance were sheathed;
And then, with voice which seemed a soul in sound
Made audible, he pled th' Almighty's cause
In words almighty as the cause he pled —
The Bible's, God's religion, not the priest's,
By craft invented and by lucre saved:
For *this* life, limb, and liberty he vowed
To sacrifice. Though earth and hell might rage,
Not Pope nor canon, council nor decree,
Would shake him. From the throne of that resolve
By fiend nor angel would his heart be hurled;
Truth and his conscience would together fight,
The world 'gainst them — and they against the world!
And then, with eyes which flashed celestial fire,
Full in the face of that assembly rolled
The fearless monk those ever-famous words
"God help me! Here I stand alone. Amen." [88]

After the glitter and glare of Worms the silence and solitude of the Wartburg. But one enemy had stolen after Luther into the fortress. No sentinel was able to keep *him* out. "On earth is not his equal." The devil sought to plague the Reformer, busy with his translation of the New Testament into German. It is quite unnecessary to determine the historicity of the inkwell throwing. If Luther did *not* throw it, he would very likely have done so, had the opportunity offered. The very rise of such a legend is a testimony to Luther's hell-defying courage. Men knew of what he was capable. Carlyle says that Luther wrote upon one occasion: "I have seen and defied innumerable devils. Duke George is not equal to one devil. If I had business at Leipzig, I would ride into Leipzig, though it rained Duke Georges for nine days running." Carlyle adds: "What a reservoir of Dukes to ride into!" [89]

---

[88] Po, L 22 f.   [89] Ca, H 165.

"FEAR WAS A TOTAL STRANGER TO MARTIN LUTHER"

There has been frequent occasion to refer to Luther's return to Wittenberg in 1522 to curb the spirit of "enthusiasm" and radicalism that was threatening the conservative Reformation. If we were to choose the incident in Luther's career that is most illustrative of his character, it would be this one. It reveals half a dozen traits of the big man's character, among them especially his courage. He returned to his troubled flock in defiance of papal excommunication and imperial ban. The Elector had told him he could not protect him. Luther replied he had not asked for any protection. He plunged into the greatest personal danger. At every turn a violent death might have overtaken him. But Luther never flinched. That is courage at its best and purest.

His contemporaries recognized it as such. Many are the expressions of admiration and awe that have come down to us. When he had scarcely begun his career, Spalatin wrote to a friend: "If you ask how he [Luther] is, for all I know, he is well, and, as I who write have found out, of too lofty and strong a mind to be turned by any blast of furious fortune from doing what he has proposed and from the path he has set for himself. For the sake of Christ and the truth he shuns no misfortune, he flees no calamity, he fears no evil." [90] The impression he made at Worms was deep and lasting. A priest is said to have embraced him and devoutly kissed his clothing three times. When Elector Frederick returned to his quarters after the hearing, he said to his intimates, full of admiration and of a concern characteristic of the cautious man: "Well did the Father, Doctor Martinus, speak in Latin and German. He is much too courageous for me." Even among Luther's enemies remarks of respect were heard. People looked with awe upon the brave monk.

Respect for the Reformer's courage rises still higher when it is observed that it was never a blind and unreasoning courage, a sort of impassioned daredeviltry. Still less was his courage rooted in a stoical indifference, a temperamental imperturbability.

---

[90] S-J, LC I:137.

It has been pointed out that Luther was a man of intense feeling and of a vivid imagination. Such natures are very susceptible to apprehension and fear. There is nothing surprising about the courage of a man who is too ignorant to see the grave danger that is threatening him or who despises it with the lightheaded optimism of a daredevil. But Martin Luther faced his dangers neither ignorantly nor flippantly. He clearly saw that, humanly speaking, the odds were heavily against him. This was plain to him when in 1518 he journeyed to Augsburg to appear before the papal legate Cajetan. But Luther went, willing to do his duty at all costs. When his interview with the Italian cardinal had convinced him that he could expect no fair hearing from the man, he hastily left Augsburg under the cover of night.[91] He considered any longer stay a needless and unanswerable exposure of his life. A hot-tempered, reckless man would have stayed on.

Luther was too sober to court danger. This appeared also in the following year. The Leipzig Debate with Eck was to be held in the summer of that year. But Luther had many bitter enemies in ducal Saxony. He therefore wrote for a safe-conduct to its head, Duke George: "As the affair has brought me danger to my life and much enmity, I pray Your Grace for God's sake to give me a safe-conduct. For I must not venture to tempt God by despising human help, for which I requite Your Grace with my humble prayer before God."[92] These words recall the famous advice of Oliver Cromwell to his soldiers: "Trust in God, but mind to keep your powder dry." Luther believed in the help and protection of God, but he also believed that we had a right to rely upon these only if and when we used to the full the protective and remedial means God placed at our disposal.

But the man who acts according to this Christian principle will at times find that "discretion is the better part of valor." Naturally, his enemies might maliciously misconstrue his caution into cowardice. Luther had been cited to appear in Rome. At first he was inclined to go. But upon second thought and after

---

[91] Se, A 136; Erl 64:364. [92] S-J, LC I:182.

consultation with his friends he refused to undertake the journey. He justified his decision by writing: "They taunt me, asking why I am timid and do not come to Rome. As if Christ ran of His own accord to Annas, Caiaphas, Pilate, and Herod and begged them to kill him. I thought it enough to stand my ground and not to flee, and to wait for them where I am till they fetched me, as they did Christ, and led me whither they would. But they say I ought to have run after them and urged them to kill me; they put everything so cleverly! Why are they not so bold as to refute my writings or to come to me and conquer me with their lofty wisdom? Ah, well, let the blind be blind!" [93]

HIS COURAGE ROOTED IN A GREAT FAITH

Luther's courage was not a natural but an acquired virtue. It was rooted in his heroic faith. It was the courage of a man who relies not upon himself, upon his own strength, but upon the omnipotent God, to whom he has entrusted his cause, nay, whose cause he has made his own. Lincoln was once asked whether his patient courage was due to the fact that he felt God to be on his side. He replied: "My concern is not to have God upon *my* side, but to be on *God's own* side." There lay the secret of Luther's courage. It did not lie in his temper, his disposition. He never loved danger for danger's sake, because of the thrill and excitement it gave him. He was not like the mercenary soldier of Europe, who often hired himself out to fight anybody's quarrel just for the mad pleasure of fighting.

LUTHER WAS NOT AT ALL QUARRELSOME AND BELLIGERENT

Perhaps it will be surprising to some to hear that Martin Luther was not a born fighter. To quote Carlyle again: "Perhaps no man of so humble, peaceable a disposition ever filled the world with contention. We cannot but see that he would have loved privacy, quiet diligence in the shade." [94] Again he says: "Luther

---

[93] Ho III:105.   [94] Ca, H 155.

to a slight observer might have seemed a timid, weak man; modesty, affectionate, shrinking tenderness the chief distinction of him. It is a noble valor that is roused in a heart like this, once stirred up into defiance, all kindled into a heavenly blaze." [95] Since Luther became involved in controversies and achieved a world-wide renown for his valor in conducting them, the average man thinks of the Reformer as an aggressive, perhaps somewhat turbulent character. But Luther did not walk about with a chip constantly on his shoulder, hoping someone would knock it off and thus give him an excuse to indulge his love of fighting. J. Froude correctly says of Luther: "He had no notion of making a disturbance in the world." [96] And Luther himself wrote to Elector Frederick in 1521: "I cannot easily express my aversion to being plunged in these whirlpools and taken from my studies." [97] Preserved Smith says: "He [Luther] was, indeed, a born fighter. His amazing strength and courage, animated by the strongest of all motives, devotion to conscience . . . found ample scope in the great load of wrong and superstition to be combated." [98] Smith seems to mean that Luther possessed the qualities of head and heart to make a fighter, if fighting had to be done. This is certainly true. But he was not belligerent by nature. "I will attack no one first; it is sufficient to me to defend myself when attacked," he wrote.[99] History bears out the truthfulness of this statement. Prierias, Emser, the theologians of Louvain and Cologne, Alfeld, Murner, Henry VIII, Cochlaeus, Erasmus, Carlstadt — all were the aggressors. Luther merely defended himself against them. Perhaps it were better to say: He defended Scripture against them, as his doctor's oath solemnly bound him to do. His entire activity from 1517 to 1546 is both accounted for and characterized when he writes: "In all my writings I have sought no more, even now I seek no more, from the Pope and all my enemies than just such confession that their cause is acknowledged to be without foundation in Scripture." [100] Again: "Let the Roman decretals

---

95 Ca, H 166. 97 S-J, LC I:478. 99 S-J, LC I:395.

96 Fro, L 208. 98 Sm, L 497. 100 Ho III:391.

leave me the pure Gospel and take away all else, I will not move a hair." [101] The judicious von Ranke says: "One must confess that it was not Luther who brought about the outbreak [of the war of controversies]." [102]

HE DEPLORED THE NECESSITY OF SO MUCH CONTROVERSY

It irked the peace-loving and conservative Luther that he had to do so much destructive work. He longed for nothing more than to be left alone, so that he might quietly study Scripture and preach and teach its Gospel to old and young. As early as 1521 he complained: "This I can boast and prove, that in this whole matter I have never started a controversy, for I have always against my will been torn away from useful, helpful occupation, so that many good people have felt sorry that I must waste so much precious time in answering my lying and malicious assailants." [103]

Even after controversies had been brought on by the enemies of the Gospel, how considerate "the prophet of fire" was, how patient with the ignorant and those of slow and weak comprehension. To a former Wittenberg student, Count Lewis of Stolberg, he wrote: "We must destroy . . . false beliefs by preaching, so that men's hearts may be drawn away from them [images, etc.] by the pure Gospel; the external thing would then go to pieces of its own accord, because it helps nobody. So long, now, as men's hearts cleave to these things, we cannot tear them out without tearing men's hearts out too." [104] Again he said: "With the wolves you cannot be too severe, with the weak sheep you cannot be too gentle." [105] Luther, it is seen, differentiated between error rooted in ignorance and heresy anchored in stubborn unbelief and rejection of the proffered truth. His fire was reserved for those guilty of the latter sin. To Spalatin he wrote in 1523: "I think the Lord's Supper ought henceforth to be freely given and received in both kinds. We have been sufficiently indulgent here-

---

101 S-J, LC I:167.   103 Ho III:291; cp. Se, A 183.   105 Ho III:221.
102 Ra, D I:277.   104 S-J, LC II:122.

tofore to the infirm, and the matter has now been made known everywhere. . . . Those who are offended by a practice that has become so well known are not weak but rather obstinate." [106]

Luther gave his enemies the benefit of the doubt as long as he could, always hoping and praying that perhaps after all God might open their eyes to the error of their way. Indeed, he always held that many were saved also in the heretical and corrupt Church of Rome. To his table companions he once remarked that no doubt many were moved to cling to Christ alone when, as was customary, a crucifix was held before their glazing eyes in the agony of death.[107] At another time he remarked: "All of us know that the Pope and the papists want us dead in body and soul. But we want all of them saved together with us in body and soul." [108]

LUTHER WAS MAGNANIMOUS TOWARDS HIS DETRACTORS

There are many instances of Luther's generous treatment of his enemies. The case of poor Johann Tetzel is well known. Karl von Miltitz had been sent to Germany in an effort to extinguish the fire the intemperate indulgence racketeer had started. He dealt harshly with Tetzel. Severe disciplining and permanent disgrace were in prospect for him. He was a broken man. Every one deserted him. Then, one day, came a letter of sympathy from — Martin Luther. In this surprising letter Luther told Tetzel not to despair because of the scandal caused by the sale of indulgences. He [Tetzel] was not solely nor even primarily responsible for the offense; "the child has an entirely different father," Luther told him.[109] This bigheartedness of Luther became well known, and not infrequently a former enemy or traducer of Luther would turn to no one but Luther himself in times of trouble. Carlstadt did this more than once. Men knew that Luther fought issues, not persons, that he hated sin but loved sinful men and was ever ready to help them, whether they were friend or foe. Jerome

---

[106] S-J, LC II:160.　　　　　　[108] In Wa, L 157.
[107] Erl 58:63.　　　　　　　　[109] Se, A 173; K-K, M I:225.

PLATE X

GEORGE SPALATIN

George Burkhardt was born at Spalt, near Nuremberg in Bavaria.
He became known as Spalatin. At the age of fifteen he entered the
University of Erfurt in 1499 and met young Martin Luther, whose
fast friend he became for the rest of his life

PLATE XI

LUTHER AS KNIGHT GEORGE

To add to his disguise, Luther grew a beard while at the Wartburg.
He was then spoken of as the "Knight George" (Junker Joerg).
Lucas Cranach has given the world a painting and a woodcut of
the Reformer's appearance at this time. The artist did his painting
during Luther's secret visit to Wittenberg in December, 1521, and
subsequently made woodcuts on the basis of his painting

PLATE XII

TITLE PAGE OF THE SMALL CATECHISM

Both of Luther's catechisms were written in 1529. It seems that
no copy of the original book edition of the Small Catechism has
survived. However, we do possess two Erfurt reprints of the first
edition in book form and High German. The above is a reproduction of the title page of this reprint.

PLATE XIII

LUTHER'S STUDY

Four centuries have dealt kindly with many Luther relics in the
Black Cloister at Wittenberg: the writing table, the quaint old iron
stove, the floor on which he walked, the very window panes of his
study are preserved

Emser was one of Luther's most inveterate and malicious enemies. The following passage is found in a reply to a bitter book of his against Luther. The Reformer tries to touch the man's conscience. He writes: "I pray you again, my dear Emser, for God's sake moderate your lying and make amends for this lie, so that you may not go too far in tempting God. I know you cannot harm me, and I would rather see you repent than perish. That I may withhold no duty which a Christian owes his enemy, and I notice that you stake your soul upon your cause, like an angry bee sacrificing its life with its sting, I will offer you now . . . leave to choose either anger or mirth; and I will give you both exhortation and encouragement, that when your last hour comes — for we are uncertain of any moment — you need not be frightened or driven to despair when my image rises up in your memory, and I assure you now that what you have done to me shall not then rise up to your hurt. I desire to do my part for the salvation of your soul." [110]

That last sentence characterizes Luther very succinctly. As a "prophet of *fire*," he no doubt often wrote and spoke; but if and when he did so, he, like Paul, wished to "use sharpness . . . to edification and not to destruction." [111] He did it because he loved souls and hated sin. "I desire to do my part for the salvation of souls" — write that as a motto over the entire activity of Martin Luther.

---

[110] Ho III:296.   [111] 2 Cor. 13:10.

CHAPTER VII

THE FRUITS OF FAITH

Luther was the embodiment of personal piety.
Thomas Lindsay, Scotch historian

THERE WERE MANY IN THE DAYS OF LUTHER WHO EXPECTED his Gospel to exert a distinctly demoralizing influence. Such an effect seemed inevitable to them. They argued on this wise: If the sinner be taught that his good works contribute nothing whatever toward making good his standing before God, he will draw the conclusion that he need no longer concern himself about moral requirements so long as he has faith in Christ. This is unexceptionable logic, Luther was told, and would open the floodgates of license and immorality. The Catholic Michelet quoted the following from a sermon Luther had preached at Leipzig in 1519: "It is a thousand times more important to believe piously in absolution than to be worthy of it and make atonement. Faith renders you worthy of it and makes atonement." The French historian called this a "dangerous doctrine" and remarked that at this time Luther propounded it "without any misgiving of the fatal consequences which resulted thence to man's liberty and morality."[1] Before and after Michelet's criticism appeared, this was a common charge against "Luther's Gospel."

JUSTIFICATION BY FAITH NOT DEMORALIZING ACCORDING TO ST. PAUL

Now, even if the vicious deduction above mentioned were demanded by the rules of logic and psychology — a point which we are not at all ready to concede — it would have to be borne in mind that a proposition may be logically correct but theologically incorrect. Christian doctrine is grounded on Scripture, not on logic or psychology; on revelation, not on reason. The fall into

[1] Mi, L 47 f.

sin did not leave man's mental powers unaffected. They are, by themselves, to be trusted as little in the field of the spiritual as that "sense organ for the ethical," a man's conscience. Their pronouncements need to be examined in the light of Scripture. But when this is done in the case in hand, what do we find? We find that men argued on this wise even in the days of Paul. We hear the Apostle ask: "Shall we sin, because we are not under the Law, but under grace?" [2] In a previous chapter (3:8) he referred to what he calls the "slanderous charge of some." There were people who said Paul's Gospel of free grace intentionally encouraged a life of sin to the greater glory of a forgiving God. What did Paul answer?

The Apostle replied: His critics knew very well that he taught no such demoralizing doctrine, wherefore their condemnation as liars was just. "God forbid," Paul cries out, that he who has received the pardoning grace of God into his heart should thereby and therefore consider himself absolved from *obedience* to the Law no less than from the *curse* of the Law! When the penitent makes Christ his own by faith, he, in turn, becomes Christ's own; and "know ye not that to whom ye yield yourselves servants to obey, his servants ye are to whom ye obey; whether of sin unto death, or of obedience unto righteousness?" [3] The point Paul makes is this: In both cases cited, obedience is rendered certain by a power superior to man's will. By justification the sinner is sanctified and receives that supernatural, spiritual life which expresses its vital power in loving service to God and man. The roots of true piety are securely anchored in an appreciation of God's gratuitous salvation. Thus Paul answered his critics.

Luther's answer was the same. He so entirely agreed with Paul that Julius Hare called the Apostle a "Luther before Luther." One would expect to find a clear statement from Luther on this matter in his *Commentary on Galatians*. Nor is one disappointed. In his exposition of the weighty words in Gal. 5:6 the Reformer says: "He [Paul] shutteth out all slothful and idle persons which

---

[2] Rom. 6:15.   [3] Rom. 6:16.

say, if faith justify without works, then let us work nothing, but let us only believe and do what we list. Not so, ye enemies of grace; Paul saith otherwise. And although it be true that only faith justifieth, yet he speaketh here of faith in another respect; that is to say, that after it hath justified, it is not idle but occupied and exercised in working through love. Paul therefore in this place setteth forth the whole life of a Christian man, namely, that inwardly it consisteth in faith towards God and outwardly in charity and good works toward our neighbor." [4]

ONLY THE JUSTIFIED ARE SANCTIFIED

Naturally, Luther's view of the nature of personal piety and good works differed greatly from that current in the Church of Rome. At times he speaks of the blasphemous impiety of which he had been guilty while in communion with Rome. Since we have heard his very enemies testify to his moral purity, this cannot mean that he lived a wayward life. Luther's characterization of his previous life must be understood in the light of his discovery that according to Scriptural standards the soul of piety is the loving gratitude of a believing heart. In common with Paul, Luther held that only the justified can be truly pious. He saw this truth clearly as soon as he had rid himself of the papal perversions of the doctrine of justification. As early as 1516 we therefore read in a letter to Spalatin: "Whatever good is done outside the faith of Christ, even if it makes Fabricii and Reguli, men who were righteous before men, yet it no more savors of justification than do apples of figs. For we are not, as Aristotle thinks, made righteous by doing right, except in appearance; but (if I may so express it) when we are righteous in essence, we do right. It is necessary that the character be changed before the deeds; Abel pleased before his gift." [5]

Autobiographically he says in his *Commentary on Galatians:* "With great rejoicing I give thanks to God for that He hath abundantly and above measure granted that unto me which I so

---

[4] Lu, G 440.   [5] S-J, LC I:43.

earnestly desired of Him when I was a monk: for He hath given unto me the grace to see not one but many saints, yea, an infinite number of true saints; not such as the sophisters have devised, but such as Christ Himself and His Apostles do describe. Of the which number I assure myself to be one. For I am baptized and do believe that Christ, my Lord, by His death hath redeemed and delivered me from all my sins and hath given to me eternal righteousness and holiness. And let him be holden accursed whosoever shall not give this honor unto Christ to believe that by His death, His Word, etc., he is justified and sanctified." [6] These words are clear and convincing, but perhaps the best-known statement of Luther on the subject of a "faith that worketh by love" is found in the introductory remarks to his German translation of the Bible. There is a note of almost apostolic assurance and exaltation in the mighty words: "Oh, there is something living, energetic, active, mighty about this faith, so that it is impossible that it be not engaged in doing good without ceasing. Nor does it ask whether good works are to be done, but before one asks, faith has done them and is constantly doing them. . . . Faith is a living, bold confidence in the grace of God, so certain that it would die a thousand deaths for it. . . . In consequence a man becomes willing and anxious, without compulsion, to do good to every man, to serve every man, to suffer all sorts of things for the love and praise of God, who has shown him such grace; so that it is impossible to separate works from faith, yea, as impossible as it is to separate burning and shining from fire." [7]

THE TAPROOT OF GOOD WORKS IS LOVING GRATITUDE

According to Luther, then, the soul of a truly good work is reverential, grateful love. Therefore he began the explanations of the Ten Commandments in his Small Catechism with the words: "We should fear (reverentially) and love God." To Staupitz he wrote: "The commands of God become sweet when we understand that they are not to be read in books only but in the wounds

---

[6] Lu, G 484.   [7] Wal XIV 99 f.

of the sweetest Savior." [8] Elsewhere he says in his blunt way: "Cursed all works that are not performed in love." [9] But if this principle is true, the prime consideration must be *why* a man performs any given work; the doing of it is not in and of itself a guarantee of its goodness. Moreover, if God judges the goodness of an act by the motive of the actor, it follows that the humblest service performed in a spirit of love is precious in the eyes of the Lord. And so it is. Says William Cowper:

> One act that from a thankful heart proceeds
> Excells ten thousand mercenary deeds.

Luther resurrected this Scriptural doctrine. It shook to their foundations monasteries and nunneries and ultimately left many of them forsaken and in ruins. It was Martin Luther who rescued the humble duties of daily life from the stigma of inferiority and exploded the medieval myth of the superior merit of a cloistered life. He wrote: "God does not consider how small or large the works are, but [He looks at] the heart, which performs in faith and obedience to God what its calling demands." [10] In his famous *Treatise on Good Works* there is this: "In faith all works become equal, and one is like the other. . . . For the works are acceptable not for their own sake but because of the faith which alone is, works, and lives in each and every work without distinction, however numerous and various they are, just as all the members of the body live, work, and have their name from the head, and without the head no member can live, work, and have a name." [11]

LUTHER A GREAT PREACHER OF RIGHT LIVING

This truth deserves to be emphasized from a slightly different point of view. The average person thinks of Luther as the restorer of the doctrine of justification by faith; and no doubt no man since Paul has more clearly stated and more successfully defended that cardinal truth of Christianity. But, like Paul, the Reformer emphasized this teaching so constantly in order not

---

[8] S-J, LC I:91.   [9] Wal X:407.   [10] Wal IX 1207.   [11] Ho I 190.

merely to insure a man's peace of conscience but also to guarantee his purification of soul, to place piety on a secure basis. Thus did Paul. Among the Corinthians he had been "determined not to know anything . . . save Jesus Christ, and Him crucified." [12] The Corinthians were as notorious for immorality as were many of the clergy in the days of Luther. To clean this Augean stable, Paul preached the justifying Gospel because it alone sanctified. So he assured the Corinthians: "He [Christ] died for all, that they which live should not henceforth live unto themselves but unto Him which died for them and rose again." [13] How great the theological immaturity of those who not only charged Luther with an overemphasis of the doctrine of God's saving grace but actually held that such teaching would generate moral indifference! Luther followed Paul and said: If you wish to further genuine piety, preach the sanctifying Gospel to penitent sinners. In consequence it is historically and doctrinally correct to say that few men have shown such zeal for piety and good works as did the Gospel preacher Martin Luther. "Throughout he preaches faith and love — not good works as having any value, any merit, in themselves, but faith and love after the example of St. Paul, in their living, inseparable unity and their active energy, perpetually bringing forth good works to the glory of God. . . . His reverence for the Moral Law, as declared in the Ten Commandments, has never been surpassed: and as it was his delight to teach the poor and simple, he made a number of attempts to set them forth in such a manner that they might be written on the hearts and minds of the people. . . . The same reverence for the Moral Law induced him to publish a versified form of the Ten Commandments in a hymnbook in 1524 and another briefer form in another hymnbook in 1525." [14]

Not only do we hear Luther tersely say: "Holiness is the greatest thing in all the world," [15] but in his introductory remarks to the exposition of the Creed in his Large Catechism of 1529 he states, looking back at the Commandments: "This [the faith

---

[12] 1 Cor. 2:2.   [13] 2 Cor. 5:15.   [14] H, V 50 f.   [15] Ho III:51.

taught in the Creed] is intended to help us do that which according to the Ten Commandments we ought to do. For (as said above) they are set so high that all human ability is far too feeble and weak to (attain to or) keep them. Therefore it is as necessary to learn this part as the former in order that we may know how to attain thereto, whence and whereby to obtain such power." [16] According to these words God adopted the plan of salvation by grace through faith in Christ because He wanted to make sure also of man's sanctification, his personal piety.

Martin Luther was a living proof of the effectiveness of this plan of the All-wise. It is said that a religion is as good as it works. Luther's must have been very good, for it certainly worked. Thomas Lindsay says: "Luther was the embodiment of personal piety." [17] This statement may seem like an exaggeration, but Luther's exceptional piety was witnessed to by his contemporaries. Melanchthon wrote that Luther was the "honored, good, and learned leader of true Christian piety." [18] And we have heard Erasmus testify: "No one who knows the man does not approve of his life." The Catholic Humanist adds that "blameless morals even among heathen find favor." [19] One hesitates to say what this statement makes some of Luther's contemporaries out to have been, for he found no favor with them. Some of the vile names they called him have been recorded above. But such vilification ought not to surprise us too greatly. It should be remembered what men called the Son of God in the days of His flesh. And the Holy One said: "If they have called the Master of the house Beelzebub, how much more shall they call them of his household?" [20]

THE SOBERNESS OF LUTHERAN PIETY

But another fact must be remembered. The sober, full-souled, sunny, unsophisticated piety of Luther was to some extent incomprehensible to the morally jaundiced leaders of the Roman

---

[16] Wal X:90 (*Conc. Triglotta* translation).
[17] Li, H I:191.   [18] S-J, LC I:115.   [19] S-J, LC I:179.   [20] Matt. 10:25.

Church. To most of the serious churchmen the ideal piety meant solitude, silence, sighs, a downcast look, a scant diet, fastings, vigils, scourgings, and sundry similar activities. Luther, the conversationalist who laughed heartily in the circle of his lingering friends around his hospitable table, who thoroughly enjoyed his beer and wine and publicly said he did; Luther, who advised the melancholy introvert Hieronimus Weller to stop brooding about his pardoned peccadilloes, to enjoy the good things of life and to thank God for them — Rome could not understand such a Reformer. The unostentatious, every-day piety of this man, which threatened to put virtual sainthood within the reach of every man and to make the halo the common property of all believers — the aristocratic, ecclesiastical monopolists resented such a "cheapening" of religion. The utter absence of the puritanical and the pietistic in this man, who proposed to reform a Church notorious for her laxness and license, seemed like a moral incompatibility to many who still took their religion seriously, after the medieval pattern.

The offensive better-than-thou attitude, found with such saddening frequency, was entirely foreign to Luther. There was nothing pharisaical about his piety. His classic description of Christian life and character is well known: "This life is not righteousness but growth in righteousness, not health but healing, not being but becoming, not rest but exercise; we are not yet what we shall be, but we are growing toward it; the process is not yet finished, but it is going on; this is not the end, but it is the road; all does not yet gleam with glory, but all is being purified." [21] Fourteen years of observation and — we may be sure — introspection did not change his views of human nature; for we hear him say, as with a sigh, in his *Commentary on Galatians:* "Grace maketh not such a change in the faithful that by-and-by they become altogether new creatures and perfect in all things; but there remaineth yet certain dregs of their old and natural corruption. . . . Indeed, many things are purged in us

---

[21] Ho III:31.

and principally the head of the serpent; that is to say, infidelity and ignorance of God is cut off and bruised, but the slimy body and the remnants of sin remain still in us." [22] Such language must have sounded strange indeed to churchmen whose common theology recognized sin and holiness to lie all but exclusively in outward acts. The shallow theologians and moralists of Rome were nonplused by a consciousness of sin so deep that it recognized imperfections in our very best works and left the sinner no other alternative than to seek comfort in the righteousness of another. But such had been the experience of Luther. His conscientiousness would not permit him to be satisfied with himself.

LUTHER'S SENSITIVE CONSCIENCE

Historians and biographers have much to say about the conscience of Martin Luther. It played a very important part in his career. Even among his enemies there are men who grant that there was nothing whatever of the hypocrite or the actor about Luther. They concede that he did what he did in good faith, however mistaken — they say — he was. The sensitiveness of Luther's conscience revealed itself very early in his life. He entered the monastery because of it, and within the monastery it made life miserable for him. The reason for his spiritual agony is to be found not in the monastic life itself but in the severe, relentless rigor of his judgment concerning himself. His unusually keen and lively sense of responsibility made monastic life with its many rules and regulations a veritable hell for him. It cannot be denied that life in a monastery could be made quite comfortable without sacrificing the glory of living in a state of superior sanctity. It is notorious that the general run of monks circumvented, neglected, or ignored many of the more irksome prescriptions. But Luther's conscience would not permit him to do this. The old monkish lesson of humility and abasement, the rigors of monkish penance, the forbidding picture of Christ, the severe Judge, all must be looked upon as impulses which caused

---

[22] Lu, G 164.

Luther's delicate conscience to quiver in a state of constant spiritual disturbance. Had Brother Martin been made of coarser fiber, the world would probably never have heard of him. But a man in such dead earnest as the gifted Luther, a man with a conscience as delicate as his, was certain to attract attention.

His conscientiousness soon became the subject of comment in his monastery. Upon one occasion, after he had not appeared among the brethren at the appointed time, the door of his cell was forced open, and the zealous monk was found prostrate on the floor, all but unconscious from rigorous self-discipline. After the opening of the dispute in October, 1517, Luther became so preoccupied that at times a week or two would pass without his having read his breviary. Thereupon the conscientious Martin would shut himself in for entire days, eat and drink practically nothing, and read to make up the arrears in one protracted sitting. His earliest portrait dates from 1520. He was thirty-six years old at the time, but he looks withered and worn out. His eyes are cavernous, his cheeks fallen in. This picture tallies with descriptions that have come down to us from some who saw Luther at Worms in the following year.

What had brought this emaciated monk into the august assembly at Worms? His conscience had driven him there. The honest among the opposition concede this fact. The Catholic Michelet quotes Luther's words to Erasmus: "I solemnly call God to witness that I should have continued to fear and should even now be hesitating, had not my conscience and the truth compelled me to speak." [23] The Frenchman has no fault to find with this explanation of the Reformer. The entire movement might be said to have been begun by the sensitive, troubled conscience of the lone monk. Such a statement is, of course, an oversimplification, but it is largely true. In 1522, when the agitation was beginning to reach an acute stage, Luther wrote to his brother monks at Wittenberg on the abuse of the Mass. At the beginning of this writing he confesses: "Oh, with how great an

---

[23] Mi, L 45.

effort and exertion, also proof from Holy Writ, I barely succeeded to justify before my own conscience that I, a lone man, dared to rise against the Pope, hold him to be the Antichrist, the bishops his apostles, the schools of higher learning his houses of ill fame! How often my heart convulsively struggled (*gezappelt*), rebuked me, and threw up to me their one and strongest argument: You alone are wise? Can it be that all the others are erring and have been erring for so long a time? What if you are erring and are leading into error so many people, all of whom would be eternally damned? [Such questionings continued] until Christ confirmed and settled me by His own certain Word so that my heart no longer struggles but confronts these arguments of the papists as a rock-bound shore the waves and laughs at their threatening and storming." [24] These are weighty words. They tell us that it was not easy for Martin Luther to begin the Reformation, that he undertook the tremendous task after fighting through its issues in his own soul with painstaking conscientiousness. They reveal that he was not at all anxious to set himself up as a reformer but that his *conscience* "would not down." He had to speak up or ever after feel branded in his conscience as a traitor to God's truth.

In August, 1518, he appeared before Cardinal Cajetan at Augsburg. Upon leaving that city he addressed a letter of explanation to the ecclesiastic, in which he stated his position, a position from which he never receded. His memorable words are: "As to the truth of my opinion, I would most readily recant, both by your command and the advice of my vicar, if my conscience in any way allowed it. But I know that neither the command nor the advice nor the influence of any one ought to make me do anything against conscience or can do so." [25] Biographers of the Reformer are not agreed upon the trait which ought to be considered the key to his character. But it were difficult to find another trait in Luther that stands out as prominently as does his downright conscientiousness. Consistently it is found to have been the motive power of his conduct.

---

[24] Erl 28:29.　　　[25] Sm, L 52.

HIS IMMORTAL WORDS OF LOYALTY TO CONSCIENCE AT WORMS

So it was at Worms. The dramatic scene need not be rehearsed again. Von Ranke says of the impression Luther had made at Leipzig in 1519: "Above all he instilled the feeling that he was seeking the truth." [26] This was the impression made upon observers also at Worms. It appeared that here was one of those rare characters who cared for nothing and no one but the truth. Emperor, Pope, Luther, — all were expected to bow before the truth. External harmony and peace in Church and State — all were secondary to the conscientious confession of the truth. Luther's very life meant nothing when the truth was at stake. Therefore the immortal words, words which will ring on through the ages, words which will remain unforgettable as long as men of conscience live: "Unless I am overcome and convicted with testimonies from Scripture or with evident reasons — for I believe neither the Pope nor the councils, since they have often erred and contradicted one another — I am overcome by the Scripture texts which I have adduced, and my conscience is bound by God's Word. I cannot and will not recant anything; for to act contrary to one's conscience is neither safe nor sincere. God help me! Amen." [27]

In later years his enemies and even timid friends frequently told Luther that he might at least keep his convictions more to himself and not cause such a disturbance by broadcasting them. To this the Reformer replied: "I have never wanted to do it and do not want to do it now. I was forced and driven into this position, in the first place, when I had to become a Doctor of Holy Scripture against my will. Then, as a doctor in a general free university, I began, at the command of Pope and Emperor, to do what such a doctor is sworn to do, expounding the Scriptures for all the world and teaching everybody. Once in this position, I have had to stay in it and cannot give it up or leave it, even yet, with a good conscience, even though both Pope and Emperor were to put me under the ban for not doing so. For what

---

[26] Ra, D I:282. [27] Se, A 353; cp. K-K, M I:419; Sm, L 118.

I began as a doctor, made and called at their command, I must truly confess to the end of my life, and I cannot keep silent or cease to teach, though I would like to do so and am weary and unhappy at the great and unendurable ingratitude of the people." [28] And as to the strife such an activity might occasion, that consideration never weighed heavily on Luther's conscience. He wrote: "I know that the Father has given me what I preach. It is His Word and doctrine. If I can say *that*, I also say: Now let matters take their course; let the entire world cave in and burn in full blaze; let bloodshed, or whatever it may be, follow thereupon — what do I care? The Lord is God and the world should obey our Lord God. Christ knows that the Word is more important than the entire world. What is a prince or an emperor, yea, the entire world, heaven and earth and all creation in comparison with the Word? Dirt is what they are." [29]

These vigorous words were no bravado. They were penned a few years after Luther had demonstrated how ready he was to act on the principles enunciated in them. The terrible Peasants' War had severely tried the uncompromising conscientiousness of the Reformer. It had clearly revealed that Luther simply would not "play politics." Luther had found both peasants and princes, ruled and rulers, guilty. Therefore he had faulted both. In 1525 he had written against the peasants: "Let everyone who can, smite, slay, and stab, secretly or openly, remembering that nothing can be more poisonous, hurtful, or devilish than a rebel. It is just as when one must kill a mad dog; if you do not strike him, he will strike you and a whole land with you." [30] Thereupon the princes had not only crushed the rebellion but had inflicted inhuman barbarities upon their victims. In consequence Luther had now felt conscience-bound to turn upon them and had written of them: "The Supreme Judge, who is using them to punish the self-willed peasants, has not forgotten them either, and they will not escape Him. . . . When I have time and occasion to do so, I shall attack the princes and lords too, for in

---

[28] Ho IV:315.   [29] Erl 48:364.   [30] Ho IV:249.

my office of teacher a prince is just the same to me as a peasant. I have already done them certain services which have not made me overpopular with them; but that matters little to me." [31] Luther had been quite right in suspecting that his popularity among the higher powers was not great. In the spring of 1525, when the storm had been brewing, he had written his *Admonition to Peace*. In this dispassionate review of the points in dispute he had told the higher powers bluntly: "In your temporal government you do nothing but flay and rob your subjects in order that you may lead a life of splendor and pride, until the poor people can bear it no longer. The sword is at your throats, but you think yourselves so firm in the saddle that no one can unhorse you. This false security and stubborn perversity will break your necks, as you will discover." [32] The governmental authorities never thanked Luther for thus publicly scoring their tyranny. The Reformer had clearly foreseen that he would lose caste with both peasants and princes by doing what he did, but his conscience had not permitted him to take any other course. His personal popularity did suffer noticeably because of his stand during the Peasants' War. Even five years later, in 1530, he found it advisable not to leave the security of Wittenberg to visit his father, who was at the point of death. He wrote him a letter instead, excusing his failure to come by a reference to the danger threatening his life from both peasants and princes. [33]

It is abundantly clear, then, that Martin Luther followed the voice of his conscience although — as men judged — he would be the loser by so doing. He often had to choose between conformity to the dictates of his conscience and the adoption of a course of compromise and concession. There was, for instance, the question of making common cause with those who indeed accepted the fundamental doctrines of the Christian faith but demurred at nonfundamentals. Luther saw as plainly as anyone else that a church union with such people would, humanly speaking, be a great accession of power and prestige. But the Reformer

---

[31] Ho IV:270.   [32] Ho IV:220 f.   [33] Erl 54:130.

was not concerned about numbers and influence. His first and highest concern was not to violate his conscience by making common cause with anyone or any group of men who, according to his honest conviction, based upon Scripture, were not entirely loyal to the clear, infallible revelation of God's Word. Naturally, men called this attitude narrow-minded, loveless, separatistic, dogmatic, and a number of other choice names. They still do. But that sad fact never made the conscientious man swerve an inch from his course.

He was human enough to be attracted by the vision of an externally united front on the part of all who loved the Lord Jesus against the utter unbeliever who rejected Him and the papist who disfigured Him. But Luther would not enter into such a union at the expense of one iota of the truth. To the Henry Clay of the Reformation, the "Great Compromiser," Martin Bucer of Strassburg, he wrote: "I cannot admit a full, solid peace with you without violating my conscience. . . . Let us rather bear a little discord with an imperfect peace than, by trying to cure this, create a more tragic schism and tumult. Please believe what I told you at Coburg, that I would like to heal this breach between us at the cost of my life three times over, for I see how needful is your fellowship to us and what damage our disunion has done the Gospel. I am certain that, were we but united, all the gates of hell and all the Papacy and all the Turks and all the world and all the flesh and whatever evil there is could not hurt us. Please impute it not to obstinacy but to conscience that I decline the union you propose. May the Lord Jesus illumine us and make us more perfectly at one." [34]

CONDUCT AT MARBURG DICTATED BY CLEAR SCRIPTURE

There are few acts for which Martin Luther has been more generally criticized than for his refusal to extend the hand of church fellowship to Zwingli and his party at Marburg in 1529. But we do not hesitate to say that there were few occasions in

---

[34] Sm, L 288 f.

Luther's active life upon which he rose to the heroic height exhibited at Marburg. With the story of that disputation about the real presence of Christ's body and blood in the Lord's Supper we are not here concerned.[35] But we *are* interested in the revelation it gave of Luther's unbending conscientiousness. When Philip Schaff wrote: "There are not a few Lutherans who have more liking for Luther's faults than for his virtues and admire his conduct at Marburg as much, if not more, than his conduct at Worms," [36] he entirely missed the point. Luther was fully as great in his defense of the Real Presence against the sacramentarians as he was in his defense of the sole authority of Scripture against the papists. The principle he contended for was, as a matter of fact, the same at both places. A faith without a God-given object is just as reprehensible as a God-given object without faith. While Papists believed in many matters which God had never made articles of faith, the Reformed refused to accept the Real Presence although it *was* clearly proposed to their faith in Scripture. However different in other respects, the Reformed and the Papists occupied common ground in refusing to let Scripture *alone* determine the content of Christian doctrine. The question was simply this: Ought a man be conscience-bound to accept God's revelation on every point at its face value, in its clear, grammatical, literal sense, without any interpretive additions, subtractions, or "clarifications"? Luther insisted upon this position. Zwingli's refusal to do so in spite of the unmistakably clear words "This is My body" fully justified Luther in saying: "You have a different spirit from ours." They did indeed, since despite their disagreement Zwingli, with tears in his eyes, asked those to make common cause with him whose doctrine of the Lord's Supper he condemned in terms we have no desire to repeat.

Many were depressed by the failure of the Marburg meeting and felt that a severe blow had been dealt the cause of the Gospel. But Luther returned to Wittenberg in the spirit of that

---

[35] See Se, A 973; K-K, M:II, 121 sq.   [36] In Sc, C 610, n. 1.

optimism which usually dominated him. He had learned to bear up and to look up under such apparent checks and failures. To Franz von Sickingen he had written in 1521 about the stubborn, blind papists: "They are so obstinate that they will neither hear nor consider. Ah, well, I have seen bubbles on the water before now, and once I saw an ambitious smoke cloud set itself to quench the sun; but the smoke is gone, and the sun still shines. I will keep on polishing up the truth and putting it forth." [37] *"Nebula est, transibit,"* one of the early Fathers had said of the Christian persecutions of his day: "It is a cloud, it will pass over." Just as firmly Martin Luther was convinced that, however lowering the skies might look at times, the cause of Christ and His Gospel would ultimately gain the victory. The Reformer somewhere says: God's ways are like Hebrew books; they can be understood only by reading them forward from the *end;* then they show a beneficent plan and prove to the believer's entire satisfaction that "He hath done all things well." The optimism of Luther was also a fruit of his great faith.

And the fruit of his optimism was his general cheerfulness. We once read in a biography on John Calvin that he regarded loud laughter as being very objectionable. Luther did not share this view. Perhaps he thought of Solomon's proverb, "A cheerful heart is a good medicine," [38] when he wrote: "A cheerful mind is a greater comfort than much riches." Also in this respect Luther practiced what he preached: he was usually cheerful. The first description we have of him contains this testimony of an eyewitness: "In daily life and manners he is cultivated and affable, having nothing of the stoic and nothing supercilious about him. . . . He is a joker in society, vivacious and sure, always with a happy face." [39] To the great disgust of his enemies, the sanctimonious ones and others, this trait continued. When a severe sickness overtook him in 1527 and he reviewed his life as in the presence of death, he said to his pastor confessor, Bugenhagen,

---

[37] S-J, LC II:40 f.

[38] Prov. 17:22 (American version).   [39] S-J, LC I:261.

that he had at times resolved to put on a more dignified front in place of his unconventional cheerfulness and playfulness. He thought such a serious demeanor might have made a greater impression on the world; but, said he, God simply had not given him the ability to put on airs.[40] We suspect Luther did not try very hard. Why should he? He believed that "true piety is as cheerful as the day." One evening he exclaimed: "Ah, how gladly I should like to have been with the Lord Christ when upon some occasion He was joyful." [41] Luther held that genuine cheerfulness is an integral part of piety; wherefore he wrote: "God loveth not heaviness . . . He hateth . . . heavy and sorrowful cogitations and loveth cheerful hearts. For therefore hath He sent His Son . . . to cheer up our souls in Him; for this cause the Prophets, the Apostles, and Christ Himself do exhort us, yea, they command us to rejoice and be glad." [42] After quoting pertinent passages he continues: "Where this joy of spirit is, there the heart . . . outwardly expresseth [it] with words and gestures."

LUTHER HAD HIS MOMENTS OF SADNESS AND SORROW

Luther thought a permanently sad Christian an abnormality. Seasons of sadness would, of course, come to the Christian too. But he would strive to do what only a child of God can do: smile a smile of genuine joy through the very tears of a temporary sorrow. How often the Reformer was called upon to do this! At times he found it difficult. He had his seasons of sadness and depression, especially in later years. The marvel is that he did not have more of them, that the burdens resting upon his shoulders did not take all the joy of life out of him. He recognized such spells of depressions as temptations of the devil. "Sadness," he told his table companions, "is a tool and an instrument of the devil by which he effects much." [43] Again he told them: "The devil is the spirit of sadness, but God is the Spirit of joy, who saves us. We have more occasion for joy than for sadness; for

---

[40] K-K, M II:168 f.   [42] Lu, G 494.
[41] K-K, M II:515.   [43] Erl 60:169.

we believe in the living God, and Christ lives, and we shall live also." [44]

The last quotation indicates how Luther sought to dispel the spirit of gloom and sadness. He turned to the Word of God for light and comfort. At times, after depressing news had arrived, he would take his beloved Psalter and retire to his study for a period of prayer and wrestling with God. He would reappear with a tear-stained face but a resigned and confident look. "Through Christ and prayer such [depressing] thoughts are to be driven away, and God's Word dispels sadness," he once remarked.[45] But in this very passage he added that occasionally he had found it difficult to rid himself of his depression. In that event, he informs us elsewhere, he would seek the company of cheerful people, or he would make love to his wife — to the horror (?) of his monkish critics — or he would turn to music to relieve the tension. Luther believed that low spirits are at times the result of physical or nervous disorders. And indeed he often had reason enough to suspect that the condition of his body was responsible for the lowness of his spirits, and that the burden of care upon his heart was not without effect upon his general health. He once said: "If the heart is worried and sad, weakness of the body will follow." [46] Precisely how much Luther's poor health had to do with his periods of depression it is perhaps impossible to determine.

The nervous strain upon the Reformer must certainly have been very great. He never spared himself, worked incessantly, and, especially in his earlier years, before his marriage, would literally drag himself, utterly fatigued, to his unmade bed. For years his meals were far from what they ought to have been for a man working under such pressure. Of recreation there was practically none at this time. Even the soundest nervous system cannot take such punishment without finally showing signs of exhaustion. It is therefore not surprising to hear Luther complain before long about spells of dizziness and buzzing noises in his

---

[44] Wal XXII:305.   [45] Wal XXII:803.   [46] Erl 61:406.

head, besides other disorders.[47] But he was not a born neurotic, who imagined himself afflicted with all sorts of ailments because he discovered in himself what his apprehension construed to be their symptoms. His soberness and common sense were revealed, for instance, in 1529, when Wittenberg was threatened with the "English sweat." Luther wrote to Nicolaus Hausmann at this time: "Many think it is epidemic here also, but I do not believe it. Our prefect has made himself ill with his own imagination, though he showed no other symptoms of illness except his own ideas. . . . Even last night I broke out in a sweat and awoke in distress, and my thoughts began to trouble me; if I had given way to them I should have taken to my bed, as others, who make martyrs of themselves, have done." [48] It was certainly not necessary for Luther to draw upon his imagination to make him feel miserable. "I am a veritable Lazarus," he once remarked, "greatly tried by sickness." [49] He was right. "Luther, from his fortieth year onwards, was a sick man. After he had suffered for six months, in 1521, from severe digestive troubles, he was attacked in 1523 by a nervous affection of the head, which soon became permanent. In 1526 he developed a severe stone in the kidneys, with all possible accompaniments — feverish rheumatism, sciatic conditions, boils, etc. In addition to this he suffered very frequently from obstinate catarrh and digestive trouble, also, transitorily, from hemorrhoids (1525), dysentery (1528), a running inflammation of the ears (1537) which for weeks deprived him of sleep and hearing, toothache, and fearful nervous constriction of the chest (1527)." [50] Luther's death was caused by a heart attack in 1546.

LUTHER'S "SICKROOM PHILOSOPHY"

When Luther entered the cloister in 1505, he subjected his body to the ascetic discipline of monkery with such relentless conscientiousness that he permanently weakened his constitution and sowed the seeds of later disorders. As a pious monk he strove

---

[47] See Erl 61:404, 409.
[48] S-J, LC II:492 f.
[49] Erl 61:407.
[50] Bo, L 186.

to drive the sin out of his soul by making his body suffer. The practice was rooted — as were other features of monasticism — in a pagan philosophy according to which the material and sensuous are the seat of moral evil. Most of the sicknesses with which the Reformer became afflicted more or less throughout his life were those to which a sedentary life together with intense mental application particularly expose a man. Thus he wrote to his confidant Spalatin from his "Isle of Patmos," his Wartburg retreat: "The trouble with which I suffered at Worms has not left me but increased, for I am more constipated than ever in my life and despair of a remedy. The Lord thus visits me that I may not be without a relic of the cross. Blessed be He. Amen." [51] We quote this letter in particular because it reveals Luther's "sickroom philosophy." The Doctor held that, as everything else in life, sickness is in the hands of the Lord. When He sees fit, He sends it; upon His command it will leave. At the same time it was Luther's opinion that in the actual infliction of the visitation God used the devil as an instrument. Naturally, as the case of Job proved, Satan could go no step farther than God permitted him to go. Luther expressed himself thus: "God sends no sickness into the world but through the devil; for all sadness or sickness comes from the devil, not from God. But God ordains it and permits it to happen. . . . Whatever pertains to death is the devil's handiwork, trick, and machination; again, whatever pertains to life is God's grace and benefaction." [52] Luther thus correctly held that sickness and disease are not merely natural phenomena to be accounted for entirely on materialistic grounds.

But he also was no enthusiast; he did not hold that a Christian ought to be too spiritual to use grossly materialistic remedies, such as drugs and chemicals. Luther was frequently attended by a physician. Of the medical profession he said: "Doctors consider only the natural causes in sicknesses . . . and want to help with their medicines; and they are right in acting thus." [53] However, parenthetically it may be remarked that also the Reformer did

---

[51] S-J, LC II:43.　　　　[52] Erl 61:406.　　　　[53] Erl 61:414.

not always follow the directions of his doctor. Throughout his life he had an independent and original way of treating his complaints. During his boyhood he once lay sick of a fever. The then medical profession considered the drinking of water by a patient who was running a temperature well-nigh fatal. Luther's parents were gone. Young Martin now took matters into his own hands. He dragged himself to the water bucket, drank freely, returned to his bed, fell into a deep sleep, and perspired profusely. Upon the return of his parents he awoke. The fever had left him. A miracle, perhaps thought the parents. Young Martin said nothing. During his severe sickness at Smalkald he had been put on a diet that seemed altogether too strict to him. His hostess was of the same persuasion and asked him what he would like to eat. He called for cold peas and fried herring, thoroughly enjoyed them, slept soundly after the meal, and apparently was none the worse for the experiment.[54] Luther somewhere says: "I eat what I please and suffer what I must." His faith in the medical profession was not very great; and it is true, the layman of Luther's day often knew as much about his disorder as did the physician, and applied time-honored and homemade remedies that would cure him or kill him as slowly or quickly as those of the professional man. When Luther was suffering excruciating torture from the stone at Smalkald in 1537, his wife recommended a mixture of garlic and horse dung. Luther wrote to her: "Your medicine did not help me." The words imply that he tried it. Martin Luther was a courageous man.

He was on the whole a patient and resigned sufferer. Towards the end of his life, when he hardly passed a day without pain, he showed some of the irritableness and querulousness which are so common in the aged. In point of years, indeed, he could hardly be called old, but at fifty-five he had done more, preached, taught, written, prayed, and fought more than most men have at seventy. Luther was no doubt prematurely old. But we never hear him question the justice of God during the throes of his

---

[54] Erl 61:408.

affliction. He never asked in rebellious impatience why God put him through such a painful schooling although he had served Him so devotedly. The thoughts he most frequently expressed during a siege of sickness were, first, that what Christ endured for us was infinitely more agonizing than anything we may be called upon to bear and, secondly, that sickness and suffering are to draw and drive us closer to God and His Word of grace. If the trials of life are used aright, they are steppingstones to a closer communion with God. It is to be doubted whether even the religion-centered Luther would have become the mighty man of prayer he was if his life had run more smoothly.

LUTHER CALLED MEN BACK TO CHRISTIAN PRAYER

In a very real sense Luther may be called the restorer of Christian prayer. The emphasis is on the word "Christian." There was enough and to spare of what passed as prayer before the restoration of the Gospel. But most of these prayers were abominable idolatry. Christ had been crowded out of the hearts of men, and His virgin mother had been put into His place. In a popular medieval prayer book, also referred to by Luther and called *The Little Garden of the Soul,* the following supplications are found: "O Mary, thou mediator between God and men, make of thyself the medium between the righteous God and me, a poor sinner! . . . O Mary, thou restorer of lost grace to all men, restore unto me my lost time, my sinful and wasted life!" [55] The prayer is much longer, but we have no desire to quote any more of it. Such gross idolatry alone were enough to justify, nay, to demand, a reformation. Is it James Froude who somewhere says: The Church of Rome had forsaken Christianity and degenerated into Maryanity? We say nothing of the lesser saints. Here was the re-establishment of the Roman pantheon with Christian nomenclature and adaptations.

Against this abomination Luther testified. He had experienced in his own soul that the "saints" were poor comforters indeed.

---

[55] In Tr., Introd., 66 b.

The dawn of day would look into his little cell and would often find him kneeling at the foot of his bed, his head resting upon his folded arms. He had been there for hours, praying to saint upon saint. Would they never hear and mediate peace of soul for him? Then, finally, he found Him who had said: "Come unto *Me*, all ye that labor and are heavy laden, and *I* will give you rest"; and again: "No man cometh unto the Father but by *Me*." [56] Through Him alone Luther henceforth went directly to the Father, and throughout the rest of his busy life he spent many precious hours in communion with Him in fervent prayer. Nor did he ever tire of preaching that only prayer offered in the name of Jesus moves the heart of the Father. Thus he wrote: "Without faith no one is able to pray a solitary letter that is worth anything before God and is acceptable to Him." [57] In 1523 he wrote to the Waldensians concerning the nature and purpose of the Lord's Supper. Towards the end of this treatise he said: "Of the intercession, adoration, and prayer to the departed saints there is nothing in Scripture. No one can deny that we have by such saint worship now come to the point where we have made utter idols of the Mother of God and the saints and have comforted ourselves more with them than with Christ Himself." [58]

After Luther had found Christ, his prayer life became as Christ-centered as his theology, as, indeed, his entire life. It is interesting, to say the least, to read the advice he gave a man who had asked him how to pray. Luther wrote: "Dear Master Peter, I shall give you the best advice I have and shall tell you how I myself conduct my praying. Our Lord God grant that you and every man may do it better. Amen. First, when I feel that because of distracting business or thoughts I have become cold and disinclined toward praying . . . I take my precious Psalter and hasten to my room; or, if it is the proper day and time, I hasten to church to the gathered multitude (*Haufen*) and begin to recite to myself, just as children do, the Ten Commandments, the Creed and, if time permits, a number of Christ's or

---

[56] Matt. 11:28; John 14:6.   [57] Wal VIII:362.   [58] Erl 28:415.

Paul's verses or Psalms. Therefore it is well to let prayer be the first work in the early morning and the last work in the evening and to guard oneself with care against the false, deceptive thoughts that say: Wait a bit, after an hour I shall pray; I must first perform this or that task. For with such thoughts one gets from prayer into business matters which thereupon hold one captive so that nothing comes of prayer on that day." [59] Another method Luther occasionally employed to warm himself into the fervor of prayer he once revealed to his table companions. He told them that he would dwell in his mind upon the ingratitude and godlessness of the enemies of the Gospel. These considerations, he assured his auditors, would so thoroughly arouse and incense him that he would burst forth into an ardent prayer to the Lord, beseeching Him to hallow His name, establish His kingdom, etc.[60]

In the advice given to Master Peter, Luther called prayer "work." He did so elsewhere. In his *Treatise on Good Works* he said: "Where now are they who desire to know and to do good works? Let them undertake prayer alone and rightly exercise themselves in faith, and they will find that it is true, as the holy Fathers have said, that there is no work like prayer. Mumbling with the mouth is easy . . . but with earnestness of heart to follow the words in deep devotion, that is, with desire and faith, so that one earnestly desires what the words say, and not to doubt that it will be heard: that is a great deed in God's eyes." [61] How true it is that "there is no work like prayer," Luther had himself experienced, particularly before he rested his faith entirely on Him of whom Paul says: "All the promises of God in Him are yea and in Him Amen." [62] After Luther had discovered the glorious certainty of sonship in Christ, he looked also at prayer with different eyes. He still felt that the best of our praying is not what it ought to be, but he could write: "The prayer of the Christian which is offered in faith in God's promises and sincerely presents the Christian's trouble, is easy and causes

---

[59] Erl 23:215.　　[60] Erl 60:107 f.　　[61] Ho I:230.　　[62] 2 Cor. 1:20.

no work."[63] Luther held that Christian prayer is the simple pleading of a child with its parent, whose love and care and understanding are among life's firmest convictions.

Close friends of Luther have recorded that he was in the habit of praying aloud to himself and that, especially in the evening, he loved to stand or kneel before the open window and there offer his prayers.[64] Did the darkness and the deep silence of the night have a soothing and quieting effect upon the troubled spirit of this man, who all the day long fought the battles of the Lord with wicked men and the devils of hell? Did he look up to the starry heavens and long to be quit of this world with its sin and sorrow, its unbelief and ungodliness, its ingratitude and incorrigibleness? Otherworldliness, heavenly homesickness was, as we have seen, an outstanding trait in Luther's character. But we venture to say that when Martin Luther poured out his big soul to his heavenly Father, he asked Him first of all and above all to give him strength to carry on in the face of all odds and to "preach in season and out of season" the saving truth as it is revealed in the Christ of God's infallible Book. Melanchthon once remarked that he had often surprised Luther at his prayers and had found him pleading with God for His Church, while tears were running over his furrowed cheeks. Luther never apologized for the tears. To a generation like ours, which sheds its tears — if it has any to shed — in theaters over a lover's frustration or over the physical misery of men, Luther's tears over the *spiritual* misery of men, who in their stubborn folly frustrate the plan of God's love and play and dance their way into the hell they deride, must seem very strange. In 1520 Luther wrote: "There is need every hour without ceasing to pray everywhere with tears of blood to God, who is so terribly angry with men. And it is true that it has never been more necessary to pray than at this time, and it will be more so from now on to the end of the world."[65] Will our generation listen to these solemn words? And will it act on them? The shadows are getting long.

---

[63] Erl 43:177 f.   [64] K-K, M II:514, 621.   [65] Ho I:237.

A few unburdenings of Luther's soul have been preserved
for us. They affect us deeply. We almost feel as though we were
rudely breaking in upon a strictly confidential, a sacred communion between a soul and its God. But the depth of devotion,
the childlike candor, the heroic faith that are to be found in these
prayers justified their publication. These characteristics of Luther's prayers have endeared him to thousands, and have made
the many shorter and general prayers which he has written the
favorites of many generations of God's children.[66] If ever we
feel "cold and disinclined to praying," we need but read some
of Luther's wrestlings with his God. They ought to warm the
coldest and soften the hardest heart.

Perhaps even Luther never lived through more critical days
than those at the Diet of Worms. He fully realized that not
merely his fate but that of the entire cause of Christ lay trembling
in the balance. In the spirit of that grand self-effacement, which
we shall yet give its due credit, his heart and mind were filled
with deep concern for "his Gospel." To his God he takes his
troubles. From Him he receives the moral courage not to retract
a word, not to retreat an inch, unless Scripture bids him do so.
Historians and biographers have practically exhausted their vocabulary in praise of Luther's heroic stand at Worms. Strangely
enough few have called attention to the source of this strength.
We follow the lone monk into the privacy of his room and there
see him look heavenward with those deep, black, soulful eyes
of his as if to penetrate to the very throne of the Disposer of
all things. Now he prays: "Almighty and eternal God! What
a contemptible thing this world is! And yet it causes men to
gape and stare at it. How small and slight is men's trust in God!
How tender and frail is their flesh! And how powerful and active
is the devil through the agency of his apostles and worldly
philosophers! How soon do the men of this world become disheartened, desert a cause and run the common course, the broad
way to hell that was prepared for the wicked! Their eyes are

---

[66] See Wal X:1482 sq.

fastened only upon whatsoever is splendid and powerful, grand and mighty, and upon whatsoever enjoys a great reputation. If I, too, were to turn my eyes to such things, I would be undone, the bell that is to toll my doom would already be cast.

"O God! O God! O my God! Thou who art my God, support me in this struggle against the reason and wisdom of all the world. Do it! Thou must do it, Thou alone. This affair is not mine, but Thine. I have no personal business here with these great lords of the world. Indeed, I, too, would spend my days in undisturbed comfort and peace. But, O Lord, this affair is Thine, and it is righteous and of eternal importance. Stand by me, Thou faithful and eternal God! I rely upon no man. Such confidence were futile and vain; for all that is carnal and smacks of the flesh is lame and halting.

"O God, O God! Dost Thou not hear me, my God? Art Thou dead? Nay! Thou canst not die. Thou merely hidest Thyself. Hast Thou chosen me for this task? I ask Thee; for I know of a certainty that Thou hast indeed chosen me. Then be it so. Thy will, O God, be done. For never in my life had I in mind to oppose such great lords, and I never had such an intention.

"O my God, stand by me in the name of Thy dear Son Jesus Christ, who shall be my Protector and Defender, yea, my mighty Fortress, through the power and strengthening bestowed by Thy Holy Spirit.

"Lord, where dost Thou keep Thyself? O my God, where art Thou? Come, oh, come! I am ready to lay down my life, meek as a lamb. For the cause is righteous and it is Thine. Therefore I shall not part from Thee forever. Be that decision made in Thy name. The world will have to leave my conscience unconquered, even though it were filled with devils, and though my body, which is the work and creature of Thy hands, should be utterly ruined. Nevertheless Thy Word and Spirit will be a sweet compensation to me. After all, only the body is concerned; the soul is Thine and belongs to Thee. It will remain with Thee eternally. Amen. God, help me! Amen." [67]

This mighty prayer *was* answered, and in immortal words Luther gave the representatives of the world of his days and all subsequent times "a reason of the hope that was within him."

But the struggle had now only been fairly begun. Many more battles were to be fought. For Luther himself the enforced retreat at the Wartburg followed. This confinement was almost a greater strain on his spirit, eager to do battle for the Lord and His Christ, than the dangers of open conflict. He returned to Wittenberg in 1522. Lowering clouds began to rise on the political horizon. The Lutherans were requested to present their views of the matters in dispute in writing at the Diet of Augsburg in 1530. Luther, excommunicated, banned, outlawed, dared not attend. In the near-by castle of Coburg he, as Moses on the mountaintop, held up his arms in prayer for those who, as Joshua, were doing battle for the Lord. A few intimates were with Luther, among them Veit Dietrich. On June 30 he wrote to Melanchthon at Augsburg about Luther: "I cannot sufficiently admire that man's unique constancy, joy, confidence, and hope in these days of most sore distress. And daily he nourishes them by diligent contemplation of the Word of God. Not a day passes in which he does not spend in prayer at least three hours, such as are most precious for study. On one occasion I chanced to hear him pray. Good Lord, what a spirit, what faith spoke out of his words! He prayed with such reverence that one could see he was speaking with God and withal with such faith and confidence as is shown by one who is speaking with his father and friend. 'I know,' said he, 'that Thou art our Father and our God. Therefore I am certain that Thou wilt confound those who persecute Thy children. If Thou dost not do it, the danger is Thine as well as ours. For the entire matter is Thine own. We were compelled to take hold of it; mayest Thou therefore also protect it.' Standing at a distance, I heard him praying in this manner with a loud voice.

---

[67] Wal X:1420 ff.; Erl 64:289 f.

Then my heart, too, burned mightily within me, when he spoke so familiarly, so earnestly, and reverently with God, and in his prayer insisted on the promises in the Psalms, as one who was certain that everything he prayed for would be done. Hence I do not doubt that his prayer will prove a great help in the desperately bad affair of this Diet." [68] It did prove a great help, and Luther said he thanked God that he had been permitted to see the day on which the truth had been publicly read before Emperor and hierarchy and its very enemies had to listen to its proclamation.

LUTHER'S FIRM CONFIDENCE IN THE POWER OF PRAYER

If one were called upon to single out the most prominent characteristic in these prayers of the Reformer, one would be tempted to choose their heroic confidence, the conviction that God not only may hear and help but that He surely would do so, nay, that He *must* do so, because He has pledged Himself to it in His own Word. This taking God at His word, this holding Him to His promises, is the secret of Luther's success in his praying. He therefore often remarked that he had prayed the Reformation to success. "Let happen what will," he once exclaimed, "we succeed in everything through prayer, which alone is the omnipotent empress. Through prayer we guide what has been decided upon, correct what has gone wrong, bear what cannot be remedied, overcome all misfortune and receive everything that is good." [69]

Someone has said: Faith moves to prayer, and prayer moves the hand that moves the world. Because of his firm faith in the power of prayer Luther so often asked others to remember him in their supplications. Many of his letters close with the brief petition: "Pray for me." Nor was this merely a conventional close, which had lost much of its meaning for both writer and addressee, as our modern "good-by," which is a contraction of the wish "God be with ye" and perhaps means little more to the average users than the termination of their communication for the present. In

---

[68] Wal XVI:1762 f. (tr. Tr., Introd., 38 a).   [69] K-K, M II:514.

1527 the plague (*Pest*) ravaged Wittenberg. The conscientious Luther stayed to care for the sick and dying. To his friend Hausmann he wrote: "I beseech you for Christ's sake that you stand by me with your prayers against Satan and his angels, who are hostile to me beyond measure, so that Christ, who has hitherto chosen me for the furtherance of His Gospel, does not forsake me but glorifies His name in my weakness either by my death or by my life. I do not request this without reason; for I need the prayers and help of the brethren." [70] He was constantly exposed to the dread disease, and some of its victims died practically in his arms. That the strain was beginning to tell on him appears from a letter to another friend. "Implore God for me," he pleads, "whom Satan's angel is buffeting, that Christ does not forsake me." [71]

But the Reformer did not only desire others to serve him with their prayers; he, in turn, was ever ready to be of assistance to them. Luther the monk, it is true, appears to have been rather self-centered. Indeed, he confesses as much. He tells us that by nature he was "inclined to crawl into some corner" and devote himself to study, letting the world take care of itself.[72] But when the Gospel with all its implications began to dawn upon him in the cloister, the glorified selfishness of monkery made him uneasy; and he began to think what he preached and taught and lived so consistently in later years: "Cursed and damned is all life that is lived and sought for its own benefit and good." [73] Henceforth his life was to be a life of service. In 1520 Luther wrote his *Treatise on Christian Liberty,* which he correctly evaluated thus: "Unless I am deceived, it is the whole of Christian living in a brief form." In this classic the Reformer says: "Thus from faith flow forth love and joy in the Lord, and from love a joyful, willing, and free mind that serves one's neighbor willingly and takes no account of gratitude or ingratitude, of praise or blame, of gain or loss. For a man does not serve that he may put men under obligations; he

---

[70] K-K, M II:173.   [72] In Wa, L 53.

[71] K-K, M II:174.   [73] Wal X:407.

does not distinguish between friends and enemies, nor does he anticipate their thankfulness or unthankfulness; but most freely and most willingly he spends himself and all that he has, whether he waste all on the thankless or whether he gain a reward." Towards the close of this treatise he says: "We conclude, therefore, that a Christian man lives not in himself but in Christ and in his neighbor. Otherwise he is not a Christian. He lives in Christ through faith, in his neighbor through love; by faith he is caught up beyond himself into God, by love he sinks down beneath himself into his neighbor; yet he always remains in God and in His love." [74] If these expressions sound a bit mystical, Luther's life demonstrated their practicableness. For it is no exaggeration to say that he unwittingly drew his own pen portrait by these words. This was Luther. Nor was it long before men discovered his kindly heart and his willingness to serve his fellow men. When a growing influence with the high and mighty was added to this accessibility, he became, as was to be expected, a man much sought after. And "the latch of his door was always hanging out."

Luther interceded for others about the most varied matters imaginable. In 1519 he sent a man to the Elector's secretary, his close friend Spalatin, with a letter in which there was this: "The bearer of this letter begs me to write to the Elector for him for license to exercise the baker's craft at Wittenberg. For I hear that the bakers have forbidden him to do so because he is son of a bathman; so exclusive is the nobility of tradesmen. Lest I should annoy the Elector, I ask you to make this petition to him, in my name, if you wish." [75]

Particularly a certain Pfaffenbeck was a very persistent suitor for Luther's help. The Elector seems to have had ample reason to treat this man severely. But his plight touched the heart of Luther. He thereupon wrote a letter in his behalf which is a revelation at once of Luther's willingness to serve others, though they had no personal claim whatever upon him, and of his candid,

---

[74] Ho II:338, 342 f.   [75] S-J, LC I:218.

unconventional approach to those in high places. Plainly speaking, it is a request for bread and butter, but the offensive spirit of begging does not appear. Luther wrote: "I fall at Your Grace's feet and humbly ask Your Grace to have pity on this poor man, and at least support him in his old age until his death. It is no good to let him be ruined and forced into beggary, for I observe that his poverty distresses him so that he may lose his mind. God has more Schneebergs [silver mines], and Your Grace's dominions need not fear that they will be impoverished by charity; it has never happened so before. The saying is true, *Date et dabitur vobis* ('Give and it shall be given you,' Luke 6:38); if the *date* is rich, *dabitur* is far richer, and to whom much is given, of him shall much be required.

"Your Grace may be sure that I shall not leave the man in this state, even though I have to go out and beg for him myself. If that does no good, I shall even rob and steal the first thing I lay my hands on, especially if it belongs to the Elector of Saxony. Therefore I ask Your Grace graciously to hear this my request for my own sake, so that I may not have to go to stealing. I would not like Your Grace to hang me for stealing one of the treasures of the Castle Church [a relic] to help this man's need.

"I hope that Your Grace will not take this thirsty [*sic! thuerstig* = bold] or foolish letter of mine amiss." [76]

It is astounding to think of the precious time the overburdened Reformer must have consumed to pen his many letters of intercession. There are letters extant that ask the Elector or some affluent friend to give clothing to one man, money to another, and employment to a third. Luther requests subsidies for needy students and higher salaries for poor pastors. To his friend Link he wrote: "You complain in your last letter that I have not answered your questions. Do not be surprised at my failure to do so. I am daily so overwhelmed with letters that my table, my chairs, benches, footstools, windows, chests, bookcases, and everything

[76] S-J, LC II:117 f.

else lie full of letters, questions, legal matters, complaints, petitions, etc." [77]

However, it were unfair to Luther to imagine that he used his influence to get his friends into prominent and lucrative positions irrespective of their qualifications. He once wrote to Spalatin: "I have promised Mattis Buchbinder that he shall be bridge master of Wittenberg when the present incumbent dies, if the thing is possible. He is a poor man and needs it, but if there is someone else better qualified, I do not wish to urge his appointment. Do whatever you can and think you ought." [78]

LUTHER LOVED TO SERVE OTHERS PERSONALLY

According to this last advice Luther constantly acted: He "did what he could and thought he ought" to help others. And he could do much and thought he ought to do still more. The man's openhandedness and hospitality were nothing short of amazing. A certain Gospel preacher by the name of Stiefel had to flee from Austria. Luther took him into his home and supported him for more than seven months.[79] For almost as long a time a refugee monk, who could find no ready placement, was Luther's guest. The Doctor never dreamed of dismissing his eccentric, lame, indolent servant Wolfgang Sieberger, although his usefulness became negligible. Aunt Lena was faithfully provided for to her very end. His hospitable home became the refuge of all needy and orphaned relatives. More than ten destitute nephews and nieces were provided for by Luther. Indeed, at times the Doctor's liberality caused his frugal and thrifty "Lord Katie" moments of concern. On one occasion, while she was in confinement, Luther gave away even the silverware presented to his children at baptism by their sponsors. To his wife's demurrings or objections he might reply: "We have a wealthy Father; He will provide," or again: "They travel best who travel lightly laden." He was known to have sold or pawned rings, plated cups, and other articles of value in order to relieve the sorely distressed.

---

[77] In Wa, L 60. [78] S-J, II:121. [79] Erl 56:xix; 54:34.

Luther's openhandedness was, of course, abused at times. It might be found that he had shown hospitality to the undeserving or given money to the unworthy. But such discoveries never made the man close his hand or his home to the needy. Indeed, "he did what he could and thought he ought" to serve his fellow man. And it was said "his Gospel" of free grace would make people morally indolent!

But did not Luther himself at times complain that the fruits of faith were not what they should have been? Did he not, towards the end of his life, become so disgusted with conditions at his own Wittenberg that he was about to leave the place forever?[80] Yes. But these facts are to be attributed in part to Luther's optimism, which led him to expect a more rapid improvement in life and morals than actually came about, in part to the sad circumstance that many had accepted "his Gospel" only outwardly and nominally — for which *they* were to blame, not the Gospel — and in part to that tendency of oncoming old age which sees especially the darker sides of life or the growing conviction of the experienced Christian that the world at large wants neither the Law nor the Gospel of God and becomes steadily worse and more hardened in sin and unbelief. Had Luther's character been less intense, had he loved the Gospel less ardently and hated sin less deeply, his life might have been far more undisturbed. But as matters stood with him, his deep emotional response to the weal and woe of mankind helped to wear him out prematurely.

Luther's impressionable heart went out to men in sympathy. Emotionally he lived the lives of his friends in addition to his own life. And he had the necessary prerequisite for genuine sympathy, sympathy in the etymological sense of the word: the emotional ability to appreciate what the sufferer is enduring. How frequently his own body was racked by pain, has been pointed out. What he endured spiritually was, if anything, still more agonizing and trying. Consequently his many letters of sympathy to sufferers of every kind rang true.[81] There was noth-

---

[80] K-K, M II:571 f., 607 f.   [81] See Erl 54:130, 232.

ing conventional about them, as though they were form letters, nothing coldly impersonal, as the printed cards of sympathy one buys in gift shops. One sensed that they had been written by a man who really entered into one's own sorrow, who wrote because the iron had entered also into his soul and who therefore appreciated what it meant to suffer.

Aside from his many letters of sympathy, letters to students and ministers and widows and princes and all sorts of bereaved, his writings abound with short remarks which are to the soul what cooling water is to parched lips. It was to be expected that Luther would be particularly adept at comforting the spiritually depressed. Perhaps he was thinking of his own experience when he once preached to his Wittenbergers: "He who has not felt the battle within him, is not distressed by his sins nor has a daily quarrel with them, and wishes no protector, defender, and shield to stand before him, is not yet ready for this food (the comfort of the Gospel). This food demands a hungering and longing man, for it delights to enter a hungering soul, one that is in constant battle with its sins and eager to be rid of them. . . . This bread is a comfort for the sorrowing, a healing for the sick, a life for the dying, a food for all the hungry, and a rich treasure for all the poor and needy." [82] Who would know this better from personal experience than the ex-monk Martin Luther?

HIS GENEROUS PRAISE OF MELANCHTHON

And he knew that he knew it. We mean that Luther was well aware of the fact that few, if any, of his contemporaries understood more clearly and entered more deeply the spirit of the Gospel than did he. We have seen above that Luther appreciated his own gifts and talents. The marvel is that despite this clear recognition of his greatness and historical significance the man was so genuinely modest. This may seem to be a psychological impossibility. We are not concerned about that difficulty. Our concern is to record that in the character of Martin Luther were present both self-appreciation and modesty. An interesting com-

---

[82] Ho II:418 f.

bination, no doubt, and the more so when we observe that both traits were very genuine and very strong. In a letter which Luther wrote to John Lang occurs a brief reference to Melanchthon which is a typical illustration of these two traits of the Reformer's unique character. Luther wrote: "This little Greek beats *me* even in theology."[83] No doubt Melanchthon's lectures on Matthew's Gospel, to which Luther had referred, were well done, but "the little Greek" lacked both the theological depth and the inspiring presentation of a Luther. He was in reality a philologist and a philosopher. But Luther modestly places him above himself even in theology. However, it is to be observed that the honest Martin considers this a notable elevation. "Melanchthon beats me even in theology," says he. There is the candid self-appreciation of the modest man.

We shall remain with "the little Greek" for a moment. Unfortunately, professional jealousy is rather common. At first Melanchthon was a member of the philosophical, not of the theological faculty of the university at Wittenberg. He had enjoyed no graduate training in theology and held no doctorate in this field. But he became increasingly interested in theology, received the Bachelor of Divinity degree in 1519, and in 1521 published what has been called the first Lutheran dogmatics, his *Loci Communes*. Professional men have often shown themselves very sensitive to such a trespassing upon their department by an outsider. But Luther was so delighted with Melanchthon's work that he said: "I find no book among all other books in which the summary of religion and all theology are found so happily put together. After Holy Writ there is no book that is better than this one. . . . Philip is more concise than I am. He is a polemicist and a teacher. I am more of a rhetorician and prattler (*Waescher*)."[84] From the very beginning of his acquaintance with Melanchthon, Luther thought very highly of Philip's gifts. In 1520, the year before the publication of the *Loci*, the Doctor wrote: "Philip is theologizing most happily, lecturing, as a first attempt, and yet with incredible success to almost five hundred auditors on Paul's Epistle to the

---

[83] S-J, LC I:264.　　　　[84] Erl 59:279.

Romans. . . . I do not think that for a thousand years Holy Scripture has been treated with the same simplicity and clearness, for his talent is next that of the Apostolic Age. . . . I lose these years of mine in unhappy wars and would like all my works to perish lest they should become obstacles to pure theology and better geniuses, although today I expound my philosophy without slaughter and blood. It is my fate that all evil beasts attack me alone, all seeking to win the laurel and palm from me. God grant that I may be David pouring out blood, but that Melanchthon may be Solomon reigning in peace. Amen." [85] In the same year he wrote to John Lang: "I am not able to determine my own place in the present movement; perhaps I am the harbinger of Melanchthon [!], for whom I shall, like Elias, prepare a way in spirit and in power, troubling Israel and the followers of Ahab." [86] To Melanchthon himself he wrote from the Wartburg: "Even though I should perish, the Gospel will lose nothing, for in the Gospel you are now greater than I, and are the Elisha, who succeeds Elijah with a double portion of his spirit." [87]

Nor did Luther ever cease to sing the praises of his co-worker in public. There are those who hold that he distinctly over-estimated the ability of Melanchthon to carry on the work of the Reformation after his death. History reveals their judgment to be sadly correct. Meanwhile, however, Luther wrote on his table in 1537:

Deeds and words, Melanchthon;
Words without deeds, Erasmus;
Deeds without words, Luther;
Neither words nor deeds, Carlstadt.

Melanchthon chanced to enter and read the lines. He remarked that Luther had spoken too highly of him and that he (Luther) also had words — how true! — and not only deeds.[88]

LUTHER'S PRAISE OF JOHN BRENZ

Another co-worker of Luther was John Brenz. He had sent his exposition of the Prophet Amos to the Doctor with the request critically to review and revise it. Luther replied: "My opinion of

---

[85] Sm, L 77 f.   [86] Sm, L 86.   [87] S-J, LC II:35 f.   [88] Sm, L 286.

your writings is such that my own become very contemptible to me in comparison with yours and with similar ones. I do not play the flatterer or the hypocrite. I do not jest, nor do I deceive myself. I do not praise the man Brenz, but the spirit that is more friendly, peaceable, and quiet in you than he is in me." [89] Even if one were to judge that Luther's criticism was well founded, the fact that he so generously recognized and published what was good and commendable in others, although his own standing might become less exalted thereby, reveals a magnanimous and modest character.

LUTHER'S MODEST APPRAISAL OF HIMSELF

This sincere modesty of the great man appeared also in his frequently depreciating remarks about himself, about his talents and attainments, when others praised him. The similarity even many of the Reformer's contemporaries professed to have discovered between him and Paul has frequently been the subject of comment. But Luther considered such praise an overestimation of his character and work. Upon one occasion he was told that someone had said that in a certain sense he actually preferred Luther to the Apostles. "Ah, no," cried Luther in abashment, "the Apostles were great, precious people! If God but permits me to be His lowliest servant! But I am not even that." [90] Upon another occasion he exclaimed: "If it is an apostolic gift to fight with devils and frequently to lie at death's door, I am indeed a Peter and a Paul in this respect, although other traits of mine are certainly not those of Apostles but those of malefactors, publicans, and sinners." [91]

While Luther declared the ultimate reason of his success to be the gracious blessing of God, he often attributed the lack of greater and more general success to himself. With characteristic modesty he wrote to Spalatin: "I try to do what I can for the Word; perhaps I am unworthy to accomplish anything. I also should prefer, if God willed, to be freed from teaching and

---

[89] In Wa, L 73.   [90] In Wa, L 75.   [91] In K-K, M II:176.

preaching; I am almost disgusted to see how little fruit and gratitude to God comes from it. Perhaps it is all my fault. Farewell, and pray for me." [92] These words are found in a letter bearing the date of 1520. Particularly in these earlier years Luther expressed himself very modestly about his gifts and attainments. Those who picture him to us as a cocksure, belligerent, dogmatic young man who, having discovered himself endowed with more than average gifts, forthwith developed the Messianic complex of an opinionated reformer, are certainly constructing a young Luther for us who is nowhere to be found in sober history. In later life Luther remarked that it was a good thing God had led him into the whole affair as one might lead a blinded horse, for if he had clearly seen from the outset what the movement involved, he doubted whether it would have been possible to drag him into it with a team of horses. The remark does not express any doubt on the part of Luther about the goodness of the cause of the Reformation, but it does reveal the fact that Luther did not begin the Reformation because of any personal ambition or self-assertiveness. At first he was so modestly distrustful of himself that some biographers even suspect a slight inferiority complex in him at this time. After writing his *Resolutions* in explanation of his Theses, Luther sent them (1518) to his superior, the Bishop of Brandenburg, accompanied by a letter in which he stated: "Since no one has responded to my universal challenge, and since I see that my propositions for debate have flown farther than I would have wished and were accepted everywhere not as inquiries, but as assertions, I have been compelled against my hope and intention to expose my lack of eloquence and my ignorance, and to publish my propositions with their proofs, thinking it better to jeopard my reputation than to let the propositions fly about in a form which might lead people to think they were positive assertions. For I doubt some of them, am ignorant about others, and deny some, while not positively asserting any, but submitting all to the holy Church." [93] Here we have modesty, open-mindedness, and a desire to learn.

---

[92] S-J, LC I:345.   [93] S-J, LC I:89.

After twelve years Luther *had* learned, had learned *much*, and found himself the leading theologian of his age. His opinions were cherished by many and had to be reckoned with by all. But his modesty had not left him, although he had grown immeasurably in self-reliance. In a sermon preached during 1532 he said: "It is a great art to moderate oneself and remain humble if God perchance endows one with gifts. . . . Thereupon such people speak as this Pharisee: 'I am not as other men are.' 'I do not want to hear such language from you,' says Christ to me and to you and to every one. 'That I have made you a doctor of Holy Writ and learned — these benefactions are My gifts, otherwise you would be as unlearned as yonder man. If you want to become proud because of My gifts, I can easily take them from you again.'" [94] To say that Martin Luther was at times tempted to be proud of the dizzy height to which he had risen, is simply another way of saying that the man was human. Characteristic and well known is his remark to Melanchthon that he [Melanchthon] had better not have the students in the lecture hall arise upon his [Luther's] entrance, since such a demonstration of respect always called for an additional prayer for humbleness from the busy Reformer. In a sermon preached in 1538 Luther told his audience with that childlike candor about which we shall have more to say: "Against this devil [of pride] I too have prayed constantly; and God has hitherto graciously protected me against him. I hope He will continue to protect and keep me to the end of my life. . . . My daily prayer since the beginning [of my career] is this, that I may not grow haughty, and God has hitherto answered my prayer and at times has humbled me almost more than I have been able to bear." [95]

Perhaps nothing is quite so flattering to a man as to be told that he is a born leader. There is credit in successfully managing one's own affairs, but glory beckons the chosen leader of many men. How eminently qualified Martin Luther was to be a leader has been proved in an earlier chapter.[96] But while preparing for

---

[94] Erl 5:32 f.   [95] Wal VII:1081 f.   [96] See p. 21 f. above.

his first public appearance as a defender of the principles of the Reformation at Leipzig in 1519, Luther wrote to Spalatin: "Even should I perish, nothing will be lost to the world. For my friends at Wittenberg have now progressed so far, by God's grace, that they do not need me at all. What will you? I fear I am not worthy to suffer and die for such a cause. That will be the blessed lot of better men, not of so foul a sinner. . . ." [97] Thank God, Luther did not perish. He lived to champion the cause of Scripture and the Gospel. But he also lived to warn every man against believing anything whatever to be true merely because the learned Doctor Luther had so preached and taught. [98]

LUTHER NEVER THOUGHT HIS OWN WRITINGS BEYOND IMPROVEMENT

A great general was once asked whether he would exchange his position and fame for that of any other man. He replied that he would prefer the glory of being the author of a book read by millions to the renown of being the conqueror of millions. The book, he added, would move hearts and control wills, whereas the power he wielded moved only bodies. Luther enjoyed the fame of being the most popular and influential writer of his day. Yet his own estimate of his writings is astoundingly low. In 1515 he was requested to publish his lectures on the Psalms. Many a young professor would have hurried them through the press with undisguised pride. But Luther demurred and delayed so successfully that the material was actually not printed during his lifetime. In fact, it was not published till 1876. [99] The Reformation was certainly not rooted in any Narcissus complex of Martin Luther. This modest evaluation of his own literary productions continued. In the preface to the collection of his Latin works which was published in 1545 he wrote: "I have long and earnestly resisted those who wished that my books, or rather the confused mass of my lucubrations, should be published, both because I was unwilling that the labors of the ancients should be overwhelmed by my novelties, and that my readers should be hindered from

---

[97] Sm., L 61.   [98] See p. 45 f.   [99] Wa, L 72.

reading them, and because now, through God's grace, there are a great number of methodical books — among which Philip's *Commonplaces* excel — whereby a divine and a bishop may be well and amply trained to be mighty in preaching the doctrine of godliness; more especially since the Holy Bible itself may now be had in almost every language, while my own books, as the disorderly course of events led, or rather compelled, me are themselves a sort of rude, undigested chaos, which I myself should now find it difficult to arrange. For these reasons I wished that all my books were buried in perpetual oblivion that there might be room for better ones." [100]

At the end of the preface to an earlier collection of his German works, published in 1539, there is a passage so characteristic of the modest man that we shall reproduce it here: "If you feel and fancy that you really have what it takes to be successful and are tickled about your own booklets, teachings, and writings, as though you have done splendidly and have preached excellently well, are also greatly pleased that you are praised before others, perhaps also desire to be praised or you would mourn and quit — if you are of that stripe, dear friend, take hold of your own ears, and if you grasp aright you will find a pair of large, long, rough ass's ears. Moreover, you ought then assume the expense of adorning them with golden bells so that, wherever you go, one may hear you, point the finger at you, and say: 'See! See! There goes the fine animal that can write such splendid books and can preach so excellently! Then you will be blessed and superblessed in the kingdom of heaven — yea, where hell fire has been prepared for the devil and his angels." [101]

These words are so strong that they may seem insincere to some. Was Luther proud of his humility? Only gross ignorance or malice would accuse the Reformer of this most odious form of pride. No; the severe language Luther uses when he speaks of the sin of pride is to be attributed to a large extent to his observation of the damnable results of pride within the very

---

[100] In H, V 86 f.   [101] Erl 1:71 f.

Church of the lowly Jesus. The lesson of sincere modesty and humility was one of the first to have been neglected and forgotten by Christendom. However, once "the devil of pride and the pride of the devil" had crept into the Church, the very spirit of Antichrist, the "man of sin," had come; for pride is the taproot of all sin. That is the reason why the Reformer preached and wrote and fought against it so mightily. That is the reason why he prayed so constantly for that genuine modesty and humility which perforce make a man live close to God and Christ, because he has such a lively sense of his own insufficiency and unworthiness. But Luther was not proud of the modesty he knew to be the inevitable result of an honest appraisal of one's own worth. When he invited his brother monks to the ceremony in which the degree of Doctor of Theology was to be conferred upon him, Luther wrote: "I do not accuse myself of unworthiness, lest I should seek praise and honor by my humility; God and my conscience know how grateful I am for this public honor." [102] The last sentence is important. It reveals wherein, according to Luther, true modesty and humility consist.

Luther did not believe that genuine modesty necessarily consisted in denying the possession of any superior gifts or talents. But he did hold that it meant the surrender of all thoughts of having *deserved* anything good from God. The sincerely modest and humble man is convinced that all his gifts and talents, everything good in his life no less than in his character, all virtuous dispositions, and all virtuous actions are gifts bestowed upon him and wrought in him by God without any merit or worthiness on his part. But Luther held it to be culpable ingratitude toward God not to recognize and acknowledge the blessings of head and heart which He has possibly bestowed upon us. Luther believed that a man would be guilty of insincerity if he were to deny his gifts, and of mock modesty if he were to hide and disparage them. No doubt this humble acknowledgment of the gifts of God's grace may at bottom be only a dissimulated form of vanity. But no one

---

[102] S-J, LC I:25.

can charge the candid Luther with such offensive hypocrisy. It is rather gratefully to be acknowledged that the Reformer restored the true, Scriptural concept of modesty and humility. He revealed the sanctimonious modesty and the hypocritical humility of monkery to be cheap counterfeits of papal moralists. Luther was too candid not to acknowledge the great things *God* had done for him and through him.

SOLI DEO GLORIA

And he was sincerely grateful for them. Luther's deep sense of gratitude were in and of itself sufficient to exonerate him from the charge of pride and arrogance. Proud men are rarely thankful. Why should they be? Whatever distinctions are conferred upon them, whatever blessings come to them are merely a just recognition of their superior talents and achievements. Why should one be grateful for merely receiving one's dues? think they. Luther must have been a grateful man, because he was modest. But we need not depend upon a psychological deduction to prove Luther's gratitude. In his letter on translating (1530) there is a beautiful passage which reflects both his modesty and his gratitude. Writing about the motives that actuated him in his Bible translating, he says: "Nor have I had any intention to win honor by it — that God, my Lord, knows — but I have done it as a service to the dear Christians and to the honor of One who sitteth above, who blesses me so much every hour of my life that, if I had translated a thousand times as much or as diligently, I should not deserve to live a single hour or have a sound eye. All that I am and have is of His grace and mercy, nay, of His dear blood and His bitter sweat. Therefore, God willing, all of it shall serve to His honor, joyfully and sincerely." [103]

Thomas Carlyle wrote of the Reformer: "I will call this Luther a true great man; great in intellect, in courage, affection and integrity; one of our most lovable and precious men. Great, not as a hewn obelisk; but as an Alpine mountain — so simple, honest,

---

[103] Ho V:18 f.

spontaneous, not setting up to be great at all; there for quite another purpose than being great!" [104] Carlyle's last words refer to what we should like to call Luther's spirit of self-effacement. This high-mindedness appeared clearly at the very beginning of the Reformation. If there ever was a man who meant only to do his duty conscientiously and to serve his God single-mindedly, irrespective of results for himself, that man was Martin Luther. In 1518, at the time of the Diet of Augsburg, Luther seemed to be fighting a losing battle as far at least as his personal lot was concerned. But this did not at all depress him. He wrote Spalatin: "As you know, I fear nothing. For even if their sycophancy and power should succeed in making me hateful unto all, yet my heart and conscience would tell me that all things which I have and which they attack, I have from God, to whom willingly and of my own accord I refer them, to whom I offer them. If He takes them away, let them be taken away; if He preserves them, let them be preserved, and may His name be holy and blessed forever. Amen." [105] These are not words of a man who is aflame with personal ambition.

LUTHER'S SPIRIT OF SELF-EFFACEMENT

When an Italian of note, Maria Da Pozo, wrote to his friend Francis Spinelli: "It is said the Pope will make him [Luther] cardinal to quiet him," [106] he proved once again that Rome understood neither the character of Luther nor the nature of the Reformation. To buy off Martin Luther with a paltry cardinal's hat! Still, how could the Romanists judge Luther but by themselves? However, we are glad for the intimation that at least some at Rome seemed to have doubted whether this popular mode of pacification would effectively silence the monk, for Da Pozo added: "provided he choose to accept the grade." No! Luther would have refused the very tiara of the Pope as an abomination, though he would not have hesitated to wear a crown of thorns if the interests of the Gospel of Christ would thereby have been

---

[104] Ca, H 168.   [105] S-J, LC I:109.   [106] S-J, LC II:210.

advanced. A few months after the posting of his Theses he wrote to Spalatin: "For the love of truth I entered this dangerous labyrinth of disputation and aroused against myself six hundred Minotaurs, not to say Radamanthotaurs and Aeacotaurs." [107] Minos, Radamanthus, and Aeacus were held to be the three judges of the infernal regions in Greek mythology. The bull of Minos was said to have been slain by the hero Theseus in the Labyrinth on the island Crete. Luther meant that he had aroused the powers of hell against himself. We are therefore not surprised to read that the Reformer suspected that his effort to call Christendom back to the Bible would end in his personal undoing. In 1519 he wrote to Elector Frederick, referring to the persecution suffered by Athanasius († 373) during the Arian controversy: "If God in those blessed times so tried the Church, I shall not be much surprised if a poor man like myself be suppressed. But the truth remains and will remain forever." [108]

But Luther no less than the truth continued to live and thrive. A dozen years later the Reformer's voice was eagerly listened to by millions and could not be ignored even by his enemies. Luther therefore called upon the German people to further the cause of an intelligent Christianity and citizenry by establishing Christian schools. In the beginning of the publication dedicated to this purpose Luther said: "I can boast before God with a good conscience that I am not seeking my own advantage, which I could attain far better by remaining silent, but am dealing in hearty good faith with you and with the whole German land, to which I have a divine commission, let men believe it or not." [109] Do the words: "I have a divine commission to the whole German land," betray the Messianic complex of the religious enthusiast? Not at all. The Reformer simply means to say: By having placed upon him the duties of a Christian preacher and a Doctor of Theology, God had made him responsible for the proclamation of the truth and for its defense against all enemies whatsoever. Only malice can read conceit and egoism into Luther's words. How very far

---

[107] S-J, LC I:71.   [108] S-J, LC I:154.   [109] Ho IV:104.

removed the Doctor was from the selfish ambition of the ecclesiastical racketeer who schemes to build up a large following for his own glory and advantage, appears from his famous criticism of the use of the name "Lutheran." "I ask that men make no reference to my name, and call themselves not Lutherans but Christians. What is Luther? My doctrine, I am sure, is not mine, nor have I been crucified for any one. St. Paul, in 1 Corinthians 3, would not allow Christians to call themselves Pauline or Petrine, but Christian. How, then, should I, poor, foul carcass (*Madensack*) that I am, come to have men give to the children of Christ a name derived from my worthless name? No, no, my dear friends; let us abolish all party names and call ourselves Christians after Him whose doctrine we have. The papists have a party name deservedly, because they are not content with the doctrine and the name of Christ but want to be papists as well. Let them be papists, then, since the Pope is their master. Christ alone is our Master, and He teaches me and all believers in one and the same way." [110] Luther was so incensed at hearing the Gospel called "*Lutheran* doctrine," as though it were an original, hitherto unknown theory of religion, instead of the old saving truth revealed to fallen man in Paradise, that he called *this* use of the expression "outrageous blasphemy." [111] No; Martin Luther did not fancy himself a theological genius whose mission it was to originate a new religion. His thankless task was to preach what we should like to call a reactionary progress, a return to the old ways, which were not necessarily true because they were old, but were old because they were true, because they were the saving truth "once delivered unto the saints."

LUTHER NO ECCLESIASTICAL DICTATOR

The modesty and the self-effacing spirit of Luther may also be seen by looking in another direction. Historians have called attention to the fact that all who have had the unhallowed ambition to tyrannize over the religious life of men have meticulously

---

[110] Erl 22, 55 f.; Ho III, 218 f.   [111] S-J, LC II:217.

prescribed the forms according to which this life was to conduct itself. A regimented conduct became an absolute requirement. The manifestation of religiousness had to appear in the same dress — often literally. Not only the Roman hierarchs but also the heads of other peculiar sects in and out of Christendom have forced their followers into such ecclesiastical strait jackets. Now, if the cultus of the Lutheran Church at the death of the Reformer is examined in the light of these considerations, it becomes evident that Luther entirely lacked the personal ambition of an anti-pope, another heresiarch. This becomes the more admirable when we bear in mind the original cast of Luther's mind, as reflected in his writings. Here was a man who plainly had many ideas of his own. Moreover, the forms of service as found in the Church of Rome could not always be continued in the purified Church, because many of them involved a sanctioning of false doctrines. But the ordering of the forms of worship was a matter not prescribed by Scripture to the Church of the New Testament. How easily a forceful and resourceful character might have imagined it to be not only its privilege but a sort of duty to regulate matters which — it might have feared — would end in a demoralizing chaos if something were not quickly done to insure order and uniformity! However, Luther did not take this view of the matter. He *was* relentless in his insistence upon complete conformity to the doctrines of Scripture when he placed them before a man. But he never stubbornly insisted upon the adoption of his views and preferences in matters not clearly prescribed by Holy Writ.

Luther had been largely instrumental in framing and introducing the new order of service in the congregation at Wittenberg. In 1523 he wrote an article about it in which the words occur: "But herewith we want to have hindered no one from adopting and following another [order of service]; yea, we heartily beseech every man through Christ that he ask us to discontinue the former [order], if something better be revealed to anyone, so that we all co-operate and further the common cause." [112] From

---

[112] Wal X:2234.

these words it appears that Luther was indeed interested in ultimately achieving a common order of service as a matter of Christian charity and co-operation but he would not impose one by virtue of his authority as Reformer. He acknowledged the possession of no such authority.

In 1539 Joachim of Brandenburg introduced the Reformation in a conservative spirit, retaining all the ceremonies not antagonistic to Scripture. The provost Georg Buchholzer asked Luther what he thought of the retention of these rites. Luther wrote to Berlin: "If the Margrave and Elector will have the Gospel preached in its purity, without human additions, and the two Sacraments administered according to their institution, and will discontinue the intercession of saints and the carrying of the Sacrament in procession and masses for the dead, and abolish holy water and consecrated salt and herbs, and will have pure responsories and hymns sung in processions, then let him go on in God's name, whether he have a silver or a golden cross carried, or wear a cap and gown of velvet, silk, or linen; and if one cap and gown be not enough, let him put on three, like Aaron; and if one procession be not enough, let him go round seven times, like Joshua; and if the Margrave should care about dancing with the music of harps and cymbals, as David did before the Ark, I am satisfied. For such things neither add anything to the Gospel nor remove anything from it, if only they be not regarded as necessary for salvation or made a matter of conscience." [113]

Of the absence of personal ambitions and selfish aims in Luther's entire career Alexander Bower has well said: "[Luther's] opposition [to Rome] bears no mark of selfish motives. It implies, on the contrary, a relinquishment and forfeiture of professional advancement. In all Luther's proceedings, various as they are, in his preachings, his treatises, and disputations, we discern no step taken for the gratification of personal advantage. All is disinterested and zealous, all is prompted by an anxiety to understand and promulgate the Word of God." [114]

---

[113] Wal XIX:1026 f. (abridged).   [114] Bow, L 282.

CHAPTER VIII

A MAN WITH HIS HEART ON HIS SLEEVE

Open as the sky, bold and fearless as the storm, he gave utterance to all his feelings, all his thoughts.   *J. Hare*, chaplain of Queen Victoria

SOME WAG HAS SAID: DIPLOMACY IS THE FINE ART OF SPEAKING in order to hide your thoughts. If this be true, Martin Luther would have made a very poor diplomat. He could hide nothing. No one ever remained in doubt very long as to what Luther thought and as to how he felt about a matter or a person. His straightforwardness at times bordered on indiscretion. At other times his frankness was almost brutal. It is not our intention carefully to evaluate this trait of the Reformer's character. There are not a few, even of his friends, who hold that Luther might often have gained by the cultivation of a cautious silence. They point out that he not infrequently furnished his detractors with welcome ammunition by expressing his views emphatically and at length on everything imaginable. But there are also many students of Luther who consider his candor one of his most endearing traits. They point out that this amazing straightforwardness makes the Reformer one of the most transparent characters in history.

FRANKNESS ONE OF LUTHER'S CARDINAL CHARACTER TRAITS

Candor was not simply another trait in Luther's character. It is one of his *outstanding* characteristics. This is the reason why we shall devote an entire chapter to a consideration of Luther's frankness. In the great crises of his life it often became the determining factor; and the role Luther played is often inexplicable if we lose sight of his irrepressible frankness. Luther

212

simply had to speak out. He could not keep his views to himself. And dissimulation of any kind was constitutionally hateful to him. For better or for worse, he had to reveal exactly what was within him. He had to be himself at all times. There was nothing whatever of the actor in Martin Luther.

Moreover, Luther's frankness was a *natural* characteristic. He did not choose to be candid after mature deliberation. His straightforwardness was not a mode of procedure which he had decided to employ because he had discovered that it would best serve his purpose. He seems never to have given his candor any particular thought until his friends called his attention to it and suggested that perhaps a little reserve might be advisable. Luther's plain speaking was therefore not an intentional bluntness but rather a childlike artlessness. The sophisticated may call it uncouthness. We prefer to call it the naivete of a truly great personality. For why do many people who are in the eye of the public assume such airs of importance, dignity, and learning? They wish to create a favorable impression by seeming to be what they want others to think they are. But it was unnecessary for Martin Luther thus to hold his own in the eyes of the public. Without being aware of it, he was in the fortunate position of being able to be himself without endangering his standing. He needed to create no *impression* that he was a great man, because he *was* a great man. And the very artlessness of the man was felt to be an integral part of his greatness.

Both Luther's words and acts may therefore be taken at face value. Their message and meaning lie on the very surface. His *Table Talk* has at times been criticized for its unabashed frankness. The Reformer has been looked upon as a sort of adult *enfant terrible* even when among his boon companions. But Luther himself did not at all view the situation in that light. What he thought of the unreserved exchange of thoughts and the free expression of one's views is indicated by a remark in this very *Talk*. He once told his tablemates that the intimate conversation of the disciples with Christ must have been on the order of their own table talk after meals. Christ, said Luther, "indulgently viewed their [the disciples'] weakness and had patience with them, although they at times spoke rudely. . . . [These conversations] were real collations and table talks, during which every one freely and unabashedly stated and revealed what was in his heart and his thoughts." [1]

Such candid revelation was not restricted to the *Table Talk* in the case of Luther. We have freely quoted Luther's views in the above to illustrate his character. In the case of many men this method of revealing their character would be open to a serious objection; for, unfortunately, most men are distinctly worse than their creed. Thus the Stoic philosopher Seneca would appear to have been a noble character if judged only by the sage advice he dispenses so freely to others in his writings. But many who have spoken less loftily have lived far nobler lives than Seneca. Ordinarily it is therefore hazardous to imagine a man's character fully and accurately reflected by his views. At best these were high ideals, unattainable here below; at worst they were low maxims, whose demoralizing implications were never realized in his life. But despite all of these considerations it may be said that few men in history may be judged so safely and truly by their ideals as Martin Luther, for few have so conscientiously lived up to their creeds. We are therefore in the fortunate position of being able to find Luther's character reflected in his writings. He always meant what he wrote, and he rarely failed to write all he meant, that is, all he thought on a subject. It is true, with the modesty we have learned to admire he said, in effect: Follow my writings, not my life. What I present as divine truth is as perfect as the inerrant Scripture from which all of it has been derived, but my life is unfortunately full of sinful weaknesses and imperfections. However, we know of few great men in history who could better afford to say with Paul: "Brethren, be followers together of me, and mark them which walk so as ye have us for an ensample." [2] In consequence we look into both

---

[1] Erl 58:48.   [2] Phil. 3:17.

Luther's life and his writings in order to reconstruct his character. There are no glaring contradictions between what he preached and what he practiced.

Luther's candidness has endeared him to many. Martin Bucer was present at the Leipzig Debate. The impression he there received of Luther he communicated to a friend in Basel, Switzerland. We quote the following from it: "His [Luther's] sweetness in answering is remarkable, his patience in listening is incomparable, in his explanations you would recognize the acumen of Paul, not of Scotus; his answers, so brief, so wise, and drawn from the Holy Scriptures, easily made all his hearers his admirers. . . . He agrees with Erasmus in all [?] things, but with this difference in his favor, that what Erasmus only insinuates he teaches openly and freely." [3] The last statement is significant. One of the commonest criticisms which was directed against Erasmus is implied in it. Both friend and foe of the Humanist complained of the unclearness, the undecidedness of his presentation. It was evident that the timidity of the learned man moved him to say less than his conscience told him was true. It was a different matter in the case of Martin Luther. He publicly confessed what he held to be true, without any timid concern about the consequences. Men might doubt his discretion and judgment, but there was no denying the man's sincerity and candor. They knew that Luther was telling them exactly what he thought and precisely how he felt. This openness of the Reformer has received due recognition ever since it amazed the world more than four hundred years ago.

Julius Hare said of the frank Luther: "No man ever lived whose whole heart and soul and life have been laid bare as his have been to the eyes of mankind." [4] After having remarked about the zeal with which Luther's admirers recorded and treasured every statement and word of his, H. Boehmer continues: "Yet all this watching, note-taking, spying and searching would have availed these inquisitive spirits but little had Luther been as

---

[3] S-J, LC I:82.   [4] H, V 239.

impenetrable as Calvin, as completely master of his very gestures and moods as the reserved and prudent Loyola. But he was a true Thuringian, by nature not one to sit mum or walk on tiptoe, nor yet a lover of fine gestures and smooth civilities. He took no anxious thought for his dignity, but spoke his mind freely before his friends and companions over everything that interested and occupied him. . . . Nor did he depart from this inborn freedom and frankness when he sat down to write." [5] According to Dr. Wm. Dallmann, Rev. F. S. Buchanan of Oxford said at the time of the quadricentennial of the Reformation: "I may say that spiritually I owe more to Martin Luther than to any of my own countrymen, and am under a greater debt to him for his bravery, for his courage, for his truth, for his humanity, and for his total absence of all hypocrisy. If you ask me what was the grand thing about Martin Luther, it was that the man had not a line, not a trace of hypocrisy in his whole composition." [6] Luther's candor, honesty, and sincerity place him among the few *truly* great men of world history. How frequently those who come down to us through the centuries as "the Great" achieved and held their position among men by cunning and dishonesty! One need but think of the career of a Herod of Judea, and a Peter of Russia, and a Frederick of Prussia to be faced by the strange phenomenon that people consent to call those "the Great" who have raised themselves upon the backs and the bones of suffering mankind.

Luther has been faulted for his great candor. His French biographer Michelet said: "Luther conceals nothing; he could not contain himself. He suffers us to see and to sound the deep plague sore inherent in our nature, and is, perhaps, the only man in whose moral structure we can find a pleasure in studying this fearful anatomy." [7] The Catholic historian, it will be observed, appreciates the candid record the Reformer has left us of his spiritual conflicts. But in a previous paragraph he scores Luther's friends for indiscriminately transmitting to posterity everything Luther has said. Michelet feels that the Reformer's frankness

---

⁵ Bo, L 31 f.   ⁶ D, L 19 f.   ⁷ Mi, L xi.

must cause Lutherans many an embarrassing moment. We hold that the anxious concern of Michelet is unnecessary. He who knows all the circumstances in the case is nonplused as little by Luther's *plain* speaking as he is by his *vehement* speaking.

At the same time it may be mentioned in passing that certain contemporaries did caution against the use of both. Nor were all these monitors timid by nature, as was Melanchthon. There were those who, sympathetic to the principles of the Reformation, believed that methods of diplomacy and legitimate indirection would be more successful in furthering the cause of Christ than Luther's frontal attacks. One of these advisers was Wolfgang Capito. His counsel is so typical of what was frequently suggested to Luther, especially in his earlier years, that we shall quote a part of it. Capito wrote in 1518: "Believe me, you will accomplish more obliquely than by a direct assault in full force. . . . Lest your splendid attempt should turn out vain, I pray you use a little artifice, by which you may fix your hook in the reader before he suspects that a hook has been baited for him. . . . The Acts of the Apostles are full of examples of this method. Thus in a tumult St. Paul answers like a turncoat; he does not say, 'I do not speak against the Law,' but, 'Of the resurrection I am called in question,' thus with wonderful prudence diverting attention from the observance of the Law. Thus great things are safely accomplished by oblique methods. Thus I wish that you might always keep some window open by which you might escape when you are harassed in debate."[8] Now, we need not enter upon an investigation of the ambitious charge that Paul, as recorded Acts 23, "answers like a turncoat," and uses the old strategy of changing the subject to escape from an embarrassing dilemma. So much is certain: Luther could not and would not employ tactics of indirection against Rome and her minions. Indirection of any kind was distasteful to him. Whether rightly or wrongly, he felt that it smacked of dishonesty. He wanted to fight with an open visor. He meant to say just what he thought and everything

---

[8] S-J, LC I:110 f.

he thought; and he insisted upon telling his adversaries to their face where and why he considered them to be wrong.

Only a few times Luther, yielding to earnest representations of friends, did not handle situations with his customary directness and candor.[9] We do not mean to say that he intentionally dissimulated. He simply did not say all he would like to have said nor act to the full the part he thought he ought have played. He was not entirely himself but "held his spirit in check." One such occasion was the Diet at Worms. It may seem strange to hear that Luther expressed dissatisfaction with a performance which has called forth the admiration of men ever since it took place. Luther's conduct at Worms has become synonymous for courage and candidness. He had journeyed to the Diet fully intending not to recant an iota. How could he? He was firmly convinced that he stood squarely on the Word of God. How could anyone prove *that* to be false? But such divine, Spirit-wrought certainty was incomprehensible to the Church of Luther's day. His blunt insistence upon it would be interpreted as stubbornness and conceit. Why not, urged his friends, declare yourself open to conviction? Why not consent to recant if you are proved to be in error? This is a more diplomatic and conciliatory way of stating your position. And it *is* your position, although you do not expressly say that no man will be able to prove you to be in error.

Luther yielded to the friendly pressure and — rued it ever after. He wrote to Spalatin from "the Wilderness" (Wartburg): "My conscience troubles me, because I listened to you and to my friends at Worms and held my spirit in check and did not show myself a second Elijah to those idols. They would hear another story if I stood before them again." [10] Luther, it appears, feared that perchance he had created the impression at Worms that he was not certain of himself. He could not rid himself of this disturbing apprehension and recurred to it in a letter written a half year later. Meanwhile the irregularities

---

9 See Erl 30:6 f.   10 S-J, LC II:57; Se, A 367 f.

at Wittenberg had arisen, and Luther professed to see a connection between them and his lack of straightforwardness at Worms. He suspected that the Wittenbergers had been so easily misled because he had not spoken up more decidedly at the Diet. Luther therefore wrote: "All my enemies, and all the devils too, however nearly they have touched me, have not wounded me as I have now been wounded by my own people; I must confess that the smoke hurts my eyes and almost chokes my heart. Here, thought the devil, I shall take the heart out of Luther and make his stubborn spirit weak; this trick he will neither understand nor beat. Ah, well, I wonder whether this too is not a punishment . . . on me . . . because at Worms, to please my friends and not to appear too obstinate, I quenched my spirit and did not make my confession before the tyrants harder and stronger, though since that time the unbelieving heathen have accused me of pride. Heathen that they are, they judge like heathen, who have never received either Spirit or faith. I have often rued my humility and the respect I showed them." [11] Martin Luther considered himself unfaithful to his trust and untrue to himself, unless he unburdened himself of everything that was within his spirit. "This man had to think aloud to satisfy his conscience," a biographer remarks.

Another illustration of Luther's straightforwardness is furnished by a letter in which he refers to the use of the address "my most gracious Lord." This was the title customarily given to the Emperor. Now, it was notorious that the Emperor had treated the cause of Christ with scant courtesy — if, indeed, one may say even so much of him. The Elector was disturbed to hear that Luther considered the continued use of this address a sort of conventional lie, so far as he was concerned. Upon having the matter explained to him, the Reformer wrote to Frederick's secretary, Spalatin: "I have been compelled to call the Emperor 'my most gracious Lord,' when all the world knows he is most hostile to me, and everybody will laugh at this evident dissimulation. Still, I would rather be laughed at and convicted of dis-

---

[11] S-J, LC II:106 f.

simulation than withstand the infirmity of the Elector, and I clear my conscience of the charge because it is the custom thus to style the Emperor. It is, so to speak, a proper name and a title, and is used even by those to whom he is most hostile. I hate dissimulation, and have made enough concessions heretofore; there is a time for plain speaking." [12]

DOES LUTHER CARRY HIS PLAIN SPEAKING TOO FAR?

More than one biographer of Luther holds that the Reformer frequently thought the "time for plain speaking" had arrived, when it had *not* come. We have in mind particularly Luther's references to private parts and matters and to sexual relations. There is no denying the fact that he speaks of these matters with a freedom and a candor which seem very strange to our generation. Nor were his remarks restricted to the inner circle of his friends. This observation simplifies matters in one respect but complicates them in another. The fact is of itself sufficient to prove that Luther was not given to telling risque stories to his intimates. The motivation must be looked for in another direction. But that circumstance somewhat complicates matters. It is not so easy to account for in a man whose piety and personal purity were all but proverbial but who nonetheless used expressions in his conversation, terms in his writings, and references in public discourse on the pulpit which are today frowned upon as improper in the privacy of many family circles and are as a rule the subject of discussion only between husband and wife or between a man and his medical adviser.

In Luther's writings are found references to the various processes of eliminating waste matters and gases from the human body.[13] They are used as illustrations of the utter despicableness and worthlessness of certain things. Again, the biological facts of life or the anguish of a mother during parturition are called upon to clarify a point in the spiritual history of man. To some people this mode of procedure seemed like a jarring ascent from,

---

12 S-J, LC II:101 f.　　　　13 Cf. Sm, L 67, 355.

not, indeed, always the ridiculous, but rather the offensive, to the sublime. Thus Luther frequently compared human reason to a harlot, who by her wiles seeks to seduce man to commit spiritual adultery against God.[14] The Reformer might upon occasion carry out the comparison with an unreserve that would be considered highly improper in a modern pulpit. Such so-called offensive terms and passages occur too frequently in the Reformer's writings to permit one to attribute them to the heat of controversy or to bursts of righteous anger. Anyone who has read Luther's works with any degree of regularity will have received the impression that this manner of expressing himself is customary with Luther. We have no desire to adduce further illustrations in proof of this statement nor is it necessary to do so. Those who wish to satisfy themselves on this point, will find abundant source material.[15]

Now, what are we to think of this at times embarrassing frankness? Is Luther to be exonerated on all counts or is his astounding outspokenness to be considered a flaw in his noble character? His adversaries, it need hardly be said, have ever striven to put the worst construction on the plain speaking of the Reformer. But merely in passing we wish to remark that also in this matter the Romanists have forfeited every moral right to find fault with Luther alone. Even if it were demonstrable that he carried his plain speaking too far, Rome ought to remain discreetly silent in accordance with the principle expressed in the homely proverb "They who live in glass houses ought not throw stones." Luther's remarks and references are positively pure and chaste when compared with the effusions of Romanists. Again we have no desire to become specific. Rome is notorious enough for her immorality. We take no delight in exposing the vile depths of her corruption. Whoever wishes to convince himself that we are not maligning "Holy Mother Church" may consult the references below. These in turn will direct him to enough additional material to satisfy the most morbid taste for filth.[16]

---

[14] E. g. Erl 16:143 ff.   [15] See e. g. Erl 26:184 f., 195.

[16] Wa, F 595—612; Ba, L 47—82; Ma, M 218 f.

LUTHER'S OUTSPOKENNESS NO INDICATION OF SALACIOUSNESS

What, then, are we to say of Luther's plain speaking? To clear his speech from the charge of salaciousness, it is sufficient to show that such a charge is flatly contradicted by everything we know of the man in this respect and that his use of such language may well be explained on other grounds. It is conceded by all that the mere employment of such expressions does not necessarily reveal immoral inclinations; and if a bad construction patently disagrees with the known character of the man, it is nothing short of slanderous imputation of motives so to interpret his language. But what are the facts in the case? The purity of Luther's morals was conceded by his very enemies, and his intimate friends frequently testified to it. Melanchthon complained more than once about what he considered the lack of professional dignity in the Reformer, but he never accused Luther of using indecent language. On the contrary, Melanchthon said after Luther's death, when the timid man had no loss of favor to fear by revealing the unvarnished truth: "His [Luther's] lips were full of grace, and, as St. Paul demands of the Christian, truthful, decent, just, chaste, pleasant, sweet-sounding — this testimony all of us and many other, outside people who have seen and known him must give of him." [17] To this witness may be added the assurance of Johann Mathesius. This earnest man observed the Doctor for years during his hours of comparative relaxation after meals. Under such circumstances, if ever, the secrets of a man's soul will rise to the surface. A man is then inclined to be off guard, so to speak, and to be entirely himself. But Mathesius tells us: "He [Luther] was hostile to unchasteness and indecent talk. As long as I was about him I heard no shameless expression from his lips. When at times offensive stories were adverted to, he had a way of politely and cleverly trimming them down. He did the same thing to proverbs which in German fashion run into

---

[17] In Wa, L 27.

indecent plainness of speech." [18] If, then, Luther's "indecent" references and expressions cannot be attributed to a taste for the salacious, we must look elsewhere for an explanation of their use.

Students of the age of the Reformation have called attention to the fact that its standards of decency were in some respects strangely unlike ours. Sermon books, books of devotional exercises, even Bibles, exhibit nude women or naked little boys upon their title pages. At times they are pictured in the act of holding up sections of the artistic scaffolding upon which the title and the author appear. At other times they serve no such practical purpose but seem to have been designed for purely artistic reasons. If an author or a publisher were to produce something like that today he would cause at least a mild sensation. Were such nudes to appear in a book of religion — well, one can only wonder into what the scandal would develop. But such nudities were considered quite inoffensive in the sixteenth century and for a considerable time thereafter. It becomes apparent, then, that Luther's language was a part of the social pattern of that age. It was the language of respectable society in Germany. The good people of those times certainly acted with a vengeance on the principle expressed in the proverb "What is natural is nothing to be ashamed of." Matters and relations that were a "public secret," it was held, might as well be discussed aloud with anyone, even in the presence of modest womanhood. Incidentally, the modest womanhood of that age seems to have possessed the delicacy of feeling to be found in the proverbial fishwife of today.

Nor were standards different in other countries during the sixteenth century. The *Heptameron* of the French Margaret of Navarre († 1549), the pious and cultured grandmother of Henry IV, contains tales which no decent woman of today would profess to relish. In England the Virgin Queen, Elizabeth Tudor, heartily enjoyed the coarse comedy of Shakespeare's *Pericles* and *Merry Wives of Windsor*. She would not berate her sailors for

[18] Ma, M 218.

saluting her with the words "Good morning, old whore!"[19] Such were the civilities of those lusty times.

Perhaps the short skirts of today would seem the very acme of indecency and suggestiveness to the people of those days. Is it simply a matter of becoming accustomed — or calloused — to such exhibitions? One often wonders. This is a subject upon which the sociologist, the student of the social and moral history of mankind, may exercise his diagnostic ingenuity.[20]

Attention has been called to the fact that also in Scripture expressions occur and language is at times used which it would be embarrassing to introduce today of one's own accord, at least before a mixed audience. Thus Paul tells the Thessalonians that the anguish which will suddenly overtake the world at the break of Judgment Day will be "as travail [coming] upon a woman with child." [21] And our Holy Lord Himself employs a reference to the pains of parturition to illustrate the sudden sorrow of His disciples at His crucifixion, and He mentions the subsequent rejoicing of the mother to illustrate the sudden joy of His disciples at His resurrection.[22] To some extent, therefore, the use of such embarrassingly frank language by a man of Luther's well-known piety must be explained on the principle of the Scripture statement: "Unto the pure all things are pure." [23] It is obvious that the mere use of such language does not with inescapable logic stamp a man as tainted.

J. HARE'S JUDICIOUS REMARKS

On this entire subject Julius Hare has written such pertinent remarks that we should like to insert them here at some length. He says: "To judge of such matters we ought, according to a favorite expression of Luther's . . . to be *boni dialectici,* so as to discern how much in the prescriptive usages of society belongs to particular configurations of manners and how much results of necessity from the principles of morals. On this point . . . different ages differ greatly, and even in the same age there are

---

19 Bo, L 180.
20 Cp. Wa, F 594 f.

21 1 Thess. 5:3.
22 John 16:21.

23 Titus 1:15.

considerable differences between different classes of society. Culture increases delicacy: as a nation becomes more cultivated, it becomes more delicate and fastidious in its language. . . . If we examine the question on the widest scale, we find that the feeling of shame did not exist in the paradisaical state any more than it does in early childhood, that it only sprang out of the Fall, being, so to say, the shadow cast by sin on the pure surface of the conscience, and that, as the consciousness of sin has deepened, so has shame. Thus we learn that though shamelessness in all ages since the first betokens a deadness of conscience, yet the increase of fastidiousness with regard to language by no means betokens an increase of moral purity but often the very contrary . . . for sensitiveness may arise from soreness as well as from a natural fineness of organization; and the sparks which would be harmless elsewhere become dangerous in the neighborhood of tinder and of gunpowder. Thus in Luther's age a plainness of speech prevailed whereby, if we look at it unreflectingly, we may easily be disgusted. But it gave no offense then, because in the greater simplicity, or call it rusticity, of men's minds, it was not provocative of impure feelings." [24]

Dr. Wilhelm Walther thinks that Luther's outspokenness and honesty were typically German traits of character. The reader may take this judgment for what he thinks it is worth. Perhaps he will be inclined to pass it by with a smile, as a bit of pardonable supernationalism and racial pride. However, it ought at least to be mentioned that Luther himself expressed the view of Dr. Walther, who quotes him to this effect: "We Germans still have a spark of the old virtue according to which we do not relish being called liars; we do not laugh at such names, as the Italians and Greeks do, nor do we turn the matter into a joke. And although the Italian and Greek mischief is making inroads among us, the fact still remains that a man can use or hear no more stern, horrible word of insult among us than the name liar.

---

[24] H, V 159 f.

And I think there is no more shameful vice upon earth than to have proved oneself to be a liar and a faithless person." [25] Dr. Walther goes on to point out that the German Luther professed to have discovered evidences of the lack of veraciousness among the Italians, French, Spanish, and English in the very manner in which these nations pronounced their words. Luther referred to the many silent letters and to the hissing and nasal sounds so common in the languages of these people, for he is quoted as having remarked: "Therefore it is said of the French: 'They do not utter what they write; and they do not mean what they utter.'" We find ourselves neither qualified nor called upon to decide the merits or the demerits of the Doctor's views. They interest us, however, as additional corroborative evidence of the man's unabashed plain speaking on everything that attracted his notice. It seems to us that this unreserve was a personal rather than a national or racial characteristic.

The artlessness of Luther's self-appreciation has been dwelt upon above,[26] and it has also been pointed out that he did not regard it incompatible with genuine modesty to recognize the gifts of head and heart which God has graciously bestowed upon us.[27] To the thoughts there developed we wish here to add the following. The Doctor's straightforwardness was often demonstrated by the naive manner in which for the encouragement of the timid and disheartened he would speak of his great achievements. Such confessions of his signal success will appear self-congratulatory only so long as one loses sight of the purpose for which they were spoken. Luther is glorifying God, not himself. He seeks to encourage his downcast friends by calling their attention to the fact that the Almighty performed such great things through a weak, lone, sinful monk. Why should they despair of succeeding in life? Luther points the moral: The strategy is to throw oneself entirely upon God; for "with might of ours can naught be done."

The impression Luther's public behavior made upon his con-

---

[25] Wa, L 206.			[26] P. 73.			[27] P. 205.

temporaries was deep. They instinctively felt here is a man who is utterly honest with himself and perfectly frank with friend and foe. This simplicity and artlessness we should like to call Luther's candor of conduct. His behavior in public and in private was as plain and natural as his speech. The debate at the University of Leipzig in 1519 was designed to be a splendid affair. There was much academic fanfare. The streets and halls were crowded with the high and mighty of Church and State. Everyone tried to appear at his best lest the world fail to take due cognizance of his importance for its continued welfare. This was an opportune moment for the lone monk to make a favorable impression by acting well his part. He did, but in a way quite his own. A politic man might have ascended the rostrum with a simulated expression of profound learning and with an imposing air of professional dignity. Luther must have known the truth of the proverb "The world will make as much of you as you make of yourself." But the candid Reformer could not and would not appear other than what he was. His artlessness surprised many. This was not the sort of man they had expected to see. How plain he was! And what was that in his hand? A small bouquet, which in the heat of controversy he would from time to time admire and raise to his nose. This man plainly had ways of his own. And why did he look so thoughtfully at that ring on his finger? Perhaps the devil was in it. There was something about this monk — people did not act that way ordinarily. Of course they did not, but this Augustinian was no ordinary man. Whatever others thought or advised about proper professional decorum was noncanonical to him. He would be his natural self.[28]

Also at Worms. Luther's artlessness at that Diet was such that Emperor Charles made the well-known remark "This monk will never make a heretic of me." [29] Charles said this before Luther had an opportunity to present his entire case. The Emperor judged by appearances, as men too frequently do. There was nothing impressive about the plain, straightforward monk.

---

[28] K-K, M I:243 f.; Se, A 185 f.   [29] Se, A 349.

Others looked deeper. After his first appearance before the Diet, a voice was heard to exclaim as he passed through the throng, "Blessed is the womb that bare thee." Others, too, were deeply impressed by the very artlessness of conduct which in the eyes of the Emperor stamped Luther as a definitely overrated man. Fixing his gaze upon the monk, the Emperor remarked to a bystander that he would never believe Luther capable of writing the books attributed to him.[30] Well, how could the "young blood Charles," as Luther called the Emperor, be expected to know that the man before him could not be measured by popular standards? The great moments and persons in history do not always come to us labeled. A man such as this Brother Martin appears every thousand years or more. How was Charles to know that?

But to return to the great candor of Luther. It becomes the more remarkable when it is observed how unhesitatingly he related matters that actually reflected upon himself, upon his judgment, or even upon his character. But after what we have learned about the Reformer's modesty we are prepared for such self-exposures. Luther is never bent upon persuading the world that he is really an exceptional character. It never enters his mind that this very fact makes him an exception. He simply does not think about himself as of prime importance. Therefore he writes in his reply to Henry VIII: "In fine, my doctrine is the matter of chief importance. With that I defy not only princes and kings but all devils as well. And, indeed, besides my doctrine I have nothing that supports, strengthens, and gladdens my heart and makes it increasingly bold and defiant. As to the other matter, my life and my conduct: I am well aware of the fact that I am sinful and cannot bid defiance to men in this respect. I am a poor sinner and am satisfied to let my enemies be pure saints and angels. Blessed are they if they can sustain the reputation." [31]

---

[30] K-K, M I:412.   [31] Erl 30:5.

LUTHER FREELY CRITICIZED HIMSELF

It has been mentioned that Luther at times yielded to the representations of friends and pursued a course that, according to his own judgment, was unwise. As a rule subsequent developments proved his view to have been the better one. Now, the average person might, under such circumstances, have laid the blame of the miscarriage upon his advisers. But Luther is too honest and candid to do any such thing. He knows that after all the act was his own, no matter how or by whom he had been persuaded to perform it. We therefore hear him complain about himself: "I am a simpleton (*Schaf*) and remain a simpleton, because I so readily believe others and permit myself to be influenced and led by them." [32] After he had been whisked away to the Wartburg and was chafing under the enforced "leisure" of his retreat, he consoled himself with the thought that his Wittenbergers were now in a position to take care of themselves. But his comfort on this head was short-lived. After the disillusioning news of the Wittenberg enthusiasts and their popularity had reached him, he did not merely berate the visionaries, but even years later (1527), after the sacramentarian aberrations of some of his friends had been added to this disillusionment, he indicted himself and wrote: "There you have it, Sir Luther! Learn sometime what it means: 'Beware of men.' Are you a Doctor professing to know the devil right well and still do not know that [no trust is to be put in men]?" [33] The Reformer never hesitated to confess errors of judgment on his part. Under similar circumstances others might also have judged themselves in error, but very likely they would have kept their judgments discreetly to themselves. Luther published his.

In 1516 the plague came to Wittenberg. For some time two or three deaths occurred in the small place every day. John Lang, a friend of Luther, advised him to flee, as others were doing. But he resolved to stay. He wrote to his friend: "I hope the world will not come to an end when Brother Martin does. I shall send the

---

[32] Erl 30:8.   [33] Erl 30:12.

brothers away if the plague gets worse. . . . Not that I do not fear the plague (for I am not the Apostle Paul, but only a lecturer on him), but I hope the Lord will deliver me from my fear." [34] The *Table Talk* introduces him as remarking: "All sadness is devilish because Christ, in whom we believe, has come to console us and to have mercy on us. Therefore the Holy Spirit must be called upon in times of sadness. He is our defense and defiance against death and dangers. If you feel sadness because of death, say: 'I shall not die but live' (Ps. 118:17) and rejoice. But, dear God, this article of faith will not [enter] into [the heart]. That is the reason why so much sadness comes to us. I am often angry with myself that although I have delivered so many lectures, have preached and written how this temptation is to be overcome, yet I cannot root out sadness when I myself am tempted." [35] With characteristic frankness we hear this great hero of faith confess that fear of death is not unknown to him. A less candid character would have been ashamed to confess any such terror. While not denying it, he would at least not have confessed it voluntarily. He might even have tried to persuade himself and especially others that at least he was superior to the fear of death. But the conscientious and candid Luther will not and cannot do that.

But is fear of death not due to lack of faith? It is; wherefore Luther did not fail to confess that also in this respect he was not what he ought to be. Nor do such confessions date only from the earlier years of his career. In later life the Reformer once remarked with a note of sadness: "I am not godly, but Christ is godly. In His name I am baptized; I receive the Holy Sacrament and am a pupil of the Catechism. He [Christ] takes care of us if only we rely upon Him. I am surprised that I cannot rely upon this doctrine. I am angry with myself because of this lack of faith, since all my disciples fancy they know it to a T." [36] Mathesius records that upon one occasion a certain minister by the name of Musa sincerely deplored the fact to Luther that he [Musa] often could not himself firmly believe what he preached to others. "Praise and thanks be to God," the Reformer is said to have re-

---

[34] Sm, L 33.   [35] Wal XXII:803.   [36] Erl 62:122.

plied, "that other people also have such experiences; I thought only I had them." [37] Mathesius adds that the disturbed minister was so greatly impressed by this remark that he never forgot it. This early biographer of Luther has recorded a somewhat similar story. A woman complained to the Doctor about what she called her unbelief. "Do you still remember the Creed of your childhood?" Luther asked her. "Yes," replied the woman and recited it. "Do you also hold these things to be true?" he asked her. Upon her answering in the affirmative the Reformer exclaimed: "Truly, my dear woman, if you hold and believe these words to be true — and, indeed, they are nothing but the truth — you believe more firmly than I do; for I must daily pray for an increase of faith." These incidents may be considered typical.

Luther never wanted to impress people with his personal importance and goodness. Many felt that since he was the Reformer of the Church, there ought to be a sort of halo of unapproachable sanctity about him. They held that for the sake of good morale men ought to be taught to consider him in a class by himself — as, indeed, he was — so that they might instinctively look to him as the infallible guide, the religious superman, to use a modern term. There were those who feared that anything that would lessen the admiration for the man Luther should be carefully avoided lest the cause of the Reformation suffer. But Luther himself did not at all agree with this point of view. He was not concerned about personal glory. If he could hearten a discouraged brother or sister who was wrestling with weaknesses of the flesh or the spirit by confessing to similar struggles, he never failed to do so. Men might thereafter think of his spiritual maturity and personal goodness in terms less exalted, but Luther was not interested in wearing a halo of superlatives which his modesty and candor told him he did not deserve. "Who is Luther?" he had asked. Men were to look to Christ, not to Martin Luther.

But what are we to say to these candid confessions of sinfulness by Luther? They are easily accounted for. As his knowledge of the spiritual demands of the Law of God deepened, as the broad

---

[37] Ma, M 220.

sweep of its requirements became ever clearer to him, Luther grew increasingly dissatisfied with himself. As the Reformer looked ever deeper into the nature of man and discovered how utterly corrupted it is, he was ready to cry out with Paul, the saint whom he so much resembles: "O wretched man that I am! Who shall deliver me from the body of this death?" [38] With these considerations in mind one must read statements of Luther such as this one: "I am quite well in body and mind, except that I should prefer to sin less. I sin more every day, of which I complain to you and ask your prayers." [39] Only the very good people know how bad they are: this is one of the many paradoxes of Christianity.

LUTHER APPROACHED EVEN GOD WITH INTIMATE FRANKNESS

Faith has been defined as taking God at His word. Luther frequently exemplified this definition. He "took God at His word" notably in his prayer for the life of Melanchthon at Weimar. This mighty spiritual effort revealed both the faith and the frankness of Luther and showed that the frankness was rooted in the faith. With the causes of Melanchthon's sickness, largely emotional and spiritual, we need not concern ourselves. To many it appeared that the end of the man was near at hand. Luther hastened to his friend's bedside from Wittenberg. Upon his arrival the dying man no longer recognized anyone. He looked like a corpse. Deeply moved, Luther exclaimed: "God forbid! How has the devil abused this instrument!" Then, turning to the window, he poured out his heart in fervent prayer. Luther considered Melanchthon indispensable at this time for the progress of the Reformation and appeared before the Throne of Grace with such emphatic representations to this effect that one may say he demanded the life of his fellow worker from God. The physicians in attendance had given up all hope. Many of the signs of oncoming death were plainly visible in the sufferer. But Luther frankly told his God that He could not, He dared not, forsake His own. To the utter amazement of all witnesses Melanchthon

---

[38] Rom. 7:24.　　　　[39] S-J, LC I:342.

"returned from the dead," to use Luther's strong words. Both he and Melanchthon believed that God had wrought a miracle in answer to the Reformer's prayer. We should like to have all the words of that prayer. The spirit in which it was offered has been preserved in the remark of Luther: "Then and there God our Lord was obliged to listen to me; for I flung the burden, too heavy for me, before His door. I besieged His ears (literally: rubbed his ears: *rieb ihm die Ohren*) with all the Scripture promises I could recall that He would hear prayer. Thus He was obliged to hear me if I was henceforth to trust His promises." [40] Luther, it is seen, retained his frankness at the very throne of God. His candor conditioned also his prayer life.

To some people such an intimate, informal approach to God may seem presumptuous. But few souls have been filled with a greater reverence for the majesty of the Eternal One than the soul of modest Martin Luther. Moreover, few have had a livelier conviction of the Fatherhood of God in Christ Jesus than had the Reformer. With the childlike candor of his great faith he "stormed unceremoniously into the throne room of the King of kings." His obtrusiveness did not show a lack of reverence and respect, but gave evidence of an utter confidence in the love and favor of his Father. We make allowance for such importunity in children; in their willingness to help, parents welcome the evidence of this great, loving confidence on the part of their children and notice not the unconventional manner of its manifestation. Throughout his life Martin Luther exhibited certain traits of a child. For years we have thought that some of the passages in his life's history were enacted commentaries on the words of Jesus: "Except ye . . . become as little children, ye shall not enter into the kingdom of heaven." [41] The man Luther was a genuine child of God. In his explanation of the introduction to the Lord's Prayer the Reformer had said: "We [Christians] may with all boldness and confidence ask Him [God] as dear children ask their dear father." Luther always meant what he wrote. He practiced what he preached.

---

[40] In Wa, L 20.   [41] Matt. 18:3.

OUTSPOKEN IN CORRECTION AND COMMENDATION

Towards the end of Luther's life a gradual change in Melanchthon's theological position placed a heavy strain upon the famous friendship between him and the Reformer. But Luther's judgment of the gifts of his co-worker never varied. However much it must have pained him to see "his Philip" slowly drifting from his sound theological moorings, he ever regarded him as one of the most talented men of the age. The Doctor once remarked about him to a friend: "Whosoever does not recognize him as a teacher must be an ass and a bacchant, who is suffering from an attack of conceit. The sun shines not upon another man on earth who has such gifts. Therefore let us highly esteem the man. Whosoever despises him must be a despised man before God." [42]

But Luther's eyes were not closed to the faults of his friends. He was as frank and free with his criticism as with his commendations. Melanchthon frequently experienced this fact. During the enforced absence of Luther from Augsburg in 1530 Melanchthon was looked upon as the theological spokesman of the reformers. The responsibility almost crushed him. Luther observed this sad state of affairs and wrote to strengthen the timid soul. In a kindly but candid manner the Reformer scored the weakness of Melanchthon's faith. He told him that he had little sympathy for him, since he was his "own worst enemy." Luther professed to be losing patience with him. He admonished him finally to stop "sucking up cares like a leech." The root of the trouble, the Doctor frankly told his friend, lay in the deplorable fact that he [Melanchthon] had too much philosophy in his system and not enough religion. [43] Melanchthon took the letter in good part. He not only knew Luther's criticism to be justified, but he was also convinced that it was offered in a helpful spirit and came from a person who dealt with his fellow men "straight from the shoulder." The kindly spirit in which Luther's corrections of his friends were given took out of them whatever sting they might have had because of the bluntness and candor of their delivery.

---

[42] In Wa, L 70.   [43] Sm, L 258; K-K, M II:216.

To cast reflections upon the physical weaknesses or malformations of even our close friends is usually considered to be not in the best of taste, since such frailties or abnormalities are, as a rule, beyond the control of man. Upon one occasion Veit Dietrich had asked the Doctor how, according to his idea, Paul might have looked. Luther replied: "I believe Paul to have been a despised person, unimpressive in appearance; a poor, dried-up little man, like Magister Philip." [44] No one seemed to have felt this to be an offensive reflection on "Magister Philip's" physique. Besides, could not everyone see that Melanchthon answered this description? No doubt. But few besides the outspoken Luther would express it so bluntly in public.

We also read of Luther's candid criticism of other friends. Johann Bugenhagen of Pomerania († 1558) was a noted fellow reformer. His fortes were pastoral counseling and preaching. Luther thought very highly of "Pomeranus," but once remarked that he wished the good man would preach shorter sermons; even a good thing may be overdone. Another friend, Justus Jonas († 1555), Luther criticized for what he called a very disturbing habit: when preaching, Jonas periodically cleared his throat as though he had lost the thread of his discourse. Melanchthon's sermons the Reformer thought excellent in content, but he found Philip's delivery lacking in vigor and positiveness. Such constructive criticisms of his friends, frankly and freely given, did not detract from, but rather added to, the respect men felt for Luther. There was something distinctly virile about his friendship. He was known to be no lickspittle. Generous praise and frank criticism might be expected from him at any time, in any place.

LUTHER'S UNABASHED STRICTURES OF THE GREAT

It is interesting to observe this candid, manly attitude of Luther revealed in his relation to the great men of his day. The Elector Frederick had expressed high satisfaction with the Reformer's two publications *The Psalms* and his *Commentary on Galatians*. Moreover, he had promised Luther a new black cowl.

---

44 Erl 58:71 f.

It never came. Luther's old one was literally falling to pieces of old age. He finally purchased a new one for himself. But the favorable reception of his publications seemed an opportune moment to remind the Elector of his overdue gift. Luther had discovered that the delay was apparently also attributable to the niggardliness of the Elector's treasurer Pfeffinger. With typical candor he wove all these data into a letter to the Elector and wrote: "I pray Your Grace to buy me at this Leipzig fair a white and a black cowl. Your Grace owes me the black cowl, and I humbly beg the white one. For, two or three years ago, Your Grace promised me one which I never got. For although Pfeffinger spoke me fair, yet either because of business or because, as people say of him, he is slow to spend money, he put off getting it. . . . In this need I humbly pray Your Grace, if the Psalter deserves a black cowl, to let the Apostle (*Galatians*) earn a white one, and pray do not let Pfeffinger neglect it." [45] Incidentally, this Pfeffinger seems really to have merited the good Doctor's disgust. Two years before the letter just quoted had been written, Luther had already complained of him to the Elector: "As Your Grace promised me a gown some time ago, I beg to remind Your Grace of the same. Please let Pfeffinger settle it with a deed and not with promises — he can spin mighty good yarns but no cloth comes from them." [46]

DISAGREEMENT WITH THE ELECTOR

While Luther was at the Wartburg, news reached him of the reopening of the sale of indulgences by Albert, Archbishop of Mayence. He instantly decided to write the dignitary a candid letter about the re-introduction of this abomination. The Court heard of this intention and requested the Reformer not to attack the prelate. Thereupon Luther wrote to Spalatin: "I have scarcely ever read a letter that displeased me more than your last. I not only put off my reply, but I had determined not to answer you at all. For one thing, I will not suffer what you say, that the

---

[45] S-J, LC I:183 f.   [46] Sm, L 34.

Elector will not allow me to write against Mayence nor anything that can disturb the public peace. I will see you and the Elector and the whole world to perdition first. . . . Your idea about not disturbing the public peace is beautiful, but will you allow the eternal peace of God to be disturbed by the wicked and sacrilegious doings of that son of perdition? Not so, Spalatin! Not so, Elector! For the sake of the sheep of Christ we must resist that grievous wolf with all our might as an example to others. . . . The question is settled, and I will not listen to you." [47]

ALBERT, ARCHBISHOP OF MAYENCE

One is curious to know just what Luther had to write to Albert. This curiosity may be satisfied to the full, for the letter soon became public property. Nor did Luther object to letting the public know what he had to say. He had nothing to hide and loved to fight in the open. There was nothing of the assassin about him. Tacitus somewhere remarks about the furious frontal attacks of the ancient Germans. The enemy never needed to surmise where or when they would strike. Luther's enemies never needed to doubt either. His candor toward them was as great as that toward his friends. He minced no words. He said with unmistakable clearness everything he meant; he meant in deadly earnest everything he said.

This was not the first time Luther had taken Albert to task. The posting of his Theses in 1517 had been occasioned by the sale of indulgences with the sanction of this prelate. A letter exists, dated on the very day of the nailing of the Theses to the door of the Castle Church, October 31, in which the protesting monk told the archbishop: "My God! thus are the souls committed, Father, to your charge instructed unto death, for which you have a fearful and growing reckoning to pay. . . ." [48] Luther inclosed a copy of the Theses for the private study of the "Father." Instead of replying to this and to a second letter from Brother Martin, Albert informed Rome of the manner in which the "presumptuous monk"

---

[47] S-J, LC II:63 f.   [48] Sm, L 43.

was carrying on. By the time Luther again wrote to him about the sale of indulgences (1521) Albert had at least learned that the "presumptuous monk" could no longer be lightly dealt with. The following is, in part, what the excommunicated and outlawed Luther had to tell the prelate: "I humbly pray Your Grace to leave poor people undeceived and unrobbed and show yourself a bishop rather than a wolf. It has been made clear enough that indulgences are nothing but knavery and fraud and that only Christ should be preached to the people, so that Your Grace has not the excuse of ignorance. . . . Let no one doubt that God still lives and knows how to withstand a Cardinal of Mayence, even if four emperors support him. He rejoiceth to break the lofty cedars and to humble the proud, stiff-necked Pharaohs. . . . And let not Your Grace think Luther is dead. He will gladly and joyfully put his trust in God and will start such a game with the Cardinal of Mayence as few people expect. . . . If you unexpectedly become a laughingstock, remember that I have warned you." [49]

How did the great churchman react to this candid criticism? Within a few weeks Luther had an answer in his hand. The proud prelate, addressing him as "my dear Doctor," replied in a manner that stamped him as either a chastened man or a consummate hypocrite. His subsequent history († 1545) forces us to accept the latter alternative as the correct one. For the present the Archbishop assures the condemned monk: "I have received your letter, and I take it in good part and graciously, and will see to it that the thing that so moves you be done away, and I will act, God willing, as becomes a pious, spiritual, and Christian prince, as far as God gives me grace and strength, for which I earnestly pray and have prayer said for me, for I can do nothing of myself and know well that without God's grace there is no good in me, but that I am as much foul mud as any other, if not more. . . . I can well bear fraternal and Christian punishment." [50] If there was any sincerity in these words, Albert's failure to mend

---

[49] S-J, LC II:74 f.   [50] S-J, LC II:80 f.

his ways make it difficult for one to believe in the man's honesty. In 1535 Luther again wrote to him, now "for the last time." The occasion which called forth the letter need not concern us here. The Reformer addressed the churchman with his customary frankness: "I wish you repentance and forgiveness of sins, most noble Prince, gracious Lord! I am moved to indite this letter to Your Holiness not in the hope that it will do you any good, but only to satisfy my conscience before God and the world and not to connive at your crimes by keeping silence. . . . If Your Holiness would hang all who speak evil and shame of you . . . you would not find rope enough in all Germany. . . . Leave off your attacks on God and His Church and let a few live until the infernal torturer gets hold of you. Amen." [51] Luther lived to consider the Archbishop of Mayence one of the most determined enemies of the Gospel.

DUKE GEORGE

Probably Luther regarded only George of Saxony worse than Albert of Mayence. Enough has been said to identify this inveterate persecutor of the Gospel of Christ. A letter of Luther to the Duke is submitted here as another illustration of the amazing straightforwardness of the Reformer's attacks upon his adversaries. The occasion was, briefly, this: Luther had written a letter to one Hartmuth von Cronberg, which contained passages interpreted by George as defamatory references to him. He thereupon wrote a letter of protest to Luther. The Reformer replied by going directly to the heart of the matter. His candor simply would not permit him any longer to address George as "Your Grace." He therefore omitted the conventional greeting entirely and said: "Instead of greeting I wish you would stop raging and roaring against God and against His Christ. Ungracious Prince and Lord! I received Your Disgrace's letter with the pamphlet, or letter, I wrote Hartmuth von Cronberg and have had read to me with especial care the part of which Your Disgrace complains. . . . As Your Disgrace desires to know what position I take

---

[51] Sm, L 298 f.

in it, I briefly answer that as far as Your Disgrace is concerned, it is the same to me whether my position is standing, lying down, sitting, or running. . . . If Your Disgrace were in earnest and did not so ignobly lie about my coming too near your soul, honor, and reputation, you would not so shamefully hurt and persecute Christian truth. This is not the first time that I have been belied and evilly entreated by Your Disgrace. . . . But I pass over all that, for Christ commands me to do good even to my enemies, which I have hitherto done with my poor prayers to God for Your Disgrace. . . . May He lighten Your Disgrace's eyes and heart and please to make me a gracious, kind prince of you. Amen." [52] This remarkable epistle was signed: "Martin Luther, by the grace of God Evangelist at Wittenberg."

ERASMUS

An opponent of a very different type was Erasmus. In some respects he was far more dangerous than the savage George. A man like Luther preferred the frank fury of George to the two-faced indetermination of the great scholar. By 1524 the rumor that Erasmus had finally consented to attack Luther publicly was widespread. The peaceable Reformer wrote to him in this eleventh hour, attempting to avoid an open and final breach. Perhaps Luther thought he had written a conciliatory, politic letter. If that had been his intention, he had largely defeated his purpose by his irrepressible candidness. To a man of Erasmus' egoistical sensitiveness some of the statements in Luther's letter must have seemed like withering sarcasm. But the Doctor was simply very frank, perhaps brutally frank. The famous letter, in part, runs thus: "Grace and peace from our Lord Jesus Christ. . . . Since we see that the Lord has not given you courage or sense to assail those monsters (papists) openly and confidently with us, we are not the men to exact what is beyond your power and measure. . . . The whole world knows your services to letters and how you have made them flourish and thus prepared a path for the direct

---

[52] S-J, LC II:158 f.

study of the Bible. For this glorious and splendid gift in you we ought to thank God. . . . Even if you cannot and dare not declare for us, yet at least you might leave us alone and mind your own business. . . . I say this, excellent Erasmus, as an evidence of my candid moderation, wishing that the Lord may give you a spirit worthy of your reputation, but if He delays doing so, I beg that meanwhile, if you can do nothing else, you will remain a spectator of the conflict and not join our enemies, and especially that you publish no book against me, as I shall write none against you." [53]

THE GERMAN PRINCELETS

This letter did not deter Erasmus from publishing (September, 1524) his attack on Luther in the book *On the Freedom of the Will*. Luther countered the blow with his *On the Bondage of the Will* (December, 1525), and the war had begun also in this direction. While Humanist and theologian were thus belaboring each other with their sharp pens, prince and peasant were drenching Germany in blood with their swords and pikes, their pitchforks and clubs. Because of the public breach with Erasmus it was evident that also the humanistic interests would henceforth turn their backs upon the Reformation. Luther had already estranged the insurgent peasants by his denunciation of their rebellion against constituted authority. Even while working on his book against Erasmus, he had to defend himself in another publication against the charge that by opposing the peasants' revolt he had made common cause with the tyranny of the princes. In this writing he therefore expressed his opinion of the oppression of the lords. Again Luther minced no words. He was so outspoken in his indictment of the maladministration of the German princelets that he estranged them too. No doubt it was impolitic to do so. But it was the honest, the candid way of handling the situation; and this was always the way of Martin Luther.

Of the princes and minor nobility Luther wrote these scorching words: "To these bloody dogs it is all one whether they slay

---

[53] S-J, LC II:228 ff.

the guilty or the innocent, whether it please God or the devil. They have the sword, but only that they may vent their lust and self-will. I leave them to the guidance of their master, the devil, who is leading them. . . . Why should I write for scoundrels and hogs like that? The Scriptures call such people *Bestien*, that is, 'wild animals,' such as wolves, boars, bears, and lions, and I shall not make men of them. I had two fears. If the peasants became lords, the devil would become abbot; but if the tyrants became lords, the devil's dam would become abbess. Therefore I wanted to do two things — quiet the peasants and instruct the lords. The peasants were unwilling, and now they have their reward; the lords too will not hear, and they shall have their reward also. Except that it would have done harm if they had been killed by the peasants, that would have been a light punishment for them. Hell-fire, trembling and gnashing of teeth in hell will be their reward eternally, unless they repent." [54]

CRITICISMS INTENDED TO BE CONSTRUCTIVE

"Unless they repent," that is a significant close. It reveals the end Luther wished to attain also by his candor. He had truly told Albert of Mayence that he took no pleasure whatever in exposing the falsehood and the wickedness of men. The only reason he did expose them with a plainness of speech that at times bordered on the brutal was to get men to see the error of their way before it would be too late. Also Luther's candor was made to serve the single purpose of his life: adjusting the relation between a man and his God. This was the dominant note in the life of Luther when he entered the cloister; it remained the dominant note when he left it; and even in the subsequent domestic life of the Reformer it continued to be the dominant note. He taught men by his own example to enrich the humblest and to ennoble the most prosaic duties and relations of domestic life by infusing into them the spiritual motives of Christian service. We therefore now follow Luther into his home.

---

[54] Ho IV:280 f.; cp. 220 f., 270 f.

CHAPTER IX

FATHER LUTHER

His domestic life was an integral part of his confession and public testimony.

J. Koestlin, Luther scholar

THE PREREQUISITE OF FAMILY LIFE IS MARRIAGE, AND THE basis of marriage is the sex relation. Probably there was no relation more fearfully disorganized in the days of young Luther than this one. The Church of Rome had herself contributed toward this unspeakable state of immorality by her antichristian decrees of celibacy. It will not be necessary again to review the doctrinal aberrations of the papal Church to prove that also the immorality of the age was one of the foul fruits of the departure of Rome from Scripture. The licentiousness of the clergy was attracting attention everywhere and was increasingly arousing disgust and resentment. The bitter indignation with which Erasmus spoke of all orders of the Church was greeted with immense applause by all but the objects of his sarcastic humor. The vices of the hierarchy from parish priest to Pope furnished the biting satirist with a congenial subject. Henry Lea has well summarized the impasse at which the Church of Rome had arrived at this time. He writes: "The corruption of the church establishment in fact had reached a point which the dawning enlightenment of the age could not much longer endure. The power which had been intrusted to it, when it was the only representative of culture and progress, had been devoted to selfish purposes and had become the instrument of unmitigated oppression in all the details of daily life. The immunity which had been necessary [?] to its existence through centuries of anarchy had become the shield of unimaginable vices. The wealth, so freely lavished upon it by the veneration of Christendom, was wasted

243

in the vilest excesses. All efforts at reformation from within had failed; all attempts at reformation from without had been success- fully crushed and sternly punished. . . . Corruptions were daily displayed before the people with more careless cynicism. There appeared to be no desire on the part of the great body of the clergy to make even a pretence of the virtue and piety on which were based their claims for reverence."[1] Somewhat later Lea speaks of "the dread experienced by every husband and father lest wife and daughter might at any moment fall victims to the lust of those who had every opportunity for the gratification of unholy passions."[2]

That such statements are not exaggerations becomes plain when we hear that priests might be found defiling the holy days by quarreling about a pretty prostitute in a tavern or a house of ill fame, and that the graduated tariff known as the "Taxes of the Penitentiary" made it possible for a priestly sinner for half a ducat, that is, for little more than a dollar, to purchase absolu- tion for incest committed with a mother or a sister.[3]

SEXUAL VICIOUSNESS OF THE ENTIRE AGE

It is not pleasant work to dig into such filth and to expose it to public view. But it must be done to prove that Luther's strong words on this subject were not outbursts of a blind hatred or an ignorant fanaticism. He knew whereof he spoke when he called clerical circles cesspools of nameless vices. Social diseases were commoner in the sixteenth century than tuberculosis in the nine- teenth century. They were regarded as class diseases of students, clerics, monks, soldiers, and statesmen. It is characteristic of the age that no one hesitated to confess to being afflicted with these shameful sicknesses. Among those who are known to have suf- fered from social diseases were men like Emperor Charles V, Francis I of France, Pope Julius II, the papal legate Aleander, Ulrich von Hutten, and cardinals too numerous to mention.[4]

---

[1] Le, H 409. [2] Le, H 427. [3] Le, H 428. [4] Bo, L 188.

It was generally conceded that the enforced celibacy of the clergy had contributed no little in the course of time to this fearful lowering of moral standards. *Qualis rex, talis grex:* Like shepherd, like flock.

The view Luther took of celibacy throws an interesting light on the development of his character. In a wedding sermon preached in 1519 he still speaks of marriage as a sacrament and says of celibacy, or "virginity and chastity," as he calls it: "Before Adam fell, it was easy to preserve virginity and chastity, but now few find it possible, and without the special grace of God it is impossible. Therefore neither Christ nor the Apostles wanted to command chastity, though they did advise it and put it up to the individual to examine himself: if he cannot contain himself, he is to marry; if by the grace of God he can contain himself, chastity [celibacy] is to be preferred." Toward the end of this sermon Luther exclaimed: "Oh, truly, a noble, great, blessed estate, the estate of matrimony, if it be properly conducted! Oh, truly, a miserable, terrible, dangerous estate, the estate of matrimony, if it be not properly conducted. The man who would consider these things would soon cease being prurient and would perhaps as readily seize the celibate state as the estate of matrimony. But youth little considers the seriousness of this matter, merely following its passions." [5]

There was still a bit of the monk in this sermon, but even at that time Luther's observation had already taught him that the blanket requirement of celibacy was an unnatural and godless ordinance. Therefore, when in the following year he defended his burning of the canon law and other papal books, he listed enforced celibacy among the damnable statutes which made the volumes he had destroyed richly deserve their fiery fate. As eighteenth charge he listed "that he [the Pope] forbids marriage to the entire clergy, whereby sin and shame have been greatly

---

[5] Erl. 16:160 f.

increased without cause, against the command of God and Christian liberty." [6] Again, in 1521, in his controversy with Ambrogio Catarino, he stigmatized enforced celibacy as "angelical in appearance but devilish in reality," invented by Satan, as predicted by Paul in 1 Tim. 4:3.[7]

THE EFFECT OF THESE VIEWS ON THE MONASTIC SYSTEM OF HIS DAY

It was to be foreseen that the proclamation of such principles would empty many a monastery and lead to many a marriage. And so it did. Nor did the Reformer at all regret this development. On the contrary, he advised erstwhile monks and nuns to disregard their false vows and to marry. He once exclaimed with evident satisfaction: "I am the father of a great people, like Abraham, for I am responsible for all the children of the monks and nuns who have renounced their monastic vows." [8] But on this point Luther was slower to practice what he preached than he had shown himself in other respects. He had, indeed, long since laid aside the monks' cowl. In April, 1523, he officiated at the wedding of his friend Link, vicar of the Augustinian order, and preached a sermon in favor of the "chastity of marriage." Why did he postpone his own marriage so long?

In his *Open Letter to the Christian Nobility* Luther had said five years before his marriage: "Human frailty does not permit a chaste life, but only angelic power and celestial might." [9] Was he speaking from personal experience? As far as unchastity of life is concerned, definitely not. Luther's life was pure. Preserved Smith says: "The example of the monk of Wittenberg was a striking contrast to the prevalent immorality." [10] Naturally Luther felt the urges of a strongly masculine nature. With the candor we have learned to admire, the honest man wrote for the public eye in 1535: "Oftentimes it cometh to pass that even they which are most sober are tempted most of all. Hereof I myself also had experience when I was a monk. The heat of unclean lusts is not

---

6 Wal XV:1625.   8 Sm, L 325.   10 Sm, L 320.
7 Wal XVIII:1495.   9 Ho II:121.

quenched by fasting only, but we must be aided also by the spirit, that is, by the meditation of God's Word, faith, and prayer. Indeed, fasting represses the gross assaults of fleshly lust; but the desires of the flesh are overcome by no abstinence from meats and drinks, but only by the meditation of the Word of God and invocation of Christ." [11] Subsequent statements of the Reformer persuade us to doubt the intensity of the biological urge in Luther at this or any other time. His intensely religion-centered and otherworldly character would move him, especially during his monastic career, to look upon even the normal assertion of the sexuality within him as something to be reprobated and utterly crushed. The very fact that Luther did not marry till 1525 more than indicates that his sex urge was comparatively slight.

This view is corroborated by a letter to his bosom friend Spalatin, in which he bids his intimate thank a certain Argula von Stauff for her inquiry about the rumor of his intention to marry. Luther says: "I do not wonder at such gossip when so many other things are said about me; please give her my thanks and say that I am in the hand of God, a creature whose heart He may change and rechange, may kill and make alive, at any hour or minute, but that hitherto I have not been and am not now inclined to take a wife. Not that I lack the feelings of a man (for I am neither wood nor stone), but my mind is averse to marriage because I daily expect the death decreed to the heretic. However, I shall not ask God to bring my labors to an end, nor shall I strive in my heart, but I hope He will not let me live long. Farewell, and pray for me." [12]

We have dwelt upon this very personal matter at some length because of the slanderous statement that has still not entirely disappeared from books on the Reformer and according to which Luther severed his connection with Rome on account of his incontinence. Someone has rather stingingly replied that in the Church of the sixteenth century it would have been quite unnecessary to go to so much trouble merely to get sexual satis-

---

[11] Lu, G 492 f.   [12] S-J, LC II:264.

faction. That was to be had by the "best" of clerics on very convenient terms. But the purity of Luther's morals was conceded by his very enemies in his days. We have heard Erasmus testify: "His character is so upright that even his enemies find nothing to slander in it." [13] We know of no contemporary of Luther who ever dared to charge him with incontinence in the sense of Scripture. That he who had vowed celibacy should marry a girl who had vowed perpetual virginity was, of course, a gross breach of morality according to *papal* standards. But that is neither here nor there. Very curious reading are statements such as that of the Catholic historian Michelet. He points out that the Reformer married during the distracting period of the Peasants' War. This struggle had indeed caused Luther many heartaches and disappointments. Michelet professed to have discovered the following connection between the strain of the war and Luther's marriage: "In this prostration of mind the flesh regained its empire; he married." [14] That marriage may be brought on by mental debility is something new to us.

But why *did* Luther marry? If we were to come upon passages in his writings which were to tell us that he finally took the step in order to satisfy the urgent demands of his masculine nature, we should be neither surprised nor shocked. And we may rest assured that such confessions would be found in the writings of the candid Luther if that had been the reason why he married his Catherine. He did, indeed, write a letter to Spalatin about two months before he took a wife in which he banteringly jokes with his friend about his (Luther's) failure to marry although he had helped to bring so many others together in matrimony and is even now encouraging Spalatin to take the step. Only a pitiful lack of the sense of humor or an inexcusable malicious intent can find anything offensive or suggestive in this letter. Luther tells Spalatin: "You write about my marrying. You ought not to wonder that I, who am such a famous lover, do not take a wife; it is more wonderful that I, who write so often about matrimony

---

[13] See p. 19 above.   [14] Mi, L 130.

and thus have so much to do with women, have not long since become a woman, to say nothing of marrying one. . . . I had three wives at the same time and loved them so bravely that I lost two of them, who are about to accept other wooers. The third I am only holding with the left arm, and she too, perhaps, will soon be snatched away from me. But you are such a laggard in love that you do not venture to become the husband even of one woman. But look out, or I, who have no thought at all of marriage, may sometime get ahead of you prospective bridegrooms. It is God's way to bring to pass the things you do not hope for." [15] Preserved Smith has pointed out that the "three wives" jestingly referred to were perhaps the two sisters Ave and Margaret von Schoenfeld and Catherine von Bora, all of whom had been under the care of Luther at Wittenberg. The last words quoted from the letter seem to indicate that the Reformer was at this time very undecided as to the advisability of his marrying. However, two months thereafter he had finally resolved to do so. With characteristic promptness he acted upon his resolve. Luther married the former nun Catherine von Bora on June 13, 1525.

We need not guess at the reasons which prompted the Reformer to take this step. He has himself recorded them with perfect frankness; and though they betray little that is of a romantic nature, they do reveal motives that are a credit to both Luther's head and his heart. It is true, his head seems to have been more engaged than his heart. A week after his marriage he wrote to Nicolaus Amsdorf: "I hope to live a short time yet to gratify my father, who asked me to marry and leave him descendants; moreover, I would confirm by my example what I have taught, for many are yet afraid even in the present great light of the Gospel. God has willed and caused my act. For I neither love my wife nor burn for her, but esteem her." [16] There are a number of noteworthy expressions in this letter. Luther assured Amsdorf that he had not married his Catherine because he had found continence increasingly difficult. It ought to be borne in

---

[15] S-J, LC II:305 f.   [16] S-J, LC II:329.

mind that Martin Luther was forty-two years old at this time. Then, too, the strenuous life he lived was not conducive to amorousness. It is also significant to note that Luther says he decided to marry in order to gratify his father's expressed desire for descendants from his illustrious son. This motive is quite in keeping with Luther's character. He often thought more of others than of himself. But of still greater importance are the words: "I would confirm by my example what I have taught."

LUTHER'S MARRIAGE LARGELY AN ACT OF FAITH AND CONFESSION

This is not the only time we hear the Reformer express the thought. The *Table Talk* quotes him to this effect: "In order to confirm the estate of matrimony, I had resolved before I was married that I should like to have myself united to a maiden upon my deathbed, in case I had to die unexpectedly and were to suffer from a fatal disease. I should have done this to spite the Pope, who with all his regulations has ruined and dishonored the estate of matrimony more than can be expressed — the godless Sodomite." [17] According to these words Luther considered his marriage an act of religious confession. He had for years testified against the unnaturalness and viciousness of celibate vows. Now he would publicly act against them, since "actions speak louder than words" — even Luther's words.

Very likely also economic and social considerations were contributing causes of the decision. At its best Luther's bachelor life in the Black Monastery must have been anything but comfortable. As his manifold labors increased, he found neither the time nor the strength to perform the most necessary domestic duties. Indeed, he was on the road to ruining himself by his irregular life, his poor meals, and his disorderly quarters. We have already mentioned that during practically the entire year before his marriage his bed remained unmade. Reminiscing in 1540, he told his table companions: "I knew nothing about it;

---

[17] Wal XXII:1127.

for I was dead tired, working away the whole day. I simply fell into my bed."

But why did Luther finally choose Catherine von Bora? This erstwhile nun had been engaged to a young man from Nuremberg, Jerome Baumgaertner, for nearly two years. She sincerely loved her fiancé, but as she was very poor, the young man broke his engagement. Luther felt bad about this development, since he had encouraged the connection. He now sought to persuade the jilted girl to marry a Reverend Glatz, pastor at Orlamuend. But Catherine now and thereafter revealed that she had views and tastes of her own. With a candor that reminds one of Luther himself, she declared one day to the no doubt somewhat embarrassed Professor Amsdorf that she would hear no more of Pastor Glatz, but that she would marry either him [Amsdorf] or Luther. This frank revelation set the Reformer to thinking. He finally decided to "take pity on the deserted woman," as he put it rather unromantically. In the ordinary sense of the word one may therefore hardly call the ensuing union a love match. But Luther felt that conjugal love as it is usually understood is largely rooted in the physical, and that a more necessary and secure foundation for matrimonial happiness is mutual respect and esteem. He held that the physical attraction of sex, so potent a factor in ardent youth, recedes and declines in the course of time, whereas the attractiveness of a sterling Christian character increases as the character develops and grows in beauty. We do not mean that the Reformer's love was purely Platonic. But in keeping with his entire view of life, he emphasized the intangibles rather than things corporeal, the spiritual rather than the physical.

Although Luther's marriage was a surprise even to many of his close friends, it was not a rash step. Melanchthon, it is true, wrote a letter to Camerarius three days after the ceremony which is not at all a credit to Luther's Philip. It is a disagreeable mixture of peevishness and querulousness and was penned in a distinctly ungenerous spirit. Melanchthon obviously felt hurt that Luther had not consulted him. But the Reformer had consulted Someone of far greater value as a counselor than Philip Melanchthon. In later years he told a friend: "My dear fellow, do as I did. When I desired to take my Catherine to wife, I earnestly prayed to our Lord God." [18] After God in answer to such supplication had convinced Luther what He would have him do, he "conferred not with flesh and blood," but promptly and confidently did it. When faultfinding enemies condemned the union and apprehensive friends doubted its wisdom, the bridegroom was not in the least disturbed, but expressed his conviction that "the angels were laughing for joy, and the devils were weeping in rage." [19] The historic union was solemnized in the Black Monastery on the evening of June 13, 1525, only Bugenhagen, the city pastor, Justus Jonas, the artist Lucas Cranach and his wife, and Dr. Apel, professor of law at the university, being present.

CATHERINE VON BORA

Catherine von Bora was twenty-six years old at the time of her marriage, sixteen years younger than her husband. Hans von Bora, her father, was of the lower nobility and found himself in somewhat straitened circumstances. Catherine lost her mother soon after her birth. In a few years her father remarried, and she was sent to a Benedictine convent at Brehna when she was only five years old. Since a relative was the abbess of the Cistercian cloister at Nimbschen, Catherine was transferred to that institution at the age of nine. An aunt, Lena, who later became a fixture in Luther's household, was a sister at this cloister. At the early age of sixteen Catherine was consecrated a nun. The education she received was fairly good. In later life she at times surprised the friends of Luther by her ability to get the drift of Latin conversations. The reformatory doctrines of Luther did not respect the walls and the secrecy of the cloister at Nimbschen, and soon the inmates longed for "the liberty wherewith Christ hath made us free." Catherine and eleven other nuns were spirited away from Nimbschen on the night of April 4, 1523. Their liberators

---

[18] Erl 61:210.   [19] In Wa, F 658.

were one Leonhard Coppe of Torgau, his nephew, and another young man. Most of the former nuns had no one to receive them, since cloisters were frequently used as places of permanent refuge by the destitute and friendless. They were in consequence taken to Wittenberg and provided with temporary homes and employment. It was hoped that suitable husbands might be found for them in time. Catherine was received into the home of a prominent Wittenberger by the name of Reichenbach. Here she soon showed herself adept at learning to manage a household.

Catherine's appearance is well known to all who have read biographies of the Reformer. She does not seem to have been physically attractive. H. Lea even says: "If the portraits after Lucas Cranach given in Mayer's Dissertation on Catherine be faithful likenesses, it was scarcely the beauty of his bride that led Luther to take this step, for her features seem rather African than European." [20] We have not seen the portraits in the old volume referred to by Lea, but the Cranach portrait (1526) in E. Kroker's biography of Luther's wife is not only distinctly "European" but shows a woman with an intelligent, determined, even somewhat pert and shrewd expression. And, as said above, Luther was far more interested in character than in comeliness. And character Catherine certainly had. "She was no man's fool." Her thrift, energy, alertness, intelligence, and piety fully deserved the praise Luther frequently bestowed upon them. Theirs was a happy marriage and a happy home.

Luther's wife has at times been accused of having been proud, domineering, and stingy. We need not examine the justifiableness of these charges. No doubt Catherine had her faults, as everybody has his imperfections. Luther does frequently refer to her as "Lord Kate." How large an ingredient of this expression was simply humor and how much of it was a reference to a domineering ambition which Luther had discovered in his good wife, it is impossible to determine. It ought to be recognized that Catherine had no mean task to perform as the manager of Luther's house-

---

[20] Le, H 425 f.

hold. And manager in a very real sense she had to be, since Luther had neither the time nor the inclination to occupy himself much with his domestic economy. Catherine's position was difficult, and often the very virtues of her husband, his softheartedness, hospitality, and liberality, increased the difficulties. But as we shall see, Catherine Luther gave an excellent account of herself.

In the eyes of Luther's papal enemies his marriage to an escaped nun was, of course, the very nadir of his disgrace and shamelessness. But to Luther himself, who now clearly saw that monkery is a pitiful perversion of the moral standards of Scripture, his marriage was the realization of that normal life which God has intended for man. In consequence the Reformer enjoyed the pleasures of married life with a perfectly clear conscience, nay, with thanks to God. With his usual candor he speaks and writes also about conjugal relations. "To the pure all things are pure." To Spalatin, who had meanwhile also entered the holy estate, Luther wrote: "Greet your wife kindly from me. When you have your Catherine in bed, sweetly embracing and kissing her, think: Lo, this being, this best little creation of God, has been given me by Christ, to whom be glory and honor. I will guess the day on which you will receive this letter, and that night I will love my wife in memory of you with the same act and thus return you like for like. My rib and I send greetings to you and your rib. Grace be with you. Amen." [21] Luther also held that no one ought to take offense at the "pretty little follies" lovers commit by the manner in which they manifest their fond affection for each other. He expressed this thought in the most mature product of his theological presentations, his lectures on Genesis.[22]

THE HEAD OF HIS HOUSE

But Luther was not weakly sentimental in his attitude to Catherine. He did indeed appreciate the love she bore him. In a course of lectures delivered five or six years after his marriage

---

[21] S-J, LC II:356.   [22] Wal I:157 sq.

he remarked: "This life has nothing more lovely and delightful than a woman who loves her husband." [23] And to his table companions he once said: "While I was attending school at Eisenach my hostess remarked: 'Nothing on earth is more precious (*lieber*) than the love of a woman.'" [24] At the same time Luther had some very strong convictions about the subordination of woman in the marriage relation. The modern "emancipation" of woman would in many respects be considered an anti-Christian abomination by him. He wrote: "A woman should either be subject to her husband or not marry . . . thus God commands and ordains through the Apostles and His Holy Writ." [25] He would refer men to passages like 1 Pet. 3:6; Eph. 5:24; and Gen. 3:16. In the spring of the year in which he was married he preached a sermon on the estate of matrimony in Wittenberg. In this discourse he said: "Now, this [subjection] is the other penalty of woman for having misled her husband. And I readily believe that women would sooner and rather, yea, more willingly and patiently, suffer the former penalties, such as pain and anguish during pregnancy, than be required to be subject and obedient to their husbands. So fond are women by nature of ruling and reigning, following in the steps of their first mother, Eve." [26]

Whatever desire "Lord Kate" might have manifested to usurp supreme authority in the Luther household must have been effectually and promptly squelched; for neither friend nor foe ever reported a disturbance of peace and harmony by any improper self-assertion of Catherine Luther. A henpecked husband once unburdened himself to the Reformer and was told that he had himself spoiled his wife by weak compliance and should remember and act on 1 Cor. 11:17. When a man whose wife was a veritable termagant was referred to, Luther remarked: if *his* wife were such a woman he should not hesitate to slap her foul mouth.[27] But his "Lord Kate" was no such woman. "I would not surrender my Catherine for France and Venice!" he once

---

[23] Wal IV:1998.   [25] Wal III:1234.   [27] K-K, M II:488; cp. Sm, L 180.
[24] Wal XXII:1158.   [26] Wal XVI:185 f.

exclaimed. "Kate, you have a man who loves you," he assured her. Upon occasion he would confess her faults as freely and frankly as his own but would conclude with the emphatic assertion that her shortcomings paled before her many virtues. Not the least important of these virtues was Catherine's domesticity. She was in her element when she managed the household. Luther appreciated this trait and gladly granted her jurisdiction over the culinary department of his large establishment. He must have spoken with a comfortable sense of security when he once remarked: "He is a martyred man whose wife and maid know nothing about the kitchen. Such ignorance is the beginning of calamity, for many evils follow from it." [28]

From what has been said it will have appeared that the Reformer expected no slavish deference from any woman, nor reserved the right for himself to lord it over his wife as a petty despot. Luther was very kind to his Catherine and bore her foibles with the patient forbearance with which she bore his. He once remarked with a sigh of resignation: "I must have patience with the Pope, ranters, insolent nobles, my household, and Katie von Bora, so that my whole life is nothing else but mere patience." [29] Luther's personal requirements were neither many nor exacting. His tastes were of the simplest. This made keeping house for him comparatively easy. He was soon satisfied. Nor did he require much looking after. At least so *he* thought. He usually wore the sixteenth-century jerkin, or short coat, and the long hose of the age, covering legs and waist. Occasionally he tried his hand at mending his own clothing, but the success was very indifferent. In fact, Catherine once complained that her husband had cut a piece of cloth from his son's trousers to patch his own. The Doctor, looking rather sheepish, tried to defend himself like this: "The hole was so large that I had to have a large patch for it. Trousers seldom fit me well; so I have to make them last long." On special occasions Luther wore a gown and on

---

[28] Wal XXII:1141.   [29] Sm. L 181.

PLATE XIV

THE KATHERINE PORTAL

This door leading into the Black Cloister at Wittenberg (the
("Luther House") was presented to Luther by his wife in 1540.
The projections at the bottom on either side served as porch chairs
and those above as canopies

PLATE XV

MARTIN LUTHER

This is another painting of Luther by Lucas Cranach. We are indebted to this German artist for almost all of our authentic reproductions of the Reformer. While there were those who excelled Cranach as portrait painters, his productions give us a fairly satisfactory idea of Luther's appearance

PLATE XVI

CATHERINE LUTHER

Catherine von Bora, Luther's wife, was the daughter of Hans von Bora and Katharina von Haugwitz, who died soon after the birth of her daughter. Catherine, thus more or less always dependent upon herself, soon developed that determination of character for which she was more noted than for any personal beauty. The picture was done by Cranach in 1526

PLATE XVII

MAGDALENA LUTHER

This picture was painted by Cranach not long before Magdalena's death. The Reformer never was blind to the faults of his children. This fact makes his high praise of Magdalena the more significant. The winsomeness of Magdalena grows upon one by a study of Cranach's painting

festive days a more or less becoming gold chain around his neck. He was also physically clean. He had a bathroom in his house and used it freely. "Why is the water so dirty after bathing?" he once asked at dinner. "Ah," he moralized, "I forgot that the body is dirt, as the Bible says: 'Thou art dust and ashes.' Why art thou proud, O man?" [30] Usually Luther was clean shaved, but during his seclusion on the Wartburg grew a beard, perhaps to aid his disguise. Also the ever-growing beard had to furnish an illustration. The Doctor said that a man's beard is like original sin: although we daily destroy its manifestation, it constantly reappears.

This was the sort of man for whom the former nun had to care. It must have been a pleasure and a privilege to live with him and for him. His heart was as large as his mind. He painted what became his own portrait when he thus characterized the faithful husband in a marriage sermon of 1525: "There [Eph. 5:25, 28] you hear how well the Apostle teaches a man to conduct himself toward his wife. He should not consider her a rag on which to wipe his feet; and, indeed, she was not created from a foot but from a rib in the center of man's body, so that the man is to regard her not otherwise than his own body and flesh. . . . And although another woman be prettier, better, more eloquent, prudent, wise, and well than your wife, you should nonetheless not love *her* as much as you love your own body. Nay, nay, *your* wife you should love as your own body. And although she does not always please you, have patience with her as with your own body." [31]

"MAN CAN BUILD A HOUSE, ONLY A WOMAN CAN MAKE IT A HOME"

Like all virile men, Luther disliked the masculine woman. He held that in creating male and female God had endowed each of the sexes with excellences peculiarly its own, and that in consequence both man and woman fulfill the design of their Creator only if they work and remain in the sphere for which God has

---

[30] Sm, L 316 f.   [31] Erl 16:181 f.

designed them. While developing this thought in the course of lectures on Ecclesiastes, Luther said: " 'A woman handles a child much better with one finger than a man does with both fists.' Therefore let everyone continue to perform the work to which God has called him and for which he was destined." [32] Naturally there would be exceptions, but Luther held that the normal sphere for the woman was the home. She had been created to be a wife and a mother.[33] The age of the Reformer with its warped monastic standards needed to be told that Scriptural truth. Nor would our own age have so many problems if it would return to this basic prerequisite of a happy and well-balanced society.

Children are like the windows of a house: they let the sunshine in. God blessed Martin and Catherine Luther's home with six children. The first-born was John, or Johannes, Luther's "Haenschen," little Hans. On June 17, 1526, ten days after his birth, Luther wrote to Spalatin with the pride and concern of a father: "From that most gracious woman, my best of wives, I have received by the blessing of God a little son, John Luther, and by God's wonderful grace I have become a father." [34] Seven months later he wrote: "My little Hans sends greetings. He is in the teething month and is beginning to say 'Daddy' and scold everybody with pleasant insults. Katie also wishes you everything good, especially a little Spalatin, to teach you what she declares her little Hans has taught her, namely, the fruit and joy of marriage, of which the Pope and all his world was not worthy." [35] Luther was a close student of child life, and many of his remarks reveal a surprising insight into human nature. In some of the Reformer's remarks we discover anticipations of modern genetic psychology. When Hans had arrived at his seventh year his father said: "My boy Hans is now entering upon his seventh year. Every seven years a person changes; the first period is infancy, the second childhood. At fourteen they begin to see the world and lay the foundation of education; at twenty-

---

[32] Wal IV:1517.
[33] Cp. Erl 57:273.
[34] S-J, LC II:373 f.
[35] S-J, LC II:391.

one the young men seek marriage; at twenty-eight they are householders and patresfamilias, at thirty-five they are magistrates in Church and State, until forty-two, when they are kings. After that the senses begin to decline. Thus every seven years brings a new condition in body and character." [36]

LUTHER'S CHILDREN

On December 10, 1527, Elizabeth was born. She died in less than a year. Child mortality in the sixteenth century was very great. It was not exceptional for a mother to lose almost half of her children before they had reached their teens. To his friend Nicolaus Hausmann, Luther wrote: "My little daughter Elizabeth is dead. It is marvelous how sick at heart, how almost womanish, it has left me, so much do I grieve for her. I would never have believed that a father's heart could be so tender for his child. Pray the Lord for me." [37] On May 4, 1529, it must have seemed to the Luthers as though the Disposer of life and death had replaced their sainted little Elizabeth, for on that day another infant girl arrived in their home. They named her Magdalena. She seems to have been one of those sweet, demure, and meek natures, altogether lovable. Luther's affection for her was deep. But "Lenchen" was loved in heaven no less than on earth, and in her fourteenth year the angel of death took her too.

The other children, all of whom survived their illustrious father, were: Martin, born November 9, 1531; Paul, born January 28, 1533; and Margaret, born December 17, 1534. The first-born, Hans, became a law student after his father's death and accepted a government position. Martin, never very strong, studied theology but did not enter the ministry. He died at the age of thirty-nine. Paul studied medicine and became a famous physician, while Margaret married a wealthy nobleman, Georg von Kuhnheim. Although none of the Reformer's children except Paul achieved renown, it is a great satisfaction to know that even

---

[36] In Br, L 100.   [37] S-J, LC II:451.

the lynx-eyed investigations of Luther's enemies have been unable
to find any stains in the lives of his offspring. His ardent prayers
for them were answered, and his great love and care found their
reward.

And Martin Luther did love his children. One is not surprised
to find him interested in *all* children. We have seen that there was
something childlike about this great, strong man. His simplicity,
his candor, his trustfulness established a bond of sympathy between him and children. We therefore find him making and
saying much of his children. Their childish prattle delights him,
their physical and mental development is full of ever new marvels
to him, and even their petty little quarrels attract him. And, of
course, everything must point a lesson. He sees great principles
and truths reflected in the most trivial occurrences. One day
when the baby had befouled the parental lap, on which it had
been sitting, the father, not at all disconcerted, bade the guests
note that this performance was sadly symbolical of the manner
in which most people treated their heavenly Father. God cared
and provided for them, and they repaid Him with the filth of
their sin and ingratitude. The same humiliating trait of human
nature Luther saw illustrated one day when his child screamed
lustily because it could not have its way. "What cause have you
given me to love you so?" the moralizing Doctor asked. "How
have you deserved to be my heir? By making yourself a general
nuisance. And why aren't you thankful instead of filling the house
with your howls?" [38]

But perhaps the classical illustration of Luther's "profound
understanding of child nature and his great ability to adapt himself to it," to enter into the feelings and speak from the view-
point of children, is his charming letter to his son Hans. The boy
was four years old at the time. This "children's classic," as Preserved Smith calls it, will take on added importance when we
bear in mind that it was written at a time when the fate of the
Reformation was again hanging in the balance, when the Re-

---

[38] Sm, L 353.

former was suffering from physical pain and was distressed by spiritual wrestlings. Moreover, his father had recently died without his having been able to see him once more. But with a power of mental abstraction which is unique Luther wrote to his Hans:

"Grace and peace in Christ. My dear little son. I am very glad to see that you are learning well and praying diligently. Continue to do so, my son, and when I come home, I shall bring you a pretty present.

"I know a lovely, pleasant garden, in which there are many children. They wear golden jackets and gather nice apples under the trees, and pears and purple and yellow plums and sing, run, and are happy and have pretty little ponies with golden reins and silver saddles. I asked the man who owns the garden whose children they were. He said: 'They are the children who gladly pray, learn, and are good.' Then said I: 'Dear man, I also have a son, whose name is little Hans Luther; may he not also come into the garden, that he too may eat such lovely apples and pears and ride such fine ponies and play with these children?' Then the man said: 'If he gladly prays, learns, and is good, he may also come into the garden; Lippus and Jost too; and if they all come together, they shall have whistles and drums and lutes and all kinds of stringed instruments. They may also dance and shoot with little crossbows.'

"Then he showed me a fine lawn in the garden fixed up for dancing, and there was hanging nothing but golden whistles, drums, and fine silver crossbows. But as it was early and the children had not finished eating, I could not wait to see them dance, and I said to the man: 'O my dear sir, I shall go right away and write my dear little son Hans about all these things so that he will pray diligently, learn his lessons well, and be good, in order that he too may come into this garden. But he has an Aunt Lena. He must bring her along.' Then the man said: 'All right, go and write him about these things.'

"Therefore, dear little Hans, learn and pray cheerfully and tell Lippus and Jost that they also learn and pray; then you will come together into the garden. With this I commend you to God. Greet Aunt Lena and give her a kiss for me." [39]

The Reformer was never too busy to find some time to devote to his children. He once remarked that children edified him more than he entertained them. In fact, there were character traits for which Luther professed to envy the little ones. Thus when his little Hans once spoke enthusiastically about the glories of heaven, the Reformer remarked: "They [children] are far more learned in faith than we old people; for they believe in all simplicity, without any disputing and doubting, that God is gracious to them and there is an eternal life after this one." [40] The Doctor also expressed his great admiration for the faith of his children in God's providence. "They are not concerned about the price of wheat," said he, "for they are certain at heart that somehow they will find something to eat." [41]

Luther did not consider a large family a misfortune. Were he living today, he would no doubt have some very strong remarks to make about the planned childlessness of many homes. In the course of his exposition of Psalm 128 he wrote: "You will find many to whom a large number of children is irksome, as though marriage had been instituted to satisfy their swinish sensuality and not for the sake of the extremely precious service which we render God and men by caring for and educating the children God has given us." [42] And in his lectures on Genesis he expresses similar thoughts. [43]

PARENTAL RESPONSIBILITY FOR CHILD TRAINING

The training and education of children, Luther held, should begin at an early age. He considered child training the immediate responsibility of parents. To him education was not identical with going to an organized school. Luther believed that the educating process should begin in the mother's arms and at — or over, if need be — the father's knees. Deep, lifelong impressions ought

---

[39] Erl 54:156 f. [41] K-K, M II:482. [43] Wal I:1079.
[40] In Wa, L 179. [42] Wal IV:1999.

to have been made upon the plastic little soul long before the child must toddle off to school. Nor could parents even thereafter transfer the ultimate responsibility for the spiritual and moral welfare of their children from themselves to anyone else. The Reformer preached and wrote some very earnest words on this subject. Thus he said in the wedding sermon of 1519 previously adverted to: "There is nothing which will more surely earn hell for a man than the improper training of his children; and parents can perform no more damaging bit of work than to neglect their offspring, to let them curse, swear, learn indecent words and songs, and permit them to live as they please. Some parents themselves incite their children to such sins by giving them superfluous finery and temporal advancement, so that they may but please the world, rise high, and become wealthy. They are constantly concerned to provide sufficiently for the body rather than for the soul. . . . Therefore it is highly necessary that every married person regard the soul of his child with greater care and concern than the flesh which has come from him, that he consider the child nothing less than a precious, eternal treasure, entrusted to his protection by God so that the devil, the world, and the flesh do not steal and destroy it. For the child will be required from the parent on Judgment Day in a very strict reckoning." [44]

Luther's deep earnestness and his highly developed awareness of right and wrong, truth and falsehood, might lead one to suspect that he must have been rather rigorous than otherwise in his child training. But Luther recalled the experiences of his own childhood and youth. He knew that undue severity was pedagogically unsound. It crushed and intimidated the tractable and filled the intractable with rankling hatred and rebellion. He once said that "the apple ought to lie next to the rod." Luther knew human nature too well to advocate the removal of the rod and the serving of apples only. That bit of pedagogical stupidity was to be reserved for subsequent "enlightened" ages. But the Reformer was moderate in his application of corporal punishment. His boys

---

[44] Wal X:643 f.

received more of it than his girls. At one time he was so indignant at a transgression of his first-born that, notwithstanding the intercessory pleas of his wife, he refused to forgive his boy for three days. Upon this occasion he made the well-known remark that he had rather have a dead son than a disobedient one. But such severity never estranged the children from their father. They knew how truly he loved them.

LUTHER VERSUS LOYOLA

H. Boehmer compares the principles that obtained in Luther's large household with those advocated by Loyola, who is well known for the unquestioning obedience his methods developed in his disciples. Very pertinently Boehmer says: "Whereas Loyola seeks to order and regulate everything in the lives of his disciples, down to the cut of their coats, the breadth of their collars, and the position of their slippers and other articles under the bed, nothing is so repugnant to Luther as giving laws of this kind for matters of outward physical life. Remembering his own experience in his Catholic days, he holds that such laws are all too apt to become chains upon the soul and fetters for unhappy consciences. All laws, therefore, so far as they are indispensable, should in principle be guided and ruled by love, and every man should strive to remain on good terms with God and his conscience. Then laws and regulations will no longer be necessary. In harmony with this view, his house was never conducted so absolutely according to rule as the Roman College. Really bad habits and serious offenses against morality could, of course, not be permitted in anyone. But severe as he could be in such cases, he was anything rather than one of those unbending domestic patriarchs who cannot rest till they have turned their house into a kind of well-managed reformatory. His children had far more freedom and pleasure than he himself had enjoyed. To the young people in his hostel he was more like an older friend than a strict disciplinarian." [45]

---

[45] Bo, L 230 f.

LUTHER ESTABLISHED THE PROTESTANT PARSONAGE

In more than one respect Luther's family life became of world importance. He established that institution whence so much that is good has gone forth: the Protestant parsonage. Of this the church historian Dr. P. Schaff has said: "The domestic life of Luther has far more than a private biographical interest. It is one of the factors of modern civilization. Without Luther's Reformation, clerical celibacy with all its risks and evil consequences would still be the universal law in all Western churches. There would be no married clergymen and clerical families in which the duties and virtues of conjugal, parental, and filial relations could be practiced. It has been proven that a larger portion of able and useful men and women have been born and raised in households of Protestant pastors during the last three hundred years than in any other class of society. Viewed simply as a husband and father and as one of the founders of the clerical family, Luther deserves to be esteemed and honored as one of the greatest benefactors of mankind." [46]

DAILY LIFE IN LUTHER'S HOME

Let us enter the Luther home and observe the pleasant routine of a representative day. No time was wasted in getting at the tasks of the day. During the greater part of the year the dawn saw Catherine bustling about the place. Luther liked to call her the "morning star of Wittenberg" because of her early rising. After prayers the Doctor devoted the morning to lecturing and preaching, while Catherine performed the never-ending duties of a thrifty housewife and a provident mother. The principal meal of the day was served at ten o'clock. There was little lingering over this since the Doctor did some of his heaviest and most intense work during the long afternoon. Frequently he would be "dead to the world" from about eleven o'clock to nearly five in the afternoon. This precious time was given to writing and

---

[46] In Br, L 93.

reading or, more rarely, to conferences and interviews. Supper was served at five o'clock. This hour ended the most strenuous labor of Luther's day. As a rule, he would relax during the meal, call upon someone of his rather numerous table companions to relate the latest news heard on the street or conveyed to someone by letter, and begin a running comment on anything and everything that was of interest to him. As was to be expected, he gave the cue and was the chief conductor of the conversation which ensued. Thus originated his famous *Table Talk*. However, at times he would find it impossible to divert his thoughts from his work and would sit at the table lost in meditation, scarcely aware of what he ate. Out of deference to him the others would remain silent or converse in whispers. Not infrequently Luther would bring a book to the table and discuss parts of it with his guests. It was customary at the time for a number of students and tutors to dine at the table of some professor, and Luther's board always had its full complement. It was frequently late before the diners arose. Even then some would not disperse. Some might continue their lively exchange of thoughts and perhaps finally join in the songs which were being accompanied by Luther on the lute. The few remaining hours of the evening were spent in reading, catechizing the children, and playing with them or, perhaps, in playing a game of chess. The regular bedtime was nine o'clock. Artificial light was poor and expensive in those days. Besides, nine o'clock was the end of a long day for those who had been active since five or six in the morning. Luther would, as a rule, close his day by offering his private prayers at the open window, if the weather permitted.

Luther was a very sociable man. Love of companionship revealed itself also in his fondness for his home. He quite agreed with the English proverb "A man's home is his castle." When at one time Wittenberg was being disturbed by certain ruffians, Luther declared in a sermon that, though he was a religious man, anyone attempting to break the peace of his home would be given a hot reception, nor would he (Luther) hesitate to dispatch the intruder, if need be, with a clear conscience.[47] Luther's candid nature increased his capacity for friendship. Had he not possessed great earnestness and will power, he could have made a poor monk and a miserable hermit. He was too communicative. His nature craved the companionship of friends. He thrived on the exchange of thoughts. Controversy exhilarated and stimulated him. Martin Luther was designed to be a friend, a husband, and a father. Preserved Smith says: "Luther's whole nature blossomed out in response to the warm sunshine of domestic life."[48] His circle of friends became very large. No wonder it did; for Mathesius assures us that men found the great man to be "a joyous, frolicsome companion."

To his friend Prince Joachim of Anhalt, who was inclined to be melancholy and to avoid company, Luther wrote: "Hausmann has told me that Your Grace has been a little unwell. . . . It often occurs to me that, as Your Grace leads a quiet life, melancholy and sad thoughts may be the cause of such indisposition; wherefore I advise Your Grace, as a young man, to be merry, to ride, hunt, and keep good company, who can cheer Your Grace in a godly and honorable way. For loneliness and sadness are simply poison and death, especially to a young man. . . . Joy and good humor, in honor and seemliness, is the best medicine for a young man, yea, for all men. I, who have hitherto spent my life in mourning and sadness, now seek and accept joy wherever I can find it. We now know, thank God, that we can be happy with a good conscience and can use God's gifts with thankfulness. . . ."[49] A month thereafter he wrote to the same friend, whose spirits had meanwhile improved: "As soon as I have fed the printer a little bit, so that I can rest, I will come to you with Pomeranian Bugenhagen and his little Pomeranians and marmots, so that my gracious lady, your wife, may see how like the old dog the puppies are and how merry. God bless you. Amen. Your Grace must really look out for that marvelous chess-player, Franz Burkhardt, for he is quite sure that he can play the game like a professional.

---

[47] Ma, M 106.   [48] Sm, L 322.   [49] Sm, L 322.

I would give a button to see him play as well as he thinks he can. He can manage the knights, take a castle or two, and fool the peasant pawns, but the queen beats him on account of his weakness for the fair sex, which he cannot deny." [50]

Luther's sociability was not aristocratic and exclusive. Any decent person was of social interest to him. He would converse with the lowliest without any airs of superiority and associate with the high and mighty without any touch of obsequiousness. The Reformer once remarked that he had rather seek the company of his swineherd John and his pigs than be alone. [51]

LUTHER FELT BOTH JOY AND SORROW VERY DEEPLY

Sociable natures are warm natures. They are hearty, sensitive. The German has a striking, rather untranslatable expression for such personalities: *gemuetvoll*. Luther's was such a nature: deeply emotional but not morbidly sentimental. His laughter and his tears were very genuine. He apologized for neither and hid neither. We have seen how matters pertaining to the kingdom of Christ enlisted Luther's deepest sympathy. Like a Psalmist or a Prophet of old, he was filled with joy and sorrow that were both profound and vocal. His reactions to his social experiences were similar. The Reformer was called upon to suffer many heartaches in his family life. Two of his children died, and he keenly felt the bereavement. Elizabeth Luther's stay on earth was brief, like that of a migratory bird, which remains a short while in transit to bluer skies and warmer climes. [52] Luther's heart had scarcely begun to entwine itself about the precious little mite when God, who had given her, took her again.

But it was different in the case of Magdalena. God seemed to have sent her to take the place of Elizabeth; and Luther seems to have loved her for her little sainted sister's sake no less than for the sake of her own sweet self, loved her, therefore, with a twofold love, so to speak. And then, after fourteen years, after Magdalena had completely captured the big heart of her father

---

[50] Sm, L 323 f.   [51] K-K, M II:493.   [52] See p. 259 above.

by her winsome personality, God took her too. She was old enough to understand the situation. Luther's conversation with her on her deathbed is part of one of the most touching scenes of his entire life. The narrative which describes it comes to us from the pen of one of the household who was present. It moves one by its very simplicity. We are told: "As his daughter lay very ill, Dr. Luther said: 'I love her very much, but, dear God, if it be Thy will to take her, I submit to Thee.' Then he said to her as she lay in bed: 'Magdalena, my dear little daughter, would you like to stay here with your father, or would you willingly go to your Father yonder?' She answered: 'Darling father, as God wills.' Then said he: 'Dearest child, the spirit is willing, but the flesh is weak.' Then he turned away and said: 'I love her very much; if my flesh is so strong, what can my spirit do? God has given no bishop so great a gift in a thousand years as He has given me in her. I am angry with myself that I cannot rejoice in heart and be thankful as I ought.' Now as Magdalena lay in the agony of death, her father fell down before the bed on his knees and wept bitterly and prayed that God might free her. Then she departed and fell asleep in her father's arms. . . . As they laid her in the coffin, he said: 'Darling Lena, you will rise and shine like a star, yea, like the sun. . . . I am happy in spirit, but the flesh is sorrowful and will not be content; the parting grieves me beyond measure. . . . I have sent a saint to heaven.' " [53]

The struggle between his two reigning passions, submission to God and love for his daughter, shook his great heart to its very depth, and for a time even prayer could not staunch his burning tears. A few days after Magdalena's death he wrote to Justus Jonas: "My dearest daughter Magdalena has been reborn to the eternal kingdom of Christ; and although my wife and I ought only to give thanks and rejoice at such a happy pilgrimage and blessed end . . . yet so strong is natural affection that we must sob and groan in heart under the oppression of killing grief. . . . Would that I and all mine might have such a death, or rather such a life.

[53] Sm, L 353 f.

She was, as you know, of a sweet, gentle, and loving nature." [54] Still later he wrote to a friend: "I have conquered the pain of a father, though only by a sort of fuming anger against death. By this counterirritant I have staunched my tears. I loved her dearly; but I dare say death will find its punishment on that Day together with him who is its author." [55]

By this time (1543) Luther must have felt peculiarly strong ties binding him to the other world. His father had died in 1530, his mother in 1531, and now two of his daughters had entered into the rest of the people of God. News of his father's death had come to him while he was at the Feste Coburg during the Diet of Augsburg. The faithful Veit Dietrich described his reaction to the news in a letter to Luther's wife. He wrote: "Although his father's death was very bitter to him, he ceased mourning for it after two days. When he read Reinecke's letter, he said to me: 'My father is dead.' And then he took his Psalter and went to his room and wept so much that for two days he couldn't work. Since then he has not given way to grief any more." [56]

In 1538 the Reformer had lost one of his dearest friends in the person of Nicolaus Hausmann, who had recently accepted a call to a congregation in Freiberg. When, on October 17, he left Wittenberg for his new charge, both he and Luther vainly tried to keep back their tears. Did they sense what was coming? During his first sermon, on November 6, Hausmann suffered a stroke and was carried out of the pulpit. He died in the evening from another stroke. Luther's friends broke the news to him gently. The Reformer exclaimed: "He was truly a very dear friend of mine"; then he could no longer contain himself but sobbed aloud. Throughout the day the death of his friend lay like a dead weight upon his heart. Luther would converse with Melanchthon and Jonas, suddenly lapse into silence, sigh, and wipe the blinding tears from his eyes.[57] In a subsequent letter Luther expressed his surprise at the fact that his friends were so

---

[54] Sm, L 354.
[55] In Wa, L 205.
[56] Sm, L 251.
[57] K-K, M II:519.

hesitant to inform him of Hausmann's death, since he (Luther) knew how entirely his friend lived in Christ, and "precious in the sight of the Lord is the death of His saints." [58] Martin Luther was no stoic. He had no desire to be one. He held that a man was born to enter into the joys and the sorrows of life with a heart that responds to both. His unembarrassed registration of joy and sorrow was another manifestation of his childlike candor. It has endeared him to many men. Luther was so human.

FALSE VIEW OF LIFE IN ASCETIC MONASTICISM

He was human also in his appreciation of the good things of this life. By word and deed he exposed the false philosophy which in monkery had made such a caricature of Christian ideals. The ascetic ideals of piety may be traced back through the Middle Ages to the post-Apostolic period. These ideals consisted largely in the abnegation of sensuous enjoyments. The pagan philosophers of Greece had taught that the body of man is the prison of his soul, that the spiritual has been enslaved and degraded by the material or sensuous. In consequence they held that the corporeal is the seat and source of sin. Under the influence of this false view early Christian theologians misunderstood the two Biblical concepts of "spirit and flesh." They fancied that "flesh" meant man's corporality and "spirit" his higher intellectual nature. These misconstructions eventuated in an entirely false conception of the ethical and the moral. Finally it was commonly held and publicly taught that the most effective way to achieve a more perfect life was to suppress and crush the sensuous and the physical in one's nature. In this manner monkery with its theoretical denial of the world and its material pleasures had ultimately become the ideal of perfection in Christendom.

Over against these aberrations Luther defended the Scriptural position, according to which God has made man a creature in which an immaterial soul is united with a material body, and the Platonic theory that evil was caused by the union of the

---

[58] Ps. 16:15.

physical with the spiritual is proved to be false. But if the corporeal is a God-intended, integral part of man, it follows that the legitimate satisfying of its wants is not merely to be connived at as a necessary evil but is to be regarded as a sacred duty. It might have been foreseen that the suppression of such satisfaction would result in moral perversions of the gravest kind. When it was consistently carried out, it either shriveled men up into inhuman beings, suffering from emotional anemia, so to speak, or it finally made their natures forcibly break through these unnatural inhibitions and then frequently turned them into monsters of vice and indulgence. The fact that monks were frequently "jolly good fellows" does not at all disprove what has been said. It merely demonstrates the instinctive rebellion of human nature against being strapped into a strait jacket, which, it was felt, God had never intended for man. The asceticism of monkery and nunnery is unnatural and inhuman.

Luther called attention to this fact with his usual emphasis. Naturally, his scoring of asceticism, celibacy, and world abnegation in general was misunderstood and misconstrued. To this day one at times meets with the old view, completely exploded by many scholars, both Protestant and Catholic, that Luther was trying to rationalize his apostasy from monkery and that the strong sensuousness of his nature sparked his rebellion against Rome. The Reformer is made out to have been a veritable glutton and a sot, a man whose capacity for food and drink was almost limitless. Even Goethe somewhere says of a man: "He fattened his paunch like Doctor Luther." [59] And it is true, about a year before his death Luther himself said he would give the worms *"einen fetten Doktor"* to eat. But careful investigations have revealed that Martin Luther's sensuous nature was surprisingly weak for a character so energetic and intense. However, this is not entirely unexplainable. We have found Luther to have been a religion-centered person from his very childhood and youth. His chief concerns were always spiritual and otherworldly. His

[59] In Bo, L 197.

vindication of a man's right to enjoy the material blessings of this life was not at all engaged in because of an uncontrollable desire on his part to indulge in sensuous delights. Luther taught thus "to keep the records straight." He merely wanted to make clear what Scripture taught also on this point. Personally the Reformer was very temperate.

LUTHER A MODERATE EATER

The "paunch" Goethe refers to is indeed a historical fact. But as H. Boehmer remarks: "This late natural development was no more a result of immoderate living with him than with most of the poor old people who labor under it today; it was simply a result of defects in metabolism caused by uric acid diathesis. . . . Spiritedly though he occasionally praised the magnificent hospitality of princes and great ones . . . he still preferred 'healthy, simple home food' to all delicacies." [60] In his lectures on Genesis he charged his generation with gluttony and drunkenness. He attributed the short expectancy of life in his days to senseless gorging of food and suicidal guzzling of wine and brandy.[61] How could he have afforded to do this at the end of his life if he had himself been notorious for such excesses? We should certainly hear of that sad fact from his contemporaries, nay, from the honest man himself, who so candidly reveals his shortcomings. No; Luther's requirement of food was surprisingly moderate for a man who consumed the energy he did. Melanchthon informs us that at times the Doctor would work to capacity all day, but would eat only a herring or two and a few pieces of bread. Luther once remarked: "My praise goes to clean, good, staple, home-cooked food." [62] His favorite meat was pork. He was fond of fruit, especially apples.

But what of Luther's drinking? His enemies have accused him of excess particularly in this respect. Did the Reformer perhaps have his own too liberal use of strong drink in mind when he complained: People "are veritable sows that disregard the

---

[60] Bo, L 197.   [61] Wal I:712 f.   [62] K-K, M II:496.

roses and violets in a garden but stick their snouts into the filth. That is how the slanderous conduct themselves: they have no eyes for the virtues of great people; but if they spy a failing or a blemish in a person, *that* they love to spread abroad, or they fatten themselves on it, that is, they thoroughly enjoy it." [63] Now, it should be remembered that Luther lived in an age in which the use of strong drink in large quantities and at frequent intervals was practically the rule everywhere. That the secular and regular clergy constituted no exception to this rule need be proved to no one. Charles V is said to have commonly washed his food down with three quarts (!) of wine at dinner. Some historians contend that this quantity represents an understatement. But we hear of no one accusing His Majesty of excess in this respect.[64] It must also be borne in mind that our common beverages, tea and coffee, were not used in the Europe of Luther. Then, too, the water was often considered unfit to drink. But none of these considerations are advanced here to divert attention from the fact that Martin Luther liked a good, refreshing, strengthening drink.

He was especially fond of good beer; and he was convinced that his own Catherine could brew as good a beer as was to be found anywhere. Commercial brewing was not nearly so common in the sixteenth century as it is now, and many homes no less than monasteries and other institutions regularly prepared their own drinks. While on a visit to the Princes of Anhalt in 1534, Luther wrote to his wife: "There is nothing worth drinking here, for which I am sorry, for I like a good drink and recall the good wine and beer I have at home, and also a fair lady (or ought I say lord?). It would be a good thing for you to send me the whole wine-cellar and a bottle of your own beer as often as you can. If you don't, I shall not return because of this new beer. God bless you and the children and household. Amen." [65] Beer was the common drink at tables throughout Germany in the days of Luther. Mathesius informs us that in later life the Reformer

---

[63] Ma, M 230.　　　　[64] Sm, L 318.　　　　[65] Erl 55:61.

also used it as a sedative before going to bed and that he would jokingly tell the "young fellows" they would have to excuse old men like the Elector and him for looking for their pillow in a glass of beer.[66]

"Luther certainly stopped short of intemperance," says Preserved Smith. This biographer also points out that no one who turned out the enormous amount of work that Luther did could possibly have been given to the excessive use of strong drink. The enemies of the Reformer have combed his writings to find something, anything, a letter, a phrase, a term, an allusion, or an intimation that might be construed into a charge of intemperance. They labored with a zeal worthy of a better cause. The "worst" passage they have been able to find is so patently wide of the mark that we shall insert it here merely to show to what length malice will go in its unhallowed effort to besmirch a good name. In 1528 Luther wrote his larger dissertation on the Lord's Supper against the Zwinglians. Toward the end of that writing the Reformer says: "In this dissertation I wish to confess my faith before God and the whole world, from article to article, in which faith I expect to persevere till my death, with the help of God to depart from the world in it, and to appear before the judgment seat of our Lord Jesus Christ. And I see the necessity of doing this in order that no one after my death may say: 'If Luther were now living, he would maintain and teach this or that article differently; for he did not sufficiently meditate on the subject.' On the contrary, I assert now as then and then as now that with the grace of God I have considered all these articles with the greatest care, compared them with the Scriptures frequently, again and again, and would as assuredly defend them, as I have now defended the Sacrament of the Altar. I am not intoxicated now nor void of reflection; I know what I am saying. I deeply feel, too, what responsibility I shall bear at the coming of the Lord Jesus Christ on the Day of Judgment. Therefore no one shall charge me with loose or careless decisions. I am in earnest." [67]

---

[66] Ma, M 226.   [67] Wal XX:1094 f.

THE CHARGES OF HIS ENEMIES ARE SLANDERS

The traducers of Luther have of course singled out of this solemn passage, which sounds like the last will and testament of the man, the clause: "I am not intoxicated now." This expression, they exclaim, proves that at times Luther was, according to his own confession, intoxicated. But this is strange logic. Do the slanderers of the Reformer also conclude that the early Christians frequently became intoxicated after nine o'clock in the morning because Peter told the scoffers at Pentecost: "These are not drunken as ye suppose, seeing it is but the third hour of the day"?[68] Luther's expression is, of course, a proverbial way of saying that one is speaking with a clear understanding of the import of one's remarks. This appears from the epexegetical words "nor devoid of reflection; I know what I am saying." The very word "sober" is used in this sense by English-speaking people in our days. Luther uses such iterations and strong words to express the positiveness of his conviction, the fact that his doctrinal position is the result of serious and sober thought.

Luther's judgment on drunkenness may be considered conveniently summarized in his exposition of Joel 2:5 f. The passage is too long to quote in its entirety. The Reformer points out that many people consider intoxication far less reprehensible than miserliness and cheating. In fact, many people, remarks Luther, "actually desire it as a sort of alleviation of their cares and labors. So judges the world. But if we consider this matter in the right way, we shall hold drunkenness to be one of the very greatest sins, which draws countless other sins in its train. . . . [Drunkards] lose the distinguishing characteristic of man, their reason, and degenerate into animals. . . . But this degeneration is still not the chief indictment against drunkenness. Holy Writ teaches us truths about this sin which the heathen could not recognize. . . . Paul says (1 Cor. 6:10): 'Drunkards . . . shall not inherit the kingdom of God.' . . . Drunkenness enervates the soul no less than the

---

[68] Acts 2:15.

body." [69] This is what Luther thought of drunkenness, an evil so fearfully common in the Germany of his days that many scarcely considered it a sin at all. Luther frequently speaks of his "drunken Germans," and "drunken peasants." He tried to arouse the conscience of his contemporaries also against this vice and its deadening effects. Entire sermons were delivered against drunkenness. Luther did not insist on total abstinence, but he did preach moderation in the use of all the pleasures and treasures of this world. While reading his writings, one is ever and again amazed at his sober, sane, and serious view of life.

Look at his attitude toward riches! The prudent prayer found at Prov. 30:8: "Give me neither poverty nor riches; feed me with food that is needful for me," [70] was, in effect, Luther's prayer throughout his life. He feared the effects of the extremes of good and ill fortune on human nature. In his *Table Talk* we hear him exclaim: "How should God deal with us? Good days we cannot bear, evil days we cannot endure. If He gives us riches, then we are proud, that no man can live near us in peace; nay, we would be carried upon men's shoulders and would be adored as gods. If He gives us poverty, then we are dismayed, impatient, and murmur against Him. Therefore, nothing were better for us than forthwith to be covered over with the shovel." [71] Again Luther is said to have remarked: "The human heart can bear neither good nor evil. If we possess money and goods, there is no rest; if we are in poverty, there is no peace." In 1532 he preached a sermon on the feeding of the five thousand to the group in his house. In the introduction he spoke of the dangers inherent in the two economic extremes, want and wealth, and said: "The wealthy despise God's Word and fancy they need neither God nor His Word. The poor say: 'How can I accept the Word and obey and follow it? I am poor and must have something to eat and drink; whoever wants to get anything out of people must speak well of them and do what they want, although he really does not like

---

[69] Wal VI:1500 sq. [70] American version. [71] Wal XXII:83.

to do it.' This attitude produces prostitutes, rogues, and godless persons, who do everything people want. In this manner, wealth to the right and poverty to the left constantly hinder the Word of God and faith." [72] Luther spoke from observation. During the Peasants' War he had had ample opportunity to see the selfishness and the insatiable greed of both prince and pauper. In reference to the covetousness and worldly-mindedness of the peasants he once remarked: "I should desire to be a little angel for just three days. I would steal all the treasures of the peasants and fling them into the Elbe. Hoity-toity! The entire supply of rope would be too small because of the rate at which the peasants would hang themselves: one here, another there." [73]

WHAT LUTHER THOUGHT OF WEALTH

But while Luther preached against the love of money, he never condemned the possession of wealth as such. He did not believe that riches were necessarily an evil in a man's hand, but he earnestly warned against letting them capture and possess a man's heart. In his practical exposition of the Book of Amos he says: "God does not condemn the possession of wealth, but the evil use of it, that is, its use merely to satisfy one's selfish desire, without coming to the aid of the poor and without being a faithful steward of that which God has given." [74] We have already learned to appreciate this character trait of Luther in a different connection.[75] He felt that a man is in the world to be of service to others, to his God and to his fellow man. A person who holds such an altruistic philosophy of life will value wealth for the good it can do. It is true, very few of those who take this view of riches ever become wealthy. They give out almost as much as they take in. This was largely the case with Luther himself. For those who hugged and hoarded their wealth and loved it for its own dear self's sake, the Reformer had little more than contempt. Of such wealth and its miserly owners he said: "Wealth

---

[72] Wal XIII:1720.
[73] In K-K, M II:510.
[74] Wal VI:1743 f.
[75] See p. 192 f. above.

is the most insignificant thing on earth, the most trifling gift that God has bestowed on mankind. What is it in comparison with God's Word, what in comparison with corporal gifts, such as beauty and health? Nay, what is it in comparison with the gifts of character, such as understanding, skill, and wisdom? Yet men are so eager to gain riches that no labor, no pains or risk, are shirked in the course of its acquisition. . . . [But] our Lord commonly gives riches to coarse asses whom He does not favor with spiritual blessings." [76]

Now, this practical contempt of wealth may by many be considered wholesome, but the Doctor's lack of any appreciation of domestic economy will not be so favorably judged. His utter indifference to achieving economic security, to say nothing of affluence, is really astounding. He seems to have had no idea whatever of the value of money. Yet Luther might have become a fairly wealthy man in a perfectly honest manner if, with only a moderate degree of interest, he had improved the many opportunities that presented themselves to him. How much money he might have amassed if he had begun the Reformation in order to enrich himself it is difficult to estimate. We believe that the sum he might have successfully demanded from Rome for his silence, had he been a different character, would run into many figures. But Mathesius informs us that also Luther's enemies had discovered that worldly riches meant nothing to him. Someone had rather naively suggested silencing the Reformer by cramming a few thousand dollars down his throat. Another who knew Luther replied: "That procedure will get you nowhere with him. The German beast thinks nothing of money." [77]

Luther seems to have had little interest in making money beyond his immediate need. He appeared to literally "take no thought for the morrow." No doubt the Reformer's attitude was rooted not merely in his intense religion-centeredness but also in his great, childlike trust in God as the Provider of all. We are

[76] Wal XXII:234.   [77] Ma, M 229.

not prepared to contend that Luther overdid matters in this respect and that he must be charged with improvidence; and we believe that H. Boehmer is going too far when he says: "Prudent calculation seems to have been inexcusably lacking in him." [78]

The economic principles by which Luther guided his life he expressed thus in his exposition of 1 Pet. 1:17: "We are to use all things on earth as a guest who goes on wearily and arrives at an inn, where he must tarry overnight and can receive nothing but food and lodging; yet he does not say that the property of the inn is his. So must we also act in regard to our temporal possessions, as though they were not ours and enjoy only so much of them as is needful to sustain the body, and with the rest we are to help our neighbor. Thus the Christian life is only a night's sojourning; for we have here no abiding city but must find it where our Father is in heaven." [79] These words may be supplemented by a passage from a letter Luther sent to Elector John: "I have delayed thanking Your Grace for the cloth you sent me. I humbly beg Your Grace not to believe those who say that I have need of such things. Unfortunately I have more, especially from Your Grace, than I can reconcile with my conscience; it becomes me as a minister not to have superfluity, and, moreover, I do not wish it. I fear Your Grace's too favorable kindness so much that I fear for myself, for I would not willingly in this life be found with those to whom Christ says: 'Woe unto you rich, for ye have received your consolation.'" [80]

But, leaving general principles, let us look at Luther's domestic establishment and its economy more in particular. Before his marriage Luther had a salary of one hundred gulden, the equivalent in our currency and present buying power of about eight hundred dollars. The gulden is worth about fifty cents, but in Luther's day its purchasing power was fifteen to twenty times as great as our half dollar today. After his marriage, in 1525,

---

[78] Bo, L 232.   [79] Wal IX:1154.   [80] S-J, LC II:490 f.

Luther's salary was doubled. It is curiously interesting to read that a wedding gift of about two hundred and fifty dollars came from Archbishop Albert of Mayence. Luther refused to accept it, but his thrifty bride heard of it and accepted it without his knowledge. When the Reformer subsequently learned of this transaction, his face must have been a study. He scarcely knew whether to register anger or amusement. He felt both. In 1532 his salary was raised to about two thousand and five hundred dollars in modern terms, and in 1536 the equivalent of another eight hundred was added in perquisites.

"About 1541 Luther's income was further increased by a pension from the Elector to him and his heirs of fifty gulden per annum on a capital of one thousand gulden. In the last year of his life a pension on the same terms was granted him by the King of Denmark. . . . He mentions a legacy of a hundred gulden left him about 1520, and Henry VIII gave fifty gulden in 1535."

As to the Reformer's holdings in real estate, "the Black Cloister was legally deeded to Luther on February 4, 1532. About the same time he bought a small garden adjacent, moved by the prayers and tears of Katie. Some time in the thirties he bought for nine hundred gulden the large house and property of Claus Bildenhauer, on the swine market, a little north of the Cloister, near the present post-office. The 'lazy brook' which flowed through it is still to be seen. Katie made a fish pond of it, in which, as her husband said, she took more pleasure than many a noble in his large preserves. About 1534 Luther bought a very small garden for his servant Wolfgang Sieberger. In 1541 he purchased for four hundred and thirty gulden another cottage and land adjoining the Black Cloister which had once belonged to Brisger. . . . In 1544 he bought a hop-garden for three hundred and seventy-five gulden. All these purchases had been in Wittenberg. About 1540 he bought from Katie's brother, Hans von Bora, the little farm of Zuelsdorf, some twenty miles south of Leipsic on the road to Altenburg. This was Katie's favorite property; she spent much time there, cultivating the land, which was richer than that around Wittenberg. The price was 610 gulden, of which the Elector gave six hundred. . . . Katie also rented a large bit of meadow land, the Boos Farm, from the Elector." [81]

A few years before his death Luther estimated his personal property at one thousand gulden, or about nine thousand dollars. He had actually made a sort of will in 1542, but had drawn it up without a notary because of his great dislike for lawyers. According to the then law such a will was invalid.

The Reformer might have realized a little fortune on his writings. At one time a publisher offered him about three thousand dollars a year for the exclusive right to print his books, but Luther declined the offer. He remarked that he wanted his books to be as cheap as possible since his desire was not to get money out of the people but to get Christian knowledge and principles into them. Again his single purpose in life appears. Furthermore, at that time professors commonly received money from the individual student in addition to their salaries. This stipend, called the *honorarium,* Luther refused to take. For some time the Doctor was also assistant pastor of the city church at Wittenberg. This position entailed considerable extra work, but Luther declined any remuneration for it, remarking that since his salary satisfied his needs, he "did not want to preach for money." [82] The Elector offered Luther a share in the rich Schneeberg silver mines, but also this offer was declined.[83] Tax exemption was offered him by the city magistracy, but he insisted upon paying taxes like other citizens. Surely, about the greatest possible display of historical ignorance would be furnished by the man who would say that Martin Luther engaged in the work of the Reformation in order to enrich himself.

"THERE IS NONE UPON EARTH THAT I DESIRE BESIDE THEE"

Princes become wealthy, publishers rich; universities become famous and people free; the needy are helped, and unto the poor the Gospel is preached because of the labors of Martin Luther.

---

[81] Sm, L 367, 369; cp. K-K, M II:490–495.
[82] Wa, L 44.   [83] Wei Tischreden 3471.

And *his* reward? The man writes to his friend Link: "Money and goods I do not have and do not desire. If I formerly possessed a good name and honor, these possessions are now being very energetically ruined. Just one thing remains, my weak body, rendered dead tired by constant adversity. If they take that, according to God's will, by cunning or force, they will perhaps deprive me of an hour or two of my life. But I am satisfied with the possession of my sweet Redeemer and Propitiator, my Lord Jesus Christ, to whom I shall joyfully sing as long as I live." [84]

The Reformer speaks of his "weak body, rendered dead tired by constant adversities." Perhaps he never realized how much he had impaired his constitution by his monastic austerities. The monk was to consider the physical base and contemptible. But after Luther had been led from medieval perversions to the light of Scripture, he saw in the Christian's body the temple of God's Spirit. [85] As such it was to be cherished and cared for, not despised and neglected. Physical exercise, diversions, and amusements were not to be considered a wasting of time. Any recreation that was not sinful in and of itself was allowable and might at times even be required and prescribed as a necessity. Such care of one's body was to be looked upon as a service rendered to God as truly as the care of one's soul. The following incident, related by Mathesius, may serve to illustrate Luther's sane views also in this respect. "When Luther, returning home with his companions from Coburg, was visiting Spalatin, and Philip [Melanchthon], constantly engrossed in thoughts concerning the Apology, was writing during the meal, he [Luther] arose and took the pen away from him, saying: 'God can be honored not alone by work but also by rest and recreation.' " [86]

WHOLESOME OUTDOOR RECREATION

According to Luther the field of recreation was very broad, extending from simple resting, as in the quotation, to the strenuous diversion of gardening. Like many people before and after

---

[84] In Wa, F 50.   [85] 1 Cor. 6:19.   [86] In Tr. Intr. 42 a.

him, Luther found working in God's earth to be a veritable tonic for frayed and tired nerves. During the strain of the winter of 1526—1527 he wrote to Link: "I am glad you promise me seed in the spring. Send as much as you can; I want it and am looking for it. If I can do anything in return, command me, and it will be done. For though Satan and his members may rage, I will laugh at him and will turn my attention to the garden, that is, to the blessings of the Creator, and enjoy them to His praise." [87] In Luther's latitude, it is true, this splendid recreation is seasonal, and during the greater part of the year relaxation and recreation must be looked for elsewhere. The Reformer had tried hunting while at the Wartburg and had even done a little target shooting with Veit Dietrich during his involuntary seclusion in "the Wilderness." But he professed not to be fond of these sports. For hunting, it is evident, his heart was too tender.[88] He strongly recommended outdoor sports to the young nobles as a substitute for their notorious protracted drinking bouts.

LUTHER'S INDOOR RECREATIONS

Indoors Luther enjoyed a game of chess in particular. He is said to have played the game very well. We suspect that pitting one's skill against his was a change of work rather than an idling of the mental mechanism. At one time the Reformer determined to try his hand at lathing and wrote to Link at Nuremberg for the necessary tools. Luther told Link that his lathing was to serve a twofold purpose. It was to be a diverting avocation, and it might also prove to be valuable some day as a way of making a living. "When the world simply will no longer support us as ministers of the Word," wrote the Reformer, "we want to know how to sustain ourselves by the work of our hands and want to serve the unworthy and the ungrateful after the example of our Father in heaven." This venture was not very successful. Some-

---

[87] S-J, LC II:388.   [88] See S-J, LC II:53 f.

what later Luther wrote to his friend to send no more lathing tools unless he could discover some that would continue to work of their own accord after Sieberger would have neglected them and fallen asleep.

ON DANCING

On dancing as a recreation Luther made some notable remarks. However, it must be remembered that the Reformer knew nothing of our modern dances. He would certainly have condemned many of them and directed them back to the dens of vice whence some of them came. The sequence of movements in many of the dances common in Luther's days it is impossible accurately to determine, but they must have been distinctly decent, for the Reformer condemned every kind of dance in which the partners circled about in close contact. At the same time the Reformer did not frown upon the element of sex attraction in dancing. On the contrary, he recognized as one of the legitimate purposes of the dance the creating of opportunities for the marriageable to become acquainted with each other under the supervision of chaperons.[89] Luther himself did not dance. It is more surprising to hear that Melanchthon ventured to do so.[90]

ON DRAMATICS

That the broad-minded, tolerant, and conservative Luther would not frown upon all dramatics and theatrical performances, was to be foreseen. He did not agree with those who found the dramatization of Biblical incidents and stories a profanation. He once pointed out that the Gospel had been diplomatically introduced by such presentations into a section of Lower Germany from which its public preaching had been debarred.[91] But even to secular drama Luther was sympathetic. Upon one occasion he was told of a teacher in Silesia who had given offense to some by proposing to perform before a Christian audience a comedy written by the pagan Terence. Luther was asked whether such

---

[89] K-K, M II:506; cp. Erl 11:40 f. [91] K-K, M II:504.
[90] K-K, M II:683; Pr, L 95.

an undertaking were proper. He answered that the pupils should be permitted to present the drama. Such plays would be of great educational value to actors and audience alike. They are a mirror of life, said Luther. Nor ought Christians be held to avoid them because at times coarse jokes and objectionable love affairs are found in them. If a man *insists* upon taking offense, even the Holy Bible may give him occasion to do so, was Luther's realistic comment.[92] There was certainly nothing prudish or puritanical about Martin Luther.

ON NATURE

Whoever would mentally reconstruct the Reformer should not visualize him merely in church, in the lecture hall, poring over manuscripts in his study, trying to plumb the depths of theological mysteries with his friends about his table, or even jesting with his wife and children. Luther should also be followed through the woods and fields; he must be observed walking and working in the garden of the Black Cloister, sowing and weeding and grafting with a zest that is written all over his face, harvesting with a joy and satisfaction that at times breaks forth in grateful song. The Reformer was a great lover of nature. Nor did he merely possess the melancholy joy of a gloomy Northener, sadly sensitive only to those phenomena of nature which depress the spirit. Nature, we have seen, was largely the workshop of the devil to him. In field and forest he sensed his presence and saw evidences of his power. But this consideration did not detract from Luther's love of nature. Though "the trail of the serpent was over it all," Luther had an eye for the beauty of a rose, an ear for the song of birds, and a heart to enjoy the thousand miracles of God's great outdoors.[93]

ON FLOWERS

He was a great lover of flowers. Into the heat of the Leipzig Debate he took a few to refresh himself by them. One of his first projects after marriage was the cultivation of a flower garden, to

---

[92] Erl 62:336 f.   [93] K-K, M II:499.

which a very productive vegetable garden was added. With the pride of a successful gardener he wrote to Spalatin in the summer of 1526: "I have planted a garden and dug a well, and both have turned out well. Come, and you will be crowned with roses and lilies." [94] Luther seems to have been especially fond of roses. Somewhere we have read that he once remarked to a friend: "When you see a rose, tell her I greet her." His *Table Talk* reveals that flowers were frequently the texts for impromptu sermonets on the omnipotence and wisdom of God.[95]

Shrubs and trees, particularly fruit trees, were likewise of great interest to Luther. He tried his hand at grafting and within his circle of friends became favorably known for his success in this field. In fact, Duchess Elizabeth of Brunswick once sent the Doctor a number of good cheeses and asked him to favor her in return with any "extraordinary" plants which he might have on hand. The gardener Luther therefore forwarded her some small mulberry and fig trees with which he had been having good success.[96]

The Doctor also kept a few beehives. The busy tenants called forth never-ending comments of admiration from him. The cleanliness, industry, order, and skill observable in the apiary reminded the Reformer of all sorts of matters and relations in Church, State, and home. Particularly the manner in which the bees would swarm around the queen and would be lost without her seemed an apt illustration to him of the loyalty of believers to their Savior, without whom there would be no "communion of saints." [97]

ON BIRDS

Also Luther's great fondness for birds was a sign of the true lover of nature. He loved to spy on birds and observe their ways and manners. "One night two little birds flew into the room but were frightened by us and would not let us approach. The Doctor

---

[94] S-J, LC II:374.
[95] E. g. Erl 57:232 f.
[96] Erl 55:211.
[97] K-K, M II:500.

said to me: 'Schlaginhaufen, these birds lack faith. They do not know how glad I am to have them here nor that I would let no harm be done them. Thus we act toward God, who loves us and has given His Son for us." [98] Upon another occasion the Doctor, sitting in his garden at twilight, noticed how two birds, which had built their nest in a near-by tree, were periodically frightened away by the passing of people. Thereupon Luther said: "Ah, you dear little bird, do not flee. I am at heart truly your friend, if only you would believe my assurance. But just so we also do not believe and trust our Lord God, though He grants and gives us everything that is good; indeed, He does not want to kill us, He who gave His Son into death for us." [99] Upon another evening a bird was more successful in finding an undisturbed branch upon which to spend the night. Luther observed it composing itself for rest as the twilight thickened into night. Finally he remarked: "That bird has had its supper and now wants to sleep in peace and security. It is not fretting and worrying at all about tomorrow. . . . It sits contentedly up there on its little branch and lets God take care of it." [100]

ON DOGS

Luther never outgrew his love for dogs. Especially while he was living alone in the Black Cloister, his dog, Toelpel, was his constant companion. He was granted liberties which Catherine a few years later no doubt found entirely too great. She noticed that some of the Doctor's books, even a Bible, had edges so ragged that only Toelpel's teeth could be considered responsible for them. But Luther loved his dog and once remarked that he hoped he would find transfigured dogs in heaven. At one time the Doctor was playing with Toelpel and, rubbing the dog's ears, said, while looking lovingly into his loyal eyes: "The dog is the most faithful of animals and would be much esteemed were it not so common. Our Lord God has made his greatest gifts the commonest." [101]

---

[98] Sm, L 337 f.　　[99] Erl 57:134.　　[100] Erl 57:238.　　[101] Sm, L 338.

LUTHER WHOLE-SOULED, LARGEHEARTED, WELL-BALANCED

"What a nature this man had!" S. Coleridge said of Luther. There certainly was nothing crabbed, narrow, and shriveled up about the character of Martin Luther. His was a big soul, his a big heart. He loved his God, his fellow man, and everything good in the world. In full draughts he refreshed himself with the beauties and benefactions of his Lord's creation. No one observing the Reformer's unconventional manners and his childlike appreciation of nature and its marvels; no one hearing him sing out joyfully in his clear tenor, while good nature beamed forth from his deep, dark eyes; no one hearing his ringing, carefree laughter at the witty remark of some friend; no one thus seeing and hearing Martin Luther would have recognized him to be one of the most serious men in the world, one of the greatest men of all times, and one of the most profoundly learned theologians of his days. But Luther's professional life, to which we now turn, proves him to have been all of that.

CHAPTER X

PROFESSOR LUTHER

Brother Martin is a man of genius.
Pope Leo X

LUTHER WAS A VERITABLE DYNAMO OF ENERGY. NOTHING BUT the hand of death seemed able to stop that powerful pen and silence those eloquent lips of his. The man's industry appears the more astounding when we bear in mind the stress and strain under which he frequently labored. There were "fightings and fears within, without." Both body and soul were racked with pain. More than once Luther and his friends fancied that the end was near. The Reformer felt enervated and used up. But the indomitable spirit within him refused to give up the fight against the powers of darkness. Even when working under physical handicaps that might have entirely incapacitated the ordinary man, Luther not infrequently turned out work that in quality, no less than quantity, is to this day the envy of men in the prime of life. Thus he wrote from the Wartburg under date of July 13, 1521, that he was so sick that unless relief would soon come, he would have to risk a journey to Erfurt in order to consult a physician. But on this very day he wrote a five-page letter to Melanchthon in which he mentions that he is laboring at a series of sermons (his postil), projecting an answer to an attack by the Catholic Emser, and, in addition, producing a translation of a Latin polemical writing of Melanchthon. The same day also witnessed him penning to Amsdorf another long letter, in which he outlined for his friend the best strategy for a reply to an attack upon him (Amsdorf). At the end of this letter he complained of his own indolence. He was dissatisfied with himself.[1] Luther seems ever to have looked forward to what he should like to do rather than backward to what he had successfully accomplished.

---

[1] Wa, L 57 f.

Probably he would have spent a more quiet life if he could have lived more in the satisfying enjoyment of his achievements than in the ever-present awareness that a world of work still remained to be done. But had Luther been less restlessly industrious, the world would have been the poorer.

LUTHER'S TIRELESS INDUSTRIOUSNESS

This tireless industriousness is observable in his character from the very beginning. In 1516 Johann Lang was informed by Brother Martin: "I need a couple of amanuenses, or secretaries, as I do almost nothing the livelong day but write letters. . . . I am convent preacher, the reader at meals, am asked to deliver a sermon daily in the parish church, am district vicar (that is eleven times prior), business manager of our fish farm at Litzkau, attorney in our case now pending versus the Herzbergers at Torgau, lecturer on St. Paul, assistant lecturer on the Psalter. . . . You see how idle I am!" [2]

The discovery of the "truth as it is in Jesus" naturally increased the industry of the busy man still more. The two Swiss students who met Luther at the inn of the Black Bear at Jena, when the Reformer was on his way to disturbed Wittenberg, observed a book lying beside him on the table. He had been reading in it intently. The volume was the Hebrew Psalter. Even on his journeys his industry would not let him rest. "There was not a lazy bone in Luther's body."

Note, for instance, the amount of work he turned out in 1523. Nervous headaches frequently made work almost impossible for him, and professional duties called him away from Wittenberg for more than a month during this year. But here is the record of his labors in 1523: He lectured regularly at the University. His exposition of Deuteronomy, much of which was delivered at this time, is 240 pages long. He addressed his fellow monks in the early morning on Sundays and the many festival days of the church calendar, preached a sermon later in the morning and

---

[2] Sm, L 32.

another in the afternoon of these days. These sermons were all newly prepared, as the copies made by some of the auditors prove. They fill over five hundred pages in the large format of the Weimar edition of Luther's works. In addition to these publications the Professor produced a few dozen pamphlets and booklets, totaling six hundred and forty pages in the Weimar edition. During this year he was also engaged upon the translation of the Old Testament books from Joshua to Esther. These Biblical books cover about three hundred pages in an average Bible. Nor is even this the full tale of his labors. Luther wrote hundreds of letters during this year. Those that have been preserved in their entirety take up more than one hundred pages in the Erlangen edition of his works. There are few who would not find the mere copying of these productions within less than one year an arduous task. But Luther had to create them and had himself to write out most of them longhand. Nor let it be forgotten that besides the time devoted to this literary work Luther gave many a precious hour to interviews and consultations. No wonder J. Hare speaks of the "almost superhuman rapidity and vigor" with which the Reformer carried on his work.

Luther was a very busy man to the very end of his life. During his last year he published no less than eleven books or pamphlets. This number does not include the many sermons and lectures delivered at the University during 1545 but published subsequently, nor the many letters written during this time, almost a hundred of which are extant. The year also saw the production of his dying blast against the Papacy. Leopold von Ranke says: "Luther owed no one an answer that he did not pay." [3] Nor was there any reason why the Reformer should fear to face any attack upon his position. We have seen above how sure he was of his ground. It had not been rashly occupied. If ever a man was well fortified and equipped to hold his own, it was Luther. The industrious Professor was one of the most scholarly and learned men of the age.

---

[3] Ra, D I:213.

LUTHER'S LOVE AND CAPACITY FOR LEARNING OBSERVED EARLY

He seems to have been studiously inclined by nature. Perhaps his father, a practical man with much common sense, observed this inclination at an early date and concluded that God had intended his Martin for one of the learned professions. Hans Luther thereupon worked long hours and spared no effort to make it possible for his gifted son to study law.

SCHOOLS ATTENDED

About Luther's primary education little need be said. He attended the village school at Eisleben, in which "the examination was like a trial for murder," to use his own expression. At the age of thirteen he was sent to Magdeburg to attend a school staffed in part by the Brethren of the Common Life, the "Nullbrueder," a monastic order whose chief aim was the teaching of the Bible to the common people, the cultivation of the vernacular — the language of the people — and the development of a pious life.[4] Perhaps it was at Magdeburg that young Martin's thoughts began to turn towards the monastery. One day the studious, serious lad saw a sight that he vividly described thirty years later. "With my own eyes I saw, when in my fourteenth year I attended school at Magdeburg, a prince of Anhalt . . . who went to beg bread in a friar's cowl on the highways and carried a sack like a donkey. It was so heavy that he had to bend to earth under its weight. But his companion walked by his side without a burden, so that the pious prince might alone serve the world as a perfect example of the gloomy, shorn holiness of monasticism. They had so crushed him that he did all the works of the cloister like any other brother, and he had so rigorously fasted, kept vigil and mortified his flesh that he looked like an emblem of death, mere skin and bones. Indeed, he presently died; for he could not bear up under so strenuous a life. In short, whoever looked at him

---

[4] See RE 3:472–507; 11:723.

fairly drooled in admiration of his sanctity and must needs be ashamed of his worldly position." [5]

In 1498 Luther was transferred to Eisenach, where he attended the school of St. George and was befriended and mothered by Frau Cotta, who had been greatly impressed by the devout singing of Martin, "serious and pious beyond his years." Luther made such satisfactory progress in this school that his father was now fully resolved to send his studious, gifted son to the renowned University of Erfurt. In 1501 Luther matriculated at this institution of learning and soon became known as "the philosopher" because of his studiousness.[6] This love of study never forsook him. His thirst for knowledge grew and at times greatly irked and embarrassed those who ought to have shared it. In the cloister, which he had entered in 1505, the monks imposed many menial tasks upon him and loved to torment him on account of his studiousness. Mathesius says they told him that "by begging and not by studying the cloister was served and enriched." [7]

IN THE CLOISTER

Luther's entry into the cloister was in more than one respect an important milestone in his career. Upon that occasion he was given his own complete copy of the Bible; and how zealously he studied it the Church of Rome was ere long to discover, and all the world now knows. It is true, his university professor, Usingen, advised him to devote more time to the Church Fathers than to Scripture. Others, however, as Staupitz, encouraged the studious monk to search the Scriptures. How rarely this was done in the days of Luther has been mentioned previously. The *Sentences* of Peter Lombard († 1160) and the *Summa Theologiae* of Thomas Aquinas († 1274) had quite displaced Holy Writ, and while the study of Scripture was, indeed, part of the curriculum, it received scant attention. The great Roger Bacon, the "Edison of the Middle Ages," offered this criticism in 1392: "Although the principal study of the theologian ought to be the text of Scripture . . .

---

[5] Erl 31:239 f.   [6] Bo, J 39.   [7] Ma, M 7.

yet in the last fifty years theologians have been principally occupied with questions [for debate], as all know, in *tractates* and *summae* — horse loads, composed by many — and not at all with the holy text of God. . . ." [8]

TO KNOW GOD'S WORD HIS SUPREME CONCERN

To Martin Luther the Bible became increasingly central to all studies. In a very real sense he became a student of one book. He saturated himself with the Bible. His ability to find desired texts in Scripture, to quote entire pages of it, and to tell one where in Holy Writ a certain statement was to be found became the holy envy of his contemporaries. It is not too much to say that few people history knows of have studied the Bible more intensively than did Martin Luther. Preserved Smith says: "Like all natures with an abnormally developed religious faculty, he found his spiritual ancestry rather in Judea than in Greece, even preferring the literature of the Hebrews, an opinion in support of which the great English poet-scholar Milton has elaborately argued in *Paradise Regained.* 'Compared to the wisdom of the Hebrews,' said the German professor, 'that of the Greeks is simply animal, for there can be no true wisdom without knowledge of the true God.' From the first years in the cloister to the day of his death, Luther's chief spiritual nourishment was the Bible." [9] Scripture became the highest court of appeal to Luther.

We do not mean to say that Luther depreciated secular knowledge. It is true, religious fanatics have frequently frowned upon all education and despised all secular studies in the superspirituality of their enthusiasm. So did Muenzer, Carlstadt, and others in the age of the Reformation. But Luther was not a fanatic. His studies and interests were and remained broad. To a friend, Eoban Hess, who had expressed concern on this point, Luther wrote: "I am persuaded that without knowledge of literature pure theology cannot at all endure; just as heretofore, when letters have declined and lain prostrate, theology

---

[8] In Br, L 48.   [9] Sm, L 341.

too has wretchedly fallen and lain prostrate; nay, I see that there has never been a great revelation of the Word of God unless He has first prepared the way by the rise and prosperity of languages and letters, as though they were John the Baptists." [10]

Luther was a good linguist, knowing German, Latin, Greek, and Hebrew. His proficiency in these four languages is indicated with fair accuracy by the order in which they are named. Probably he never knew enough Greek to enjoy reading Thucydides or Aeschylus in the original, but neither could the renowned Humanists of the Italian Renaissance read them. The poet Petrarch found it easier to fondle and kiss Homer's *Iliad* than to construe it. With the Latin language the Reformer was well acquainted. It was the language of the classroom in the sixteenth century. Luther spoke it fluently. He had read Latin authors widely and carefully, as his remarks and criticisms indicate. Cicero and Vergil were among his favorites. Of the great Roman statesman he said: "Cicero is the best philosopher, for he felt that the soul is immortal. He wrote best on natural, moral, and rational philosophy. He is a valuable man, reading with judgment and able to express himself well. . . . I hope God will forgive such men as Cicero their sins. Even if he should not be saved, he will enjoy a situation in hell several degrees higher than that destined for our Cardinal of Mayence." [11] The Reformer was of course widely read in the authors who wrote church Latin. He thought most of Augustine and least of Jerome.

Luther was also well acquainted with church history and exercised his independence of judgment on many of its persons and passages. He had received a very thorough training in logic, nor had general psychology, mathematics — which he disliked — astronomy, the theory of music, philosophy, and political and

---

[10] S-J, LC II:176.   [11] Sm, L 342; cp. Erl 62:341, 351.

domestic economy been neglected. His course of study was, in fact, broader than the courses required today of a well-educated man. When one remembers not only Luther's love of study but the extraordinary gifts with which he had been endowed, it is not surprising that he made a profound impression upon his age and that to this day he casts his spell over those who study him closely. Martin Luther was a genius. H. Boehmer does not hesitate to say: "Even regarded purely as an intellectual character, he was a phenomenon that has no equal." [12]

The Professor loved to move in the realm of the mind and the spirit. He was a student in the best sense of the word, searching for the roots of things, analyzing their nature, and determining their relation to human life and destiny. He had no ambition to play a conspicuous part on the public stage of world affairs. As a real student, he rather wished to be left alone so that he might pursue his studies without disturbance. To the Elector Frederick he wrote: "I cannot easily express my aversion to being plunged in these whirlpools and taken from my studies." [13] But the entire world has reasons to be thankful that Martin Luther was not permitted to live and work in monastic obscurity. Like a rare flower, hidden in some out-of-the-way place, Luther's genius might have passed through the world unnoticed and unknown.

> Full many a flower is born to blush unseen
> And waste its sweetness on the desert air. (Gray.)

But fortunately God's providence intended the world to be the beneficiary of Luther's mighty powers. And the world has recognized and acclaimed the genius of the modest, studious "friar of Wittenberg."

CONTEMPORARY FRIENDS AND FOES TESTIFIED TO LUTHER'S GENIUS

His contemporaries testified to the phenomenal intellectual gifts of the man, aside entirely from any nobility of character and greatness of influence. We have heard his very enemies bear

---

[12] Bo, L 162.   [13] S-J, LC I:478.

witness to the exceptional purity of Luther's life. To these witnesses may be added Johann Faber, conscientious Catholic bishop of Vienna, who wrote: "I greatly wish that all men were truly Lutheran, that is, learnedly pious and piously learned." [14] At about the same time Erasmus was trying to account for his failure to write against the Reformer by telling a friend: "I was not qualified" to do so. The more this Humanist read and heard of Luther, the more he became convinced that the Professor was a most formidable antagonist. To Pope Adrian VI he wrote in 1523: "As to writing against Luther, I have not learning enough." [15] Even if this statement were hypocritical and partly rooted in the cowardice of the timid Erasmus, Luther's learnedness must have been very generally conceded if an Erasmus could hope successfully to use it as an excuse for not writing against him.

In some respects there was an affinity of spirit between Erasmus and Melanchthon. Luther's friend Philip had been a Humanist before he became a theologian, and many hold that he remained too much of a Humanist, in the objectionable sense of the word, after having become a theologian. He shared Erasmus' caution to a large, at times to an alarming extent. But Melanchthon said of the Reformer, to whom few were closer than he was: "Luther is too great, too wonderful, for me to depict in words." Again he said: "One is an interpreter; one, a logician; another, an orator, affluent and beautiful in speech; but Luther is all in all — whatever he writes, whatever he utters, pierces to the soul, fixes itself like arrows in the heart — he is a miracle among men." [16] These words pay tribute to the versatility of Luther. The many-sidedness of his genius is, indeed, one of the most amazing traits in his character. As a rule genius implies something abnormal, the overdevelopment of a certain faculty at the expense of others. But the Reformer reveals what one may call a native symmetry of faculties. He was not a genius who was brilliant and eccentric in one direction, but rather a man who could handle a multitude of interests with outstanding masterfulness.

---

[14] S-J, LC I:320. [15] Fro, L 294, 317. [16] In Kr, C 85 f.

THE ANGLICAN FROUDE

Lest anyone think that these words of high praise are dictated by the uncritical admiration of a blind partisan, we shall here insert the testimony of a few who ought not lightly to be suspected of prejudice. The Anglican James Froude, one of England's greatest historians, has this to say of Luther's mind: "Luther's mind was literally world-wide: his eyes were forever observant of what was around him. At a time when science was scarcely out of its shell, Luther had observed nature with the liveliest curiosity. He had anticipated by mere genius the generative functions of flowers. Human nature he had studied like a dramatist. His memory was a museum of historical information, of anecdotes of great men, of old German literature and song and proverb. Scarce a subject could be spoken of on which he had not thought and on which he had not something remarkable to say." [17]

THE JESUIT DENIFLE

Roman Catholic scholars have, of course, little good to say of the Reformer. As a rule they simply ignore his gifts of intellect and proceed to an interpretation of his motives which is dominated by a poorly concealed hatred. To expect fairness and objectivity from such adversaries is naturally expecting too much. A notable exception is Dr. J. Doellinger. Long before his conscience drove him from the Church of Rome because of her antichristian decree of papal infallibility in 1871, he said of Luther, whose doctrinal position he never shared: "In the presence of the superiority and creative energy of this genius, the rising and enterprising part of the [German] nation bowed down in meek reverence and full confidence." [18] One of the most determined enemies of Luther was the German Catholic priest Heinrich Denifle. In 1904 this Dominican published a work on Luther and Lutheranism the sophistry of which would be a credit to any Jesuit. As Dr. W. Walther points out, Denifle read just enough of

---

[17] In Br, L 271 f.   [18] In Br, L 275.

Luther to be able to say that he had worked with source material, and he quoted just enough of Luther to create the desired false impression of the man. But one thing even Denifle could not persuade himself to do: he could not deny the intellectual greatness of Luther. The Dominican had to confess: "I do not contend that he [Luther] was not gifted, yea, in certain respects even very gifted." [19] These intellectual gifts of the Reformer, witnessed to by friend and foe, shone forth particularly in his professional life and labor.

PROFESSOR LUTHER WAS WELL PREPARED FOR CLASSES

For obvious reasons the records of Luther's earliest work as a professor are incomplete. But fortunately they are complete enough to give us a fairly clear picture of the young lecturer at Wittenberg. Luther's early lectures indicate great conscientiousness of preparation. Certain books from his library which have been preserved for us corroborate this thoroughness. The volumes show evidence of having been used very much. It is plain that the young professor *worked* his way through his books. To many people these volumes may look unsightly, but they are a distinct delight to the student. Many of the margins are black with notes, exclamations, and question marks. There is much underlining, and some expressions or sentences are crossed out. This young professor evidently did his own thinking. Such thoroughness of preparation naturally bore fruit in the classroom.

Professor Luther was an excellent lecturer. His presentations were so interesting that students were tempted to neglect taking notes and simply listen to the outpourings of his well-stocked mind. Luther's offerings were no mere regurgitations of dry facts or the views of other men. Nor were they presented as the surmises of a man who had himself not as yet arrived at a clear understanding of the truth. Expressions like "My conjecture is," or "as I see it," or "possibly" — expressions which cast such a tantalizing haze of uncertainty over the lectures of certain pro-

---

[19] In Wa, F 539; cp. 77 f., 449, 453, 458.

fessors — were rarely heard in Luther's classroom. There was no learned floundering about. Professor Luther spoke clearly, pointedly, and directly. What he said came from the depth of a profound personal conviction, based upon intensive and extensive study and thought. Students admired this virile positiveness. They knew well enough that in the case of this great student and scholar it was not unreasoning dogmatism. Standing beside the dead Luther in the church of the castle at Wittenberg, Melanchthon said: "He was of such high and keen understanding that he alone could, in confused, obscure, and difficult disputes, see quickly what was to be advised and done." [20]

Preserved Smith characterizes the Professor thus: "He is interesting. Similes, illustrations, examples from current events, apt translations into German, with careful summaries at the end of each subject, made the lectures a wide departure from the ordinary. The students flocked to them with enthusiasm." [21]

One of Luther's students, Johann Mathesius, assures us that in spite of his decidedness the Reformer was not overbearing in the classroom. Anyone who differed from him was given the privilege of defending his position at length, while the Professor listened with patience and kindliness. The people who fancy that Luther roared down any and all opposition in a dictatorial manner do not know the bigness of his character. Luther's severity was reserved for those who, according to his observations, were closed to conviction. [22]

In 1512 the Professor received the degree of Doctor of Theology and presently began his lectures on the Bible. He chose to treat the Psalms first. These early efforts in a field in which Luther was subsequently to become world-renowned may be read in their original Latin form in volumes 3 and 4 of the Weimar edition. They are a bit stiff and create the impression that the young lecturer is feeling his way. As the expositions continue, Luther finds himself and warms up to his subject. Certain Scriptural views are expressed upon which "Holy Mother Church" will

---

[20] In Fr, M 127.   [21] Sm, L 25.   [22] Ma, M 197.

presently frown. The text used by Luther was the Latin Vulgate. The Hebrew original is rarely referred to. Luther's knowledge of that language was rudimentary at this time. To his students the Doctor gave a brief dictation, an outline of his preparation, and then elaborated upon this. A few students' notebooks containing the material are still in existence.[23] Naturally, the theological position Luther occupies in these early lectures is not that of the Genesis exposition completed in 1545.

Luther the professor and theologian has often been called unsystematic. Calvin is acclaimed the great systematic theologian of the sixteenth century. So far as the charge against Luther is concerned, it is true that he never systematized his theology in the sense of publishing a dogmatics of his theological views, although his Catechisms and certain other of his writings are steps in this direction. Then, too, it must be remembered that the Reformer's doctrinal views changed and developed in the course of his career. J. Koestlin has traced this development in his well-known work *Luther's Theology*. In consequence it is easy enough to find contradictory statements in the voluminous writings of Luther. But unless we misunderstand H. Boehmer, Luther is not chargeable with an undiscovered or unreconciled contradiction between his doctrine of justification and his teachings on the Sacraments.[24] Luther was satisfied to draw his doctrines from the Bible and considered it neither the duty nor the privilege of the theologian to "systematize" them in the sense of removing all "contradictions" from them. If gaps are discovered in the "system" of Lutheran doctrine, they are lacunae which have been taken over from Scripture and about which Luther was too good a theologian to rationalize or be disturbed. We frankly confess that, for us, the charge of unsystematic thinking and writing advanced against Luther is becoming tiresome. The centrality of the doctrine of justification by faith, as taught by the Reformer, together with the teachings antecedent to it and consequent upon

---

[23] Br, L 83; cp. Re, L 101 f.   [24] Bo, L 246 f.

it, gives the Lutheran body of doctrine a glorious consistency and coherence. With this "system" we ought to be satisfied. Greater systematization must be achieved at the expense of Scripturalness — a price no theologian who is worthy of the name ought to be willing to pay.

HIS SYMPATHETIC INTEREST IN HIS STUDENTS

But to return to Luther the professor. Particularly in Germany, the "land of professors," there is frequently a great gulf fixed, both by custom and by choice, between the cathedra and the bench. The relation between professor and student is often coldly impersonal; and the interest of the men of learning in those who sit at their feet is purely professional. It was different in the case of Professor Luther. His warm, sociable nature moved him to take a personal interest in his students. He became their spiritual mentor in and out of the classroom, exercising a fatherly supervision particularly over their moral life and cautioning them against the pleasant but perilous vices of adolescence and early manhood. The students appreciated such interest and would ask the Doctor to act as judge in their differences and difficulties. They had learned in the classroom to have confidence both in his head and his heart. He once remarked: "Some masters rate the proud youngsters to make them feel what they are, but I always praise the arguments of the boys, no matter how crude they are, for Melanchthon's strict manner of overturning the poor fellows so quickly displeases me. Every one must rise by degrees, for no one can attain to excellence suddenly." [25]

This sympathetic and considerate approach won many friends for Luther, and he soon became a very popular professor in the best sense of the word. The growing enrollment at Wittenberg also testified to this deserved renown. The institution had opened its doors in 1502, and at the end of its first year it had 416 names on its books. For some reason this number dropped considerably during the following years. It was felt that new blood was needed

---

[25] Sm, L 331.

in the faculty. In 1512 Luther succeeded Dr. Staupitz as professor of theology at the school. Ten years later Wittenberg University had an enrollment of over one thousand. It had become Germany's most famous university. During these years the average number of students at Leipzig was one hundred and fifty, at Erfurt fifty.[26] Luther's lecture room was crowded to capacity. It became known far and wide that this university was different. The students went about armed with the Bible rather than the sword. Such order and decorum were something new to people acquainted with life at the ordinary German university. The improved conditions were largely due to the mighty influence of Doctor Luther's Gospel.[27]

However, lest anyone imagine that the Wittenberg student body was rapidly approaching the ideal, we submit a letter Luther wrote to Elector John Frederic during the 1535 summer session. A slight epidemic of the plague was adding to the heat and ennui of the season. Luther wrote: "Your Grace's chancellor, Dr. Brueck, has communicated to me the kind invitation to visit you while the plague is here. I humbly thank Your Grace for your care and will show myself ready to comply if there is real need. But your bailiff, Johann von Metsch, is a reliable weathercock; he has the nose of a vulture for the plague, and would smell it five yards under ground. As long as he stays, I cannot believe that there is any plague here. A house or two may be infected, but the air is not tainted. There has been neither death nor new case since Tuesday, but as the dog days are near, the boys are frightened; so I have given them a vacation to quiet them until we see what is going to happen. I observe that the said youths rather like the outcry about the plague; some of them get ulcers from their school satchels, others colic from their books, others scurvy from the pens, and others gout from the paper. The ink of the rest has dried up, or else they have devoured long letters from their mothers and so get homesickness and nostalgia; indeed there are more ailments of this kind than I can well

---

[26] Wei 30, pt. 2, 550, n 2.　　　　　　[27] Li, H I:206, 311.

recount. If parents and guardians don't speedily cure these maladies, it is to be feared that an epidemic of them will wipe out all our future preachers and teachers, so that nothing will be left but swine and dogs, which perchance would please the papists." [28] From this letter it appears that the Wittenberg students of 1535 were very much like the students of 1935 and 1948. It also becomes clear that Professor Luther knew his students as well as the subject he was teaching them. Indeed, few have looked more deeply and discerningly into human nature than did the Reformer.

LUTHER'S PHILOSOPHY OF EDUCATION

This fact helped to make him one of the greatest educators of the world. F. Painter says: "Luther brought about as important a reformation in education as in religion." [29] We should like to say that to Luther true education could not be divorced from religion. To him they were not two fields at all, but one. The Reformer believed that the truly educated man is religious, and that only the religious man is truly educated. This view may not seem to contain anything very revolutionary. However, in the pre-Reformation papal Church, education not only was not conterminous with religion, but the objectives of education were different from those proposed by Luther. The principal aim of education in the medieval Church was not the development of the mental and moral faculties of man toward a responsible individualism, but the training of docile and faithful members of "Holy Mother Church." For the medieval people at large, life was essentially corporate in the Church no less than in the State. Over against this organizationalism, this ossified ecclesiastical Christianity, the free evangelical individualism of Scripture was now again resurrected and emphasized. The educational aim of Luther was the development of the individual, not the perpetuation of an institution. He held that the Church exists to serve the *man*, not the system. Luther's entire educational philosophy was

---

[28] Sm, L 332.   [29] Pa, L iv.

based upon the major premise of the worth and dignity, the right and privilege, the duty and responsibility, of the individual.

From this position followed the necessity of a general education that would, at least up to a certain level, recognize neither age nor sex. Elementary education ought to be universal. And the surest way to realize this desideratum would be the introduction of compulsory education for children and young people. In 1526 the Reformer wrote: "I believe that among outward sins none so heavily burdens the world in the sight of God nor deserves such severe punishment as the sin we commit against our children by not giving them an education." [30] Plans to attain this end engaged the attention of Luther particularly during the twenties. He wrote almost all of his great educational treatises during that critical decade.

Of course, there was opposition. It came particularly from the older generation, which had largely been "educated to ignorance and superstition" by the hierarchy. At times the Reformer all but despaired of ever effecting much with these people. To the Elector John he wrote in 1526: "We must have schools and pastors and preachers. If the older people do not want them, they may go to the devil; but if the young people are neglected and are not trained, it is the fault of the rulers, and the land will be filled with wild, loose-living people. Thus not only God's command but our own necessity compels us to find some way out of the difficulty." [31]

A "difficulty" it certainly was. Under the Papacy the schools no less than the clergy had been supported largely by enforced contributions. People were glad to be relieved of these. But many were neither eager nor ready to assume the burdens of voluntaryism. Nor were many of the congregations of the Reformation sufficiently organized to take over the support and management of schools. In view of such conditions Luther wrote his famous *Letter to the Councilmen of All Cities in Germany that They Establish and Maintain Christian Schools*. This publication

---

[30] Ho IV:109.   [31] S-J, LC II:383.

appeared in 1524 and is by F. Painter called "the most important educational treatise ever written." It reveals Luther as an educator of broad sympathies and clear vision. But to enter into a detailed discussion of the Reformer's educational views does not lie within the scope of our book. We wish merely to point out the following as illustrative of his character. Four years earlier, in 1520, the Reformer had said in his equally important *Letter to the Christian Nobility:* "Where the Holy Scriptures do not rule, there I advise no one to send his son. Everyone not unceasingly busy with the Word of God must become corrupt; that is why the people who are in the universities and who are trained there are the kind of people they are. . . . I greatly fear that the universities are wide gates of hell if they do not diligently teach the Holy Scriptures and impress them on the youth." [32] Resisting with difficulty the temptation to dwell upon the timeliness of these words in 1948, we wish to call attention to the religion-centeredness of Luther's educational program.

EDUCATION SHOULD BE ORIENTED BY RELIGION

In urging the teaching and appreciation of religion, the Reformer addressed words of earnest exhortation to his countrymen. They have become classic, and subsequent history proved them to have been sadly prophetic. Luther wrote: "Buy, dear Germans, while the fair is at your doors; gather in the harvest while there is sunshine and fair weather; use the grace and Word of God while they are here. For, know this, God's Word and grace is a passing rainstorm, which does not return where it has once been. It came to the Jews, but it passed over; now they have nothing. Paul brought it to the Greeks, but it passed over; now they have the Turk. Rome and the Latins had it, too; but it passed over; now they have the Pope. And you Germans must not think you will have it forever; for ingratitude and contempt will not suffer it to remain. Take and hold fast, then, whoever can; idle hands cannot but have a lean year." [33] Ever there appears this emphasis

---

[32] Ho II:153.   [33] Ho IV:108.

on the religious: children are to learn how to read so that they may read Scripture; the ancient languages are to be cultivated so that Scripture may be read in the original tongues by preachers. Therefore, says Luther, "in proportion as we prize the Gospel let us guard the languages. . . . And let us be sure of this: we shall not long preserve the Gospel without the languages. The languages are the sheath in which the sword of the Spirit is contained; they are the casket in which we carry this jewel; they are the vessel in which we hold this wine; they are the larder in which this food is stored. . . . Since the languages have been restored, they bring with them so bright a light and accomplish such great things that the whole world wonders and is forced to confess that we have the Gospel quite as purely as the Apostles had it and that it has altogether attained to its original purity." [34]

TEACHING A GLORIOUS PROFESSION

While at the Feste Coburg during the Diet of Augsburg in 1530, Luther wrote his *Sermon on Keeping Children in School.* This production is not a sermon at all but a treatise on schools and education. Luther exalts the difficult office of schoolteaching in a passage so beautiful that we shall reproduce it here. For the comfort and inspiration of every teacher of childhood and youth the Reformer writes: "I would be brief and say that a diligent and pious schoolteacher, or master, or whoever it is that faithfully trains and teaches boys, can never be sufficiently rewarded or repaid with money, as even the heathen Aristotle says. Nevertheless, this work is so shamefully despised among us as though it were nothing at all. I myself, if I could leave the preaching office and other things, or had to do so, would not be so glad to have any other work than that of schoolmaster, or teacher of boys, for I know that this is the most useful, the greatest, and the best, next to the work of preaching. Indeed, I scarcely know which of the two is the better; for it is hard to make old dogs obedient and old rascals pious; and that is the work at which the preacher must

---

[34] Ho IV:114 f.

labor, often in vain. But young trees can be better bent and trained, though some of them break in the process. Let it be one of the greatest virtues on earth faithfully to train other people's children; very few people, almost none, in fact, do this for their own." [35]

LUTHER'S CLASSIC SMALL CATECHISM

Even while the Reformer was penning these words, he was becoming one of the world's most influential schoolmasters through the spread of his Catechisms, especially his Small Catechism. And to this day Martin Luther is teaching children throughout the world the fundamentals of the faith by that "little gem of the Reformation"; for the Small Catechism has been translated into a very large number of languages and dialects.[36] "It is an interesting historic fact that Luther's Small Catechism was the first book to be translated into a native American language, being translated into the language of the Delaware Indians in the year 1648 by Rev. John Campanius, a Swedish pastor in the Swedish settlement in Delaware and early Lutheran missionary among the Indians. It was not, however, published until 1696, eleven years after the publication at Cambridge of Eliot's translation of the Bible into the Indian language." Campanius' translation was ultimately published at Stockholm. Luther's Small Catechism has been acclaimed one of the most influential books ever written. McGiffert, an American biographer of Luther, says of it: "It contains a most beautiful summary of Christian faith and duty, wholly devoid of polemics of every kind, and so simple and concise as to be easily understood and memorized by every child. . . . The versatility of the Reformer in adapting himself with such success to the needs of the young and immature is no less than extraordinary. Such a little book as this it is that reveals most clearly the genius of the man." [37] What McGiffert says is true. We should like to add that one can scarcely dip anywhere

---

[35] Ho   IV:173 f.

[36] See Reu, J. M., *Dr. Martin Luther's Kleiner Katechismus*, Muenchen, Kaiser, 1929, pp. 261—306.   [37] In Br, L 184.

into the writings of Martin Luther without sensing the workings of an extraordinary mind.

The Reformer's works are so voluminous and are written in such a surging style that one may suspect them to have been dashed off with little effort. But we shall see that this is true only in a certain sense. Although Luther was a genius, or perhaps we ought to say, just because he was a genius, he found mental work to be hard work. It has been said that genius is the capacity for taking infinite pains with one's work. The Reformer did that. Therefore he could say of the minister, as he conceived him: "Also a preacher works in the sweat of his face; indeed, working with the head is the hardest kind of labor." [38] Luther had found this to be so in the pulpit, on the cathedra, and in his study. To those who fancied mental labor considerably easier than manual labor the Professor said: "Some think that the office of writer is a light and little office, while it is real work to ride in armor and endure heat, frost, dust, thirst, and other discomforts. Of course! That is the old story! No one sees where the other's shoe pinches; every one stands agape at the other man's good luck. True it is that it would be hard for me to ride in armor; but, on the other hand, I should like to see the horseman who could sit still the whole day and look into a book, even though he had nothing to care about, to dream, to think, or to read. Ask a writer, preacher, or speaker whether writing and speaking is work; ask a schoolmaster whether teaching and training boys is work. The pen is light, that is true. Also there is no tool of any of the trades that is easier to get than the writer's tool; for all that is needed is goose feathers, and there are enough of them everywhere. But the best part of the body (which is the head) must lay hold here and do the work, and the noblest of the members (which is the tongue), and the high faculty (which is speech). In other occupations it is only the fist or the foot or the back or some other such member that has to work; and while they are at it, they can sing and jest, which the writer cannot do. 'Three fingers do it,' they say of writers; but a man's whole body and soul work at it." [39]

---

[38] Erl 16:181.   [39] Ho IV:170.

LUTHER'S WRITING TECHNIQUE

At times we catch glimpses of Luther's method of composition. In Lauterbach's notations of the Reformer's remarks during 1538 we are told under date of December 12: "During these days Luther was worried and uneasy so long as he was planning the composition of the booklet against the Bishop of Mayence. But as soon as he had begun to write, the pen fairly flew. Questioned about the speed of his composition, he replied: 'I travail while sketching my writings.' " [40] Having carefully fixed in his mind the thoughts he wished to develop and having arranged them in logical sequence, Luther would sit down to write. Thereupon ideas would fairly gush from his keyed-up mind. A memory upon the amazing retentiveness of which we have admiring comments from his contemporaries made this method of literary composition possible for Luther.

LUTHER'S LATIN

Many of Luther's works were written in Latin. The Erlanger edition of his writings contains almost forty volumes in that tongue. This number constitutes more than one third of the entire edition. In the days of Luther the learned quite regularly not only wrote but also spoke Latin. In a letter written to an acquaintance in 1516 Luther depreciates his Latin style and apologizes that "this barbarous Martin, accustomed only to cry out among geese," should possess the temerity to write to a man as learned as the addressee.[41] The modesty of Luther guided the pen when he wrote these words. While he did not write nor, indeed, cared to write the polished Latin of the Humanists, the then enthusiasts for the classical literary heritage of the ancient world, he did write correct Latin, the church Latin of his day. The pedantic style of a Cicero which often smacks of affectation and artificiality must have been uncongenial to his disposition. Luther's candor did not forsake him when he sat down to write. Not only what he wrote, but also how he wrote what he wrote

---

[40] Wal XXII:1804.   [41] S-J, LC I:36.

revealed the man. He had to be himself; and if anyone desires to prove to himself how true the saying is that "the style is the man," he ought to read Luther's writings. Luther's Latin has the vigor and the verve of a living language. The Reformer poured his dynamic personality into a tongue which in his days was frequently written with a dryness and tediousness that made it almost unreadable.[42]

THE GERMAN LANGUAGE OWES MUCH TO LUTHER

Luther's relation to the German language is unique. While it would be an overstatement to call him the singlehanded creator of modern High German, his influence in remolding the language that existed at the time of his rise to prominence and power can hardly be exaggerated. The German language of Luther's days reflected the political scene of his times. It was rather chaotic, split up into many dialects. There was no dialect that was so national in scope that it might have been considered *the* language by all German-speaking people, however much their local brogues and provincial peculiarities might deviate from it. Three major dialects were generally recognized: High, Middle, and Low German. They differed so greatly not only in their pronunciations but even in their vocabularies that it was often difficult for people separated by no more than a few dozen miles to understand one another. By the time Luther came to the fore, it is true, these principal dialects were beginning to seek a common level, and the promise of their ultimately merging into *one* dialect, or rather each contributing its bit to *the* German language, was already present. Luther's own contributions toward achieving this end were great and enduring; and men like Klopstock and Goethe have remarked that the modern German still largely speaks the language of Martin Luther.[43]

But few even of the German literary lights have used that language more expertly than did the Reformer. We say without

---

[42] Cp. K-K, M I:38.   [43] Cp. Re, Lu 138 f.

fear of contradiction that Martin Luther is one of the greatest writers of all times. The impact of his writings upon the thought and life of his days, as the presses poured them out in an amazingly steady stream, is perhaps unparalleled in history. Nor is the secret of this success far to seek.

It is true, the Professor has been accused of verbosity and repetitiousness. And the charge comes from no one less than the Reformer himself. "I do not like my exposition of the Psalms," he once exclaimed. "It is a lengthy prattle. In former times I could so speak that I might have chattered the entire world to death. Then I could chatter more of one flower than I now do of an entire meadow." [44] We suspect that the Reformer at times was simply too preoccupied to sketch a rigidly logical disposition of what he proposed to write. At other times the pressure of his convictions was apparently too great to admit of a longer season for deliberation. He *had* to give vent to his thoughts. Then digressions occur in his writings, and he becomes somewhat diffuse. But he is logical enough always to return to his central thought. In such instances he experienced what a wit once expressed thus: "I would have said less if I had had more time."

And yet we would submit our deliberate conviction that Luther's style does not degenerate into mere garrulity. His "verbosity" is very often intentional. He was aware of the depth of ignorance and the density of superstition with which he had to contend. He therefore frequently repeated the same thought in a somewhat different form to insure its being neither overlooked nor misunderstood. One teaches children in this manner, and many of Luther's contemporaries were little more than children in spiritual understanding. Then, too, it must be remembered that Luther's was an intense nature. He was so entirely aglow with the eternal importance of the great truths he had rediscovered for a benighted Christendom that even he at times despaired of finding words emphatic enough to describe their transcendent consequence. In such moments he gropes about for ever clearer,

---

[44] Erl 59:279.

stronger, more incisive ways of expressing himself. In the manner of certain primitive languages which have no superlative, he seeks to achieve this degree by emphatic repetition. "The style is the man."

HIS LANGUAGE AS STRAIGHTFORWARD AS HE WAS

Among the many excellencies of Luther's style we should like to mention its sincerity. It is a reflection of the corresponding trait in his character. We have seen how Luther abominated all shams. Every striving after effect for the sake of appearing clever or learned was disgusting to him. Luther's rhetorical questions, anacolutha, aposiopeses, and apostrophes were not pedantically patterned after grammars; they welled up from the Reformer's fervent soul. He would have written thus although books on rhetorical devices had never been published. There was nothing artificial about the Professor. He never meant to be impressive; he meant to impress the truth upon his readers. In consequence he rarely revised and polished his manuscripts, as did Melanchthon.[45] If men found literary and linguistic errors here and there in his writings — he was not concerned about his reputation as a finished author. Did men see the *truth* of what he wrote? They did? Then he was satisfied; for *that* is why he had written: to exalt the truth.

And how he sweeps one along by the racy vigor of his style! "A resistless energy of soul vibrates in every paragraph; it bears down opposition and forces conviction. . . . It bends with every changing emotion; sometimes, when the great soul of the writer is shaken with a mighty thought or emotion, it thunders and crashes like a storm; and again, when a buoyant joy has settled down upon his heart, it gently plashes like the wavelets of a sunlit sea." [46]

HIS STYLE INTENSELY ALIVE

These words of Painter call attention to another characteristic of Luther's style: its colorfulness or dramatic intensity. The Reformer's exposition of the story of Joseph should be read in its

---

[45] Pa, L, 111.   [46] *Ibid.*

entirety.[47] The pathos and drama inherent in this history lose
nothing by Luther's retelling. Then there is his highly dramatic
narrative of the destruction of Sodom, tense in its brevity: "The
Sodomites drank, danced, rejoiced. They would not have wished
Lot a penny — just like our burghers, peasants and noblemen
today. Lot said: 'God will submerge you in fire.' Then they
laughed at him and replied: 'You dear old simpleton!' What
happened? Early in the morning, as the sun rose above the
horizon, the heavens turned black: a great tempest arose. Splash!
dash! — they were in hell." [48] Such passages indicate the ability
of Luther to enter into the feelings of others, to sense the atmosphere of a situation, so to speak. He possessed a lively and true
imagination. There was much of the artist about Luther.

LUTHER'S WELL-DEVELOPED SENSE OF HUMOR

We should not be surprised to find such a man endowed also
with a fine sense of humor. And Luther's wit and humor *were*
very active. In 1517 he wrote to a friend: "A little nonsense now
and then fosters and even perfects friendship as much as gravity
does. . . ." [49] No doubt the Reformer owed more to this "saving
grace of humor" than has been recorded by himself and others.
It must very frequently have served as a sort of emotional safety
valve. One of Abraham Lincoln's biographers remarks that the
President's sense of humor kept him from losing his mind under
the nervous strain of the Civil War problems. We do not know
how true the statement is, but we do know that Luther's vein
of humor saved many a delicate situation. Of course, there were
those who accused Lincoln of clownishness; and Luther was
faulted for what Melanchthon called his buffoonery. But we
need not be disturbed by this Melanchthonian criticism. Poor
Philip lacked all sense of humor and was firmly convinced of the
necessity of professional gravity. The Reformer's bursts of wit
and humor seemed unworthy of a great theologian to him. At the
time of Luther's marriage Melanchthon wrote about him to a

---

[47] See Wal II:1130 sq.　　[48] Wei 36:380, 8.　　[49] S-J, LC I:61.

careful. . . . An excellent story illustrating the point is told about a man who said he had seen some bees as big as sheep. When asked how they could get through the little holes in their hives, he replied: 'Oh, I let them think of that for themselves.' " [54]

PAPAL ABSURDITIES RIDICULED

In a letter to Spalatin, Luther referred to a certain *Dialogue*, a publication in which the vices of the hierarchy were held up to scorn and ridicule. For the following reason Luther did not like the writing: "I have determined, dear Spalatin, never to communicate the *Dialogue* to anyone. My only reason is that it is so merry, so learned, so ingenious (that is, so Erasmian), that it makes the reader laugh and joke at the vices and miseries of Christ's Church, for which rather every Christian ought to pray and weep." [55]

But the Reformer felt it to be another matter when vice was not derided, but the absurdity of papal superstitions was held up to deserved scorn and ridicule. He did not fail to do this himself, well aware of the fact that you cannot worship the ridiculous and preposterous. No doubt it is true that one ought to be careful not to ridicule what others hold sacred. But there are limits beyond which it is impossible to expect a man to keep a sober face; and the papal Church had in many instances gone very far indeed beyond these limits. There was, for instance, the deception practiced upon the "faithful" with relics — genuine, suspect, and bogus. Against Albert of Mayence Luther wrote the following travesty, mimicking bulletins that in those days would appear from time to time concerning the acquisition of new relics. "There is a persistent rumor," wrote Luther, "that among the recently purchased treasures of Albert the following are to be seen: three flames from Moses' burning bush on Mount Sinai; two feathers and an egg of the Holy Ghost; half a feather of St. Gabriel, the archangel; a whole pound of the wind which blew for

---

[54] Sm, L 326.   [55] S-J, LC I:63.

Elijah in the cave on Mount Horeb; thirty notes of the drum of Miriam, Moses' sister; a great big piece of the shout of the children of Israel with which they cast down the walls of Jericho; and sundry other marvels." [56]

LUTHER'S HUMOR WAS NOT POINTLESS

But Luther could also be seriously humorous. We mean what Melanchthon referred to in a letter to Spalatin. He remarked: "It is my opinion that he [Luther] never jokes but that some serious meaning lies behind the jests." [57] The Professor's sprightly introductory words to his *Letter to the Christian Nobility* may serve as an illustration. There Luther writes: "I know full well that I shall not escape the charge of presumption in that I, a despised monk, venture to address such high and great Estates on matters of such moment. . . . I shall offer no apologies, no matter who may chide me. Perchance I owe my God and the world another piece of folly, and I now have made up my mind honestly to pay that debt, if I can do so, and for once to become court jester; if I fail, I have one advantage — no one need buy me a cap or cut me a comb." [58] The last words contain an ironical comparison of the monk's cowl and tonsure with the headdress of the jester. Another example of Luther's serious humor may be found in a letter to Spalatin. The Doctor complains: "We have so much trouble in translating Job on account of the grandeur of his sublime style that he seems to be much more impatient of our efforts to turn him into German than he was of the consolation of his friends. Either he always wishes to sit on his dunghill, or else he is jealous of the translator who would share with him the credit of writing his book." [59]

HIS SENSE OF HUMOR WAS INDESTRUCTIBLE

Luther's humor rarely forsook him. It went with him into the classroom and cropped out even in the pulpit. Nor did it leave him on the bed of sickness and pain. During his suffering at

---

[56] Sm, L 397 f.   [57] S-J, LC I:306.   [58] Ho II:62.   [59] S-J, LC II:221.

Smalkald in 1537 Melanchthon arrived. Stepping to his friend's bedside and seeing marks of disease and suffering on Luther's face, Philip burst into tears. Luther regarded him in silence for a while and then said, smiling wryly: "Johann Loeser is in the habit of saying that it is no achievement to drink good beer, but that the real test is drinking bad beer. Well, I must practice drinking the bad beer now. Have we received good at the hands of the Lord, and shall we not also receive evil? As the Lord willed so it has come to pass; blessed be the name of the Lord." [60]

Proscription and persecution threatened the confessors of Christ. They were asked to give an account of their position at Augsburg. Luther, outlawed and banned, wrote a letter to the circle in his home which is a pure delight to read. What a heroically Christian character this Martin Luther had, to be capable of such fanciful humor under the circumstances. This is what he wrote: "Veit Dietrich, Cyriac Kaufmann, and I did not press on to the Diet of Augsburg but stopped to attend another diet here. There is a coppice directly under our windows like a little forest, where the daws and crows are holding a diet; they fly to and fro at such a rate and make such a racket day and night that all seem drunk, soused, and silly. . . . I think they must have assembled from all the world. I have not yet seen their emperor, but nobles and soldier lads fly and gad about, inexpensively clothed in one color; all alike black, all alike gray-eyed, all alike with the same song, sung in different tones of big and little, old and young. They care not for a large palace to meet in, for their hall is roofed with the vault of the sky; its floor is the carpet of green grass, and its walls are as far as the ends of the world. They do not ask for horses and trappings, having winged chariots to escape snares and keep out of the way of man's wrath. They are great and puissant lords, but I have not yet learned what they have decided upon. As far as I can gather from an interpreter, however, they are for a vigorous campaign against wheat, barley, oats, and all kinds of corn and grain. . . .

---

[60] K-K, M II:388.

It is pleasant to see how soldierly they discourse and wipe their bills and arm themselves for victory against the grain. I wish them good luck — to be all spitted on a skewer together. I believe they are in no wise different from the sophists and papists who go for me with their sermons and books all at once. . . ." [61]

LUTHER'S WIT AND HUMOR A MIGHTY FORCE

Luther's wit and humor were the delight of his friends and the terror of his foes. Every form of humor was at the Professor's command. His pen was as sharp as his tongue. Upon occasion he could treat his malicious, hypocritical adversaries with stinging sarcasm or biting irony. Thus he once wrote: "This Luther is the man whom everybody may use to achieve honor and attain salvation. No blockhead is so unlearned but what he turns learned so long as he writes against Luther. No wanton rogue ever was so wicked and despicable but what he turns out to be pious and a dear child if he writes against Luther. No one was ever so utterly disgraced but what he turns out to be a crown of honor if he writes against Luther. There are those at the courts of kings, princes, and bishops who possess great wealth and honor but who should perhaps be devouring husks with the swine if it were not for Luther. This Luther is an extraordinary man. I suspect he is God; for how could his writing and name otherwise be so mighty as to turn beggars into lords, asses into doctors, rogues into saints, dirt into pearls, and those who are a disgrace to society into glorious people?" [62] Preserved Smith is quite right: "Luther remains one of the greatest of writers. His fury and mirth are alike Titanic." [63]

THE PROFESSOR LOOKS AT HIMSELF AS AUTHOR

Luther's estimate of himself as an author may appear contradictory to one who does not remember that the Reformer considered the Bible to be in a class by itself, supreme, and unapproachable. When he suspects that his own writings may per-

---

[61] Sm, L 249 f. [62] Erl 30:375 f. [63] Sm, L 334.

chance keep someone from devoting to the study of Scripture what little time he has, he passes a very hard judgment on his literary productions. This fact has already been brought out.[64] He told the citizens of Wittenberg and Augsburg, who had requested him to publish a complete edition of his works, that so far as he was concerned his writings might perish so that only the Bible to which they were to direct men might be read. After much coaxing he finally relented to the extent of consenting to supervise such a complete edition, but death overtook him after only two volumes had appeared.

However, when the matter in hand was a comparison of his writings with those of other theologians, Luther often used very different language. It is true, he accorded the productions of Melanchthon, Brenz, and other fellow workers praise that has seemed fulsome and exaggerated to some. But it is not so far as Luther's own convictions were concerned. Luther sincerely believed that men like Brenz and Melanchthon were more than his equals in the presentation of the Gospel in writing. There are many who hold that this judgment was dictated by the Reformer's modesty. We need not argue the point. But it had been strange indeed if the good Professor had discovered no excellence in his own writings, and equally strange if the candid man had said nothing about it. He did. In the introduction to his German works, dated 1539, and therefore written when some of the most mature products of his pen had not yet appeared, he frankly said: "I may boast in God and glory without arrogance and lying that I should not concede much of a superiority over me to some of the Church Fathers so far as writing books is concerned." [65] The context of these words plainly indicates that Luther was speaking primarily of the evangelical contents of books, not merely of literary style and finish. He was too serious and sensible a man to call a book excellent merely because it conformed to all the rules of grammar and rhetoric. His first interests were those of a practical theologian, not a literary artist.

---

[64] See p. 45 above.   [65] Erl 1:69.

THE MORE OF CHRIST IN A BOOK THE BETTER THE BOOK

This is proved also by the standard of evaluation which he applied to his own books. He once told the circle gathered around his table: "If printers would follow my advice, they would print only those of my books that contain doctrine, such as my works on Galatians, on Deuteronomy, and also my sermons on John, chapter four. The rest of my books may be read in order to understand the history of the revelation of the Gospel [the Reformation], so that one may see how Gospel teaching again began. . . ." [66] Luther ever considered those books and authors the best that said most of Christ. Even in Scripture Luther's favorite books and penmen were those who dwelt longest upon the doctrine of salvation through faith in the Savior. The Reformer recognized that doctrine as the very heart of the Bible; and we recognize faith in it as the very heart of Luther's character. Even the excellencies of Luther as a writer — his incisiveness, his positiveness, his confidence, his vigor, and other attributes of his style — stem from his heroic, all-transforming faith in Christ. However little many historians and biographers say about this key to Luther's power as a writer, they are, one and all, agreed that he is one of the world's greatest authors.

CARLYLE'S AND FREYTAG'S JUDGMENT OF LUTHER AS A WRITER

Eccentric, rugged old Thomas Carlyle, who admired power of any kind in anyone, naturally thought very highly of Luther also as an author. He says of the Reformer: "Luther's merit in literary history is of the greatest; his dialect became the language of all writing. They are not well written, these four-and-twenty quartos of his; written hastily, with quite other than literary objects. But in no books have I found a more robust, genuine, I will say noble, faculty of a man than in these. A rugged honesty, homeliness, simplicity: a rugged sterling sense and strength. He flashes out illumination from him; his smiting idiomatic phrases

---

[66] Erl 59:279.

seem to cleave into the very secret of the matter. Good humor too, nay tender affection, nobleness, and depth." [67]

A historian of a very different type, Gustav Freytag, has this to say: "The swing of his [Luther's] style, the power of demonstration, the fire and passion of his convictions, carried everything before them. . . . His language adapted itself to every mood, to every key, now terse and condensed and sharp as steel, again in ample breadth, a mighty river, his words penetrated the people. His imagery and striking comparisons made the most difficult things intelligible. His was a wonderful creative power." [68]

THE GREAT RANKE'S EVALUATION

And lest the testimony of Carlyle and Freytag be suspected because of the eccentricity of the former and the evident sympathies of the latter, we shall add the evaluation of Leopold von Ranke, generally considered one of the world's greatest historians, a model of accuracy and impartiality. Von Ranke wrote: "When one reads these sentences [the Ninety-five Theses], one sees how dauntless, magnificent, and determined a spirit is at work in Luther. Thoughts flash forth as do sparks from hammer blows on an anvil." Again this judicious historian says: "In no nation or age has a more commanding and powerful writer appeared, and it would be difficult to find any other who has united so perfectly popular and intelligible style and such downright homely good sense to so much originality, power, and genius: he gave to German literature the character by which it has been distinguished ever since: thorough investigation, depth of thought, and bold attack of error." [69]

THE VERDICT OF A MODERN LUTHER AUTHORITY

One of the greatest modern Luther students is Dr. Hans Preuss. After having devoted many years to the study of Luther's voluminous works, this eminent German scholar wrote: "His [Luther's] style is not intricate and confused with many sub-

---

[67] Ca, H 164.   [68] Fr, M 44 f.   [69] Ra, D I:210; II:56.

ordinate clauses. He goes directly to the point at issue. The great cause which he represents sweeps him off his feet, hurries him along, gives him the right word, the fitting construction. Nothing is artificial, all is home-grown, all a gift. What troubles, think you, they must pass through who feel that they must decline to espouse Luther's cause and yet read this style which must surely sweep also them off their feet! But what an irresistible joy comes to those who assent also to the contents of his writings! He grasps the reader by the hand and rushes away with him, upward. While reading him, one feels as though one were carried along on some mighty billow or as though one were wafted through the air from a high hill." [70] Anyone who has read Luther with any degree of frequency will know exactly what Dr. Preuss is trying to express, because he has experienced it himself. Those who hold that Luther must necessarily be a dry and tiresome writer since he wrote four hundred years ago and dealt with issues many of which now have little more than historical value for the specialist do not know Martin Luther. Dr. Preuss has correctly characterized the Reformer's delightfully readable *style;* and an American scholar, Donald Mackenzie, has succinctly summarized the *contents* of Luther's writings.

In his important book, *Christianity the Paradox of God,* Mackenzie says on page 200: "Not until Luther came, do we find anyone who can at all be classified with Augustine for the wealth and depth of his insight into the paradoxical subtilty of the nature of man and of the manifold wisdom of God's activity both in nature and redemption and, above all, for his power of self-expression in memorable words. Is not that the reason why essentially his writings are never out of date?"

ON READING LUTHER

We entirely agree with Mackenzie. It is true, to read Luther's works in the original German is unfortunately becoming increasingly difficult even for a large number of theologians in that

---

[70] Pr, L 184.

Church which has both the honor of bearing his name and the responsibility of preserving his doctrinal legacy of uncompromising loyalty to the Word of God. And it is equally true that it is difficult satisfactorily to translate the writings of any man as original and idiomatic as Luther. But the Reformer's genius was so strong that even a fairly faithful rendering of his weighty words makes the reader feel more than a modicum of his power. And those Lutherans who are able to read Luther's original German or Latin must indeed be peculiarly constituted if they cannot assent to the confession of the Catholic historian Michelet, who, though unsympathetic to many of the Reformer's fundamental views, exclaimed: "The happy years I spent reading Luther have left me a strength, a vigor, which I hope God will preserve to me until death." [71]

It is not our intention to lapse into a homily at this point. Yet we cannot but deeply deplore the fact that even in the Lutheran Church Luther is not known and read as he ought to be, as he richly deserves to be. We should have more of the mighty outpourings of this great soul in English translations. The great theologians of the age of the Reformation, the Brenzes, the Flaciuses, and the Chemnitzes, owed their theological depth and maturity, next to Scripture itself, to Luther's influence and writings. It is a public secret that alarmingly many in modern Christendom lack that spirit of positiveness, that clear and deep apprehension of revealed truth, that saturation with both the letter and the spirit of Scripture and that unbending loyalty to it which made Martin Luther the man of God he was. We do not contend that a millennium would descend upon Church and State, but we have often wondered what conditions would be like if one could say of our generation what Erasmus could say of his days: "No one would believe how deeply Luther has crept into the minds of many nations, nor how widely his books have been translated into every tongue and scattered everywhere." [72]

---

[71] In Sm, L 359 f.   [72] S-J, LC I:495.

LUTHER AND THE LATIN BIBLE, THE VULGATE

The most famous of Luther's books was itself a translation. It was the German Bible. When, in 1512, he was made a Doctor of Theology, one of the insignia given him was a copy of Scripture. The Book was first handed to him closed and was then opened. Perhaps no one, including Luther himself, realized how profoundly appropriate the symbolism of the ceremony was. The act was in reality an undesigned prophetic epitome of Luther's subsequent career. He was to restore the open Bible to Christendom, not merely by proclaiming its message with apostolic purity and fervor but also by translating Scripture into German.

Unfortunately the available source material does not tell us when Luther first saw a complete Bible. The entire relation of Luther to the Bible has been carefully investigated by the German Dr. W. Walther and the American Dr. M. Reu. All Luther students are deeply indebted to these scholars for their exhaustive researches. Dr. Reu holds that it is possible that young Martin saw his first complete Bible during his stay at Magdeburg. Luther was then fourteen years old. The traditional view, according to which Brother Martin first accidentally came upon a Latin Bible chained to a desk in the cloister at Erfurt, must in consequence be somewhat modified. Books were indeed frequently attached to desks by small chains in order to make them always available, since copies were costly and scarce. The fact that Scripture was literally chained in the days of Luther no doubt offers tempting homiletical possibilities to a preacher fond of allegorizing, but, historically speaking, we cannot say that the Bible had actually been chained by Rome to keep it from being used. The guilt of the papal Church is damnable enough without our increasing it by charges which, for once, cannot be substantiated.

But to return to Luther: we know that a Bible was given young Martin when he was admitted as a novice into the monastery at Erfurt in September, 1505. Years later this moment was still so vividly present to the Reformer that he recalled the very color of the binding of the Latin Vulgate then given him.[73]

---

[73] Re, Lu 89 f.

GERMAN BIBLE TRANSLATIONS OF THE MIDDLE AGES

The oldest German translation that has come down to us dates back to the eighth century. It is, of course, in the form of a manuscript. Unfortunately we possess portions only of the Gospel of St. Matthew. This is the more to be regretted since scholars assure us that the translation is a remarkably good one and much better than most subsequent attempts. The unknown translator was clearly a linguist. From the following centuries we have little or nothing of note. The fourteenth century has bequeathed us most of our medieval Bible manuscripts. During the second quarter of this century no fewer than four translations of the entire Bible into German were made. The work of the fifteenth century, at the close of which Luther was born, seems to have consisted mainly in copying existing translations. Over one hundred manuscripts have been preserved from this period.[74] On the value of these translations we shall let Dr. W. Walther speak. He tells us: "Even those who attempted to speak good German, with few exceptions, had no idea as to what was required of a good translation. They were satisfied if they were readily understood. That the German Bible must also be a work of art, that the different moods of the originals were to be reproduced . . . was a knowledge of which we find only very slight traces in a very few of the translators. Most of them were fearfully prosaic, all on one note, and insufferably tedious." [75]

GERMAN TRANSLATIONS BEFORE THE REFORMATION

With the invention of printing a new era dawned also for the Bible. About seventeen years before the birth of Luther the first German Bible appeared; and before the Reformer's own complete translation became available, after 1534, more than a dozen versions in High German and four in Low German had been printed. When we say that Martin Luther gave the open Bible to Christendom, we therefore do not mean that no German

---

[74] See RE 3:64 sq.   [75] In Re, Lu 26 f.; cp. 279.

translations existed before his times, or that the existing versions were unknown and unused. The Reformer's translation was so superior to previous renderings, and his clear apprehension of Scripture truth was such an advance on the haziness of medieval theologians that one is in danger of losing sight of what little good those ages of comparative ignorance and superstition still possessed. It appears, then, that the use of the Bible was not uncommon in the Middle Ages. The reading of Scripture was an ancient rule in monasteries. Moreover, Bible manuscripts were privately owned by religious persons of means. At death such copies were frequently bequeathed to monasteries. Since they were usually in Latin, the prominent layman who perchance possessed one of them was not particularly profited by it. Some of these precious manuscripts, however, were written in German. How much of their content reached the laity is a matter of conjecture. We know that some of it did.

But how could Luther in the face of such facts say that the Bible had been "benched" under the Papacy? This expression, which has greatly exasperated the Catholics, is found in the Reformer's exposition of Zech. 8:19, delivered in 1527. But the context sufficiently indicates the sense in which Luther used the phrase. He said: "They rage and will not listen when they are told that Scripture was quite contemptuously neglected by them (*unter der Bank gelegen*), and their mad dreams alone have taken the place of authority." [76] The Reformer deplores the fact that Scripture was denied *supremacy* in the Church. He does not deny the existence of copies of the Bible. He does indeed at times complain of their scarcity during the Middle Ages, of the woefully deficient knowledge of Scripture possessed by very many of the clergy and of the total ignorance of the Bible found among not a few. The gradual drifting away of Christendom from the *sola Scriptura* has been touched upon in a previous chapter.[77] It will be sufficient to say here that the appearance of "heretics"

---

[76] Wei 23:606.   [77] See pp. 25, 52 f., above.

who demanded and practiced Bible reading in the vernacular by
the laity caused the hierarchy to forbid what might easily bring
it into the awkward position of having to justify its many departures from a book which it still officially professed to reverence as the very Word of God. In 1199 Innocent III therefore
issued a papal decree against indiscriminate reading of the Bible
by the laity.[78] At this point the difference in the attitude of
Luther and the Church of Rome clearly appears. Rome held that
only the Church was to determine what was the truth as taught
in Scripture; Martin Luther held that only Scripture was to
determine what was the truth that was to be taught by the
Church. A typical statement of the papal position was given by
the Dominican John Mensing, who wrote in 1528: "Scripture can
deceive [!], the Church cannot deceive. Who does not perceive,
then, that the Church is greater than Scripture and that we can
entrust ourselves better to the Church than to Scripture?" [79]
Such words breathed the very spirit of Antichrist to Luther. To
help counteract this rank heresy, he undertook the gigantic task
of translating the Bible into German.

He had begun to translate portions of Holy Writ earlier than
is generally known. He first turned the seven penitential Psalms
into German in 1517. That he began his work with just these
Psalms is a revelation of his character the significance of which we
should like to point out at greater length if space permitted. How
early in his career Luther resolved to translate the entire Bible the
records do not tell us. It is not surprising that the Professor
began with the New Testament rather than with the Old. Translating it alone from the Greek was less difficult under the circumstances than rendering the Old Testament into German from the
less-known Hebrew. But there was another reason. The New
Testament contained the ultimate revelation of the grace of God
in Christ Jesus. With that straightforwardness which went directly
to the heart of things Luther began by preference to translate
this final message of God to man. As far as we are able to deter-

---

78 RE 2:702, 35 f.   79 In Re, Lu 73.

mine, he had a German translation of 1475 and the Latin Vulgate before him in addition to the original Greek in the New Testament edited by Erasmus in 1516. The translation was completed in about three months: from mid-December, 1521, to about mid-March, 1522. Dr. Reu thinks: "It still remains an achievement that Luther could not have accomplished without the special assistance of the Holy Ghost." [80]

THE RAPID SALE OF LUTHER'S NEW TESTAMENT

Upon his return to Wittenberg from the Wartburg, Luther began to polish the translation with the assistance of Melanchthon. By September 21, 1522, the first printing was off the press. This first edition is known as the "Septembertestament." Luther's name is not printed out on the title page, nor is the date of publication given. It was a book of 222 leaves in folio format, with forty-five lines to the page. The chapters are not divided into verses but into paragraphs, unequal in length. The edition was sold out in less than three months. The size of the edition cannot be determined, estimates varying from three thousand to five thousand copies. The price, somewhat less than ten dollars, was high, particularly since Luther, as always, neither desired nor asked nor received any royalty. From 1522 to 1546 no fewer than ninety-five editions of Luther's New Testament appeared. A conservative allowance of three thousand copies for each edition would give us the grand total of no fewer than 285,000 copies of the New Testament alone over a period of twenty-four years. This would mean that almost one thousand copies of the Book were sold every month for twenty-four years. Surely, the printing press, the publishers, and the book market are indebted to Martin Luther. We say nothing of the gratitude the readers owed the Professor. That debt was too great for payment.

In addition to his masterful translation Luther had given the reader a general preface to the New Testament and an introduction to each book. In the general preface occur words that are

---

[80] Re, Lu 158.

characteristic of Luther's entire theology. They mark the era of a new approach to Holy Scripture, or rather of the return to the old approach referred to by Paul at 2 Tim. 3:15. The Reformer tells the reader: "Gospel is a Greek word and means in Greek a good message, good tidings, good news, a good report, which one sings and tells with rejoicing. So, when David overcame the great Goliath, there came among the Jewish people the good report and encouraging news that their terrible enemy had been smitten and they had been rescued and given joy and peace; and they sang and danced and were glad for it. So the Gospel too is a good story and report, sounded forth into all the world by the Apostles, telling of a true David who strove with sin, death, and the devil and overcame them and thereby rescued all those who were captive in sin, afflicted with death, and overpowered by the devil. . . . For this they sing and thank and praise God and are glad forever. . . ." [81]

THE OLD TESTAMENT

Even while the first edition of his German New Testament was in the press the industrious Professor began the translation of the Old Testament. He worked with the original Hebrew and not, as the medieval translators had done, with the Vulgate, already a translation, and, as Luther discovered, often a faulty one. The Doctor labored with his usual scholarly thoroughness. He had asked Spalatin for the loan of certain of the Elector's jewels to help him in the translation of Revelation, chapter 21. He now went to a butcher to observe the slaughter of several sheep and to learn the exact German word for each part of the animal. The Professor found the Old Testament far more difficult to render faithfully into a smooth German than he had the New Testament. Fortunately, he was now in a position to consult with learned colleagues at the University and elsewhere. He did not fail to do this. The very minutes of some of these consultations have been found.[82] They tell us that Luther's friends served as ad-

---

[81] In Re, Lu 167.   [82] See Re, Lu 214, 217.

visers, the ultimate form of the translation depending upon the decision of the Reformer, so that the Bible is correctly considered *his* translation. Prominent among these advisers were Dr. J. Bugenhagen, Dr. Justus Jonas, Dr. C. Creuziger, and Magister Melanchthon. This group seems to have met frequently. For example, from mid-January to mid-March, 1531, it convened no fewer than sixteen times for the revision of an earlier translation of the Psalms by Luther. The great work was finally completed in 1534, after about a dozen years of arduous labor. In print it became a stately folio of 908 pages, when bound with the New Testament. There were about fifty lines to the page. The Psalms and parts of Proverbs were printed in double columns. The precious volume was printed in Wittenberg by Johann Lufft. A facsimile of its title page, reduced in size, may be seen in an appendix of illustrations to Dr. Reu's book.[83]

In the spirit of a true scholar, who is never satisfied with his work, Luther continued to polish and perfect his translation throughout his life. In the summer of 1539 the sessions with his colleagues were resumed. By February, 1541, no fewer than sixty meetings had been held. They were subject to call by Luther, who also outlined the work to be done and led the discussion. In the spring of 1541 the New Testament was again worked through by this "commission." The revisions finally adopted were incorporated in the edition of the German Bible that appeared in 1545, a year before the Reformer's death. This, then, was the final text so far as Luther himself was concerned.

LUTHER HOLDS THAT GOOD TRANSLATING IS A GIFT

We are eager to hear something about Luther's principles of translation. To begin with, the Professor held that the ability to translate well is largely a gift. He once said: "Because someone has the gift of languages and understands them, that does not enable him to turn one into the other and to translate well. Translating is a special grace and gift of God." [84] If anyone ever

---

[83] Re, Lu.   [84] In Re, Lu 268.

had this "special grace and gift of God," it was Doctor Luther. But the difficulties to be overcome were so great that even he at times all but despaired of meeting the many requirements of a good translator. In 1522 he wrote: "I have undertaken to put the Bible into German. I had to do it; otherwise I might have died with the mistaken idea that I was a scholar. All those who think themselves learned ought to do some such work." [85]

The most detailed statement by Luther of his method of translating is found in his *On Translating: an Open Letter.* Written while at the Feste Coburg, this treatise represents the experience of more than ten years of translating. The Doctor begins with a glance at the criticism offered by papists, which was a curious mixture of malice and envy. With the blunt candor so characteristic of him he says: "I translated the New Testament to the best of my ability and according to my conscience. . . . No one is forbidden to do a better piece of work. If anyone does not want to read it, he can let it alone. . . . If I have made some mistakes in it — though I am not conscious of any and would be most unwilling to give a single letter a wrong translation intentionally — I will not suffer the papists to be the judges. Their ears are still too long and the hee-haws too weak for them to criticize my translating. I know very well, and they know even less than the miller's beast [the ass], how much knowledge, work, reason, and understanding are required in a good translator; they have never tried it. . . . It takes patience to do a good deed for the world at large, for the world always wants to be Master Wiseman and must always be putting the bit under the horse's tail, directing everything, able to do nothing." [86]

After having thus put his criticasters, the "shameless nincompoops," into their place, he refers to the great difficulty of the work thus: "In working at the Book of Job, Master Philip, Aurogallus, and I could sometimes scarcely finish three lines in four days. Now that it is translated and complete, anyone can read and criticize it, and one now runs his eyes over three or four pages

---

[85] S-J, LC II:109.   [86] Ho V:11.

and does not stumble once. . . . It is good plowing when the field is cleaned up; but rooting out the woods and the stumps and getting the field ready — that is work that nobody wants. There is no such thing as earning the world's thanks; God Himself can earn no thanks from it with the sun, with heaven and earth, or even with His own Son's death. . . ." [87]

It is true, Luther had not undertaken the gigantic work to gain fame and recognition from men, although he was not untouched by their commendations. The noble man of God had engaged in the arduous work because of his love to the Redeemer and his desire to bring Him to others. These thoughts he expressed in a passage that is so beautiful and contains such a revelation of the man's innermost character that we shall quote it at length although part of it has been cited previously.[88] Luther wrote: "This I can testify with a good conscience — I have been faithful and diligent to the utmost in this work and have never had a false thought. I have not taken a single heller for it, or sought one, or made one by it. Nor have I had any intention to win honor by it — that God, my Lord, knows — but I have done it as a service to the dear Christians and to the honor of One who sitteth above, who blesses me so much every hour of my life that if I had translated a thousand times as much or as diligently, I still should not deserve to live a single hour or have a sound eye. All that I am and have is of His grace and mercy, nay, of His dear blood and His bitter sweat. Therefore, God willing, all of it shall serve to His honor, joyfully and sincerely. Scrawlers and papal asses may abuse me, but pious Christians and Christ, their Lord, praise me! And I am repaid all too richly if only one single Christian recognizes me as a faithful workman. I care nothing for the papal asses; they are not worthy to recognize my work, and it would grieve me to the bottom of my heart if they praised me. Their abuse is my highest glory and honor. Still, I would be a doctor, nay, a wonderful doctor; and that name they shall not take from me till the Last Day; that I know for sure." [89] This

---

[87] Ho V:14 f.   [88] P. 206 above.   [89] Ho V:18 f.

candid confidence in the excellence of his work the Professor frequently expressed. Thus he once remarked: "My translation of the Bible — not to praise myself, for the work praises itself — is so good and precious that it is better than all Greek and Latin versions." [90]

Luther was correct. Regarded merely as a work of literary art, his translation of the Bible stands in the front ranks of German classics. He had said: "I will get rid of Hebraisms, so that no one can say that Moses was a Hebrew. Good translating means adapting the statement to the spirit of the language." [91] The Doctor certainly kept that promise. His translation is the German Bible rather than the Bible in German. The German language was like clay in his hands, like a violin played by a virtuoso. The sighs and sobs of some of the Psalms; the high hallelujahs of others: hymns to the God of salvation; the majestic cadences of Isaiah; the lamenting notes of Jeremiah; the profound depth beneath the simple diction of John; the tremendous power of the tense, stormy, telescopic style of Paul — Luther's translation has all of these in German. But it is remarkable that Luther never creates the impression that he is imitating the original. He had so thoroughly absorbed the spirit of Holy Writ, had entered so deeply into the genius of the inspired writers that his translation reads like an original.

LUTHER'S TRANSLATION A MODEL OF SIMPLICITY AND SCHOLARLINESS

The learned Professor's language is simple. He once remarked: "Christ spoke most simply, and yet He was eloquence itself. Nor do the Prophets use high and heavy language." [92] But the German of Luther's Bible is classically pure and, moreover, beautifully melodious. The Reformer translated for the ear no less than for the eye. He realized that "his" Bible would be read aloud in church and in family devotion, wherefore he would make the very sound of it pleasing to the ear. He therefore avoided all harsh constructions, all unbalanced sentences and disturbing sub-

---

[90] Wei Tischreden 5324.   [91] In Re, Lu 269.   [92] Wei Tischreden 5099.

PLATE XVIII

MARGARETE VON KUNHEIM

Margarete Luther was only eleven years old at the time of her father's death. Married to the wealthy nobleman George von Kunheim, she transmitted the blood, if not the name, of Luther to posterity to the present day

PLATE XIX

PAUL LUTHER

Paul Luther studied medicine and became a noted physician at the courts of Brandenburg and Saxony. He also taught medicine for some time at Jena. Descendants of his are still living

PLATE XX

HOUSE IN WHICH LUTHER DIED

On February 18, 1546, Luther died in the house of one John Albrecht, a city official of Eisleben. The Reformer was lodging in this house while reconciling the Counts of Mansfeld

PLATE XXI

ROOM IN WHICH LUTHER DIED
Luther departed this life in his birthplace, Eisleben

ordinate clauses. The result was a rhythmic flow of language. For instance, Ps. 33:18 Luther translated: "Des Herrn Auge siehet auf die, *so* [not "die" again] ihn fuerchten, *die* auf seine Guete hoffen." Matt. 5:44 he avoided a similar cacophony by translating: "Bittet fuer die, *so* euch beleidigen und verfolgen." However strong and commonplace his language was in the circle of his friends, he used more polished speech in his translation. There *Kot* is used for *Dreck,* and *Haupt* for *Kopf.* His amazing wealth of vocabulary was an invaluable asset to Luther in translating. Reu points out that Luther uses no fewer than ten synonyms for the word *Leid* (sorrow).[93] At the same time he does not choose a different word merely for the sake of variety. The Professor carefully notes the shade of difference in synonyms and makes his selections accordingly. Dr. W. Walther called attention to this scholarly method. "The *Pferde* (horses) are held in with bit and bridle, but fiery *Rosse* (chargers) carry Elijah to heaven in a fiery chariot, and it is the strong *Gaeule* (work horses) whose neighing is heard (James 3:3; 2 Kings 2:11; Jer. 50:11)." Such excellencies soon eclipsed former German translations and have to this day, four hundred years later, made it possible for Luther's Bible to hold its own in spite of all advances in scholarship and linguistic research and development.

In consequence the praises of Doctor Luther's German Bible have been sung for over four centuries. It is an enduring monument to both Luther's great faith and his great scholarship. Since it was *Luther's* translation, Rome, of course, had to condemn it — at least in public. Duke George's chaplain and secretary, Hieronymus Emser, boasted that he could prove no fewer than one thousand and four hundred "heretical errors and lies" to be in Luther's version. When pressed to make good his charge, he produced a list of — *corrections* Luther had made of faulty translations in the Vulgate. Duke George thereupon requested Emser to publish a translation of his own. The chaplain began to work independently, but his patience (and his scholarship?) were soon

---

[93] Re, Lu 278.

found to be unequal to the task. In 1527, however, Emser actually published a translation of the New Testament. But what was it? *Luther's* translation, "corrected" to agree with the inaccuracies of the Latin Vulgate. This plagiarized Bible became the basis of the German Catholic version. The Reformer smiled broadly when he found Emser's translation to be essentially his own. In 1530 he wrote: "It is a feather in my cap that I have taught my ungrateful pupils, even my enemies, how to speak." [94]

APPRECIATIVE REMARKS OF AN HONEST CATHOLIC

Since those days the beauty and power of Luther's masterpiece have at times overcome the prejudice and the malice of Catholic scholars, and they too have borne testimony to the great merits of the work. Thus the French Catholic Audin, on the whole a severe critic of Luther, wrote: "The translation of the Bible is a noble monument of literature; a vast enterprise, which seemed to require more than the life of man, but which Luther accomplished in a few years. — The poetic soul finds in this translation evidences of genius and expressions as natural, as beautiful, and melodious as in the original language. Luther's translation sometimes renders the primitive phrases with touching simplicity, invests itself with sublimity and magnificence and receives all the modifications which he wishes to impart to it. It is simple in the recital of the patriarch, glowing in the predictions of the Prophets, and colloquial in the Epistles of St. Peter and St. Paul." [95] Even the modern German Jesuit Hartman Grisar, who wrote a large negative biography on the Reformer about thirty years ago, cannot but remark: "The excellence of Luther's translation of the Bible from the point of view of the text is unquestionable." [96]

This was the Bible Luther loved, the Book in which he lived, the One Volume which he preached and expounded with a force and a clarity that have rarely been equaled and perhaps never excelled. We shall now follow the Professor into church and sit at the feet of Luther the evangelist.

---

[94] Ho V:10.   [95] In Br, L 144 f.   [96] In Br, L 145 f.

CHAPTER XI

LUTHER THE EVANGELIST

Preaching was the center and spring of his power.　　　*J. Ker,* Presbyterian scholar

IN A PREVIOUS CHAPTER A LETTER WHICH LUTHER WROTE TO his adversary Duke George of Saxony was quoted. The Reformer subscribed himself "by the grace of God Evangelist at Wittenberg." Luther exalted his office no less than did Paul. He considered the Gospel ministry the greatest profession on earth. There had been more or less of preaching throughout the Middle Ages. But a new era for sermonizing began at the time of the Reformation. The proclamation of the Gospel became the most important part of the church service, and liturgical and sacramental functions became subsidiary to it.[1] The elaborate ritualism of the papal Church was not merely rooted in an appreciation of ecclesiastical art and a normal development of the sense of the beautiful and aesthetic. As the centuries of the Middle Ages wearily rolled on, the clergy found it increasingly easier and in certain particulars safer to edify the eyes of their auditors than to instruct their minds, to fill them with awe by casting a veil of sacred mystery over their religion than laboriously to indoctrinate them. The one lesson the faithful were to learn was obedience to the hierarchy. An impressive and mysterious ritual would contribute considerably toward that end by enveloping those in holy orders in the odor of an inviolable sanctity.

THE REFORMATION EXALTED THE MESSAGE

But when the centrality of justification by faith became recognized, the sacrificing and mediating priest became a mere servant of the Word, and the entire character of the church

---

[1] RE 15:658, 6 f.

service was changed. Luther rightly said: "The faithful proclamation of the Word of God is the proper cult of the New Testament." Preaching the Gospel of a free, full, and final salvation through faith in Christ crucified was now recognized to be the precious privilege and principal purpose of the holy ministry. In the eyes of the people this altered position of the clergy might entail a loss of power and importance. Men would no longer look upon Gospel ministers as indispensable conveyors of God's salvation. But what did it signify, asked Luther, that in the eyes of *men* the gorgeous medieval priest with his pomp and circumstance was of greater consequence than the preacher of the evangel? In the eyes of *God* the simple proclamation of the Gospel of free grace is the most glorious of all professions.

THE HOLY MINISTRY GLORIOUS THOUGH DESPISED

Of this fact the Reformer was firmly convinced, wherefore he exclaimed: "Who can tell all the glory and the virtue that a real and faithful pastor has in the eyes of God? There is no dearer treasure nor any more precious thing on earth or in this life than a real and faithful pastor or preacher." Again: "Nay, if all the world calls him a heretic, a deceiver, a liar, a rebel, it is so much the better and is a good sign that he is an upright man and like his Lord Christ. For Christ too had to be a rebel, a murderer, and a deceiver and be judged and crucified with the murderers. What would it matter if I were a preacher that the world called me a devil if I knew that God called me His angel? Let the world call me a deceiver as long as it will; God calls me His true servant and steward, the angels call me their comrade, the saints call me their brother, believers call me their father, wretched souls call me their savior, the ignorant call me their light; and God says, 'Yes, it is so,' and the angels and all creatures join in." [2]

Naturally a man's evaluation of the holy ministry will depend

---

[2] Ho IV:146, 148.

upon his appreciation of the Lord whom it glorifies in the Gospel it preaches. If a person considers the message of the Cross the one thing needful, he will treasure and support the holy ministry as a precious institution of God. "For," says Luther, "what else are the Gospel and the preaching office that we have than the blood and sweat of our Lord? He won them by His anguished, bloody sweat, earned them by His blood and cross, and gave them to us. We have them without any cost to ourselves and have done nothing for them nor given anything. Ah, God, how bitter it was for Him, and yet how kindly and gladly He did it! How greatly the dear Apostles and all the saints suffered in order that these things might come to us! How many have been put to death for them in our own time! To speak of myself too, how many times I have had to suffer death for them so that I might serve my Germans with them! But all this is nothing compared with what Christ, God's Son and our dear Heart, has spent on them. And yet, by all this suffering He will have earned from us only this — some persecute this office and condemn and slander it and wish it to the devil, while others keep hands off, support neither pastors nor preachers, and give nothing toward their maintenance." [3]

QUALIFICATIONS TO BE LOOKED FOR IN A MINISTER

One would expect the writings of Luther to abound with advice to ministers young and old, promising and unpromising. Before characterizing Luther himself as a preacher, we shall here insert a few summary statements of the Reformer on the traits to be looked for in a good minister. We shall later find that he possessed most of them himself. Thus he says: "A good preacher should have these properties and virtues: first, to teach systematically; secondly, he should have a ready wit; thirdly, he should be eloquent; fourthly, he should have a good voice; fifthly, a good memory; sixthly, he should know when to stop preaching;

---

[3] Ho IV:176.

seventhly, he should be sure of his doctrine; eighthly, he should venture and engage body and blood, wealth and honor, in serving the Word; ninthly, he should suffer himself to be mocked and jeered by everyone." [4]

LUTHER'S FAMOUS "VESTRY PRAYER"

As to preaching in particular, Luther cautioned against long introductions, a diffuse treatment of the text, and above all against a parade of learning. He often said in effect that the best sermons were written on one's knees; that is, they are granted in answer to fervent prayers for God's guidance. Beautiful and well known is the prayer of the Reformer that hangs in many a Lutheran vestry. It runs thus: "O Lord God, Thou hast made me a pastor and teacher in the Church. Thou seest how unfit I am to administer rightly this great and responsible office; and had I been without Thy aid and counsel, I should surely have ruined everything long ago. Therefore do I call upon Thee. How eager and anxious I am to yield and consecrate my heart and mouth to this ministry! I desire to teach the congregation. I, too, desire ever to learn, to keep Thy Word my constant companion and earnestly to meditate thereon. Use me as Thy instrument in Thy service. Only do not Thou forsake me; for if I am left to myself, I shall certainly ruin everything. Amen." [5]

LUTHER'S DIFFIDENCE UPON BEING ASKED TO PREACH

From these words it appears that Luther considered preaching the assumption of an awesome responsibility. Probably to this fact rather than to any groundless feeling of inferiority on his part is to be ascribed the hesitancy with which he met the first requests of his superiors that he himself begin to preach. Even in later life he felt the weight of this responsibility. "Believe me," said he, "preaching is not something men can perform in their own power; for though I now am an old and experienced preacher, I nonetheless am fearful when I am to preach." [6] One day Magister

---

[4] Erl 59:194.   [5] Wal X:1496.   [6] Erl 59:188.

Lauterbach, in reply to a direct question of the Doctor, deplored the difficulty and diffidence which he experienced when he had to mount the pulpit. Thereupon Luther reassuringly said: "Ah, dear friend, I experienced the same thing; I feared the pulpit as much as you do, but I had to mount it. They forced me to preach. At first I had to preach to the monastery brethren in the refectory. Oh, how I feared to mount the pulpit! . . . Under this very pear tree I had at least fifteen arguments with which I wanted to refuse Dr. Staupitz when he called upon me to preach. Finally, when I said: 'Dr. Staupitz, you are killing me, I shall not live a fourth of a year,' he replied: 'Go to, in God's name! Our Lord God carries on a big business. He is in need of wise people also in heaven.'" [7]

Thereupon Luther regularly took his turn as one of the preachers of the monastery. The room in which he laid the foundation of his world-wide fame as a preacher was not prepossessing. It was an old, dilapidated frame structure, thirty by twenty feet in size, propped together and daubed with clay. The pulpit he ascended in this bare, unattractive hall was constructed of rough boards and raised three feet above the floor. Soon Brother Martin was being favorably spoken of beyond the monastery walls. When the pastor of the City Church at Wittenberg began to be in poor health, Luther was called to supply the pulpit during his absence. In 1515 the city council called the Doctor to serve as regular assistant in the *Stadtkirche*.

THE MEDIEVAL CHARACTER OF HIS FIRST SERMONS

Luther's earliest sermons were, of course, essentially Catholic in doctrine and scholastic in form. They quite lacked the evangelical fire for which he subsequently became famous. Moreover, they were not free from that fanciful allegorizing which the Reformer so severely condemned in later years. Thus he once preached on the story of Solomon's reception of his mother in the throne room. In the deference the king showed Bathsheba upon

---

[7] Erl 59:185.

that occasion by bowing to her and seating her at his right hand, the monk Luther told his auditors to see a type and prophecy of the honor and reverence Jesus was to accord His mother.[8] These early sermons also contain much philosophizing and speculating about doctrinal and moral matters, quite in the spirit of the monastic preachers of the day.[9] His earliest recorded sermons that were preached before a lay congregation date back to 1514 and 1515. These discourses are far more practical, and an approach to evangelical Christianity is discernible in them.[10]

LUTHER'S SERMONS BECAME CHRIST-CENTERED

After the eyes of Luther's understanding had been opened and the Gospel of a free salvation had become clear to him, his sermons never departed very far from the Cross of Christ. He now began to preach in reality as Luther the evangelist. Early in 1517 Duke George of Saxony had asked Staupitz to send someone to preach in the chapel of his castle at Dresden. Luther came. He preached with such unction and persuasiveness on the certainty of salvation in Christ that one of the lady attendants of the duchess declared at the dinner table that she could die in peace if only she might hear another sermon like that one. But the Catholic Duke George growled that he would be willing to pay a large sum not to have heard the discourse at all. Within four weeks after this incident the devout attendant of the duchess departed this life. In the course of years many more testified to the truly edifying doctrinal contents of the Reformer's sermons. Although his text perchance did not refer specifically to God's plan of salvation, Luther felt it his duty nonetheless to introduce it at some point in his sermon. This mode of procedure was perhaps not exegetically correct, but it was evangelically sound.

The history in his text, notably in the Gospels of the church year, Luther the evangelist treated briefly so that he might devote the greater part of his sermon to the exposition of doctrine. He felt that his contemporaries had heard sufficient history, canon-

---

[8] K-K, M I:118.   [9] Wei 4:595 ff.   [10] K-K, M I:119.

ical, apocryphal, and spurious history, under the Papacy. Their most immediate need was a thorough indoctrination in fundamentals. Such instruction would necessarily include the exposure of heresy and superstition wherever found; and we meet many a trenchant polemical passage in the Reformer's sermons. In the *Table Talk* we are told that he once was asked whether it were better to warn against false doctrine in a sermon or to encourage and comfort the weak. The Doctor replied: "Both are very good and necessary although it is of greater benefit to comfort the disheartened, but the weak are also edified and improved by controversial matter. Both doctrinal and exhortatory preaching are a gift of God." [11]

POLEMICS NOT TO BE AVOIDED IN THE PULPIT

The Reformer has given all generations of orthodox preachers the soundest of advice as to the proper use of polemics in the pulpit. He said: "I do not attack mainly the life but the teaching of the adversary, examining his orthodoxy.... So long as the doctrine remains pure, the life may be corrected again, though something therein be amiss. . . . The only way in which I succeeded in overthrowing the Papacy was by teaching aright. . . . And though we were externally more pious than the papists, one should not press that as an argument (for also heathen and Turks may appear to be pious from without), but one should emphasize doctrine. That breaks the neck of the Pope." [12] But Mathesius informs us that he had repeatedly heard Luther say that in public discourse the positive and thetical ought to be emphasized, and a sermon ought never to degenerate into a mere tirade against absent adversaries. The Reformer was an enemy of all extremes.

ALSO IN THE PULPIT LUTHER MINCED NO WORDS

After what has been written about Luther in the foregoing it will not be necessary to prove at length that his entire preaching was characterized by the same directness of speech which we

---

[11] Erl 59:191 f.; cp. RE 15:660.   [12] Erl 59:246.

noted in his writings. He called a spade a spade in the pulpit no less than out of the pulpit. There were those who took greater offense at the former than at the latter bluntness. They complained about his becoming too personal in the pulpit. Some of his fellow monks fairly winced under his searching exposition of the Ten Commandments; and some of the students resented his frank exposure of their illicit relations with certain girls of the town.[13] But for all that the aggrieved returned to hear again this extraordinary monk, so deadly in earnest, as the fire flashing from his dark eyes and the penetrating voice, vibrant with deep conviction, proved him to be. Of course, it did not escape the young preacher that his outspokenness was making him enemies. In later life he once remarked, no doubt in the light of personal experience: "If pious, God-fearing, faithful preachers censure sin, they are called quarrelsome, snappish blasphemers of God and man, who attack the honor of people, make the government suspected, incite uproar and what not." [14]

The last thought in this statement is significant. In strictly modern times the Reformer has frequently been represented as an apostle of totalitarianism; and certain writers who knew more clearly what they would like to have had Luther teach than what he actually did teach and write, have pictured him as prohibiting every criticism of oppression and maladministration on the part of government. But this charge is unfair to Luther. We are told that upon one occasion he was asked whether a preacher had the right to fault his government in public discourse. The Doctor replied: "Yes, indeed! For although it is God's ordinance, He has reserved the right for Himself to censure its vices and whatever is wrong about it. Therefore secular rulers are to be censured if they permit the goods of their poor subjects to be ruined and allow them to be sucked dry by usury and maladministration. But it does not lie within the province of a preacher to prescribe orders to government and to teach at which price bread ought to

---

13 K-K, M I:121.   14 Erl 59:232 f.

be sold and how much meat ought to cost. In general he ought to instruct the individual diligently and faithfully to do what God has commanded him to do in his particular station in life." [15] This is certainly sound and sober advice and deserves to be more widely known than it is.

HIS HIGH EXPECTATIONS OF SUCCESS WERE NOT ALWAYS REALIZED

If Luther as a preacher is to be faulted for anything, it may be his overoptimism. But this is a failing common to young, sincere, and ardent preachers. It is another of those "faults that lean to virtue's side." After Luther's eyes had been opened to the glories of the Gospel of a certain salvation and he had entered into the heavenly peace to which this evangel introduced him, he fancied that all the world was waiting to share this bliss with him. Then came the disillusionment, until he exclaimed one day: "A preacher had better know the world well, know that she is desperately wicked and at best belongs to the devil. He ought not to be such a simpleton as I was, who at first knew no better than to fancy the world to be so pious that she would hasten to accept the Gospel as soon as she would hear it. How shamefully I was deceived I am now experiencing with great pain." [16] But Luther continued to preach in spite of all unbelief and lack of appreciation; and he meant to preach so plainly that even the simplest could not excuse his rejection of the Gospel by saying that he did not know what Luther had meant.

Well known are the words which the Reformer spoke in answer to the question of a certain Doctor Alberus upon that minister's departure to a charge at which he would have to preach before a great nobleman. The Doctor's advice was this: "All your sermons ought to be very simple. Do not address the prince, but the plain, rude, unlearned people. After all, the prince will be found to have been cut from the same cloth. If I were to deliver my sermons with an eye to Philip Melanchthon and other doctors,

---

[15] Erl 59:238.   [16] Erl 59:242.

I should do no good. But I preach to the unlearned in all simplicity, and that sort of sermon pleases all. Though I could use Greek and Hebrew, I keep that in reserve until we learned ones convene; and then we become so profound (*machen wir's so krause*) that our Lord God is surprised at such a display of learning." [17] Again, Luther said: "Poor little children, girls, old women and men come to church. Difficult doctrine is of no benefit to them, nor do they comprehend anything of it although they may say: 'Ah, he presented an excellent matter and preached a good sermon.' But when you ask them: 'Just what was it?' they reply: 'We don't know.'" [18]

Correctly to understand the advice to emphasize little more than the fundamentals of Christian doctrine on the pulpit, we must remember that the generation to which the early reformers preached was religiously ignorant to a degree that is difficult for us to appreciate. With these considerations in mind, outbursts such as the following will not seem unduly strong to us. The Doctor once remarked with great warmth: "Cursed and confounded be all preachers who seek after high, difficult, and subtile matters in their churches and bring them before the people in their sermons, seeking their own honor and fame and desiring to please one or two in the audience who thirst for the honor (of being preached to in this 'superior' manner). When I preach here at Wittenberg, I descend to the lowest level; I do not consider the doctors and masters of which about forty belong to this parish, but the mass of young people, children, and servants, of whom there are hundreds and thousands. To these I preach, according to them I gauge my sermon, for they need it. If the others do not care to hear it — the door is open." [19] The Reformer might have called such discourses plain black-and-white sermons. He once referred to a comment of the artist Albrecht Duerer, who had expressed his dislike for pictures that were highly colored, saying that he preferred the plain black-and-white ones. Luther

---

[17] Erl 59:205.   [18] Erl 59:259.   [19] Erl 59:272 f.

added that his taste for sermons was similar. He did not relish a sermon that went beyond the depth of the hearers or was full of the bright coloring of rhetorical tricks and devices.[20] How perfectly this simple taste fits into the picture of his character!

LUTHER'S SERMONS LARGELY HOMILIES

And this combination of simplicity and directness of Luther was reflected also in the structure of his sermons. The Reformer's discourses lacked that formal disposition which many today regard the all but indispensable prerequisite for the writing of a homiletically correct sermon. Luther's sermons were usually homilies, distinguished from what we ordinarily think of as a sermon by the prevalence of exposition over systematization. The danger of such a treatment is that unity of thought may be lost or obscured by the detailed explanation of subordinate clauses and thoughts. Then the homily will seem to lack coherence. Many truths may be taught; but since they are not made to revolve about a common center in the minds of the hearers, much may be quickly forgotten. But because the preacher appears to stay closer to his text in a homily than in a synthetic sermon, the former is thought to be more easily prepared. It is indeed more easy to make a homily than a sermon, but we venture to say that it is more difficult to make a *good* homily than a *good* sermon: to do justice to all the thoughts, primary and secondary, as they follow in the text, and yet to achieve unity of thought. The homily was the most popular type of public discourse in the Church of Rome. "Homiliarium" was the name given to collections of such sermons, which were designed to be read in case the preacher found it impossible to deliver a discourse of his own.[21] Luther's *Church Postils* were to serve a similar purpose in evangelical congregations.

The Reformer's treatment of the text, then, was expository. Luther clearly recognized both the advantages and the dangers of this manner of preaching. One day his wife remarked that she

---

[20] Wei Tischreden 7036.   [21] See RE 8, 308 sq.

preferred a certain John Polner, a relative of Luther, to Dr. Johann Bugenhagen as a preacher because Polner stayed with his text. Thereupon Luther remarked: "He is a foolish preacher who must tell everything that occurs to him. A preacher ought to stay with his text and deliver what is before him, so that the people may clearly understand it. But a preacher who will say everything that comes into his mind is like maids who go to market. When another maid meets them, they stand and gossip with her, and if a second one meets them, they engage her too in conversation; they do the same with a third and a fourth and thus slowly arrive at the market."[22] Luther means: a preacher should stay with his text and emphasize its central thought. He should get at this central thought without diverting the attention of his audience by lingering over truths that have little or no bearing on the *main* truth.

HOW HE PREPARED HIS SERMONS

As a homilist Luther had himself to guard against this danger. His general success is evidenced by his extant sermons. It is true, many of these are characterized by a certain leisurely breadth. But the Reformer rarely loses sight of the central thought of his text. This will seem the more remarkable when it is borne in mind that, as a rule, Luther did not write out his entire sermon. And our surprise increases upon being told that he also did not for himself pursue the thoughts of the text into all their implications and presuppositions before mounting the pulpit. He once remarked that if he were to do that, he might preach an entire sermon on every subordinate clause.[23] But this method of preparing his sermons at times led the Reformer to develop thoughts that he had not intended to dwell upon. Such a departure from what he had mentally outlined for himself would arouse his disgust. He once accused himself in his drastic manner: "I have often spit upon myself after leaving the pulpit and said: 'Shame on you! How did you preach? Oh, you truly performed wonderfully well! You did not stay with the outline you had made for yourself!' "

---

[22] Erl 59:196 f.; cp. RE 15:661, 5. 43.   [23] K-K, M II:295; Erl 59:190.

But, the Reformer added, that perhaps that very sermon would be praised by people as one of the best he had yet delivered. "Everything is good so long as it is orthodox," he concluded, "according to the analogy of faith, and in agreement with Holy Writ." [24]

We owe very many of Luther's sermons to copyists. Upon reading their record of what he had said, he at times would contend that their transcriptions must contain more than he had offered, for he had not preached that well. The copyists must have added thoughts of their own, he modestly averred.[25] In the fervor of his presentation he scarcely realized the excellence of his offerings.

HOW LONG IS A LONG SERMON?

Perhaps he occasionally was unaware also of the length of his sermons. Few are unacquainted with the apothegm attributed to him: "Tritt frisch auf, tu's Maul auf, hoer bald auf," which may be freely rendered: "Come forward energetically, open your mouth, stop preaching soon." No doubt Luther would have heartily subscribed to the statement of the wit who said: A bad sermon ought not be long and a good one need not be long. But the question is: When *is* a sermon long? Sermon length is largely something relative. The longest discourse of today might have been the shortest in the days of the Reformation. Mathesius records that Luther once told him: "When you observe that the auditors are listening to you with great earnestness and delight, then conclude your sermon. Next Sunday people will return the more gladly for it." A certain preacher had caught his gown on a nail in the pulpit and had torn it. Upon being informed of the mishap, the Doctor commented: "I thought he was nailed to the pulpit because he would not stop preaching." [26] Referring to Dr. Bugenhagen's long sermons, upon a certain occasion, Luther said: "Some plague the people with sermons that are indeed too long, for hearing sermons is a delicate matter. One soon becomes surfeited and tired, although Dr. Pommer [Bugenhagen] always adduces this text as a pretext for his long sermons: 'He that is of God heareth God's words' (John 8:47), but moderation

---

[24] Erl 59:227 f.   [25] Erl 59:190.   [26] Ma, M 216.

is good in all things." [27] When one Johann Foerster complained to Luther about the difficulty he experienced in preaching, the Reformer replied: "If you cannot preach an hour, let it be a half hour or a quarter hour." [28] From this advice it would appear that Luther did not at all consider a sixty minute sermon too long. Many of his contemporaries almost doubled that length.

LUTHER IN THE PULPIT

To Luther himself, carried away by his subject, and to many of his auditors his sermons seemed shorter than they were in reality. The Doctor was a dynamic pulpit orator. His contemporaries testify to the spell he would cast over his hearers. His masterful handling of the language, his pointed, incisive manner of expressing old truths, his clear, conclusive way of presenting new ones, made him the most celebrated preacher of the day. When Mirabeau heard Robespierre make an impassioned appeal at the time of the French Revolution, he remarked to his neighbor: "Observe that man. The world will hear more of him, for he speaks as one who believes every word he says." People who sat before Luther's pulpit said the same of him. His dead earnestness was the first trait by which one was impressed. To this day his sermons make impressive reading. But how unforgettable and irresistible they must have been when delivered by the lively and magnetic evangelist Luther himself, all aglow with the fervor of faith, while his searching eyes seemed to penetrate to one's very heart, and his ringing, challenging, pleading voice called one's soul to rise to life and salvation! Naturally, Luther's enemies regarded as presumptuous and offensive the masculine joy in God that put the note of confidence and triumph into his preaching. Hieronymus Emser said he had never in his life heard a more audacious preacher than the Reformer.[29] No doubt Emser was utterly disgusted at Luther's lack of that unctuous humility, that sweetish sanctimoniousness, which made monastic sermonizing so nauseating.

---

[27] Erl 59:222.   [28] Erl 59:187 f.   [29] Wa, F 536.

NON-LUTHERANS PAY TRIBUTE TO LUTHER THE PREACHER

A contemporary said of Luther's preaching: "Everyone . . . who hears him once desires to hear him again and again, such tenacious hooks does he fix in the minds of his hearers." [30] The Englishman Alexander Bower aptly summarized the traits of Luther as preacher in these words: "If we pass from the examination of his mind to a view of the different capacities in which he came before the public, we shall see him to greatest advantage in the character of a preacher. He mounted the pulpit full of his subject and eager to diffuse a portion of his stores among his audience. The hearer's attention was aroused by the boldness and novelty of the ideas; it was kept up by the ardour with which he saw the preacher inspired. In the discourse there was nothing of the stiffness of laboured composition; in the speaker no affectation in voice or gesture. Luther's sole object was to bring the truth fully and forcibly before his congregation. His delivery was aided by a clear elocution, and his diction had all the copiousness of a fervent imagination." [31]

Tastes have changed, and modes and manners of sermonizing have not been unaffected by the passing of centuries, but Luther the evangelist is still recognized as one of the world's greatest preachers. The modern American Baptist scholar E. C. Dargan says: "As a preacher Luther stands in the first ranks of those who by the ministry of God's Word have molded the characters and destinies of men. Among all of his other offices and achievements — as scholar, theologian, author, and leader — we must not forget that first of all and chiefly he was a preacher. At first he could hardly be persuaded to preach, but when he once got at it, nothing could stop him. . . . The tone and spirit of Luther's preaching were what his character and views would lead us to expect. He believed, and therefore he spoke — out of his experience and convictions — out of his sense of duty — out of love to God and men, and without the fear of man before his eyes." [32]

How true it is that after Luther had recognized the grace of

---

[30] S-J, LC II:115. [31] Bow, L 290 f. [32] In Br, L 193.

God in Christ Jesus, he never wearied of its proclamation! Every conceivable means was used to bring Christ, the Savior and Sanctifier, into the hearts and lives of men. Luther was not satisfied to preach the Gospel in the pulpit, to write about it in books, and to lecture on it in the classroom. He drafted also the fine arts into the service of the Gospel. He called upon painting and sculpture and music and poetry to bring contributions to the "queen in the kingdom of knowledge," religion. The Doctor loved to decorate his home with all sorts of Bible passages and pithy proverbs. Above his tile stove in the living room he wrote these maxims: "Whoso is faithful in little things will also be faithful in great things, and who is unfaithful in little things will be unrighteous in great things. The reason is: Dogs learn to eat by lapping. . . ." — "Who esteems not a penny will never have a gulden." — "Who wastes an hour will waste a day." — "Who despises the small will never get the large. . . ." [33]

HIS APPRECIATION OF THE ARTS

The Reformer cultivated no art for purely aesthetic purposes. He knew nothing of the spirit that fosters "art for art's sake." To Luther the fine arts were to serve as means to higher ends. It is true, we have but a few references of the Reformer to the arts, but they are sufficient to reveal his general point of view. Thus he once remarked with some warmth that it was a shame to use moneys given to the church for religious purposes to pay instead for such works of art as the well-known Apollo Belvedere, a nude representation of the Greek ideal of masculine physical perfection. To the religion-centered Luther, Pope Leo's beautification of Rome with such treasures of art at a time when millions lacked the bread of life, both literally and figuratively speaking, seemed like an unanswerable waste of time, interest, and money. We do not mean to say that the Reformer had no eye for the beautiful. Perhaps Preserved Smith is overstating the case somewhat when he speaks of Luther's "fondness for music and relative

---

[33] Sm, L 365.

indifference to other arts." [34] It is true enough that the Reformer does not refer to the other arts so frequently in his writings as he does to music. But there was a good reason for this, as we shall see. Preserved Smith very correctly says: "If Luther was little appreciative of the arts appealing to the eye, the fault was rather in his limited opportunities than in his nature." [35] Perhaps the most detailed study of the Doctor's artistic tastes and talents is the book by Dr. Hans Preuss. After a microscopic study of all the references to art and artistic matters in the Reformer's works, this German scholar arrived at the following conclusion: "We must say that Luther possessed a rather extensive knowledge and a broad appreciation of works of art"; and referring to his own book, Dr. Preuss adds: "You see, one must always bear in mind that what we have offered here is merely casual remarks of Luther, and they naturally are very far from representing the sum total of what he knew and passed judgment on." [36]

RELIGIOUS FANATICS AND ENTHUSIASTS WERE ICONOCLASTS

It is well known that the radical enthusiasts inveighed against the religious use of the fine arts in the days of the Reformation. Not a little of their fanaticism carried over into the ordinarily more sober Calvinistic churches, and soon the houses of worship were stripped of everything that "smacked of popery." Organs, pictures, crucifixes, images, and altars were removed by the radicals. Many priceless works of art were ruthlessly destroyed by the "zeal without knowledge." Part of the disturbances at Wittenberg which Luther hurried to quiet in 1522 consisted in the demolition of the "images" in the churches. The Reformer deeply deplored not merely the havoc that was being wrought there but above all the spirit that was giving rise to such blind and blundering destruction. He was fully aware of the fact that the provocation had been great, that what had in previous centuries served merely as an incentive to worship had now in many instances actually become an object of worship. He recognized that

---

[34] Sm, L 335.   [35] Sm, L 349.   [36] Pr, L 50.

the crying need of Christendom was liberation from the spiritual tyranny of the hierarchy and from a formalism which was increasingly choking all spirituality out of religion, a mechanizing formalism which was coining a pretentious counterfeit of true religion by deforming and deflating it into fashions and formulas and making it dependent upon the sensuous: the image, the relic, and the rite. We are therefore not surprised to find that at first also Luther was rather unsympathetic to pictures and images. Their idolatrous abuse made him exclaim at one time: "Images are a matter of Christian liberty, although it were better we had none of them because of the miserable and cursed abuse and unbelief to which they give rise. I am not partial to them."[37] But the Reformer's dislike gradually disappeared.

LUTHER CONSIDERED SYMBOLS OF OUR FAITH NATURAL

Perhaps the very extremes of the fanatics were not without influence upon the development of Luther's views. Did they make the smashing of images and the breaking of crucifixes a sacred duty? In that event such "witnesses, memorials, and symbols of our faith," as Luther called them, ought to be upheld also on principle and in defense of Christian liberty. It is therefore not surprising to find that the Reformer came to regard works of ecclesiastical art as distinct aids to piety and devotion. Indeed, he regarded the crucifix as a natural, inevitable representation of the faith in a man's heart, saying: "When the Christian hears of Christ, a picture of the Savior involuntarily arises in his mind. Whether I want to or not, when I hear of Christ, I project a picture of a man hanging on a cross in my heart. Now, if it be not a sin but something good that I have a picture of Christ within my heart, why should it be a sin to have Him before my bodily eyes?"[38] Luther's appreciation of the pedagogical value of such artistic symbols of our faith demonstrably increased.

In 1522 he told the iconoclastic enthusiasts in Wittenberg: "Now, although it is true and no one can deny that the images are

---

[37] Wei 10:3, 26.　　　[38] Wei 18:82, 23.

evil because they are abused, nevertheless we must not on that account reject them nor condemn anything because it is abused. That would result in utter confusion. God has commanded us not to lift up our eyes unto the sun, etc., that we may not worship them, for they are created to serve all nations. But there are many people who worship the sun and the stars. Shall we, therefore, essay to pull the sun and stars from the skies? Nay, we will not do it. Again, wine and women bring many a man to misery and make a fool of him. Shall we, therefore, kill all the women and pour out all the wine? Again, gold and silver cause much evil; shall we, therefore, condemn them? Nay; if we would drive away our worst enemy, who does us the most harm, we would have to kill ourselves, for we have no greater enemy than our heart. . . ." [39]

In 1524 he wrote a preface to the first hymnal, in which he was directly interested, and expressed principles according to which he consistently acted: "I am not of the opinion," said the conservative Reformer, "that all arts are to be cast down and destroyed on account of the Gospel, as some fanatics protest; on the other hand, I would gladly see all arts, especially music, in the service of Him who has given and created them." [40]

In 1528 appeared Luther's *Dissertation on the Lord's Supper.* This writing professedly contains his final position on many of the burning questions of the day. At the end of it we are told: "Images, bells, robes, for the Mass [the Communion service is meant], church ornaments, altars, candles, and the like, I regard as things indifferent. Whoever wishes may omit them. Drawings, however, from the Scripture and from good histories I consider useful; yet these should be left to the choice or option of every one; for I do not agree with those who strip churches of such ornaments." [41]

Luther's reference to "drawings" reminds one of the value he attached to good illustrations in a book. Dr. Preuss holds that there are good reasons to believe that the woodcuts in Luther's

---

[39] Ho II:408. [40] Ho VI:284; Wal X:1424. [41] Wei 26:509, 9.

German Bible were largely chosen by the Reformer himself,[42] who held that a good picture could preach no less than the text and could, moreover, convey its message more quickly than the printed word. Luther believed that "pictures are the laymen's Bible." [43] He spoke from experience. He had been deeply impressed by a large picture done in stone on one of the outside walls of the City Church at Wittenberg. For years he had passed it more than once every day. In a truly medieval spirit it portrayed Christ enthroned upon a rainbow as Judge of the world. A sword and a whip were seen projecting from his mouth as symbols of judgment and condemnation. They were hardly necessary to give point to the picture, for the expression on the face of Jesus the Judge was so severe as to appear almost savage.[44] Luther's criticism of this monstrosity was severe on both artistic and theological grounds. But still stronger was his wrath at the popular pictures of Mary showing her breasts to her Divine Son in order to assuage His anger and others representing her shielding emperors, kings, princes, and lords against Him with her mantle.[45]

THE VISIBLE SUBSERVES THE INVISIBLE

Aside entirely from any direct evidence, one would expect a man of Luther's balanced judgment to have placed the fine arts under contribution to the Church and her Gospel. According to Holy Writ it pleased the Creator to make man a being consisting of a material body and an immaterial soul. The soul is, indeed, the seat of human life and the bearer of man's personality, but it manifests and exercises its life in and through the visible and physical. Similarly, Luther observed, God reveals the spiritual and invisible to man through the material and visible, through the Word of God as it is seen in Scripture by the eye or heard during the delivery of a sermon by the ear or seen in a picture or religious symbol. God thus leads us up to the invisible by means of the visible,[46] wherefore Augustine could call the Sacra-

---

[42] Pr, L 25.   [44] Pr, L 37.   [46] Pr, L 63.
[43] Wei Tischreden 3674.   [45] Pr, L 32.

ments "the visible Word of God." Moreover, the invisible God became visible to a creature of sense such as man is in the Personal Word of God, Jesus Christ. Fanaticism and an unscripturally exaggerated spirituality may profess to find God intuitively, immediately, and directly, but God has nowhere promised to communicate with man in any other way than *by means*. Why, then, should we condemn the use of works of art as mute preachers and eloquent symbols of our faith? They are not of themselves means of grace, but they may well remind us of these channels of grace and silently call us to them.

The very church buildings may serve this purpose, pointing upward with their stately spires, constant reminders of the heaven toward which we are journeying and for which we should prepare ourselves. "Set your affection on things above, not on things on the earth" [47] — these words may well be considered the silent sermon of church spires everywhere. In the days of Luther, church buildings were more conspicuous than they are today. The mighty cathedrals of medieval times have never been surpassed in architectural beauty. However, many of them were not only unnecessarily expensive in view of the generally low level of economic life, but their interior construction reflected a mode of worship which largely defeated the purpose for which the Church had been established and the ministry had been instituted. Of central importance in a New Testament church service is the preaching of the Word. Luther said: "Where God speaks, He dwells. Wherever the Word is proclaimed, God is present, there is His house." [48]

Now, in the smaller parish churches of the days of Luther the priest might be readily enough understood, but in the larger churches, and particularly in the great cathedrals, it was difficult even to see the officiating cleric and often impossible to understand him. But from the standpoint of medieval Catholicism this state of affairs did not greatly impair the value of a service.

---

[47] Colossians 3:2.   [48] Wei 14:386, 28; cp. Wal V:414.

Increasingly the priest addressed the eye of the worshiper rather than his ear. The service consisted largely in elevating the emotions of the faithful, in stimulating within him a feeling of awe and devotion toward the mysteries of a religion which he was too ignorant to understand and too fearful to neglect. Against this slighting of the preached Word, which alone can make a soul beautiful in the eyes of God, Luther protested. The Reformer expressed his dissatisfaction with the cathedral of Cologne because it was almost impossible to hear a preacher in that masterpiece of medieval architecture.[49] The height of the cathedral aisle is no less than 154 feet, while the length of the building is 480 feet and its width 228 feet. How much money has been used in the construction of this cathedral in the course of centuries is impossible accurately to determine.

Also such great expenditures were criticized by the Reformer. He was too sober and practical to appreciate these immense structures because such vast sums of money were lavished upon them while millions were eking out a miserable existence both physically and spiritually. Luther's interest in the artistic was largely utilitarian in the good sense of the word. In the *Resolutions* which the Reformer wrote to his Theses in 1518 he stated that moneys ought not to be devoted to the erection and beautification of costly churches until the needs of men had been satisfied.[50] Luther knew well enough that the vast amounts spent on churches were frequently given under the false and foolish impression that the building of houses of worship was a meritorious deed in the eyes of God. In 1521 he complained that the Pope taught that one is made pious and just before God by building churches.[51] A few years later he recurred to the charge and added: "Our blind leaders come along and preach that one ought to build churches here and there to honor the dear saints." [52] Luther does not object to the erection of a memorial in honor of a deceased loved one, but what does rouse his ire is the notion

---

[49] Wal XXII:1698.
[50] Wei 1:525 f.

[51] Wal XVIII:1548; Erl 7:210 ff.
[52] Wal IX:1222.

of meritoriousness which in the papal Church so commonly attached to such building of churches and chapels. If he had reasons to believe that the erection of a sanctuary had been falsely motivated, its art looked hideous to him. The Reformer looked at the heart. Character was art and beauty to him. A beautiful face could not atone for a sinful soul.

DESPITE ALL ABUSE LUTHER FOSTERED THE ARTISTIC IN THE CHURCH

But this point of view does not imply that Luther lacked all appreciation for the art in the artistic. The Reformer merely held that artistic enjoyment should be a secondary consideration. He thoroughly enjoyed the beautiful, other things being equal, wherever he found it. He believed that also church services might legitimately be made to impress the worshiper by their dignified orderliness and decorous beauty. The form of the order of the Lutheran service was therefore not merely the result of the Reformer's conservatism but must also be attributed to Luther's love of the beautiful. His retention of the church calendar with its cycle of festivals must also be explained largely on these grounds. He called the church calendar a "good and laudable arrangement." [53] But the principal reason why Luther retained the church year was again practical and pedagogical. He held that it would be easier for the unlearned mass of people (*den groben, gemeinen Haufen*) to remember the great facts and truths of our redemption if they would be presented to them annually in a systematic, chronological manner.[54] The Reformer was also in favor of retaining the ancient custom of making the sign of the cross before one offered prayer. He encouraged children to do so in his Small Catechism, saying: "In the morning, when you get up . . . in the evening, when you go to bed, make the sign of the holy cross and say [your prayers]." [55] We are informed that Luther continued to cross himself also when asking God to protect him from some imminent danger. After having been told that the Turkish Sultan, who was threatening

---

[53] Wei 31:1, 397, 20.   [54] Wei 32:431, 28.   [55] Wei 30:1, 392.

to overrun Europe, had remarked that Luther would find him a gracious lord, the Reformer crossed himself while saying: "God protect me against this gracious lord." [56]

HIS APPRECIATION FOR THE ARTISTIC IN SECULAR RELATIONS

Luther also had an eye for the artistic and beautiful in secular matters and relations. He particularly enjoyed the wonders of the heavens and often challenged all artists to match the beauties of a sunset or a sunrise. The inimitable coloring in flowers and in the plumage of birds also excited his lively admiration. Nor did the grace of the human figure pass unnoticed. Scattered throughout his writings are brief remarks about the beauty of the human body, both male and female, and about the manner in which the very shape and structure of a man and a woman's body indicate the sphere of activity for which the Creator had designed them.[57]

It is impossible for us to reconstruct in detail the entire interior of Luther's house, but to judge by a letter he wrote to his friend Amsdorf in 1542 it must also have reflected the Reformer's love of the artistic. The Doctor introduced a painter named Sebastian to his friend with the words "I know not whether you want his services. I should like, however, to see your dwelling more tasteful and ornamented, on account of the flesh, which is the better for some recreation, provided it be sinless and unobjectionable." [58]

LUTHER'S GREAT LOVE FOR MUSIC

Among the "sinless and unobjectionable recreations" that graced Luther's home was especially that fine art in which he attained a notable proficiency, music. Michelet calls music the Reformer's passion. The expression is hardly too strong. One of the first authentic notices we have of young Martin introduces him as a serenader of the good burghers of Eisenach in the ex-

---

[56] Wei Tischreden 2537.　　　[57] See Pr, L 83 f.　　　[58] In Mi, L 195.

pectation of food. It was nothing unusual for young students to band together in little groups and go about singing. But apparently one Frau Cotta did not think young Martin's clear voice and devout song so usual. This pious matron belonged to a distinguished mercantile family that had originally come from Italy. Perhaps this circumstance permits us to surmise that Frau Cotta and her family were themselves great lovers of music. Be that as it may, Ursula Cotta was deeply impressed by the musical talent and the obvious sincerity of this dark-eyed, intelligent lad. In church she had observed how devoutly he prayed for a youth of his age. And so young Martin sang and prayed himself into the heart and home of the Cottas in Eisenach. No doubt there was much singing. In later life Luther often referred to the songs of his youth. Many of their melodies still haunted him, though his eyes had been opened to the idolatry with which the text of these medieval songs were often tainted. He deplored the fact that error should be set to such captivating tunes.[59]

ESPECIALLY FOND OF SACRED SONGS

The love of music never left Luther. Many and beautiful are the tributes he paid to this fine art. In 1538 the Reformer wrote a poetical exaltation of sacred vocal music as an introduction to a poem of his friend Johann Walther. This musical colaborer of Luther had also written a poem in praise of music. The Doctor wrote:

Of all the joys that are on earth
Is none more dear nor higher worth
Than what in my sweet songs is found
And instruments of various sound.

Where friends and comrades sing in tune
All evil passions vanish soon;
Hate, anger, envy, cannot stay,
All gloom and heartache melt away;
The lust of wealth, the cares that cling,
Are all forgotten while we sing.[60]

The poem is considerably longer, but these opening lines are suf-

---

[59] Wei 42:377; 35, 480.   [60] K-K, M II:503; tr. in Br, L 267 f.

ficient to characterize it. The Reformer sings the praise particularly of vocal music, which seems always to have interested him more than instrumental music. Perhaps this preference was due to that practical bent of his character which wished to get the maximum of good out of everything. The voice that praised God in song was engaged in an act of worship while at the same time enjoying the exhilarating exaltation that comes to us on the magic wings of melody. There can be no doubt about it: Luther loved music so ardently because it too could be made to pay tribute to God and His glorious Gospel.

APPRECIATED INSTRUMENTAL MUSIC

But the reason why the Reformer made fewer references to instrumental music may also be that this type of music was at that time comparatively undeveloped. The ancestors of some of our modern instruments then existed in a crude form. But they were rarely to be found in private homes. Between 1480 and 1530 the violin was receiving the shape it has essentially retained to this day. As to the symphony orchestra — two centuries were to pass before its matchless music would set the transported listener to wondering whether its strains are the evening breeze of this life or a breath of the morning air of the future one. But though these musical instruments were yet to cast their full spell over man, there were some instruments already in common use. Among them was the lute, a now obsolete string instrument. It resembled the mandolin and guitar in shape but was somewhat larger. This instrument, played by plucking its strings, had a rather pleasing and somewhat plaintive sound. While Luther was recovering from an accidentally self-inflicted wound, he with characteristic industry taught himself how to play the lute.[61] He soon became very proficient on it and commonly accompanied himself and others with it when singing sacred and secular songs. He loved to do this particularly in the evening after supper. We are told that the Reformer also played the fife (*Querpfeife*) very well.[62]

---

[61] K-K, M I:44.   [62] Pr, L 100.

LUTHER OBSERVED THE POWER OF MUSIC OVER MAN

Luther, it appears, loved music for both its religious and psychological value. A close student of human nature, he observed the profound effect of music on the emotional life of man. Upon one occasion he remarked: "Satan is a sad spirit and makes people sad; therefore he cannot bear joyfulness. In consequence he also flees as far as possible from music; he does not stay when one sings, especially spiritual songs. Thus David alleviated Saul's temptation with his harp when the devil plagued him." [63] Again, he said: "Music is one of God's best and most glorious gifts. The devil is a great enemy of music, with which one can dispel many temptations and evil thoughts. . . . Music is the best restorative for a depressed person. Through it the heart becomes content, revived, and refreshed again." [64] Referring to the gloomy fanatics who despised music as childish frivolousness, Luther said: "I am not satisfied with him who despises music, as all fanatics do; for music is a gift of God, not of man. It expels the devil and makes people joyful; one forgets all anger, unchasteness, conceit, and other vices while listening to music. Next to theology I assign the highest place and the greatest honor to music. We see how David and all the saints have wrought their godly thoughts into verse, rhyme, and songs." [65] Luther fully recognized the great cultural value of music, its refining effect upon the emotional life of man. On this subject he wrote the significant words: "Experience testifies that after the Word of God only music ought justly to be praised as the mistress and empress of those emotions of the human heart by which men are controlled and often carried away. We cannot conceive a greater commendation of music than this one. For if you desire to revive the sad, startle the jovial, encourage the despairing, humble the conceited, pacify the raving, mollify the hate-filled — and who can enumerate all the lords of the human heart, I mean the emotions of the heart and the

---

[63] Wei Tischreden 194. [65] Wei Tischreden 7034.
[64] Wei Tischreden 968.

urges which incite a man to all virtues and vices — what can you find that is more efficacious than music?" [66] In the spirit of these words the Reformer recommended music and sports to young nobles as worthy, satisfying, and truly edifying substitutes for their demoralizing gambling and debauchery.[67]

Whenever Luther writes about the value of music, one senses that he speaks as a man who had himself frequently experienced its power. And so he certainly had. How susceptible he was known to be to music is illustrated by an incident that occurred not long before his marriage. The Reformer had been wrestling with painful spiritual problems and had locked himself into his room to meditate without being disturbed. For three days he remained in seclusion. Finally two friends forcibly opened the door. They found him lying on the floor. He was unconscious. Efforts to revive him failed. But to the strains of his beloved music he revived.[68] He once told his friends that beautiful music often filled him with an ardent desire to preach.[69] Upon another occasion he exclaimed after having listened to certain music as though he were entranced: "If God has placed such noble gifts into the cesspool of this life, what will come to pass in that eternal life where everything will be perfect and most pleasing?" [70]

ADVOCATED MUSICAL TRAINING FOR THE YOUNG

Luther naturally did everything he could to advance the knowledge and appreciation of good music. He strongly advocated putting music into the curricula of all schools. As an educator he recognized the advisability of teaching this fine art to children at an early age not only because of their receptivity at that time but particularly also because of the pedagogical value of music, of which he once remarked: "Music is a semi-discipline and a schoolmistress; she makes people milder and

---

66 Wal XIV:429 f.

67 Wei Tischreden 3470.

68 Wa, L 191.

69 K-K, M II:501.

70 Wei Tischreden 4192.

gentler, more modest and more reasonable." [71] In consequence
a good teacher must know music. "I have always loved music,"
said the Doctor. "He who appreciates music is good-natured.
Music must of necessity be kept up in schools. A schoolmaster
must be able to sing, or I shall not look at him." One day Luther
was a guest at the table of a friend. After the meal there was
some singing. Luther was delighted. "Youths should be trained
in this art," he said in his emphatic way, "for it makes fine, clever
people." [72]

LUTHER HIMSELF HAD NO MEAN EDUCATION IN MUSIC

The Reformer knew whereof he spoke, for he had himself
received the benefits of a by no means indifferent musical training.
One may call music Luther's first love. He had learned to know
and appreciate it years before the beauties of the Word of God
had been revealed to him. We know that he had received a
thorough course in singing and in the art of musicography for
at least a dozen years in the schools he attended. He was therefore quite at home in the technique of composition, as it was then
understood. Again, the Augustinian order, of which he subsequently became a member, was noted for the great emphasis
it placed on music, and Brother Martin was thus enabled profit-
ably to continue a study for which he obviously possessed a
natural talent. With characteristic soberness and modesty Luther
confessed that his love of music far outran his proficiency in it.
"Next to theology," said the Reformer, "music is God's most
significant gift to man. I would not surrender my little knowledge
of music for a great deal." [73] Only he who knows what Martin
Luther thought of theology will see a very strong statement in
these words. Luther loved theology with an intensity the world
has rarely seen. It completely absorbed him, filled his entire
mental horizon, and gave color and direction to everything he

---

[71] Erl 62:308.

[72] Wei Tischreden 6248, 3815.

[73] Wei Tischreden 3815.

did and said and thought. If such a man says only theology is more precious than music, he means to express the ultimate in praise of this fine art, so far as he is concerned.

Luther's love of music appears in a delightful manner in some of the letters which he wrote to noted musicians and composers of his day, asking their advice or thanking them for sending him some of their productions. The surrounding in which the addressee of the following letter, the then noted musician Ludwig Senfel, found himself in Catholic Munich heightens the significance of Luther's writing. The Doctor wrote: "Although my name is so hated that I must fear, my dear Ludwig, that this letter will not be safely received and read by you, yet my love of music has overcome my fear, and in musical talent I see that God has richly endowed you. It is this that makes me hope my letter will bring no danger to you, for who even in Turkey would be offended at me for loving art and honoring an artist? Moreover, I greatly honor and esteem your two Dukes of Bavaria, although they are not very favorable to me, because I see they love and foster music. I doubt not that there are many seeds of virtue in a mind touched by music, and I consider those not affected by it as stocks and stones. We know that music is hateful and intolerable to devils. I really believe, nor am I ashamed to assert, that next to theology there is no art equal to music, for it is the only one, except theology, which can give a quiet and happy mind, a manifest proof that the devil, the author of racking care and perturbation, flees from the sound of music as he does from the exhortation of religion. This is the reason why the Prophets practiced no other art, neither geometry nor arithmetic nor astronomy, as if they believed music and divinity near allied; as indeed they declare in their psalms and canticles. Praising music is like trying to paint a great subject on a small canvas, which turns out merely a daub. But my love for it abounds; it has often refreshed me and freed me from great troubles." [74]

---

[74] Sm, L 346 f.

Another letter that is characteristically Lutheran in its genialness, sprightliness, and playful humor was written to one Matthew Weller, who had sent the Reformer one of his compositions. After having thanked him for his gift Luther continued: "We sing your song as well as we can at table and afterwards. If we make a few mistakes, it is not your fault but that of our skill, which is small enough even after we have sung the song over twice or thrice. Vergil says we are not all equal to all things. No matter how well our composers do, we are too much for them and sing their songs badly. If indeed all the governments of the world were to punish us, and if God and reason were to write the tunes, nevertheless we would make such mincemeat of them as might be sold at the butcher's and make people wish us and our tongues hung as high as church bells. You composers must not mind if we do make howlers of your songs, for we insist on trying them whether we fail or not. My dear Katie says she hopes you won't take offense at my jokes, and she sends you her kind regards. God bless you." [75]

LUTHER'S PRINCIPLES OF MUSIC CRITICISM

In the course of time Luther developed a very sensitive and critical ear for good music. The judgments he passed on certain compositions of his day and on certain techniques are still considered sound and discriminating by professional musicians. He particularly insisted upon it that the melody of a song had to reflect the mood expressed in the words of the composition. Then, too, he had a great distaste for any music that was very involved. The plain and natural always attracted him. He felt that music ought to be so simply scored that the average man, who knows nothing of technical niceties, can follow its movements and enjoy its melody. Luther held that music was to be composed in such a manner that it might be enjoyed without much learned comment. We have met with the principle of this view before: the Reformer expressed the same thought about the

---

[75] Sm, L 348.

character of a good discourse. Also a good sermon, thought he, ought to contain nothing too heavy and involved. And Luther practiced what he preached in both sermonizing and composing.

HIS MUSICAL MASTERPIECE, "A MIGHTY FORTRESS"

No doubt the most famous composition of the Reformer is his melody to "A Mighty Fortress Is Our God." That Luther *did* produce both the tune and the words of this immortal hymn has been demonstrated beyond doubt by the research of scholars.[76] Musical critics have also pointed out how perfectly the mighty melody of this masterpiece reflects the heroic thoughts of the text. The stubborn, challenging insistence upon the first note, which Luther strikes three times, the comparatively high note of C above the middle C, is certainly the deathless courage and confidence of the Reformer translated into the language of music. Listen also to the musical description of the slithering approach of "the old evil Foe," and the thud of the following notes: a musical picture of the grim conflict that ensues and the panting of the contestants. Attention has been called to the fact that perhaps no composer ever succeeded in epitomizing more perfectly the pervading spirit of an age in the language of music and in words than did Martin Luther when he gave to the world his immortal "battle hymn of the Reformation." [77]

HIS CONTRIBUTIONS TO MUSIC ACCLAIMED

No wonder John K. Paine, professor of music at Harvard, has said: "We have reaped the fruits of the Reformation not only in our modern religious and social freedom but also in some of the highest forms of musical art." [78] And no one less than "the great Handel acknowledged that he had derived singular advantage from studying the compositions of the great Saxon Reformer." [79]

---

[76] Pr, L 112.

[77] Pr, L 114 f.

[78] In D, L 51.

[79] Edinburgh Encyc., in Kr, C 55.

It would appear, then, that Preserved Smith is not exaggerating when he says: "Luther was a thorough master of one of the fine arts — music." [80]

LUTHER ALSO LOVED POETRY

Music has been called the poetry of sound. Both the musician and the poet are apostles of harmony and rhythm. Not infrequently therefore a man is both poet and composer. Luther was. The Reformer liked poetry. In 1537 Eoban Hess had sent him a Latin translation of the Psalms in poetical form. Luther was pleased with Hess's work and wrote in his letter of grateful acknowledgment: "I confess to being one of those who are more strongly moved and more deeply delighted by poetry than by prose, one upon whose mind poetry makes a more permanent impression than prose, though it were the prose of a Cicero or a Demosthenes." [81] Many literary critics hold that he who truly appreciates poetry is himself a poet although he writes no verse. The Reformer frequently confessed his fondness for poetry but at times denied that he was himself a poet. However, such disavowals of the poetic gift must be understood in the light of the connection in which they were spoken. The Reformer denied that he was a poet in the sense of the Humanists, who strove to write verse with the polish of their classical masters, whom they all but idolized. However, a few fragments also of this nature have come down to us from the pen of Luther. As an instance Dr. Preuss cites what he paradoxically calls the "gruesomely magnificent" verse:

"Pestis eram vivens (vivus), moriens ero mors tua, papa." [82]

These strong words may be thus rendered:

"I was your plague while I lived, at death I shall be your death, O Pope."

But Luther never cultivated classical models in poetry, however much he enjoyed reading them. And he did enjoy his Vergil and Terence. The former poet he took with him into the cloister at

---

[80] Sm, L 346.   [81] Wal XXI b:2182.   [82] Pr, L 146.

Erfurt,[83] and the latter he would often read in the evening to ease his mind before retiring for the day.

The practical Luther was especially fond of simple didactic poetry. Perhaps we had better simply call it rhyming. The "prose poetry" of Aesop's fables with its appended morals found such favor with him that he bracketed it with a translation of Old Testament prophets, upon which he was engaged while at the Feste Coburg, and expressed his hope to turn to publishing Aesop next.[84] Luther took great delight in the homely wisdom of proverbs, of which he made a little collection for his own use. In this private anthology we come upon such rhymes as this one:

> Schweig, leid, meid und vertrag,
> Deine Not niemand klag,
> An Gott nicht verzag,
> Deine Hilf' kommt alle Tag.[85]

More profound is the melancholy little rhyme:

> Ich lebe und weiss nicht wie lang;
> Ich muss sterben und weiss auch nicht wann;
> Ich fahr' von dannen, weiss nicht wohin;
> Mich wundert, dass ich so froehlich bin.

Luther, applying a Christian corrective to the paganism and agnosticism of the last lines, said they ought to read thus:

> Ich fahr' und weiss, Gott Lob, wohin,
> Mich wundert, dass ich so traurig bin.[86]

The thought as expressed by the Reformer is this:

> I live and know not how long;
> I must die but do not know when;
> I pass on, and, thank God, I know whither;
> I marvel that I am so sad.

In the original poem lines three and four had run thus:

> I pass on and know not whither;
> I marvel that I am so cheerful.

---

[83] Wei Tischreden 166.   [85] Wei 35, 583.
[84] Sm, L 253.   [86] Wei 48:159; cp. Tischreden 5798.

HIS EARLIEST ORIGINAL POEM HONORS TWO LUTHERAN MARTYRS

Luther's earliest original poem was a requiem in honor of the youthful martyrs Johann Esche and Heinrich Voes, burned in Brussels on July 1, 1523.[87] Very touching are the words the Reformer wrote to the countrymen of the martyrs. "Praise and thanks be to the Father of all mercy, who at this time lets us see His wonderful light, hitherto hidden on account of our sins while we were compelled to submit to the terrible power of Antichrist. But now the time has come when the voice of the turtle is heard in the land and flowers appear on the earth. Of what joy, dear friends, have you been the participants, you who have been the first to witness unto us. For it has been given unto you before all the world not only to hear the Gospel and to know Christ but to be the first to suffer, for Christ's sake, shame and injury, wrong and distress, imprisonment and death."[88] There is in these noble words that spirit of almost apostolic exaltation that had found expression in the poem dedicated to the sufferers.

LUTHER AS A WRITER OF CHORALES

During the following year, 1524, more hymns were written by Luther than during any subsequent twelvemonth. Perhaps it was not a mere coincidence that this year also witnessed the publication of Luther's first translation of the Psalms, the hymnal of the Old Testament Church. The Reformer is credited with a total of about forty hymns.[89] That Christ is the center of Luther's hymns need hardly be said, "for there's none other God." Nor need it be demonstrated at length that the theology of these hymns is better than their poetry. Again we observe that Luther is far more concerned about matter than manner. His emphasis is on content rather than on form. He sits down to bring the beautiful Savior into the hearts and lives of men by writing Christian songs. Therefore Luther the evangelist is often more evident than Luther the poet. Many of his chorales are in con-

---

[87] K-K, M I:607. [88] Sm, L 228. [89] See Erl 56; Wei 35.

sequence largely didactic versification. Others are more or less poetical treatments of certain Psalms with their obvious limitations of thought. Still others are translations and revised versions of medieval hymns. Luther was too modest and sober to regard originality as an indispensable prerequisite of a good hymn. Like Shakespeare, he never hesitated to adapt promising material to needs. No doubt many of Luther's hymns were the children of necessity and not the creations of sudden, unpredictable poetic impulses. The purified Church needed purified hymns, the more so since henceforth the congregation at large was to raise its voice in praise and supplication as "priests and kings" in a manner not witnessed during the dark period of priestly domination in the Middle Ages.

In January, 1524, the Reformer wrote with considerable concern to his Spalatin: "There is a plan afoot to follow the example of the Prophets and the Fathers of the early Church and compose for the common people German psalms, that is, spiritual songs, so that the Word of God may remain among the people in the form of song also. We are seeking everywhere for poets, and since you are gifted with such knowledge of the German language and command so elegant a style, cultivated by much use, I beg that you will work with us in this matter, and try to translate some one of the Psalms into a hymn, like the sample of my own which you have here. But I wish that you would leave out all new words and words that are used only at court. In order to be understood by the people, only the simplest and commonest words should be sung; but they should also be pure and apt and should give a clear sense, as near as possible to that of the Psalter. The translation, therefore, must be free, keeping the sense, but letting the words go and rendering them by other appropriate words. I lack the gift to do what I wish to see done, and so I shall try you and see if you are a Heman or an Asaph, or a Jeduthun."[90] Spalatin's compliance with this request being rather

---

[90] S-J, LC II:211 f.

indifferent, Luther had little opportunity to compare him with the Old Testament worthies mentioned in his letter. And so the Reformer found that if a man wants something done, he had better do it himself.

LUTHER'S LIFE AND CHARACTER REFLECTED IN "A MIGHTY FORTRESS"

By far the best known of Luther's hymns is "A Mighty Fortress Is Our God" (Ein' feste Burg ist unser Gott). This chorale, gloriously defiant of the powers of darkness, was written some time between 1521 and 1529, at a time "when further unjust and oppressive strictures on religious liberty and freedom of conscience were enacted." It is based on Psalm 46 and reflects its spirit and thought. This hymn now appears in every church hymnal of consequence and has been translated into over one hundred and seventy languages and dialects. There are more than seventy English translations. Its soul-stirring music has been spoken of previously. We would submit that both melody and thought are an extraordinary faithful reflection of Luther's character: complete self-effacement, utter reliance upon Jesus Christ, a death- and devil-defying courage, and an immovable conviction of the ultimate triumph of the cause of Christ. This is Luther.

THE MIGHTY INFLUENCE OF LUTHERAN CHORALES

He has received well-deserved recognition as a hymnist also from beyond the borders of his own Church. The praise which Dr. Philip Schaff, the Presbyterian church historian, bestows upon the Lutheran Church belongs to a large degree to the Reformer. The eminent scholar writes: "The Lutheran Church draws the fine arts into the service of religion and has produced a body of hymns and chorales which in richness, power, and unction surpasses the hymnology of all other churches in the world." And no one less than the noted Roman champion Cardinal Bellarmine wailed: "The fine songs of Luther have seduced more souls from the [Roman] Church than the archheretic [!] with his preaching." [91] Bellarmine has not said too much concerning the influence of Luther's hymns. Luther the evangelist not only wrote, preached, and taught; he also sang the Gospel to his and to all subsequent generations. If the world does not know the way to salvation, never let it blame Martin Luther for its ignorance. He used all the means at his disposal to glorify Christ. Nor did his testimony cease when he observed that most people would "not have this man to reign over them." In fact, the premonition that after his departure the light of the Gospel would again be largely obscured made the Reformer labor the more ardently "while it was day."

LUTHER'S PREMONITION OF EVIL DAYS

There are statements in Luther's writings which have at times been called prophetic. They were not so in the technical sense of the word, nor did the Reformer ever profess to have been favored with private revelations from God concerning the future. However, the good Doctor had been a close student of Scripture, history, and human nature; and the prophetic gift, properly speaking, was not necessary to predict in a general way the course that future events would very likely take. It was not a bright picture the Restorer of the Gospel sketched. Among other things he said: "I do not hold that Judgment Day will come while the light of the Gospel shines as brightly as, thank God, it does now. But a horrible darkness will follow upon this bright sun, although it will call itself and profess to be enlightenment. This can soon come to pass. Blessed are they who meanwhile fall asleep in the Lord." [92]

But this battle-scarred veteran of the Church Militant was confident that his God would spare him so sad a sight in his own days and that he would be gathered to his fathers in peace before bloodshed and heresy would devastate and defile the land. In the circle of his theological fellow laborers he once expressed

---

[91] In D, L 50 f.   [92] Erl 58:84.

himself to this effect: "The papists are frantic and foolish; they want to defend their doctrine against us with long spears and force because they cannot produce anything worth while against us with the pen and the truth. I have prayed to God with great earnestness and continue to do so every day that He may defeat their counsel and not permit any war to break out in Germany during my lifetime. And I am certain that God will surely answer my prayer. After I have died, when I am at rest and asleep, you ought also to pray." [93]

HE PREDICTED THE LOSS OF PURITY OF DOCTRINE

Luther was certain that there would be increasing reason to pray. In his exposition of John 7:33, the Reformer used words that remind one of the famous admonition to "his Germans" which has been quoted above. There is a certain solemn sadness about the words: "We shall tell the Pope: It would not be necessary for you so to rant and to rave against us and to play the tyrant against the doctrine of the Gospel; for even without such measures the Gospel will remain with you briefly enough, particularly after we who now preach it shall have pillowed our heads in the grave. After our death the Gospel will not remain; indeed, it is not possible for it to remain. For the Gospel runs its course from one city to another. Today it is here, tomorrow at another place, just as a local shower moves onward and brings rain now to this community and presently to another, giving moisture to the soil and making it fertile." [94] These earnest words were written about 1530. As the shadows of the Reformer's life lengthened, he found no reason to believe that the immediate future would, after all, be somewhat brighter. At the end of the last sermon he preached in Wittenberg, on January 17, 1546, remarks are appended in the printings of 1549 and 1558 to the effect that Luther had frequently predicted the defection from orthodoxy of the pro-

---

[93] Erl 52:395.   [94] Erl 48:186 f.

fessors even at Wittenberg after his death.[95] How correct Luther's predictions were is now notorious history. It is not surprising that in view of such an outlook the Doctor increasingly longed for a blessed end.

In fact, for many years he thought he had reasons to expect the end at any time, suddenly, by violence. It were strange indeed to read that Luther's life had never been attempted. The age in which he lived became notorious for deaths by poison and poniard. Even some Popes achieved the unenviable reputation of being highly adept at disposing of their enemies by deadly dram and dagger. We mention only the infamous Alexander VI. It was a foregone conclusion that attempts would be made to take the great Reformer's life. Is it groundless assumption to hold that more were made than either he or we are aware of? Mathesius records two such attempts in his anecdotal biography of Luther. Both were made by Jews in the year 1543.

At that time Luther's incisive book *Schem Hamphoras* appeared and no doubt incensed many Jews by its bluntness. The Reformer, incidentally, was not prejudiced against this peculiar people. On the contrary, in 1540 he told one of the very Jews whom Mathesius accused of having had designs upon Luther's life: "I am partial to all Jews for the sake of one godly Jew, who was born of your people, though from a chaste virgin and *alma,* according to the prophecy of Isaiah (7:14). But you Jews are rarely fast color." [96] The last remark referred to the expressed desire of this Jew to be instructed and to receive Christian Baptism. Mathesius doubted the sincerity of their profession. But however well founded the suspicion of Mathesius and others might have been concerning the murderous plots of the two Jews, nothing happened. The colorful particulars may be read in Mathesius' life of Luther.[97] In that chatty book the reader will also find references to other threats against the Reformer's life.

---

[95] Erl 16:149.   [96] Ma, M 261.   [97] Ma, M 261 ff.

Upon one occasion a man who had been following Luther stopped him at the entrance of the Black Cloister and asked him why he went about alone and unguarded. The Doctor looked the man squarely in the face and replied: "I am in the hands of God. He is my Guardian and Protector. What can man do unto me?" Thereupon the man paled, began to fidget and tremble, turned abruptly, and departed.[98] Luther himself believed that his life had "without a doubt" been attempted several times by poison. But the great servant of God was not to die in such a manner. It is a miracle of God's providence that this man lived in a world of deadly and unscrupulous enemies, exposed to innumerable dangers for almost fifty years, but nonetheless died a natural death.

LUTHER BEGAN HIS FINAL JOURNEY IN ORDER TO SERVE OTHERS

When the angel of death came for him, in 1546, he found Luther serving others, as usual, at the expense of his own convenience and comfort. At the end of 1545 the Reformer had been applied to by the Counts of Mansfeld. The brothers, Albert and Gebhard, had fallen out over a dispute about money and knew of no one who would more wisely judge and more justly decide their differences than Dr. Luther. In the dead of winter the Reformer set out for Eisleben, where he was to meet the brothers. Luther's sons, Hans, Martin, and Paul, went with him to spend the time with relatives in Mansfeld while their father was engaged in the arbitration. On January 25 Luther had leisure to write to his wife: "Dear Katie, we arrived at Halle this morning at eight o'clock but have not journeyed on to Eisleben because a great lady of the Anabaptist persuasion met us, covering the land with waves of water and blocks of ice and threatening to baptize us. We could not return on account of the Mulda and so lie here between waters. Not that we venture to drink it, but we take good Torgau beer and Rhenish wine while the Saale is trying to make us angry. All the people, the postillions as well

---

[98] Ma, M 292.

as we ourselves, are timid, and so we do not betake ourselves to the water and tempt God; for the devil is furious against us and lives in the water and is better guarded against before than repented of after; and it is unnecessary for us to add to the foolish joy of the Pope and his gang." [99] The Doctor was evidently in good spirits when he wrote this letter.

HE WROTE HIS LAST LETTERS TO HIS WIFE

After three days' delay they pushed on and were escorted into Eisleben by the Counts of Mansfeld with more than a hundred horsemen. Just as they were entering his native place Luther, who had been walking and was overheated, chilled severely and was prostrated by such faintness and oppression on the chest that he had to be hurried to a near-by house. There he responded to the treatment of rubbing with hot cloths. By the next Sunday he was able to preach. The business of reconciliation prospered at first but was checked by the covetous spirit betrayed by the disputants and the equivocations and quibblings of the lawyers. These developments greatly depressed Luther. His wife became aware of this fact and was apprehensive about its possible effect on her husband's health. But under date of February 10 Luther wrote to her jocosely: "Grace and peace in Christ. Most holy lady doctoress! I thank you kindly for your great anxiety which keeps you awake. Since you began to worry, we have almost had a fire at the inn, just in front of my door, and yesterday, due to your anxiety no doubt, a stone nearly fell on my head, which would have squeezed it up as a trap does a mouse. For in my bedroom lime and cement had dribbled down on my head for two days, until I called attention to it, and then the people of the inn just touched a stone as big as a bolster and two spans wide, which thereupon fell out of the ceiling. For this I thank your anxiety, but the dear angels protected me. I fear that unless you stop worrying the earth will swallow me up or the elements will persecute me. Do you not know the Catechism and the Creed?

---

[99] Sm, L 418.

Pray, and let God take thought, as it is written: 'Cast thy burden on the Lord, and He shall sustain thee,' both in Psalm 55 and other places.

"I am, thank God, well and sound, except that the business in hand disgusts me, and Jonas takes upon himself to have a bad leg, where he hit himself on a trunk: people are so selfish that this envious man would not allow me to have the bad leg. God bless you. I would willingly be free of this place and return home if God will. Amen. Amen. Amen. Your holiness's obedient servant." [100]

The good-natured banter of this letter was no doubt designed to put "Lord Katie" at ease. Beneath its jocoseness lies an unmistakable seriousness. The spirit of the letter is typical of much that Luther wrote.

On February 14 the Reformer announced to his wife the success of his mission in the last letter he was ever to write. It began with the words: "Dear Katie, we hope to come home this week if God will," and it concluded with the benediction "God bless you." [101] On February 16 a treaty was signed by Albert and Gebhard of Mansfeld. On the same day the Reformer preached for the last time and received Holy Communion. During February 17 he kept to his rooms. He appeared to have overcome the effects of another attack of faintness. But he seemed to sense that all was not well. He requested the local pastor, Michael Coelius, to read certain comforting passages from the Psalter, his constant companion. He had heavily lined his favorite verses for ready reference. On the evening of the seventeenth the pain and oppression on the chest returned, but he gained some relief from vigorous rubbing.

GOD CALLS HIS SERVANT HOME

At about 1 o'clock in the morning of February 18, Luther awoke and soon was in extreme agony. Wringing his hands in anguish and looking heavenward, the Doctor cried: "O my God,

---

[100] Sm, L 421.   [101] Sm, L 421 f.

how agonized I am! Dear Dr. Jonas, I think that here at Eisleben, where I was born and baptized, I shall die." Great beads of perspiration rolled down Luther's forehead. "No," pants the Reformer in answer to a hopeful remark of his friends, "they are not — a sign — of recovery. They are — the cold sweat — of death." Silence. Suddenly, with eyes half opened, the man of God prays: "Lord Jesus Christ, accept my soul. O heavenly Father, though I must leave this body and be torn from life, yet I know for sure that I shall abide eternally with Thee, and no one can take me out of Thy hands." His strength now rapidly left him. But he was heard to pant three times: "Father, into Thy hands I commend my spirit. Thou hast redeemed me, Thou faithful God." That seemed to have exhausted all his strength. Dr. Jonas and the minister Coelius try to arouse him once more. They bend over him and ask aloud: "Reverend Father, do you remain fixed in faith in Christ and in the doctrine that you have preached?" "Yes," replies the Reformer. Silence, while the angel of death enters, and the soul of Martin Luther goes to its eternal rest. The fire leaves those leonine eyes, the lips stiffen into silence, the cheeks grow white, but friends comment with bated, awesome breath on the look of serenity that settles on the face of the dead one. Some say he died of a stroke; others speak of certain complications in the lungs. Still others simply say: "God took him." *They are right.*

"THIS DEAR AND PRECIOUS MAN"

Martin Luther was buried in the Castle Church at Wittenberg on February 22, 1546. Since that day millions have stood before his grave in reverent silence. Through the centuries, emperors and statesmen, scholars and artists, the high and the low, men and women and children, have called his name blessed. The tributes that have been paid to him would fill volumes. But we venture to say that they would not, because they could not, adequately describe what the world owes to this man of God.

That was no doubt the opinion of the woman who was most

immediately affected by Luther's death. On April 2, 1546, Catherine Luther wrote to her sister Christina: "Who would not be sorrowful and mourn for so noble a man as was my dear lord, who served not only one city or a single land but the whole world? Truly, I am so distressed that I cannot tell my great sorrow to any one and hardly know what to think or how to feel. I cannot eat nor drink, neither can I sleep. If I had had a principality and an empire, it would never have cost me so much pain to lose them as I have now that our Lord God has taken from me, and not from me only, but from the whole world, this dear and precious man."[102]

"This dear and precious man"! Centuries later, after a clearer perspective had become possible, and without exposing himself to the suspicion of loving partiality, which naturally attaches to the judgment of a wife, the Scotchman Thomas Carlyle re-echoed the words of Catherine Luther and exclaimed: "I will call this Luther . . . one of our most lovable and precious men."[103]

"THE IMMORTAL LUTHER"

We have frequently had occasion to quote Luther's letters in the translation of Preserved Smith. The English-speaking world is greatly indebted to the labors of this modern student of Luther. Though not a Lutheran, Dr. Smith became so deeply impressed by the monumental character of the Reformer that he publicly stated: "(Luther's) personality led and dominated his time as scarcely any other man has ever done. . . . We must all admit that the Saxon reformer was one of the greatest of the sons of men. In all that momentous age of transition his brain was the most active, his heart the most passionately earnest, his will the most indomitable."[104] F. Painter concurred in this judgment and said that Luther was "a man among men, yet towering above them in unapproachable grandeur," and that he was "the one Titanic form on the crowded canvas of the sixteenth century."[105] Henry

---

102 Sm, L 424. 104 In Br, L 273.
103 Ca, H 168. 105 Pa, L 191, 95.

Cole was one of the first to translate a number of Luther's major works into English. He fell under the spell of Luther's compelling personality. In the introduction to the Reformer's *Bondage of the Will* this Englishman simply calls the Doctor "the immortal Luther." [106]

"WE SHOULD NEVER LEAVE HIM FROM OUR HEARTS"

To study Luther's character at close range is an unforgettable experience. It is said of the Earl of Chatham that no one ever left a consultation with him without having become wiser and better. The study of Luther will have the same effect upon a man. The Reformer's noble character is a source of inspiration, and in his writings lie thousands of gems of thoughts. In 1931 Dr. Hans Preuss wrote: "We share the conviction of the complete indispensableness of Luther for the unparalleled troubles of our time." [107] These words will bear restating in 1947. Modern clothing covers hearts that are no different from the hearts that beat and ached in the sixteenth century. Were the great Reformer to reappear among us today, he would find many things strange and startling. But the troubles of the human nature he knew so well and the ills of the human society he observed so closely would be sadly familiar to him. And — depend upon it! — he would insist with all the vigor and eloquence that made him famous that there is still but *one* hope for the world: "his Gospel." Luther the theologian and evangelist is ever modern because our ills are ever the old ones.

Looking through tear-dimmed eyes at the serene corpse lying before him in the Castle Church, Philip Melanchthon said: "We should keep this our dear father in our memories steadily and forever, and never leave him from our hearts." [108]

---

[106] Lu, B 12.   [107] Pr, L 5.   [108] Fr, M 128.

Abbreviations and Bibliography

Ba, L   Bauslin, David. *The Lutheran Movement of the Sixteenth Century.* Philadelphia: The Lutheran Publication Society, cop. 1919.

Bay, M   Bayne, Peter. *Martin Luther: His Life and His Work.* London: Cassell, 1887. 2 volumes.

Be, M   Beard, Charles. *Martin Luther and the Reformation in Germany until the Close of the Diet of Worms.* London: Green, 1896.

Bo, J   Boehmer, Heinrich. *Der Junge Luther.* Gotha: Flamberg, cop. 1925.

Bo, L   Boehmer, Heinrich. *Luther and the Reformation in the Light of Modern Research,* tr. by E. S. G. Potter. New York: Mac Veagh, 1930.

Bow, L Bower, Alexander. *The Life of Luther with an Account of the Early Progress of the Reformation.* London: Baldwin, 1813.

Br, L   Bruce, Gustav Marius. *Luther as an Educator.* Minneapolis: Augsburg Publishing House, cop. 1928.

Ca, H   Carlyle, Thomas. *Heroes, Heroworship and the Heroic in History.* Burt, n. d.

D, L   Dallmann, William. *Luther the Liberator.* Milwaukee: Northwestern Publishing House, 1919.

Da, L   Dau, W. H. T. *Luther Examined and Reexamined: A Review of Catholic Criticism and a Plea for Revaluation.* St. Louis: Concordia Publishing House, 1917.

En, P   Engelder, Th., and others. *Popular Symbolics.* St. Louis: Concordia Publishing House, 1934.

Erl   *Dr. Martin Luther's saemmtliche Werke.* Nach den aeltesten Ausgaben kritisch und historisch bearbeitet von Dr. Johann Konrad Irmischer. Erlangen: Heyder, 1826–1854. 67 Baende. (The "Erlanger Luther.")

Fr, M   Freytag, Gustav. *Martin Luther;* tr. by Henry E. O. Heinemann. Chicago: Open Court Publishing Co., 1897.

Fro, L   Froude, James A. *Life and Letters of Erasmus.* New York: Longmans, Green & Co., 1900.

H, V   Hare, Julius. *Vindication of Luther Against His Recent English Assailants,* 2d ed. London: Parker, 1855.

Ho   *Works of Martin Luther with Introductions and Notes.* Philadelphia: Holman, ca. 1915–1932. 6 volumes. (The "Holman" or "Philadelphia" edition.)

K-K, M Koestlin, Julius. *Martin Luther, sein Leben und seine Schriften;* 5. neubearbcitete Auflage, nach des Verfassers Tode fortgesetzt von Dr. Gustav Kawerau. Berlin: Duncker, 1903. 2 Baende.

Ko, M   Kolde, Theodor. *Martin Luther.* Gotha: Perthes, 1884. 2 Baende.

Kr, C   Krauth, Charles P. *The Conservative Reformation and Its Theology.* Philadelphia: United Lutheran Publishing House, cop. 1913.

Le, H   Lea, Henry C. *An Historical Sketch of Sacerdotal Celibacy in the Christian Church,* 2d ed., enlarged. Boston: Houghton, cop. 1884.

Li, H   Lindsay, Thomas M. *A History of the Reformation,* 2d ed. Scribner's, 1910. 2 volumes.

Lu, B   Luther, Martin. *The Bondage of the Will;* tr. by Henry Cole, with slight alterations from Edward Thomas Vaughan; corrected by Henry Atherton. Grand Rapids: Eerdmans, 1931.

Lu, G   Luther, Martin. *Commentary on St. Paul's Epistle to the Galatians.* A new ed., corrected and revised by Erasmus Middleton. Grand Rapids: Eerdmans, 1930.

Ma, M   Mathesius, Johann. *Dr. Martin Luthers Leben.* St. Louis: Concordia-Verlag, 1883.

Mi, L   Michelet, Jules. *The Life of Martin Luther Gathered from His Own Writings;* tr. by G. H. Smith. Appleton, 1846.

Pa, L   Painter, F. V. N. *Luther on Education.* Including a Historical Introduction and a Translation of the Reformer's Two Most Important Educational Treatises. St. Louis: Concordia Publishing House, 1928.

Po, M   Polack, W. G. *Martin Luther in English Poetry.* St. Louis: Concordia Publishing House, 1938.

Pr, L   Preuss, Hans, *Martin Luther der Kuenstler.* Guetersloh: Bertelsmann, 1931.

Ra, D   Ranke, Leopold von. *Deutsche Geschichte im Zeitalter der Reformation,* 6. Auflage. Leipzig: Duncker & Humblot, 1881. 6 Baende.

RE   *Realencyklopaedie fuer protestantische Theologie und Kirche,* dritte verbesserte und vermehrte Auflage. Leipzig: Hinrichs, 1896—1913. 24 Baende.

Re, L   Reu, Michael. *Luther and the Scriptures.* Columbus: Wartburg Press, 1944.

Re, Lu   Reu, M. *Luther's German Bible: An Historical Presentation Together with a Collection of Sources.* Fourteen plates. Columbus: The Lutheran Book Concern, 1934.

Sc, C   Schmauk, Theodore E., and Benze, C. Theodore. *The Confessional Principle and the Confessions of the Lutheran Church.* Philadelphia: General Council Publication Board, 1911.

Se, A   Seckendorff, Veit Ludewig von. *Ausfuehrliche Historie des Lutherthums und der heilsamen Reformation.* Leipzig: Gleditsch, 1714. (Translated by Elias Frick from the original Latin.)

S-J, LC   Smith, Preserved, and Jacobs, Charles M. *Luther's Correspondence and Other Contemporary Letters.* Philadelphia: Lutheran Publication Society, cop. 1913—1918. 2 volumes.

Sm, L   Smith, Preserved. *The Life and Letters of Martin Luther.* Boston: Houghton, cop. 1911.

Sm, R   Smith, Preserved. *The Age of the Reformation.* New York: Holt, ca. 1920.

Tr.   *Concordia Triglotta.* The Symbolical Books of the Ev. Lutheran Church, German-Latin-English. Published as a Memorial of the Quadricentenary Jubilee of the Reformation anno Domini 1917 by resolution of the Evangelical Lutheran Synod of Missouri, Ohio, and Other States. St. Louis: Concordia Publishing House, 1921.

W, P   Wace, Henry. *Principles of the Reformation, Practical and Historical.* New York: American Tract Society, n. d.

Wa, F   Walther, Wilhelm. *Fuer Luther wider Rom.* Handbuch der Apologetik Luthers und der Reformation den roemischen Anklagen gegenueber. Halle: Niemeyer, 1906.

Wa, L   Walther, Wilhelm. *Luthers Charakter,* 3. und 4. Auflage. Leipzig: Deichert, 1917.

Wal   *Dr. Martin Luthers Saemmtliche Schriften.* Herausgegeben von Dr. Joh. Georg Walch. Neue revidierte Stereotypausgabe. St. Louis: Concordia Publishing House, 1881—1910. 25 Baende. (The "St. Louis Walch.")

Wei   *Dr. Martin Luthers Werke.* Kritische Gesamtausgabe. Weimar: Boehlhaus Nachfolger, 1883—1939. (Still incomplete; at present about 100 volumes. This is the "Weimar Luther.")

INDEX